Objective-C for iPhone® Developers

A Beginner's Guide

James A. Brannan

McGraw Hill

New York Chicago San Francisco
Lisbon London Madrid Mexico City
Milan New Delhi San Juan
Seoul Singapore Sydney Toronto

The McGraw·Hill Companies

Cataloging-in-Publication Data is on file with the Library of Congress

McGraw-Hill books are available at special quantity discounts to use as premiums and sales promotions, or for use in corporate training programs. To contact a representative, please e-mail us at bulksales@mcgraw-hill.com.

Objective-C for iPhone® Developers: A Beginner's Guide

1 2 3 4 5 6 7 8 9 0 DOC DOC 1 0 9 8 7 6 5 4 3 2 1 0

ISBN 978-0-07-170328-4
MHID 0-07-170328-4

Sponsoring Editor Roger Stewart

Editorial Supervisor Janet Walden

Project Editor Emilia Thiuri

Acquisitions Coordinator Joya Anthony

Technical Editor Billy Myers

Copy Editor Robert Campbell

Proofreader Paul Tyler

Indexer Jack Lewis

Production Supervisor George Anderson

Composition Glyph International

Art Director, Cover Jeff Weeks

Cover Designer Jeff Weeks

For my wife and kids.

About the Author

James A. Brannan has more than 15 years of experience working in IT. He has programmed using everything from AWK to Objective-C, including stints as a web designer and Oracle PL/SQL developer. He currently works full time independently on both his own and clients' iPhone and iPad projects. He is only 999,700 dollars from being the next App Store instant millionaire.

About the Technical Editor

Billy Myers has been programming for about 15 years, and his most recent work of note is his task manager program for the iPhone called To Do's by AustinBull Software, which is one of the most popular free task managers available in Apple's App Store. He began writing code in junior high and high school, and is now working on completing a second degree in Computer Science at Texas A&M Commerce in Commerce, TX.

Contents at a Glance

Contents

Acknowledgments

Thanks to all the folks who helped me with this book—particularly the technical editor, Billy Myers, who had infinite patience when correcting my memory leaks over and over again. Thanks to Neil Salkind, my book agent, for helping keep my foot out of my mouth and finding the opportunity for me to write this book. Also, thanks to the entire McGraw-Hill staff, including: Emilia Thiuri, Joya Anthony, Roger Stewart, Janet Walden, Robert Campbell, and the rest of the staff. And of course, as always, thanks to Everaldo and his open-source Crystal Project icons (www.everaldo.com). Your icons truly add the finishing touch to my books and software. Finally, thanks to the high-school student, Daniel Shaffer, for letting me profile him in the book's introduction.

Introduction

Apple opened the App Store on July 11, 2008. Since then it has offered over 100,000 Apps. An App's price can range from free to $999.99 U.S. Individuals, small companies, and large companies can all release Apps on the App Store. The App Store truly makes software development a cottage industry for many developers.

But you must remember that the iPhone, iPod touch, and iPad are all computers. Computers require programs to make them do something interesting. Apple's language of choice is Objective-C, a superset of C. In this book, the goal is getting you comfortable with basic programming, the C programming language, and the Objective-C programming language.

About This Book

This book's focus is Objective-C, not developing iPhone applications using the iPhone SDK. However, it uses the iPhone SDK to teach Objective-C. Throughout the book you use simple iPhone SDK template applications to illustrate the chapter's presented topics. The goal is that by the book's end, you will be knowledgeable and comfortable enough with Objective-C and the iPhone SDK to begin working through an iPhone SDK book such as my *iPhone SDK Programming: A Beginner's Guide* (McGraw-Hill/Professional, 2009).

Each Chapter's Content

Chapter 1 begins the book by exploring the iPhone SDK and presenting a few basic programming concepts. You must be a registered iPhone developer to download and begin using the SDK. You must be a paid developer to test applications on your device and to upload applications to the App store. You should note that in this book, I present no examples requiring paid membership; all projects are developed for the iPhone simulator only.

After presenting the essentials, Chapter 1 then jumps into a crash course on beginning programming using the C programming language. The material is terse, so if you have never programmed before, you should consult some of the other referenced material in the chapter for more help.

Chapters 2 and 3 discuss basic programming concepts in Objective-C. The material should be familiar to you if you have some C or Java experience. Chapter 2 begins the book's Objective-C coverage by discussing the language's primitive data types and operators. As Objective-C is a superset of C, if you know some C, then much of the material should prove familiar. Chapter 3 discusses Objective-C's flow control statements, arrays, and structures. This chapter, much like Chapter 2, should be familiar to you if you have some C programming experience.

Chapter 4 begins Objective-C's departure from standard C by discussing classes, objects, and messaging. The chapter begins by demonstrating procedural programming and then switches to object-oriented programming. It also uses simple Unified Modeling Language (UML) diagrams throughout to help illustrate the chapter's content.

Chapter 5 discusses memory management and properties. If you come from a Java or scripting language background such as PHP or ColdFusion, then you would be well advised to pay particular attention to this chapter. You must understand Objective-C's memory management if you wish to program quality iPhone applications. Remember, the iPhone has much less memory than a desktop computer; if you fail to manage memory properly, your application will crash when running on an iPhone.

Chapters 6 and 7 explore object-oriented programming using Objective-C. Chapter 6 explores the object-oriented principle of inheritance. Inheritance allows much code reuse and makes your programs easier to build, debug, and maintain. Chapter 7 discusses Objective-C's protocols and categories. If you are familiar with Java, then simply think of protocols as interfaces; they are fundamentally the same concept. Categories, though, are something of an afterthought in Objective-C and have no corresponding Java construct. Categories let you arbitrarily extend a class' functionality without inheriting from the class. If this doesn't make sense, it should by the end of Chapter 7.

Chapters 8, 9, and 10 introduce you to several Foundation framework concepts. Beginning with Chapter 8, the book diverges from presenting Objective-C language concepts and begins presenting fundamental classes and concepts for programming for the iPhone. These classes are all part of the Foundation framework, a collection of Apple-provided code that makes writing applications easier. The concepts presented are tailored to iPhone development, so no desktop-only classes or concepts are discussed. Chapter 8 explores several Foundation framework classes. These classes make string manipulation, managing collections of objects, and reading and writing from files much easier. Chapter 9 presents the Foundation framework classes used for reading and writing to files. The chapter also discusses the iPhone directories you have available and provides specific code examples for working with those directories. Chapter 10 continues presenting Foundation framework classes. In this chapter you learn about property lists, the `NSCopy` protocol, and how to archive and de-archive your application's objects to a file.

Chapter 11 introduces you to selectors and targets. Selectors and targets are initially one of Objective-C's more confusing aspects. However, you should take the time to carefully learn these concepts, as they allow significant programming flexibility. In essence, what these concepts allow is for a program to dynamically decide at runtime what objects and methods to call. If you are familiar with Java's reflection, then selectors should not appear foreign. In fact, having worked extensively with both, I find using Objective-C's selectors and targets much easier than working with Java's reflection.

Chapter 12 returns to basic object-oriented principles by discussing the Model-View-Controller (MVC) design pattern. I end the book with the MVC for good reason. It is fundamental to how you write programs for the iPhone SDK. Moreover, this design pattern has a rich history and is arguably the single most influential concept leading to the Mac and Windows operating systems. Without MVC, we just might still all be using DOS prompts.

Accompanying Tutorial Videos

This book is only one of many books recently released on the Objective-C programming language. Moreover, it is relatively late to arrive, as there are several other high-quality beginner books already on the shelves. So why buy this book? First, as the author, of course I believe this book to be superior to the other books. But more objectively, this book offers video tutorials for all its Try This examples. Oftentimes, steps get lost in a numbered list of printed steps. Moreover, small details are often missed. By offering video tutorials, I hope to reinforce the tutorials presented in the book.

The tutorials are available through my web site at www.jamesabrannan.com and are offered free of charge. Links to the video and the Xcode projects are provided. The videos themselves are hosted on Vimeo at www.vimeo.com. You can watch the embedded videos online; however, if you wish to download the video to watch offline, you need to sign up as a Vimeo member. Vimeo's basic membership is free.

The tutorials are also packaged as both an iPad application and an iPhone/iPod touch application. Both are downloadable from Apple's App Store for a nominal charge. The App bundles all the videos into an organized tutorial that follows the book's Try This steps. You should note, though, that the written Try This steps are not presented in the App. For that you should buy the book. The tutorial Apps are intended as a supplement to this book, not a replacement. As an aside, I know that as a reader, I rarely actually complete a book's tutorials. Well, in this book you don't have to; you can just watch them after reading the steps. Of course, officially, I recommend completing all examples using Xcode.

Realistic Expectations

You are probably not going to get rich writing iPhone Apps. The iPhone App Store is maturing, and instant sales because of the App Store's novelty is no longer the norm. Or is it? Before I try to instill an understanding of what I consider reality, consider an application like "Pocket Girlfriend" by Atrium Designs LLC.

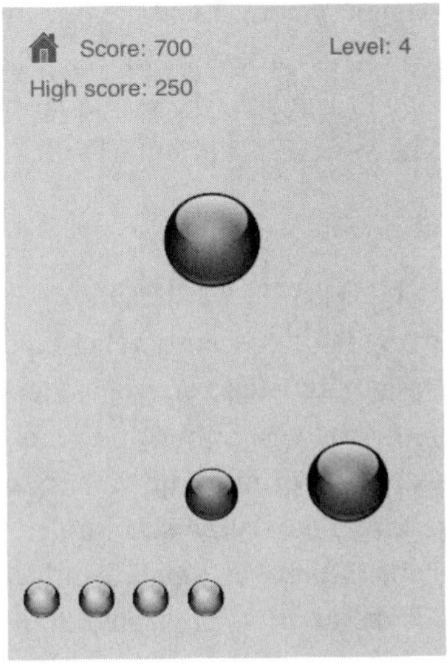

The application is rated two-and-a-half stars. A typical review says, "it blows" or "don't buy" or "a waste." Of course, there are 7728 reviews as of December 12, 2009, and at 99 cents a download, that is over $3500 earned from people who hate the game. Moreover, for every review, there are probably countless folks who bought the App and didn't leave a review. Not bad for a product that folks universally condemn as dumb and a waste of time. The reviews literally warn you not to buy it, but folks—presumably men—do anyway.

But before you say, "aha, sex sells," search the App Store using the keyword "girls." You will be disappointed; there are pages of time-wasting Apps featuring bikini-clad figures, most of which make the authors little to no money. So even if you do write the next "virtual girlfriend" App, having it stand out from all the others will prove difficult and time consuming. That's the App Store's reality. Moreover, every few months you hear of Apple purging the store of questionable material, so why risk it?

Getting noticed these days requires a quality product, with advertising and exposure. Although there are exceptions, you should approach iPhone development with a realistic perspective. Getting rich writing iPhone Apps requires hard work. Moreover, the quality of your App doesn't necessarily ensure success. Just like any other product in any other market, these days, most Apps require advertising. And advertising is not cheap. And even then, chances are, you will not earn enough money to quit your job or drop out of school. At least not immediately.

Getting rich writing an App presupposes a quality App. Writing a quality App requires understanding the iPhone SDK and Cocoa Touch. Understanding the iPhone SDK and Cocoa Touch requires understanding basic Objective-C. So before you rush out and buy a book on "opening your iPhone business" you should first learn Objective-C's fundamentals. This book teaches those fundamentals.

A Teen Developer

But you can make money on the App Store; even if you're in high school, with your parents' support, you can sell Apps on Apple's App Store. Daniel Shaffer, a senior in high school in NYC, has made over $14,000 and has sold over eleven Apps. His Apps include iMprint illusions, Utilitybox, and several others.

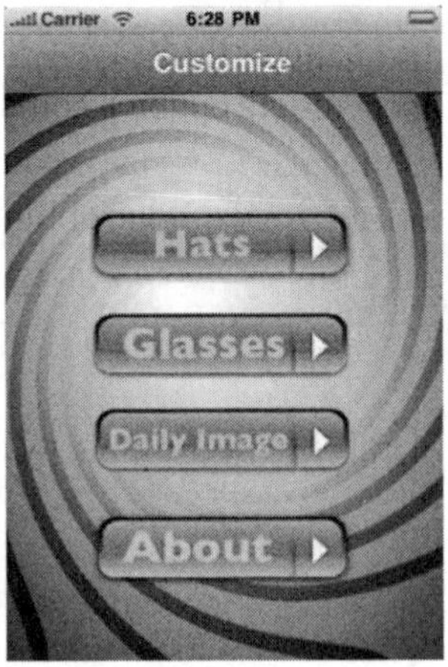

Now true, 14K is not enough to support a family, but it beats working at the local burger joint while in high school. At the very least, you can make enough money to help pay for your hobby, and perhaps more.

Summary

Hopefully I wasn't too discouraging. But you should have realistic expectations before setting out to learn iPhone programming. The iPhone is a computer, and computers require computer programming created using a computer language to get them to do something. The iPhone OS X operating system uses Cocoa Touch, which is written using Objective-C. Before developing an iPhone application of any complexity, you must have a basic understanding of Objective-C.

In this book you learn Objective-C, not the iPhone's SDK in depth. But you are probably excited to begin programming the iPhone immediately, and so this book uses very basic iPhone applications to illustrate Objective-C principles. You will not gain a good understanding of the UIKit and how to develop a complex App, but you will understand how to write a simple, single-view iPhone application. And more important, you will obtain a solid understanding of Objective-C, as it applies to the iPhone SDK.

Chapter 1

Exploring the iPhone SDK and Basic Programming

Key Skills & Concepts

- Downloading and Installing the iPhone SDK
- Understanding Where to Get Help
- Understanding Basic Programming Concepts Using C
- Reviewing C's Pointers
- Writing a Basic Objective-C Program in Xcode
- Understanding Where to Get More Information on Xcode

This chapter covers several topics needed prior to delving into Objective-C. The first topic discussed is how to join the iPhone Developer's Center. The chapter then discusses several resources you can use to help you as you learn Objective-C and iPhone programming. Chances are, you are ready to begin programming now, and not when you have completed this book. So rather than waiting until the book's end, I list several resources up front. These resources are invaluable for both beginners and more advanced developers, and they will help you get started immediately.

After covering the SDK and online resources, the chapter begins its Objective-C discussion by discussing C. In this chapter, though, I only discuss the most basic C concepts. For instance, I briefly discuss header files, preprocessor statements, comments, and C pointers. The chapter does not do any single subject justice, and you should seek out other beginner resources on C programming if you have never programmed using C. However, if you can follow and understand this chapter's simple examples, then you should have no problems with the remainder of this book. Objective-C is much more intuitive than C.

I do not presume that you know C or Java. However, writing a complete beginner's book, geared toward a novice, is a difficult task, and I'm afraid this book by itself might be insufficient if you have never written a computer program before. So to help you understand basic programming better, I reference several resources you might consult if you have never programmed. These resources, combined with this book, should hopefully prove sufficient for you to begin learning how to program. Programming the iPhone is great fun, but Objective-C is not the easiest language for a beginner to learn.

After reviewing some basic C concepts, this chapter takes a brief Xcode tour. This tour is not comprehensive, though. Its purpose is to merely introduce Xcode. I also instruct you in configuring Xcode so that it matches the configuration used in this book. If you know a little about debugging and using debuggers, you will notice this chapter does not cover using Xcode's debugger. This chapter's purpose is simply to provide enough information for you to begin using Xcode to complete this book's Try This projects.

Downloading the SDK

I'm not going to begin this chapter by providing step-by-step instructions on downloading the SDK. I'm certain you have the skills required to go to Apple's web site and determine how to register, download, and install the iPhone SDK. But I will help you get started. You should then find Apple's online installation instructions sufficient. As with most software, you can find installation instructions in the download's "readme" file (Figure 1-1).

NOTE

Installing the iPhone SDK requires an Intel-based Mac running OS X.

Before downloading the software, register as a developer at Apple's iPhone Dev Center (Figure 1-2). The URL is http://developer.apple.com/iphone. Registration is free and allows you to download and install the SDK. Membership also provides access to resources such as the iPhone SDK developer's forum. If not a member already, you should register now.

If you wish to install applications on your iPhone or iPod Touch, you must also join the Individual iPhone Developer Program. Membership in this program is 99 dollars

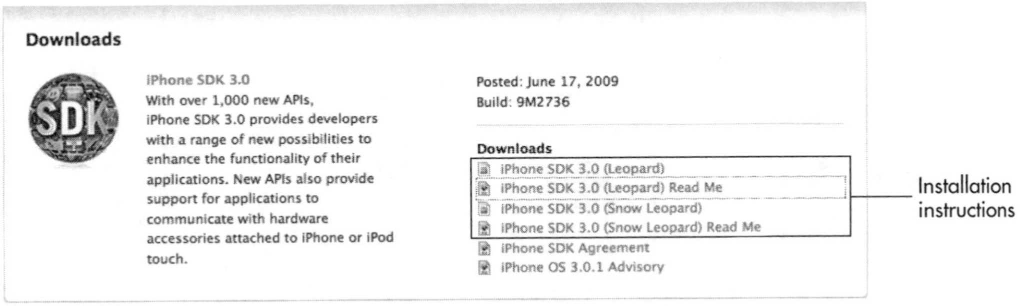

Figure 1-1 Apple's installation instructions

Figure 1-2 The iPhone SDK Dev Center

and allows you access to the iPhone Developer Program Portal. Here you will find all the information needed to install applications on your device and how to submit your application to the App Store. You should pay the membership fee and enroll if you wish to write programs you can run on your iPhone or iPod Touch.

In this book, only the free membership in the iPhone Dev Center is required. You will not write any applications that use the Accelerometer, the iTunes media player, or any other API that requires installing the application on a device to run.

TIP

Before continuing, if you have not registered with the iPhone Dev Center, do so now. Then download and follow the instructions for installing the iPhone SDK. When this is complete, continue reading.

Documentation and Getting Help

If you are just beginning programming, I have a secret to tell you. Most developers are not necessarily all-knowing on the language for which they are developing, the author included. A senior developer might claim in his or her book's bio to have had experience with OS X since in diapers, but in reality, most have not. What these senior developers have learned, though, are the broader principles behind programming. They have also learned how to access online help and distinguish between good help and bad help. Moreover, they can translate the help into reaching their own particularly needed solution. But believe me, except for the rare genius, a senior developer is not writing a program by accessing his or her brain's vast encyclopedic knowledge without consulting documentation. I still have to consult my last book, *iPhone SDK Programming: A Beginner's Guide* (McGraw-Hill Professional, 2009), when writing iPhone applications. There are simply too many things to know about the iPhone SDK for me to have remembered them all. Keeping these limitations in mind, here are some information sources I reference frequently.

SDK Documentation

The iPhone SDK comes with considerable documentation. Download it and read it—books like the one you are reading now should supplement and not replace the documentation. And if you prefer a book's familiarity, the documentation has links to related Apple manuals that are freely downloadable as PDFs. In fact, most of what you need to know about Objective-C, the iPhone SDK, and Cocoa are covered in these documents.

TIP

In the United States, the FedEx Store (formerly Kinko's) charges about five dollars to bind documentation. Print Apple's PDF documents as you need them and have them bound. As my wife will attest, I have these coil-bound documents scattered throughout my home office, kitchen, bathroom, and bedroom. The printed documentation is invaluable, as last time I checked, you would be ill-advised to take a PDF on your laptop in the bath with you to read.

Apple's Online Documents and Forums

Apple's iPhone Dev Center contains all the documentation needed to begin. It also has example applications that you can download. These applications are good as both learning tools and sources to glean source code from for your own applications (provided you comply with Apple's code licensing). The site also features important content and lets you search the site for specific content.

The iPhone Development forum on Apple's site is another vital location for information. These forums are where a developer can ask for help with specific problems he or she might be having. Other developers then reply with solutions to the problem. You can often find a solution to your problem by searching through previously solved problems other developers might have had. You should note that Google does not seem to index this forum very well, and so you cannot rely upon Google finding specific posts in these forums. But the forum is particularly useful, as Apple has staff members who regularly respond to many postings, so when faced with a problem, you should visit the forums, as chances are someone else already had the problem and somebody posted an answer to it.

Google

Despite Apple's comprehensive information, I usually "google" when faced with a problem or I have a question about technology. Google searches usually return the relevant documentation, any tutorials or blogs discussing the issue, and forum posts from others with the same question you might have. The iPhone is currently a hot topic; you will find many resources on the web. But be certain the information is current, as the iPhone SDK has changed dramatically since its inception and will continue changing.

Wikipedia

Although Wikipedia contains much dubious information about your favorite actors and athletes, its information on technology is usually accurate and in-depth. Its C coverage is

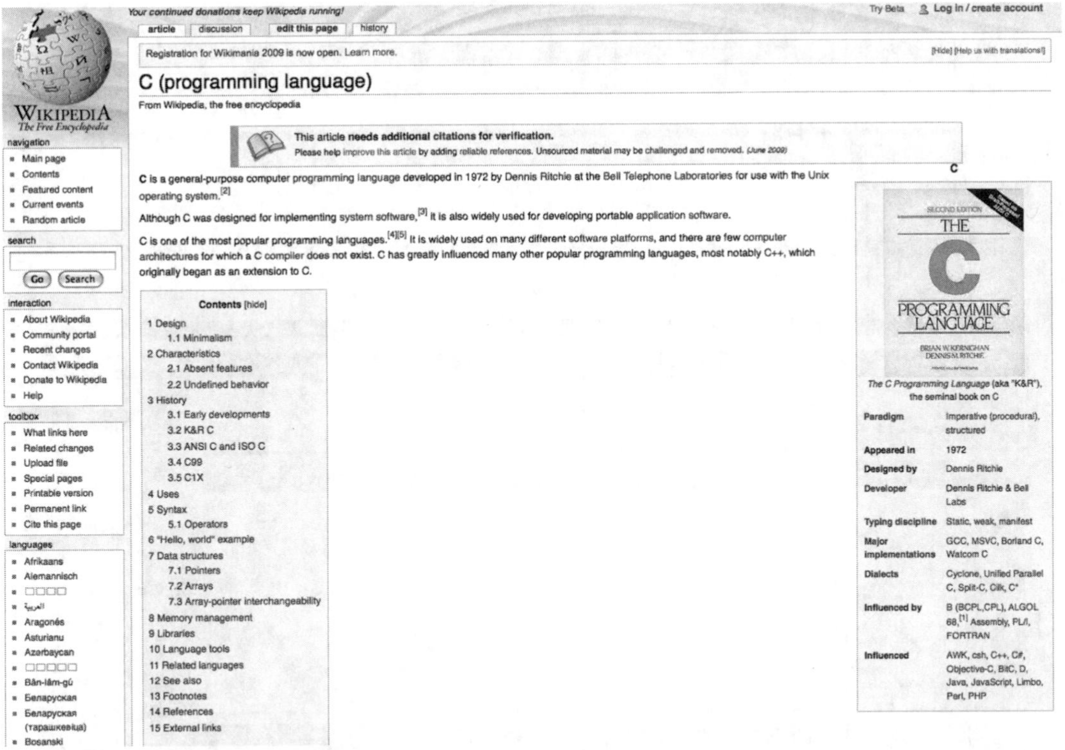

Figure 1-3 Wikipedia is a good source for C information.

very good (Figure 1-3). Many times you will find yourself needing to understand some simple C concept; Wikipedia is a good starting point for information on C.

Wikipedia also has some information on Objective-C. But the information is mostly limited to fundamental Objective-C and not Apple's particular flavor. You are better served going to Apple's developer site directly for any information related to Objective-C.

The iPhone Dev SDK Forum

The iPhone Dev SDK Forum, www.iphonedevsdk.com/forum, is my favorite location for tutorials, asking questions, and conducting research on all things related to iPhone programming (Figure 1-4). It has forums where both advanced developers and beginners

Figure 1-4 The iPhone Dev SDK forum

can have their questions answered. It even has threads discussing other developers' experiences submitting their applications to the App Store. This is invaluable, as you learn firsthand what causes Apple to reject an application. You should bookmark this resource, as I have found that any question I have has usually already been addressed on this site.

Ask the Expert

Q: Can I really write and sell an App on the App Store?

A: Yes, you can. Notice the applications listed at the page's top in Figure 1-5. After reading this book, there are several applications listed there that you could write if you wanted. If you do not have the skills required to make your iPhone belch, pass gas, or display a simple interface by this book's end, I will personally reimburse your purchase price. Easily programmed Apps with dubious value litter the App Store. You can write one too.

There is little barrier to your writing and selling Apps on Apple's App Store. For instance, consider my application, iStockMonkey (Figure 1-6).

To many, myself included, this application probably seems useless. You shake your iPhone and it randomly selects a stock. You then click the banana with a check mark and it fetches the stock from a free stock-quote web service. And that is all it does. The application only took a weekend; the only difficult part was making the picker spin automatically and calling the web service, and of course I had to randomly select a stock. But, point is, it is a simple, silly application that took a weekend. Moreover, even though I wrote it in August 2009, nobody else had thought of it first.

So yes, you can write Apps to sell on the App Store with little experience. Moreover, there are still original ideas that have not yet been implemented.

TIP

Before you begin writing useless applications, note that the App Store's novelty has worn off; many novelty applications are falling flat. Apple is even rejecting some novelty applications outright these days.

Figure 1-5 Advertisements for a few iPhone Apps

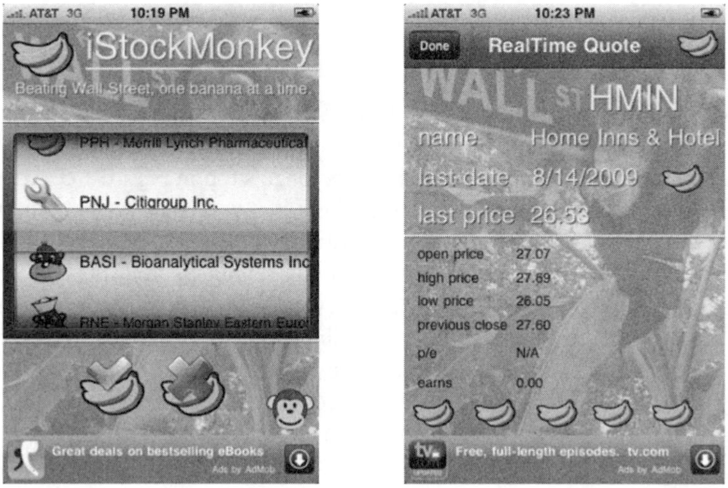

Figure 1-6 iStockMonkey

Basic Programming Concepts Using C

Enough on iPhones that break wind; this is a book on Objective-C! If you wish to write iPhone Apps, you must know Objective-C. Objective-C is not hard, but its ancestor, C, is. Luckily, you need to understand only a few basic programming principles before getting started. In this section, I cover these principles.

TIP

If you have never programmed, a good reference is *Absolute Beginner's Guide to C* by Greg Perry (Second Edition, Sams, 1994). It teaches programming and C at about the right level needed for this book. Try working through that book concurrently with this book. Also, if you do not wish to purchase a beginner's book on C, a good online tutorial is "How C Programming Works" on the howstuffworks web site (http://computer.howstuffworks.com/c.htm).

Objective-C is a superset of C. By calling Objective-C a superset, I mean that Objective-C is C, with a few additions. Those few additions make Objective-C a fully functional object-oriented programming language. Code usable in a C program is also usable in Objective-C. In fact, you can freely mix C code in Objective-C, which you do throughout this book.

A Simple C Program

A computer program is an instruction list for a computer to follow. You write the program using a language such as C or Objective-C. After writing the program, you compile

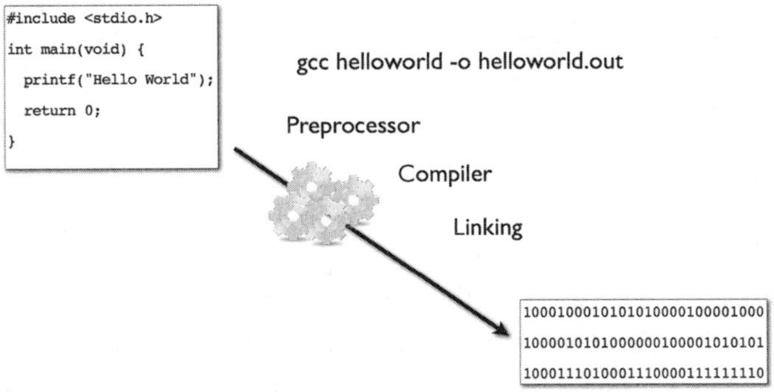
#include <stdio.h>
int main(void) {
printf("Hello World");
return 0;
}
gcc helloworld -o helloworld.out
Preprocessor
Compiler
Linking
1000100010101010000100001000
1000010101000000100001010101
1000111010001110000111111110

Figure 1-7 Workflow for a simple C program

the program. Compiling the program translates your human-readable code into machine-readable code. Figure 1-7 illustrates the workflow involved in writing and compiling a simple C program.

You first must write the text file containing the program's code. After finishing, you then compile the program using a compiler. In Figure 1-7 you are using the Gnu C Compiler (GCC), which comes standard in most UNIX and Linux operating systems (Mac OS X is a UNIX variant). The compiler preprocesses the text file and then compiles it. Usually a program will use other, already-compiled code (called libraries), and so the compiler links the program to the needed libraries. The final result is an executable program.

Try This Writing a Simple C Program

1. Open TextEdit and create a new file. Copy the code in Listing 1-1 to the file. From TextEdit's menu, select Format | Make Plain Text. Save the file as **helloworld.c**. Be certain to save the file to your home directory. The home directory is the directory named your username. For instance, my home directory is jamesbrannan.

2. Navigate to your computer's Utilities and open the Terminal application (Terminal.app in the Utilities folder). Then, using the terminal's command line, navigate to the folder where you saved the file. On my computer, for instance, I type **cd ~ to navigate to my home directory**.

3. Type **gcc helloworld.c –o helloworld** to compile the program.

4. Execute the program by typing **./helloworld**.

(continued)

Listing 1-1 The helloworld program

```
#include <stdio.h>
int main(void) {
  printf("Hello World\n");
  return 0;
}
```

Every C program must have exactly one `main` function. This function is the first method called by the operating system when running the program. The { and } symbols delineate a code block. The `printf` function sends output to the terminal. In Listing 1-1, the `printf` function writes "Hello World" to the terminal. When complete, `main` returns zero, signifying success to the operating system.

Variables

Variables are locations in memory that hold values. When you create a variable, you are telling the computer you wish to store something at that location in memory. Variables have a name and a type. For instance, the following declares a variable named `myvar` of type `int`:

```
int myvar;
```

You learn more on Objective-C's primitive types in Chapter 2. For now, simply realize an `int` is an integer, or a whole number.

You can also assign a variable a value.

```
myvar = 2;
```

If you wish, you can combine declaring and assigning a variable into one statement.

```
int myvar = 2;
```

Variables can be named almost whatever you wish, but they cannot begin with a number and can include only letters, numbers, and underscores. You also cannot name variables the same as an Objective-C reserved word such as `int`, `enum`, `do`, `while`, or other words that have a specific meaning in an Objective-C program.

NOTE

Words used by a language, that you cannot use in your code, are called "reserved words."

Functions

Functions operate on variables; they are the instructions that tell your computer to do something. Consider the following function:

```
int doubleIt(int valtodouble) {
  return valtodouble * 2;
}
```

The first line declares a function named `doubleIt` that returns an integer. It also declares that `doubleIt` takes an integer named `valtodouble` as a parameter. Everything occurring between the opening and closing braces is the function's definition. Functions that return values end with a `return` followed by the value to return.

Functions might also not return a value. You signify a function that doesn't return a value using the `void` keyword. For instance, consider the following function:

```
void sayhi() {
  printf("Hi");
}
```

The function does not return a value, and so there is no return statement. Moreover, in the function's declaration, notice the `void` keyword, which signifies there is no returned value.

Programs operate by calling functions, which in turn call other functions. For instance, in Listing 1-1 the `main` function calls the `printf` function. The `printf` function is declared in the stdio.h header file (you learn about header files later). You can also write and call your own functions, as the next Try This illustrates.

Try This Modifying helloworld.c

1. Open helloworld.c in TextEdit and modify the file to match Listing 1-2.
2. Save, open Terminal, and navigate to the file's location.
3. Type **gcc helloworld.c –o helloworld** to compile the program.
4. Execute the program by typing **helloworld**.

(continued)

Listing 1-2 The helloworld program

```
#include <stdio.h>
int doubleIt(int amounttodouble) {

  return amounttodouble * 2;
}
int main(void) {
  int original = 5;
  int amount = doubleIt(original);
  printf("Hello World %i\n", amount);
  return 0;
}
```

The program first defines a function called `doubleIt`. The `doubleIt` function takes an integer as a parameter and returns an integer. The `main` method declares a variable named `original` that has the value 5. It then declares a variable named `amount`. Only this time, rather than assigning `amount` a literal numerical value, it assigns `amount` the results from calling `doubleIt` on `original`. The `doubleIt` function doubles 5, returning 10, and the `printf` function prints "Hello World 10" to the terminal.

Do not worry if you do not understand everything in Listing 1-2. You will explore each concept in detail later in this chapter and Chapter 2. What is important is that you understand the program's flow.

Ask the Expert

Q: What is the \n character used in Listings 1-1 and 1-2?

A: The \n character is what is called an escape sequence. You use an escape sequence to indicate things such as a newline, tab, single quote, or backslash. The \n escape sequence tells the computer that it should print a newline after printing "Hello World." For more information on escape sequences, refer to Wikipedia (http://en.wikipedia.org/wiki/Escape_sequence).

Objective-C's Main Method

Objective-C programs, like their C ancestors, begin with a `main` method. In fact all applications you will write for the iPhone begin with a `main` method in the main.m file. The `main` method is the first method called by the operating system when executing your application. Rather than explaining `main` any further, the easiest way to get started is by example; so complete the following Try This.

Try This Understanding an iPhone Application's Starting Point

1. Open Xcode and select File | New Project from the menu to open the New Project dialog.
2. Under iPhone OS, select Application and then View-based Application (Figure 1-8). Click Choose.

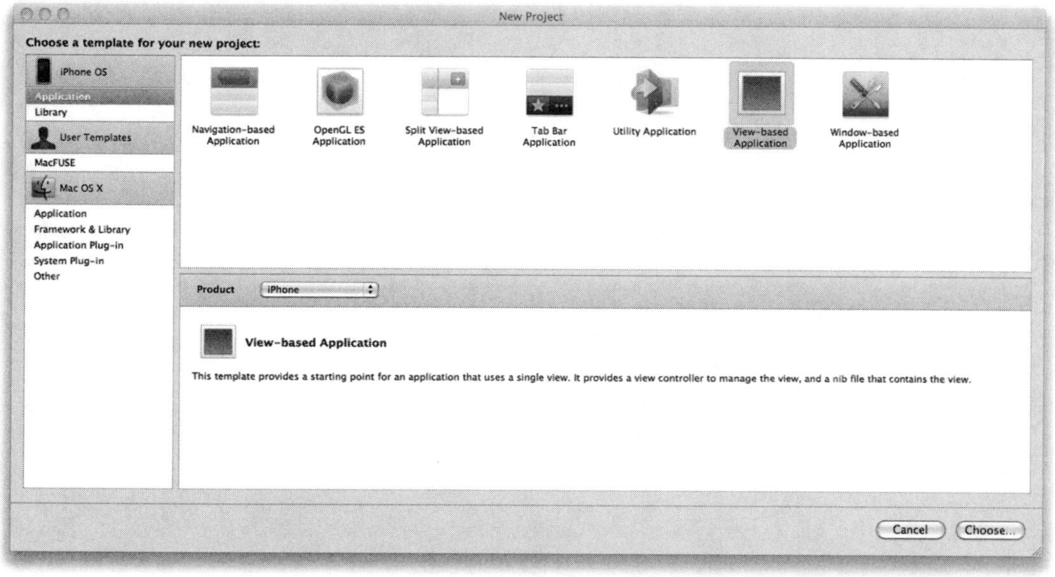

Figure 1-8 Selecting View-based Application in the New Project dialog

(continued)

3. Name the project **HelloWorld** and click Save. Xcode builds an iPhone application named HelloWorld.
4. Expand the Other Sources folder in Groups & Files and select main.m to reveal the file's content in the editor pane (Figure 1-9).
5. Modify the file to appear like Listing 1-3.
6. Select Build | Build and Debug from Xcode's menu. Xcode first asks you if you wish to save the file. Click Save All and Xcode saves the file, compiles, and runs the application (Figure 1-10).
7. If the debugger console is not visible, select Run | Console from Xcode's menu.

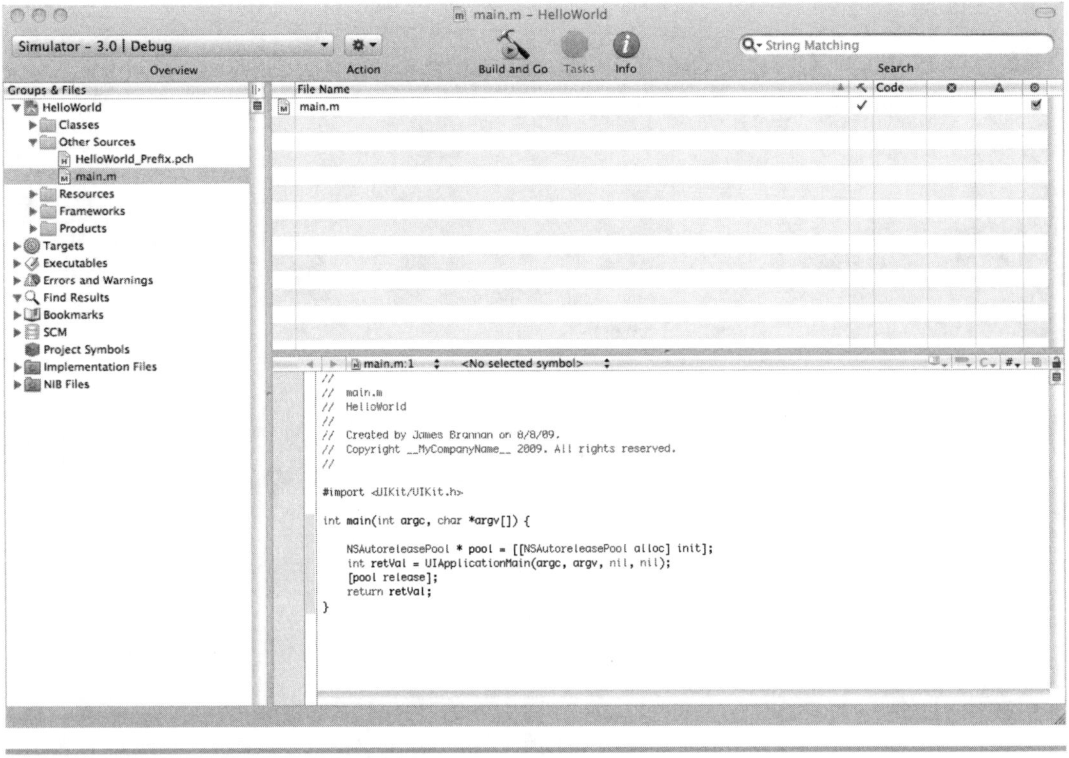

Figure 1-9 Selecting main.m in Groups & Files

Figure 1-10 Running the application in the iPhone Simulator

Listing 1-3 The `main` method in main.m is an iPhone application's starting point.

```
int main(int argc, char *argv[]) {
  NSAutoreleasePool * pool = [[NSAutoreleasePool alloc] init];
  // Log hello world to the debugger console
  NSLog(@"Hello World");
  int retVal = UIApplicationMain(argc, argv, nil, nil);
  [pool release];
  return retVal;
}
```

Notice the `main` function is simply a C function. Like C's `main`, it takes an integer and an array of C strings. It also returns an integer, where 0 usually indicates success and non-zero indicates an error. You almost never modify `main` when writing an Objective-C program for the iPhone, but understanding how an iPhone program begins is fundamental. Starting an iPhone application is the same as starting any other C or Objective-C application; it all begins with `main`.

NOTE

Apple slightly modifies the Xcode interface with every minor release. Your Xcode interface will most likely appear slightly different than this book's.

Header Files and Source Files

Objective-C, like C, consists of header files and source files. Header files contain method prototypes and variable declarations and end with the .h file extension. Source files contain method implementations and variable implementations and end with the .m file extension. Objective-C, unlike C, uses header files to declare class interfaces and source files to declare class implementations. Listings 1-4 and 1-5 illustrate an Objective-C header file and source file defining a SayHello class.

Listing 1-4 An Objective-C Class interface in a header file

```
#import <UIKit/UIKit.h>

#define GREETING @"Dawg"
#define AGE 40
@interface SayHello : NSObject {
  NSString * test;
}
- (void) sayHello: (NSString *) name;
@end
```

Listing 1-5 An Objective-C Class implementation in a source file

```
#import "SayHello.h"
@implementation SayHello
- (void) sayHello: (NSString *) name {
  NSLog(@"Hello %@, %@. You are %i years old.", name, GREETING, AGE);
}
@end
```

Although Objective-C classes and class methods are not discussed until Chapter 4, notice from the preceding two listings that Objective-C methods look different from C functions and Java methods. As you will learn in greater detail in Chapter 4, Objective-C uses what is called infix notation.

Preprocessor Directives and Compiler Directives

Preprocessor directives begin with a # character. Compiler directives begin with an @ character. Both are important to an Objective-C program's structure.

The code also uses `#import` rather than C's `#include`. Objective-C uses `#import`; the `#import` preprocessor directive is identical to `#include` but will not include the same header file more than once. Also notice the compiler directives; Objective-C relies heavily upon compiler directives.

Preprocessor Statements

The `#include` and `#import` statements are both *preprocessor directives.* When you compile your program, the compiler's preprocessor processes statements with a # sign before compiling. For instance, `#import <file.h>` or `#import "file.h"` tells the preprocessor to replace the statement with file's contents.

You can also use preprocessor macros. For instance, the `#define` preprocessor directive is a commonly used macro. In Listing 1-4, you defined two constants, `GREETING` and `AGE`. When you compile this program, the preprocessor literally replaces all `GREETING` and `AGE` occurrences with their respective values.

```
[Session started at 2009-08-08 16:53:47 -0400.]
2009-08-08 16:53:49.430 HelloWorld[745:20b] Hello James, Dawg. You are
40 years old.
```

Compiler Directives

Compiler directives are what make Objective-C different than C. A *compiler directive,* like a preprocessor directive, instructs the compiler to do something before it actually compiles. Compiler directives begin with the @ character. Objective-C has its own preprocessor that processes these special directives. The `@interface` and `@implementation` statements in Listings 1-4 and 1-5 are compiler directives, for instance. You do not really need to understand how compiler directives work under the covers. Just realize that compiler directives actually take your Objective-C code and turn it into regular C code.

Ask the Expert

Q: What is a preprocessor?

A: A *preprocessor* is a separate program from the compiler that runs prior to the compiler running. It handles preprocessor directives, replacing import statements with file contents, executing conditional statements such as `#if`, and processing definitions. Preprocessors can also conditionally compile code; however, that discussion is outside this chapter's scope.

TIP

Print and bind Apple's "The Objective-C 2.0 Programming Language" document and "Object-Oriented Programming with Objective-C." Read both after reading this book; but realize neither has much example code and both documents, although comprehensive, are terse.

Comments

Objective-C *comments* are the same as Java and C comments. Single-line comments begin with a double forward slash, while multiline comments begin with a forward slash followed by a star. A multiline comment ends with a star followed by a forward slash. The following code snippet illustrates:

```
// This is a single-line comment
/* This is a multiline
comment */
```

You use Objective-C comments the same as you would for most other programming languages. You use them to annotate your code and to mark code that you do not wish to delete but do not want the application to run. By commenting the code, you assure that the compiler does not compile the commented code. Because the code is never compiled, it never executes.

Pointers

Pointers are important in Objective-C. However, successfully using them in Objective-C does not require a deep knowledge. In this section, I briefly discuss pointers.

A *pointer* points to a location in memory. Consider an iPhone's memory as one large cubbyhole; similar to the one you most likely had in kindergarten. Each cubbyhole is a location in memory. The cubbyhole's content is the actual value. For instance, the following statement assigns a value to a cubbyhole's content.

```
int cubbyHoleOne = 32;
```

But now suppose each cubbyhole is numbered by a row and column. A pointer points to the cubbyhole's address. So a pointer to `cubbyHoleOne` would look like the following:

```
int * pointerToCubbyHoleOne = &cubbyHoleOne;
```

This statement creates a pointer to an integer and then assigns the pointer `cubbyHoleOne`'s address. Note that it is `cubbyHoleOne`'s address, not `cubbyHoleOne`'s value. When declaring a pointer variable, you indicate that it is a pointer by using the `*` operator. When you precede a variable by the `&` operator, you are indicating that you are referring to the variable's address and not the variable's value. Finally, if you wish to refer to the value a pointer points to you, precede it with a `*`. The following NSLog statement illustrates accessing the `pointerToCubbyHoleOne's` actual value.

```
NSLog("The value: %i", *pointerToCubbyHoleOne);
```

You do not really need to understand much more about pointers than that. In future chapters, when you use objects, you will be strictly using pointers to objects, and not the objects themselves. Basically, all you need to remember is that pointers allow Objective-C to pass objects around by reference and not the actual object, saving considerable memory.

Xcode Fundamentals

Xcode is Apple's Mac OS X integrated development environment (IDE). It comes packaged with the OS X install DVDs as a separate install. You can also download it from Apple's Developer Connection. As of this book's writing, Xcode is bundled with the iPhone SDK. If you have not already downloaded and installed the iPhone SDK, you should do so now. You can find Xcode in the /Developer/Applications folder. You should add Xcode to your computer's Dock so that you can access it easily. Figure 1-11 illustrates Xcode's Project window.

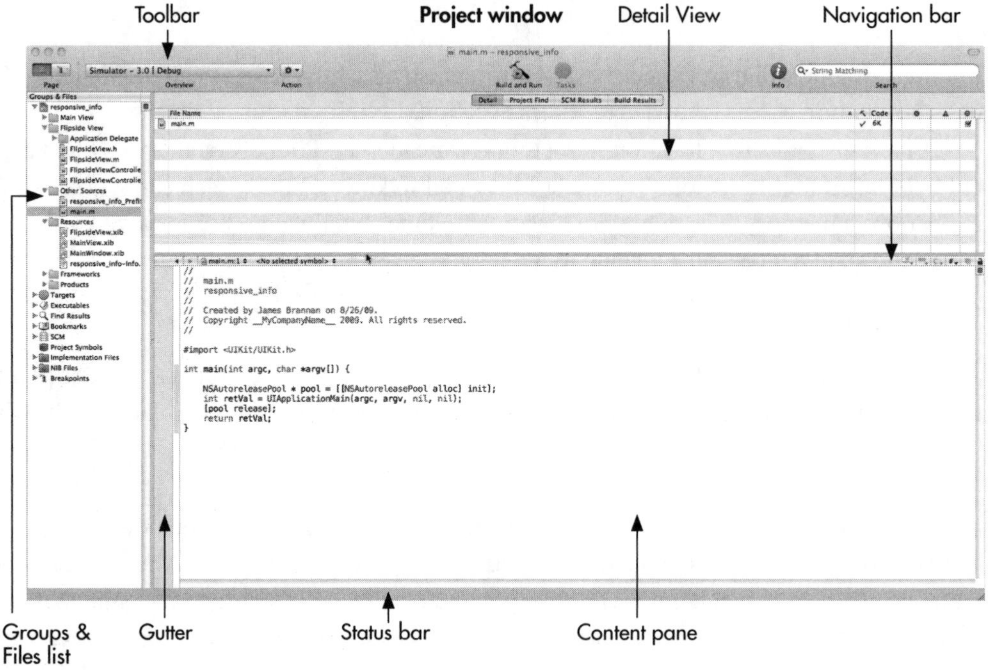

Figure 1-11 Xcode's Project window (Default layout)

You use the toolbar to select what target you will compile to. For instance, in this book you will only use the iPhone simulator in debug mode, and so you will always choose Simulator – 3.0 | Debug. After you've chosen it once, unless you change it, Xcode remembers your choice. The Groups & Files list contains the project's source files, resources such as images, and XIB files. The gutter is where you will add something called breakpoints in later chapters. And the Content pane is the editor, or where you will edit source files. For more comprehensive information on the editor, see the document "Xcode Workspace Guide," referenced later in this chapter.

Before using Xcode, you should configure it so that it matches your work style. Figure 1-11 illustrates the project window displayed using what is called the Default layout. This layout is not the layout you will use in this book's remaining Try This examples. Instead, you will use what is called the All-In-One layout. In the next Try This example you configure Xcode to use the All-In-One layout.

Configuring Xcode's Display

There are three ways you might configure Xcode's layout: Default, Condensed, and All-In-One. In the book *iPhone SDK Programming: A Beginner's Guide,* I use the Default layout. However, in this book, since you will be using the debugger console more extensively, you should use the All-In-One layout.

Try This Assigning Xcode the All-In-One Layout

1. Open Xcode. From the menu, select Xcode | Preferences to display the preferences dialog.
2. Select General and then All-In-One from the Layout drop-down. Ensure the check boxes are all selected (Figure 1-12).
3. Click Apply.
4. Select Text Editing and ensure the Show Gutter check box is selected (Figure 1-13).
5. Click Apply and then OK.
6. Open the HelloWorld project and Xcode should now show two small buttons at its upper left (Figure 1-14).

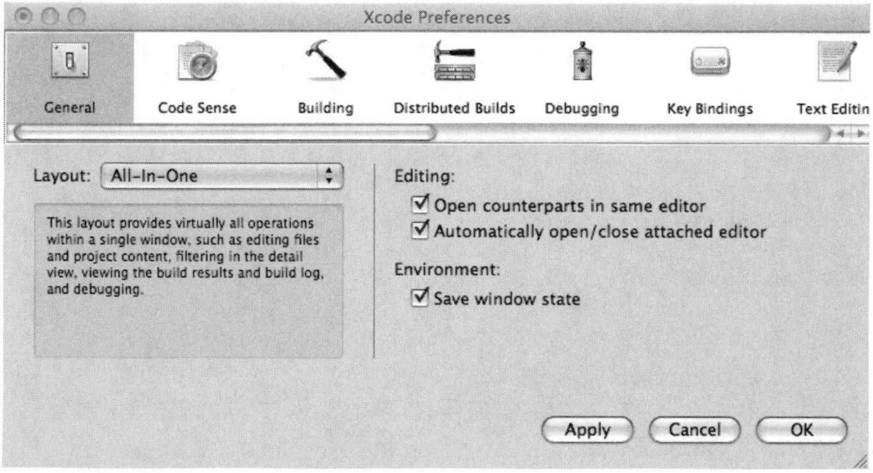

Figure 1-12 Selecting All-In-One for Xcode's layout

(continued)

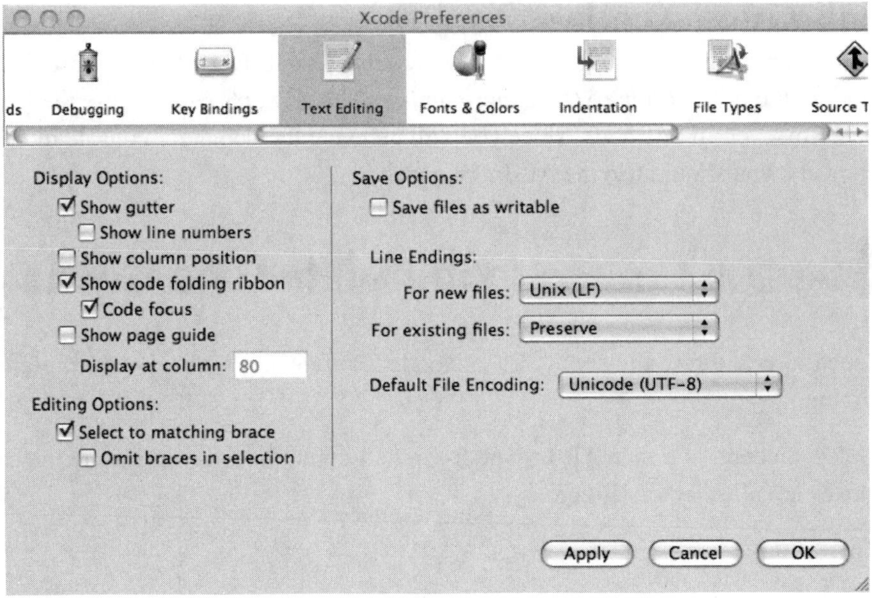

Figure 1-13 Ensuring Xcode shows the gutter

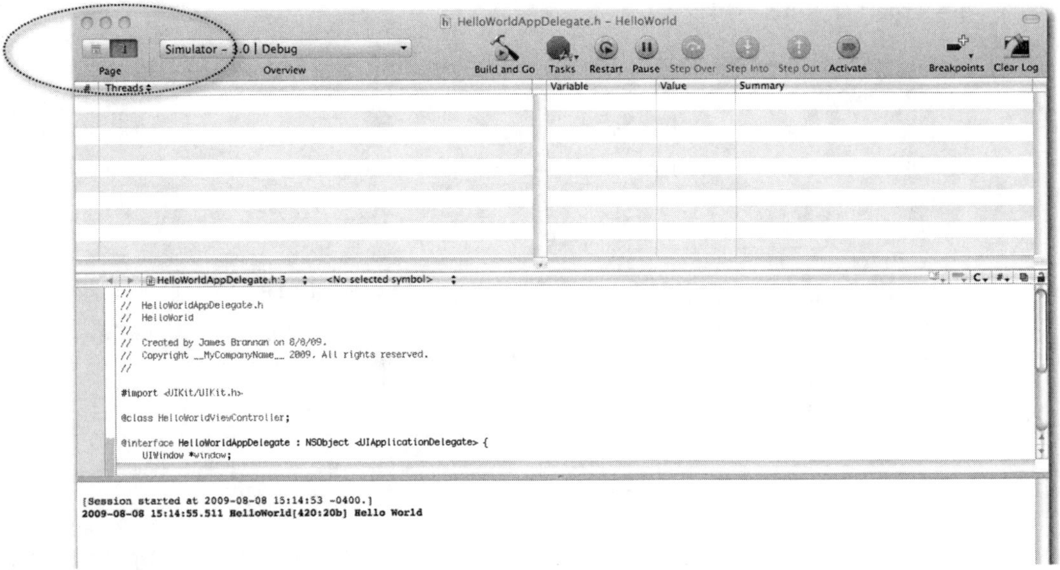

Figure 1-14 The edit and debug buttons

7. Click Build And Debug to run the application in debug mode. If the button says Build and Run, then select Build | Build and Debug from XCode's menu. Notice Xcode's appearance changed (Figure 1-15). Notice the button with the spray can image is depressed.

8. Click the other button to the left and the editor pane is displayed. Toggle between the two buttons a few times.

9. Quit the application by clicking the red Tasks button. Notice that the iPhone Simulator remains running.

10. Select the simulator, and then end it by selecting iPhone Simulator | Quit iPhone Simulator from the simulator's menu.

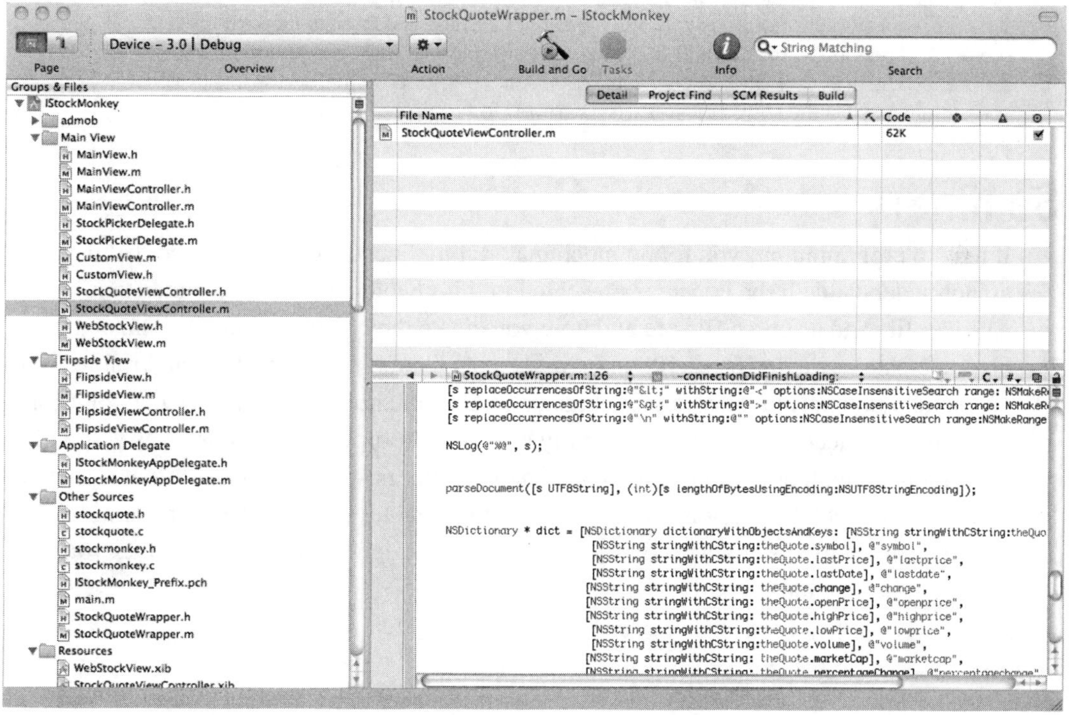

Figure 1-15 Xcode running in debug mode

(continued)

Exploring Xcode Further

Apple has good documentation on using Xcode. You should read that documentation. Apple's "Xcode Workspace Guide" is a comprehensive Xcode document that you can read online or download. You do not need to read it fully—I never have—but you should skim it for things that can help you use Xcode more productively.

This document has many tidbits you might miss that make working with Xcode easier and quicker. For instance, the document covers the keyboard shortcuts, how to reset Xcode, and how to take a snapshot of your project. The document is worth reviewing.

TIP

You can take a snapshot of your work by selecting File | Make Snapshot. This saves your project's current state should you require reverting your project back to a previous state. I use this feature religiously; many times I have made a complete mess of my project and needed to restore it to a known, more stable state. Should you need to restore, you select File | Snapshots from Xcode's menu to display the Snapshots dialog. You can then select the snapshot you wish to revert to.

Summary

If new to programming, you found much material to digest. Do not be concerned if you do not understand all the concepts presented in this chapter. You should understand what a header file and a source file are and how you create them. You should also understand how to create a simple Xcode iPhone project from a template, compile it, and run it. And you should understand that main.m contains a `main` method that is the starting point for all iPhone applications. If you do not fully understand pointers, that is okay, as you will learn more about them in the next couple chapters. For now, just remember that a pointer points to a variable's location and not the variable's value. In future chapters, almost every topic presented in this chapter will be covered in more depth. In the next chapter you explore primitive data types.

Chapter 2

Primitive Data Types and Operators

Key Skills & Concepts

- Understanding Integers
- Understanding Floats and Doubles
- Understanding the BOOL Data Type
- Understanding the Arithmetic Operators
- Understanding the Equality and Logical Operators
- Understanding the Assignment Operator
- Understanding the Conditional Operator
- Using the iPhone SDK's Window-Based Application Template

In this chapter, you explore Objective-C's primitive data types and operators. Objective-C's primitive data types and operators are the same as C's. Therefore, if you understand C's primitive data types, you also understand Objective-C's primitive data types. After exploring Objective-C's primitive data types, you explore Objective-C operators. Like the primitive data types, Objective-C's operators are the same as C's operators.

Primitive Data Types

A *data type* tells a computer the data type a variable is to represent. By telling a computer a variable's type, the data type is informing the computer how much memory it must reserve for a variable and the range of possible values a variable might contain.

NOTE

Realize that how much memory is required—and how many values a primitive data type can represent—might vary on different platforms. However, in this book, as you are using the iPhone SDK, I can assume you are using an Intel-based Mac running OS X Snow Leopard. And so I can confidently state each data type's size and value range.

Numeric Types: Integers

An integer is any whole number. The integer data type is represented by the `int` keyword. For instance, consider the following statement.

```
int x = 4;
```

The `int` keyword identifies the primitive's type, an integer, and 4 is the literal. The equal sign assigns x the literal value 4. You can also write the statement in two steps if you prefer.

```
int x = 0;
x = 4;
```

Integers can be further defined using the `short`, `long`, and `unsigned` qualifiers to form a short integer, a long integer, and an unsigned integer. Table 2-1 summarizes Objective-C's integer data types.

Type	Range	Bytes	Formats (printing in NSLog)
`short int`	–32,768 to 32,768	2	`%hi`
`unsigned short int`	0 to 65,535	2	`%hu`
`unsigned int`	0 to 4,294,967,295	4	`%u`
`int`	–2,147,483,647 to 2,147,483,647	4	`%i`
`long int`	–2,147,483,647 to 2,147,483,647	4	`%li`
`unsigned long int`	0 to 4,294,967,295	4	`%lu`
`long long int`	–9223372036854775807 to 9223372036854775808	8	`%lli`
`unsigned long long int`	0 to 18446744073709551615	8	`%llu`

Table 2-1 Integer Data Types

Ask the Expert

Q: When will I ever use an unsigned long long?

A: You will actually use an unsigned long long if you use the iPhone's `MPMediaItem` class. Songs on an iPhone or iPod Touch are accessible to iPhone developers through the `MPMediaPlayer` class. The `MPMediaItem` class encapsulates each of the media player's individual songs. The `MPMediaItem` has an `id` property. Every iTunes media item has a persistent unique `id` called the `MPMediaItemPropertyPersistentID`. That `id` is an unsigned long long.

Try This Exploring Integer Types and Using the sizeof() C Method

1. Open Xcode and select File | New Project from the File menu.
2. Select Application | Window-based Application in the New Project dialog (Figure 2-1).
3. Click Choose and then name the project **ExploreIntegers**.

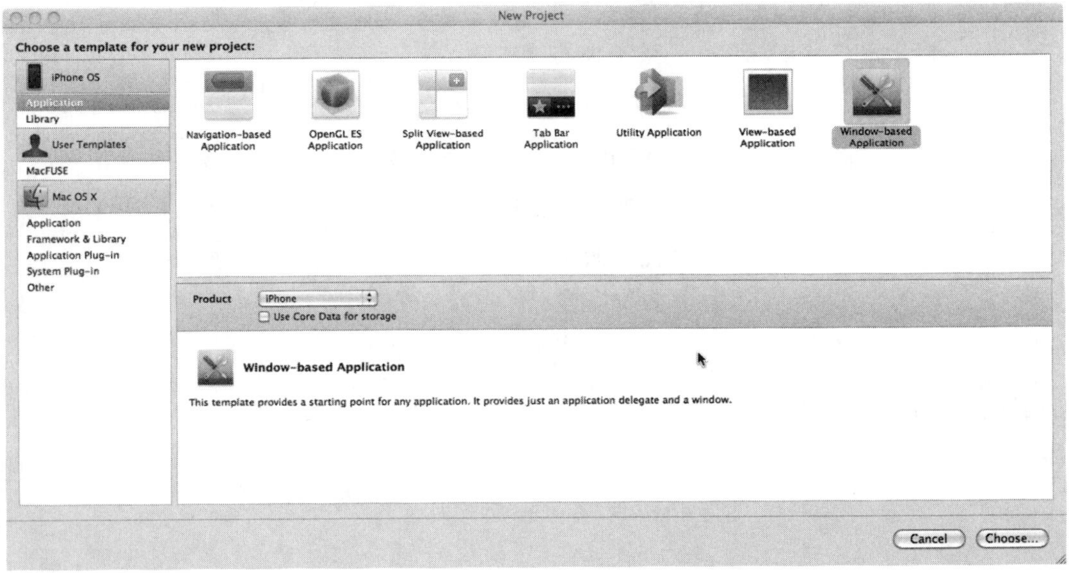

Figure 2-1 New Project dialog

4. In Groups & Files, expand Other Sources and select main.m to reveal the file's content in the editor.

5. Modify main.m to match Listing 2-1. Be certain you write the code before the `main` method. Also, be certain you add code to the `main` method that calls the `exploreIntegers` method (Listing 2-1).

6. Click Build and Debug to compile and run the application in the iPhone Simulator. The debugger console's logging should resemble Listing 2-2 (I exclude the console's date, time, and filename prefix from the logging).

Listing 2-1 The explore_integers.c source file

```
#import <UIKit/UIKit.h>
void exploreIntegers(void) {
  short int y = SHRT_MIN;
  short yy = SHRT_MAX;
  int x = INT_MIN;
  int xx = INT_MAX;
  long int z = LONG_MIN;
  long zz = LONG_MAX;
  unsigned long p = 0;
  unsigned long int pp = ULONG_MAX;
  long long int q = LLONG_MIN;
  long long qq = LLONG_MAX;
  unsigned long long rr = 0;
  unsigned long long ss =  ULLONG_MAX;
  NSLog(@"--- shorts ---");
  NSLog(@"y:%hi (sizeof):%i\n", y, sizeof(y));
  NSLog(@"yy:%hi (sizeof):%i\n", yy, sizeof(yy));
  NSLog(@"---int ---");
  NSLog(@"x:%i (sizeof):%i\n", x, sizeof(x));
  NSLog(@"xx:%i (sizeof):%i\n", xx, sizeof(xx));
  NSLog(@"---longs---");
  NSLog(@"z:%li (sizeof):%i\n", z, sizeof(z));
  NSLog(@"zz:%li (sizeof):%i\n", zz, sizeof(zz));
  NSLog(@"p:%lu (sizeof):%i\n", p, sizeof(p));
  NSLog(@"pp:%lu (sizeof):%i\n", pp, sizeof(pp));
  NSLog(@"---long longs---");
  NSLog(@"q:%lli (sizeof):%i\n", q, sizeof(q));
  NSLog(@"q:%lli (sizeof):%i\n", qq, sizeof(qq));
  NSLog(@"rr:%llu (sizeof):%i\n", rr, sizeof(rr));
  NSLog(@"ss:%llu (sizeof):%i\n", ss, sizeof(ss));
}
```

(continued)

```
int main(int argc, char *argv[]) {
  exploreIntegers();
  NSAutoreleasePool * pool = [[NSAutoreleasePool alloc] init];
  int retVal = UIApplicationMain(argc, argv, nil, nil);
  [pool release];
  return retVal;
}
```

Listing 2-2 The debugger console logging

```
[Session started at 2009-08-07 07:13:56 -0400.]
--- shorts ---
y:-32768 (sizeof):2
yy:32767 (sizeof):2
---int ---
x:-2147483648 (sizeof):4
xx:2147483647 (sizeof):4
---longs---
z:-2147483648 (sizeof):4
zz:2147483647 (sizeof):4
p:0 (sizeof):4
pp:4294967295 (sizeof):4
---long longs---
q:-9223372036854775808 (sizeof):8
q:9223372036854775807 (sizeof):8
rr:0 (sizeof):8
ss:18446744073709551615 (sizeof):8
```

The code illustrates the integer data types. For instance, the logging reports a short as two bytes and an int as four bytes. The code also illustrates using the `SHRT_MIN`, `SHRT_MAX`, and `LONG_MIN` constants in Listing 2-1. These constants are all defined in the C header file, limits.h, which UIKit.h imports.

Another thing to notice is that when declaring a short, long, or long long, you can omit the `int` keyword and the compiler interprets the type the same. This is important, as when you see Objective-C or C code, you will usually see only the qualifier and not the qualifier and `int`.

```
//you almost always see this
long x = 200000000;
//you don't usually see this
long int x = 200000000;
```

Ask the Expert

Q: In Step 5 of the previous Try This, you instructed me to be certain to place the `exploreIntegers` method above the `main` method. Why?

A: As discussed in Chapter 1, Objective-C programs, like C programs, contain source and header files. Source files end with a .m extension, while header files end with a .h extension. Header files declare things, while source files implement them. One thing header files can contain is function prototypes. A *prototype* lets the compiler know that a source file will define a function. For instance, in the previous Try This you might have declared the function `exploreIntegers` in a header file, explore_integers.h.

```
void exploreIntegers(void);
```

You could have then modified main.m to import the header file by adding an import statement to the file's top.

```
#import "explore_integers.h"
```

When compiling the code, the compiler would then know a source file is to define the `exploreIntegers` function. You could then place the `exploreIntegers` method after `main` if you preferred.

But in the previous Try This there is no header file, and so the compiler has no way of knowing that `exploreIntegers` is to be defined. Therefore, you must define `exploreIntegers` before calling it in the `main` method. Had you not placed `exploreIntegers` before calling it, the compiler would have complained that the method was undefined.

TIP

You can use a short instead of an int or a long int to save memory. A short takes two bytes, while an int and a long int both take four bytes.

Numeric Types: Float and Double

The float data type is a 32-bit (single precision) floating-point number. In computer science, rather than saying decimal, you say floating-point, but you can just think of a float as a small to medium-sized decimal number. A double, like a float, is also a floating-point number; however, it is a 32-bit floating-point number. Think of a double as a large to very large decimal number.

You can use either, but a float uses less memory than a double. A float uses four bytes, while a double uses eight bytes. Generally, unless you need scientific precision, you should use a float because of the memory savings. Although not important on a desktop, on an iPhone or iPod touch, this memory savings can be significant.

NOTE

You log doubles and floats to NSLog using `%f`.

Try This Logging a Double and a Float to NSLog

1. Open ExploreIntegers in Xcode and add the code in Listing 2-3 to main.m. As with the `exploreIntegers` method in the previous Try This, be certain you place `exploreFloats` before the `main` method.
2. Replace the `main` method's call to `exploreIntegers` with `exploreFloats` (Listing 2-4).
3. Click Build and Debug.

Listing 2-3 The `exploreFloats` method

```
void exploreFloats(void) {
  float x = FLT_MIN;
  float y = FLT_MAX;
  double z = DBL_MIN;
  double r = DBL_MAX;
  NSLog(@"x: %f sizeof:%i", x, sizeof(x));
  NSLog(@"y: %f sizeof:%i", y, sizeof(y));
  NSLog(@"z: %f sizeof:%i", z, sizeof(z));
  NSLog(@"r: %f sizeof:%i", r, sizeof(r));
}
```

Listing 2-4 The `main` function in main.m

```
int main(int argc, char *argv[]) {
  //exploreIntegers();
  exploreFloats();
```

```
  NSAutoreleasePool * pool = [[NSAutoreleasePool alloc] init];
  int retVal = UIApplicationMain(argc, argv, nil, nil);
  [pool release];
  return retVal;
}
```

Listing 2-5 The debugger console logging

```
x: 0.000000 sizeof:4
y: 340282346638528860000000000000000000000.000000 sizeof:4
z: 0.000000 sizeof:8
r: 17976931348623157000000000000
--- snip 280 zeros omitted ---
0.000000 sizeof:8
```

As Listing 2-5 illustrates, the double type provides significantly greater precision than a float. For most of your needs, a float is sufficient and saves you four bytes.

Characters

The char data type, actually one of the integers, stores a single character. For instance, the following stores the letter *c* in the `myChar` variable.

```
char myChar = 'c';
```

You enclose char types in single quotes. You print a char to NSLog using %c. When writing C programs you use characters, and character aggregations (C strings and character arrays), extensively. When writing Objective-C programs for the iPhone, you will rarely use characters or character aggregations. Instead you will use NSString. If not familiar with NSString, do not worry, by book's end you will be.

NOTE

If you are coming from Java, note that neither Objective-C nor C has a byte data type. Instead, C programmers use an unsigned char to represent a single byte. As you will learn in later chapters, Objective-C programmers usually use a higher-level foundation framework class called `NSData`.

Ask the Expert

Q: What about C strings, are they char data types?

A: C strings are character arrays. I discuss arrays and C strings in Chapter 3.

The BOOL Data Type

The BOOL data type is an Objective-C addition. It is not a true data type, as it is a C preprocessor definition. Whether BOOL is or is not a data type is unimportant here, though; what is more important is how you use it.

A BOOL evaluates to YES or NO. You use a BOOL where you would normally use a 0 or 1 when using C. Later chapters, after you learn about classes and objects, will explain BOOL further.

NOTE

BOOL is actually a type definition—typedef—for a signed char data type. If you look in the objc.h header file, you will see the following preprocessor definitions and typedef:

```
typedef signed char BOOL;
#define YES (BOOL)1
#define NO (BOOL)2
```

Operators

You use operators with variables to create expressions that are more complex. Operators operate on variables. In this chapter, I discuss arithmetic, unary, and assignment operators.

NOTE

This chapter omits bitwise operators, as you will probably rarely use them. This chapter also omits memory operators (pointer-related operators).

Arithmetic Operators

Arithmetic operators work as you might expect. Table 2-2 summarizes them.

Operator	Description
+	Addition
–	Subtraction
++	Increment by 1
––	Decrement by 1
*	Multiplication
/	Division
%	Modulus, the remainder from division

Table 2-2 Objective-C Arithmetic Operators

Try This Using Arithmetic Operators

1. Open the preceding Try This project, ExploreIntegers, in Xcode.
2. Replace `exploreFloats` with the method `arithmetic` in Listing 2-6.
3. Click Build and Debug.

Listing 2-6 The `arithmetic` method

```
void arithmetic(void) {
  int x = 20; int z = 4;
  x = x + 2;
  NSLog(@"x:%i", x);
  x = x - z;
  NSLog(@"x:%i", x);
  x = x * z;
  NSLog(@"x:%i", x);
  NSLog(@"x:%i", x++);
  NSLog(@"x:%i", x);
  NSLog(@"x:%i", ++x);
  NSLog(@"x:%i", --x);
```

(continued)

```
    x = x/2;
    NSLog(@"x:%i", x);
    x = x % 5;
    NSLog(@"x:%i", x);
}
```

Listing 2-7 The debugger console logging

```
x:22
x:18
x:72
x:72
x:73
x:74
x:73
x:36
x:1
```

The `arithmetic` method assigns `x` the value 20 and `z` the value 4. It then adds 2 to `x`, resulting in 22. It then subtracts `z` from `x` and `x` becomes 18. After subtracting, the method multiplies `x` by `z` and the new value becomes 72.

The next line combines logging `x`'s value to the debugger console and incrementing `x` by 1. However, note that the increment occurs after `x`'s value is printed, as the value printed remains 72. Conversely, two lines down, `x` is incremented by 1 before being printed and the value printed reflects the added value and prints 74.

Unary Operators

A unary operator is a preceding + or – that indicates a value is positive or negative. Adding a unary operator in front of a variable essentially multiplies the variable by a positive or negative 1. For instance, consider the following code and its output in the debugger console:

```
int x = 40;
x = -x;
NSLog(@"x:%i", x);
```

```
x:-40
```

Equality and Logical Operators

In Chapter 3, when you explore logical statements, you will use these operators. I introduce them here, for completeness. You use these operators to test for equality. Table 2-3 summarizes them. In later chapters, you will use these operators to test two variables' equivalence.

Although I do not introduce conditional statements until Chapter 3, consider the following code:

```
int x = 20; int z = 4;
NSLog(@"x equals z: %i", x = = z);
```

The logging statement prints `x equals z: 0` to the debugger console. The code, `x = = z`, asks the question "does `x` equal `z`?" If it does, the program returns 1 (true). If it does not, the program returns 0 (false). The same logic applies for the other equality operators.

Now consider the following code containing a logical or operator.

```
int x = 20; int z = 4; int p = 20;
NSLog(@"x equals z: %i", x == z || x == p);
```

The logging statement prints `x equals z: 1` to the debugger console because the question is now "does `x` equal `z` or does `x` equal `p`?"

Operator	Operator's Meaning
<	Less than
>	Greater than
= =	Equal to
<=	Less than or equal to
>=	Greater than or equal to
!=	Is not equal to
&&	Logical and
||	Logical or

Table 2-3 Equality and Logical Operators

Assignment Operators

An assignment operator assigns the value on the right of the assignment operator to the variable on the right. For instance, the following three statements are all assignments:

```
int x = 19; int z = 4; int p = 20;
```

The first statement assigns x the value 19, the second assigns z the value 4, and the third assigns p the value 20.

You can also combine the assignment operator with additive operators to create compound assignment operators. For instance, consider the following statements and their equivalent using one of the compound assignment operators (Listing 2-8).

Listing 2-8 Assignment operators example

```
int x = 20; int z = 4; int p = 20;
x = x + 2; //x = 22
x += 2; //x = 24
z = z - 2; //z = 2
z -= 2; //z = 0
p = p * 2; //p = 40
p *= 2; //p = 80
p = p/2; //p = 40
p /= 2; //p = 20
```

Table 2-4 illustrates the assignment operators. Note that in reality, you are combining the arithmetic operator with the assignment operator, but out of convenience, just refer

Assignment Operator	Example Statement	Statement's Effect	Equivalent Statement
=	`int myvar = 2;`	Assignment	
+=	`myvar += 3;`	Add 3 to value	`myvar = myvar + 3;`
–=	`myvar -= 3;`	Subtract 3 from value	`myvar = myvar -3;`
/=	`myvar /= 2;`	Divide value by 2	`myvar = myvar/2;`
*=	`myvar *=2;`	Multiply value by 2	`myvar = myvar * 2;`
%=	`myvar %= 2;`	Obtain remainder from division by 2	`myvar = myvar % 2;`

Table 2-4 Assignment Operators

to these as assignment operators rather than an arithmetic operator combined with an assignment operator.

TIP

You will often see op= in books when explaining the combined operators. The proper term for this assignment is compound assignment.

Data Type Conversions

There are often times when you might wish to convert a primitive from one type to another. For instance, you might have a situation where you sum sales figures.

```
int numberSold = 20;
float costPerItem = 23.22;
float amount = numberSold * costPerItem; //amount = 464.399994
```

The runtime knows to convert the integer to a float before multiplying. Programmers call this a widening conversion because you can widen an int to a float with no information loss. The converse is not true and often results in an incorrect value or a rounded value. Programmers call this a narrowing conversion.

```
int amount = numberSold * costPerItem; //amount = 464, it rounds to int
double grams = DBL_MAX;
float amount = grams; //amount = #INF00 or infinity
```

TIP

When a value falls outside the range supported by the specific data type, you obtain infinity, or `#INF00`.

Although a compiler can usually figure out your intentions, you should always cast if you wish to convert a value to a narrower type. Casting is explicitly changing a variable's data type from one type to another when using the variable. Casting does not affect the original variable's type. Casting is essentially saying, "I know you are an integer, but for this division I want you to temporarily be a float." For instance, you might divide two integers and assign the results to a float.

```
int points = 95;
int papers = 10;
float grade = points/papers;
NSLog(@"%f", (float)grade);
```

Because `points` and `papers` are both integers, the compiler throws away the 0.5 remainder. What the compiler is doing is saying, "Hmm, two integers, the result must be an integer, so I'm throwing away the 0.5; oh, when I'm done I need to assign the result to this float, so let me change it to a float." However, the damage was done, and the 0.5 was lost. Instead, you should cast the integers.

```
int points = 95;
int papers = 10;
float grade = (float)points/(float)papers;
printf(@"%f", (float)grade);
```

When casting the integers as floats the compiler now says, "Hmm, I need to treat these as floats, so let me add a 0.000 to both, divide, and treat the result as a float." As an aside, note that you are not required to cast both `points` and `papers` as floats; you can cast one and the compiler recognizes it should treat the result as a float.

If this all seems slightly confusing, do not worry about it. Just remember this rule: always explicitly cast when using different data types in the same expression. Doing this will prevent errors and make your code easier to read by other developers. Besides, casting does not make your code any slower.

The UIWindow Application Template

In this chapter, without explanation, you used the Window-based Application template. This template creates a bare-minimum iPhone project. It creates a xib containing the Interface Builder graphical user interface components and a `UIApplicationDelegate` class that handles the application's life-cycle events. A *life-cycle* event is a system event that affects your running application. For instance, the application running low on memory, the phone receiving an incoming call, or the phone's orientation changing from portrait to landscape are all life-cycle events. Figure 2-2 illustrates a typical iPhone application's life cycle.

The `main` method in the main.m file starts the iPhone application. The application loads the window and the window's delegate. The window and delegate remain active until the application terminates. As external events occur and affect the application, the application's delegate responds to those events. In reality it is slightly more involved than Figure 2-2, but not much.

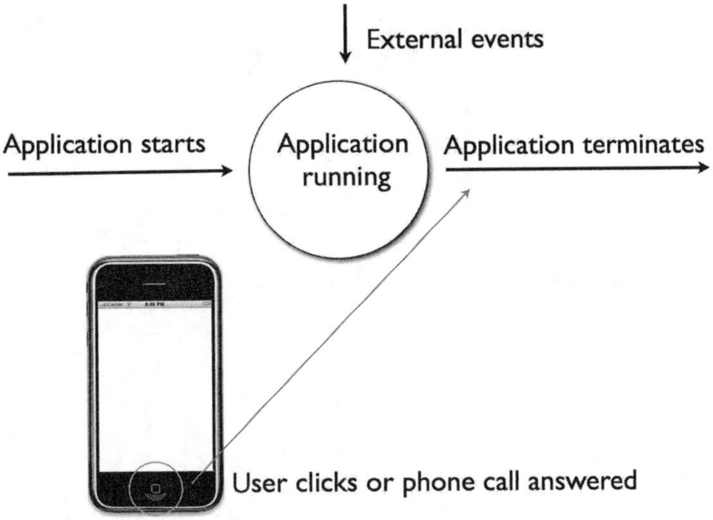

Figure 2-2 An iPhone app's life cycle

Try This Using the Window-based Application Template

1. Open Xcode and open any previous Try This from this chapter.
2. Expand Classes and select <projectName>AppDelegate.m; for instance, ExploreIntegers is named ExploreIntegersAppDelegate. Notice the applicationDidFinishLaunching: method.
3. Expand Resources and double-click MainWindow.xib to open it in Interface Builder.
4. Although you will probably see other windows, notice the document window and the window's canvas (Figure 2-3). Close Interface Builder.
5. Click Build and Debug and the application should compile and launch in the iPhone Simulator (Figure 2-4).

(continued)

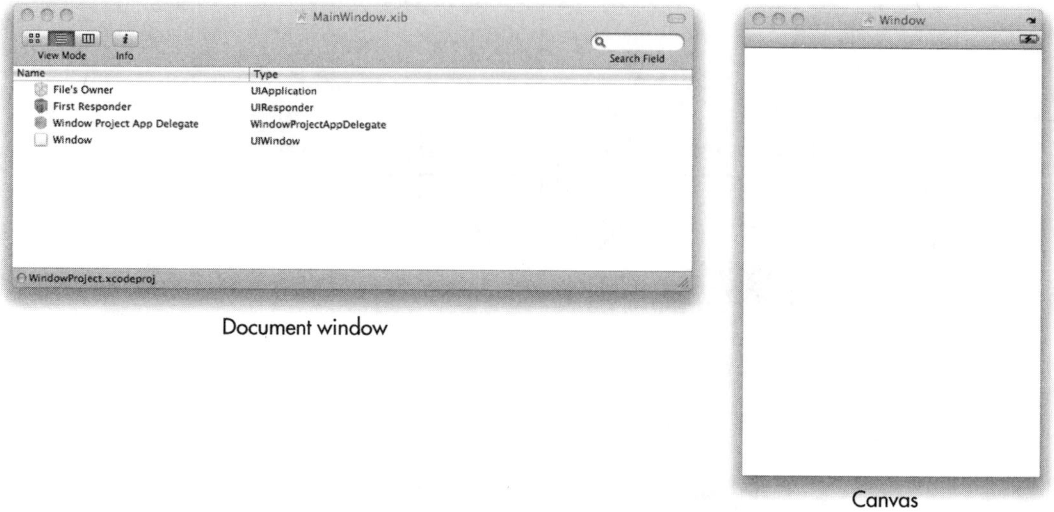

Figure 2-3 The document window and canvas in Interface Builder

Figure 2-4 The blank window displayed in the iPhone Simulator

The Window-based Application template creates an iPhone application consisting of an application delegate and a window. Every iPhone application has a single window. That window displays a single view at a time. As you shall see in later chapters, you can change that view. But in the Try This projects in this chapter you created an empty window. Notice that the template created files called <project name>AppDelegate.h and <project name>AppDelegate.m. These files contain the project's application delegate. As you will see in later chapters, the header file contains the delegate's interface, while the source file contains the delegate's implementation.

The application delegate responds to life-cycle events while your application is running. If you wish to write code that responds to a life-cycle event, you place it in one of this class's methods. For a more detailed explanation, see Chapter 6 in *iPhone SDK Programming: A Beginner's Guide.*

Summary

In this chapter, you explored the primitive data types and operators available to you in Objective-C. They are identical to the data types and operators available to you in C. This is for good reason; Objective-C is a superset of C. In the next chapter, Chapter 3, you put these primitives and operators to good use when you explore looping and conditional statements. If you do not understand the primitive data types and operators, then you should definitely consult more resources before continuing. Understanding the concepts presented in this chapter is crucial for the remaining chapters. You ended the chapter by learning about an iPhone project's main window, the UIWindow. Although you haven't learned about classes and objects yet, UIWindow should hopefully seem intuitive. The window is what will contain all views that you display in your application.

Chapter 3

Flow Control Statements, Arrays, and Structures

Key Skills & Concepts

- Understanding Boolean Expressions
- Understanding Looping Using the For Loop
- Understanding Looping Using the While and Do While Loops
- Understanding the Break and Continue Statements
- Understanding Conditionals Using If, Else If, and Else
- Understanding the Switch Statement
- Understanding Arrays and Structs

Much like Chapters 1 and 2, this chapter will seem like you are exploring C rather than Objective-C. But that is because Objective-C's control structures are the same as C's. In this chapter you explore Objective-C's looping and conditional statements (control flow statements).

A program's control flow is the order that it executes its individual instructions. Looping statements cause a program to repeat a code block. Conditional statements cause a program to choose among alternative paths.

Both looping and conditional statements rely upon Boolean expressions. Although it is outside this book's scope to fully discuss Booleans (there are entire college classes devoted to Boolean logic), this chapter does begin by discussing their fundamentals and where you can obtain more information on them.

After exploring looping and conditional statements, you take a slight detour to explore arrays and structs. You will probably rarely use either when programming using Objective-C. Instead, you will use NSArray in lieu of arrays, and classes in lieu of structs. But arrays and structs are the basis for many data structures you will come across in your programming career. Moreover, if you do not understand a basic array, then you simply cannot claim yourself as a programmer. Arrays are a fundamental programming concept. Besides, in future chapters, when you explore the Foundation Framework's NSArray and NSMutableArray, you will need to understand arrays.

Boolean Expressions

A *Boolean* expression results in a Boolean value—true or false. For example, the expression "Apple equals Orange" evaluates to false, as an apple does not equal an orange. Another example, 5 > 3 evaluates to true, as 5 is greater than 3. Both statements result in a true or false value.

You can combine Boolean expressions to form more complex Boolean expressions. For instance, you might write "Apple equals Orange AND 5 > 3." It evaluates to false because even though 5 is greater than 3, an apple is not an orange.

Boolean expressions joined by an AND must both be true. Boolean expressions joined by an OR must have one or the other expression evaluate to true for the entire expression to be true. For instance, the statement "Apple equals Orange OR 5 > 3" evaluates to true because even though an apple is not an orange, 5 is greater than 3.

You might group Boolean expressions using parentheses. For instance, consider the following Boolean expressions.

```
(3 > 5 AND 5 < 9) OR ("a" == "a" AND "b" == "b")
(4 == 4 AND 5 < 7) AND (7 == 7 AND 8 > 2)
```

The first statement evaluates whether it is true or false that 3 is greater than 5 and 5 is less than 9. Because 3 is not greater than 5, the first expression grouping evaluates to false. But the second grouping evaluates to true because *a* equals *a* and *b* equals *b.* A false or a true evaluates to true, and so the Boolean expression is true.

The second statement evaluates if 4 equals 4 and if 5 is less than 7. Both are true, and so it evaluates the first expression to true. The second expression is also true, as 7 equals 7 and 8 is greater than 2. Because both expression groupings are true, the Boolean expression as a whole evaluates to true.

Understanding basic Boolean algebra is fundamental to understanding conditional logic and control flow. If you have never taken a computer science course, then you should seek out a tutorial or two on the web. A good place to start is Wikipedia's page on truth tables (http://en.wikipedia.org/wiki/Truth_table). A truth table is nothing more than a table that evaluates True/False combinations and their ultimate Boolean evaluation. But do not worry about the more difficult combinations, as they are not required for this book. If you understand the little bit discussed in this section, you should be okay to continue with looping and conditional statements. However, if you do not understand, be certain to first seek out some other resources, as simple Boolean logic is fundamental to looping and conditional statements.

Looping

Objective-C uses the same basic looping constructs as Java and C++. After all, all three languages' lineage is C, so it is only fitting they share the same looping constructs. Objective-C, being a C superset, uses C's for, while, and do while loops.

Loops allow repeating a block of code multiple times. For instance, a car engine left running will idle until the car's gas runs out. Or, for every roach in your kitchen, you might wish to crush the roach. Loops allow a program to repeat some behavior while a Boolean condition is true. In the next several pages you explore the for, while, and do while loops. Each loop, although similar, allows slightly different behavior.

The For Loop

The *for* loop repeats a block of code and is under the control of a counter variable. A for loop consists of the for statement followed by the loop body. A for statement has the following form:

```
for(initialization; logical test; update){ <body> }
```

The for loop's body is everything between the opening brace that immediately follows the for statement and its accompanying closing brace. For instance, consider the following code:

```
for (int i = 0; i < 5; i++) {
  NSLog(@".");
}
```

The variable `i` is declared and assigned the value 0. Each loop logs a period to the debugger console. Before each loop, `i` is tested to ensure it is less than 5. At the end of each loop `i` is incremented by 1. The loop repeats five times.

You can omit parts of a for loop statement. Although I personally do not recommend writing code this way, consider a few variations of the for loop.

```
int j = 0;
for(;j<=27;j++) {
  NSLog(@"x");
}
```

In the preceding example, the `j` variable is initialized before the for loop's initialization; therefore, you can skip initializing it in the for loop statement. Now consider a skipped initialization and a different logical evaluation.

```
int q = 0;
for(;q != 7;) {
```

```
  q++;
  NSLog(@"*");
}
```

The q variable is initialized before the for loop. Rather than looping while q is less than some value, looping continues while q is not equal to 7. Remember, the evaluation statement can be anything; the only requirement is that it evaluate to true or false.

Now, consider an error. The following for loop loops indefinitely:

```
int q = 0;
for(;q != -1;) {
  q++;
  NSLog(@"*");
}
```

The q variable's initial value is 0. Each loop increments q by one. But the logical test will always evaluate to "true" because q will never equal –1, and so the loop repeats indefinitely.

Finally, consider the worst kind of for loop, something that hopefully you never do. The following, although an endless loop, is perfectly valid C/Objective-C.

```
int q = 0;
for(;;) {
  q++;
  NSLog(@"*");
}
```

Because there is no evaluation, the loop continues indefinitely, eventually causing your application to crash.

The previous three examples, though shown, are something in practice you shouldn't do. In my opinion, use a for loop only when you have a situation that requires initialization, a logical test, and an update. Although a simplification, I like to think of it as a situation where I repeat through *n* number of "things" and not a situation where I loop until some condition changes.

```
for (int i = 0; i < 5; i++) {
  NSLog(@"Vanilla for loops are the best loops.");
}
```

The While Loop

The *while* loop has the following form:

```
while ( logical test) {<body>}
```

The while loop, like the for loop, performs a logical test before entering the loop's body. If the test evaluates to not zero, or "true," then the statements in the body are executed. The loop then loops and evaluates the logical test again. This repeats until the logical test evaluates to zero, or "false." For instance, consider the following code snippet:

```
float r = 2.3;
while(r < 33.99) {
  r *= 1.2;
}
```

When executed as part of a program, the program first assigns the variable `r` the value 2.3. The program then enters the while loop. The while loop then evaluates if `r` is less than 33.99. It is, and so the program multiplies `r` by 1.2. The while loop then continues looping until `r` is not less than 33.99.

Notice that the while loop performs its logical test before executing the statements in its body. If the logical test evaluates to false, then the while loop's body is skipped. For instance, the following while loop never executes the logging because `t` is equal to `X` and so it skips the loop's body.

```
char t = 'X';
while(t != 'X') {
  NSLog(@"I ran A.");
}
```

The Do While Loop

The *do while* loop is similar to the while loop, only it always executes its body statements at least once and then performs the logical test. The do while loop has the following form:

```
do{ <body> } while(logical test);
```

Consider the following example.

```
char t = 'X';
do {
  NSLog(@"I ran B.");
} while(t != 'X');
```

When run as a program, the program first assigns `t` the value `X`. It then enters the do while loop and executes the logging statement. After logging, the program evaluates the logical test, which evaluates to false. Because the test failed, the program does not loop but continues with the statements after the do while loop.

Try This Using a For, While, or Do While Loop

1. Open Xcode and create a new Utility Application (Figure 3-1). Name the project **LoopingExample**.
2. Open the file MainViewController.m in the editor and add the `viewDidLoad` method (Listing 3-1).
3. Build the application.

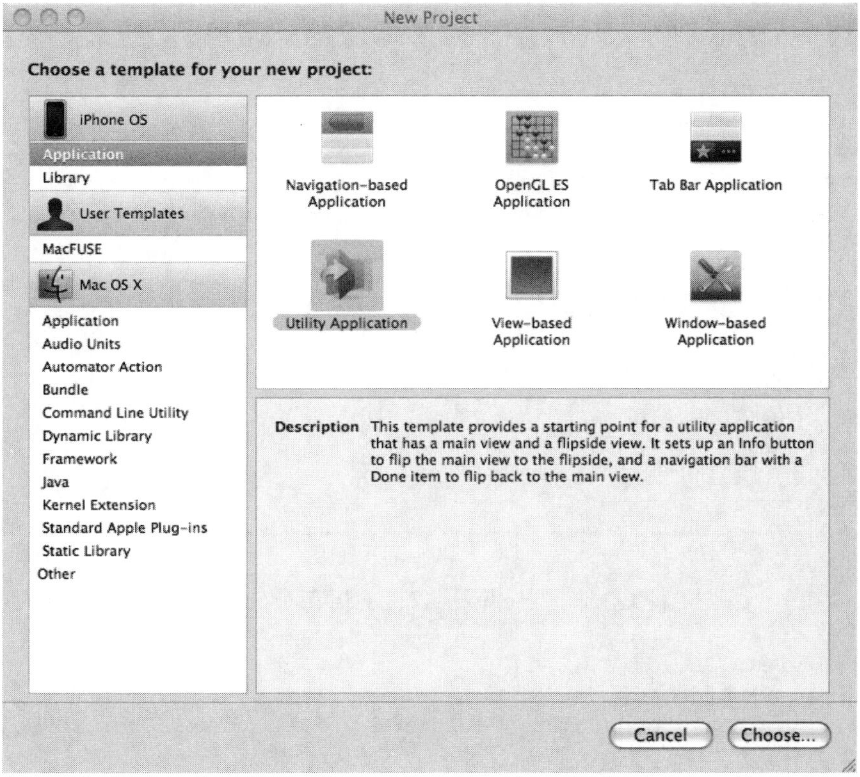

Figure 3-1 Utility Application template

(continued)

4. Open the file FlipsideViewController.m in the editor and modify the `viewDidLoad` method to match Listing 3-2. Don't worry about the line setting the backgroundColor that Xcode's template created; you don't need it for this example; it merely sets the view's background color.

5. Add the method `viewDidAppear` in FlipsideViewController.m (Listing 3-3).

6. Click Build And Go to build and run the application.

7. Click the info button in the lower-right corner and then Done. Repeat several times. Notice the logging in the logging console (Listing 3-4).

Listing 3-1 The `viewDidLoad` method in MainViewController.m

```
- (void)viewDidLoad {
  [super viewDidLoad];
  for(int i = 0; i < 5; i++) {
     NSLog(@"i's value:%i",i);
  }
  int i = 5;
  while(i++ < 8) {
    NSLog(@"i's value:%i",i);
  }
  i = 3;
  do {
    NSLog(@"i's value:%i",i);
    i++;
  } while(i < 3);
}
```

Listing 3-2 The `viewDidLoad` method in FlipsideViewController.m

```
- (void)viewDidLoad {
  [super viewDidLoad];
  self.view.backgroundColor = [UIColor viewFlipsideBackgroundColor];
  int r = 9;
  do {
    NSLog(@"r's value:%i", r);
    r /= 3;
  } while(r != 3);
}
```

Listing 3-3 The `viewDidAppear` method in FlipsideViewController.m

```
- (void) viewDidAppear: (BOOL) animated {
  [super viewDidAppear:animated];
  BOOL quit = NO;
  for(int i = 0;!quit;i++) {
    NSLog(@"an endless loop without break...%i",i);
    quit = YES;
  }
}
```

Listing 3-4 Debugger console logging

```
i's value:0
i's value:1
i's value:2
i's value:3
i's value:4
i's value:6
i's value:7
i's value:8
i's value:3
r's value:9
an endless loop without break...0
r's value:9
an endless loop without break...0
r's value:9
an endless loop without break...0
```

The logging in Listing 3-4 illustrates the method's processing. When the method executes, the for loop loops 4 times and logs 0 through 4 to the debugger console. The while loop then logs 5 through 8 to the debugger console. Notice that the while loop increments the `i` variable after evaluating if it is less than 8. This subtlety is important. If you replaced the while loop with `while(++i < 8)`, then `i` would be incremented before being evaluated if it is less than 8. In that situation, the maximum value logged to the debugger console would be 7. The `viewDidLoad` method then illustrates a do while loop; it logs 3 to the debugger console.

When you click the info button, the application displays the FlipsideViewController. When it loads into the window, it performs the do while loop and logs 9 to the debugger console.

True or False and BOOL

Before continuing, pause to consider what "true" or "false" really means. C has no true or false but instead has zero or not zero, where zero is "false" and not zero is "true." You must remember this fact when evaluating primitives.

A trick that C programmers often do is to define a typedef for a Boolean value. For instance, consider the following:

```
typedef int bool;
#define FALSE 0
#define TRUE (1)
```

Now, in subsequent code a developer can write code that uses TRUE and FALSE.

```
for(;(q != 7) == TRUE);) {
  q++;
  NSLog(@"*");
}
```

TIP

For everything you wanted to know about Boolean data types and more, go to Wikipedia's page on the subject (http://en.wikipedia.org/wiki/Boolean_data_type).

Objective-C took this C programmer trick and defines a BOOL type. As you already saw in Chapter 2, a BOOL is simply a typedef where 0 is false and 1 is true. It is important you note, though, that only 1 is true, not every value but 0. More on BOOL after you learn about classes in Chapter 4; using BOOL will be second nature by the book's end.

Conditional Statements

There are often points in a program where it must make a choice and conditionally process one set of statements or another. For instance, consider the following pseudocode.

```
If time is morning then prepare breakfast.
Else if time is afternoon then prepare lunch.
Else if time is evening then prepare dinner and go to bed.
```

The statement prior to the word "then" is the conditional statement. It tells the program, "If this is true, then execute the following statement(s)." Conditional statements control an application's flow of execution.

The If Statement

The *if* statement is the most common conditional statement; it takes the following form:

```
if ( logical test ) { <body> }
```

The statement says, "If a logical test evaluates to true, then execute the statements in the immediately following statement block." Remember, the statement block is everything between the opening brace immediately following the test and the corresponding closing brace. If the logical test, or the condition, evaluates to false, then a program skips the statement block immediately following the if statement. The following is a typical if statement:

```
int x = 0;
if(x < 9) {
  NSLog(@"x < 9");
  NSLog(@"This was a test.");
}
```

When run as part of a program, the program first assigns x the value 0. It then tests if x is less than 9. It is, and so it executes the two logging statements in the immediately following statement block.

Nested If Statements

A statement block following an if statement can also contain if statements. These if statements are called *nested* if statements. The compiler is smart enough to distinguish which closing curly brace goes with which opening curly brace.

```
int x = 0;
int * p = &x;
if(x < 9) {
  NSLog("This is a test.");
  if(sizeof(p) == sizeof(x)) {
    NSLog("x < 9 and is the size of an int");
  }
}
```

CAUTION

When evaluating a logical condition, be certain to use == and not =. Remember, one equal sign is assignment, while two is evaluation.

Compound If Statements

Sometimes multiple conditions must be met for a program to execute a code block. You use the logical operators discussed in Chapter 2 (&&, ||) when writing compound if statements. Consider the following two statements:

```
int x = 0;
int * p = &x;
if(x < 9 && sizeof(p) == sizeof(x)) {
  NSLog(@"compound if...and");
}
if(x < 9 || sizeof(p) == sizeof(x)) {
  NSLog(@"compound if...or");
}
```

The first statement says, "If x is less than 9 and the size of p is equal to the size of x, then execute the following statement block." The second statement says, "If x is less than 9 or the size of p is equal to the size of x, then execute the following statement block." You can combine the logical && and || operators to form complex conditional statements if you wish.

Short-Circuit Evaluation

Objective-C, like C, short-circuits conditional statements. Short-circuiting relies upon a technique called lazy evaluation. Lazy evaluation doesn't perform unnecessary computations. So, if evaluating a compound conditional statement, and the first part of the statement evaluates to false, then—depending on whether the compound is an *and* or an *or* statement—a program can skip evaluating the rest of the statement. For instance, the following statement uses a logical && operator.

```
int x = 2;
if(x != 2 && (x/0)==7) {
  //never reached, no error
}
```

The program knows when executing that two conditions joined by an && must both be true. However, x is equal to 2 and so the first condition is false. And so the program knows the conditional statement will evaluate to false and it skips the immediately following statement block.

Notice that the preceding code shows an interesting side effect of short-circuiting. Division by zero is a runtime error, but because the statement is never evaluated, the program never raises the error.

Now consider two statements joined by a logical or operator.

```
int x = 2;
if(x != 2 || (x/0)==7) {
  //never reached error
}
```

The program knows when executing the conditional statement that both conditions must be evaluated, as they are joined by an || operator. After evaluating the first statement, despite being false, the program evaluates the second condition, which divides by zero. And so it raises an exception because division by zero is undefined.

The If Else Structure

Sometimes a program should do one thing if one conditional statement is true and another thing if it is false. The else keyword allows this type of processing. Consider the following code snippet.

```
if(x == 3) {
  NSLog(@"x == 3");
}
else {
  NSLog(@"x != 3");
}
```

The code snippet says, "If x is equal to 3, then log 'x is equal to 3' to the debugger console; otherwise, log 'x is not equal to 3' to the debugger console."

The If Else If Else Structure

You can also combine if and else to create more complex structures. Consider the following code snippet:

```
if(x == 3) {
  NSLog(@"x == 3");
}
else if(x == 4) {
  NSLog(@"x == 4");
}
else {
  NSLog(@"x != 3 nor 4");
}
```

As the code illustrates, you can follow an if statement by as many else if statements as desired.

In summary, the if statement, combined with the else statement, takes the following forms:

```
// Pseudo Code
if condition then
<statements>
else if condition then
<statements>
else if condition then
<statements>
...
else
<statements>
end if
```

```
Objective-C/C
if (condition)
{ <statements> }
else if (condition)
{ <statements> }
else if (condition)
{ <statements> }
  ...
else
{ <statements> }
```

Try This Using Conditional If Statements

1. Open the previous Try This project, LoopingExample, in Xcode.
2. Remove the `viewDidLoad` methods from both MainViewController.m and FlipsideViewController.m (don't worry, it doesn't hurt anything).
3. Build and Go just to prove to yourself that the application still works correctly.
4. Open FlipsideViewController.m and implement the `viewDidAppear` method so that it matches Listing 3-5. Also add a variable, named `i`, in FlipsideViewController.
5. Build and Go. Navigate between the screens at least five times and notice the debugging statements (Listing 3-6).

Listing 3-5 The `viewDidAppear` method

```
int i = 0;
- (void) viewDidAppear: (BOOL) animated {
  [super viewDidAppear:animated];
  if(i == 0) {
    NSLog(@"first time appearing...");
  }
  else if(i == 2) {
    NSLog(@"third time appearing...");
  }
  else if(i < 4) {
    NSLog(@"less than 4 times appearing...");
  }
```

```
    else {
      NSLog(@"appearing...");
    }
    i++;
  }
```

Listing 3-6 The debugger console logging

```
first time appearing...
less than 4 times appearing...
third time appearing...
less than 4 times appearing...
appearing...
```

The Switch Statement

The switch/case construct is an easier alternative to multiple if and else if statements when evaluating simple integers. Listing 3-7 illustrates.

Listing 3-7 A switch statement

```
int x = 0;
while (x < 6) {
  switch(x) {
    case 1:
      break;
    case 2:
      printf("x:%i\n",x);
      break;
    case 3:
      break;
    case 4:
    case 5:
      printf("x:%i\n",x);
      break;
    default:
      printf("default\n");
  }
    x++;
  }
}
```

A switch statement evaluates an integer and routes a program's execution flow according to the integer's value. A switch's evaluation takes the following form:

```
switch(myInt){ <body> }
```

Within the body, several case statements provide values to test against the switch's variable to be tested. A case statement takes the following form:

```
case <value to test>:
```

If the case statement's value matches the switch statement's value, then the code block following the case statement executes.

A switch statement might also have an optional default statement.

```
default:
```

If a switch statement has a default, then if there is no exact match, then the code following the case statement executes.

Now, here is the tricky part with switch statements. Notice the keyword, `break`, in Listing 3-7. The `break` keyword forces the switch statement to terminate, and control returns to code following the switch statement. However, if you do not provide a break statement in a case statement's body, then upon completing the case statement, the switch statement evaluates the next case statement. In the preceding code, although the following case statements all evaluate to false, the default statement's body is still entered and the program executes the statements in default's statement block. Unless you explicitly wish following case statements to be evaluated by your program, always end a case statement's code block with a break statement.

Consider Listing 3-7's behavior in more depth. Listing 3-7 illustrates a switch statement and its control flow. When executed as part of a program, the program first assigns `x` the value 0. It then enters the switch statement, using `x` to evaluate against the case statements. On the first loop, `x` equals 0, and so that it matches none of the case statements and the program executes the default statement's logging statement. On the second loop `x` equals 1, and so the first case statement evaluates to 0 and the program executes its break statement. The break statement forces the program to exit the switch statement immediately, and so the program never reaches the default statement. The loop continues until `x` is not less than 6. With each loop, the program enters the switch statement and performs the relevant processing.

Try This Using a Switch Statement

1. Open LoopingExample in Xcode and open FlipsideViewController in the editor.
2. Add the `viewDidDisappear` method so that it matches Listing 3-8.
3. Click Build And Go to build and run the application. Tap the info button and then the Done button one time and the debugger console displays the statements in Listing 3-9.

Listing 3-8 The `viewDidDisappear` method

```
- (void) viewDidDisappear: (BOOL) animated {
  [super viewDidAppear:animated];
  int x = 0;
  while (x < 6) {
    switch(x) {
      case 1:
        break;
      case 2:
        NSLog("x:%i",x);
        break;
      case 3:
        break;
      case 4:
      case 5:
        NSLog("x:%i",x);
        break;
        default:
        NSLog("default");
    }
    x++;
  }
}
```

Listing 3-9 The debugger console logging

```
first time appearing...
default
x:2
x:4
x:5
```

The Break and Continue Statements

You can use the `break` keyword in other places than switch statements. When looping, you can exit a loop early using the break statement. You also can force a loop to skip the remaining statements in its body and continue to the next loop using the continue statement.

The Break Statement

To exit a loop immediately, use the break statement. The following code snippet illustrates:

```
for(int x = 0;x != 1000;x++) {
  if(x == 5) { break; }
  NSLog(@"x");
}
```

When executed as part of a program, under normal circumstances, the for loop in the preceding code would loop 1000 times, from x = 0 to x = 999. Here, however, when the `x` variable's value reaches 5, the logical if statement evaluates to false. When false, the program enters the code block preceding the if statement and executes the break statement. The break statement forces the program to exit the for loop immediately. And so the program only logs 0 through 4 to the debugger console. On the fifth iteration, the program exits the for loop.

The Continue Statement

To exit a loop's body and return to a loop's logical test immediately, use the continue statement. The following code snippet illustrates:

```
for(int x = 0; x < 10; x++) {
  if(x==3) { continue; }
  NSLog(@"x=%i",x);
}
```

When run as part of a program, the program loops 10 times. Each loop, except when `x` reaches 3, logs the `x` variable's value to the debugger console. When `x` evaluates to 3, the logical if statement evaluates to true and executes the continue statement, which forces the program to skip the remaining statements in the loop's body and return to the loop's logical test.

Try This Using the Break and Continue Statements

1. Open LoopingExample in Xcode and open the FlipsideViewController.m file in the editor.
2. Add a method called `viewWillAppear` to the file (Listing 3-10).
3. Click Build And Go to run the application. Tap the info button one time and the debugger console should log the statements in Listing 3-11.

Listing 3-10 The `viewWillAppear` method

```
- (void)viewWillAppear:(BOOL)animated {
  int i = 0;
  while(YES == YES) {
    i++;
    if(i == 3) continue;
    else if(i==5) break;
    NSLog(@"endless loop: %i", i);
  }
}
```

Listing 3-11 The debugger console logging

```
endless loop: 1
endless loop: 2
endless loop: 4
default
x:2
x:4
x:5
```

Arrays and Structures

C arrays and structures are valid in Objective-C. Although you will usually use Apple's NSArray when creating your own array and you will usually create your own class rather than create a structure, there are situations where you might be required to use these C data structures. Besides, understanding an array is fundamental to understanding the Foundation Framework array classes.

Arrays

Sometimes you wish to use a series of values rather than a single value. *Arrays* help you work with multiple values easily. For instance, you might have a time series representing your expenses over the past ten days.

```
-(void) expenses() {
  float expenses[10];
  for(int i = 0; i < 10; i++) {
    expenses[i] = 100.0 + i;
  }
}
```

The function's first line allocates space for ten float values. The for loop then assigns the value 100.02 + i to each of the values, the results being the series: 100.0, 101.0, 102.0, . . . , 109. Note that i has the value 0 in the first loop, and so the value added to the expenses array is n – 1.

After assigning values to individual array elements, you can refer to those elements directly. For instance, the following code accesses the seventh array element and assigns it to a variable, for which, from expenses' preceding initialization, you know the value is 106.

```
float x = expenses[7];
```

Arrays and Pointers

One way C programmers often access array elements is through *pointers*. Accessing arrays through pointers is important if you wish to understand C strings. If you wish to do any substantial C programming, it also becomes important, as C programmers use pointers in seemingly undecipherable ways.

Consider the following code:

```
void expenses() {
  float expenses[10];
  for(int i = 0; i < 10; i++) {
    expenses[i] = 100.00 + i;
  }
  float * expensePointer = &expenses;
  for(int i = 0; i < 10; i++) {
    printf("%f\n", *(expensePointer+i));
  }
}
```

The function's first half assigns values to each array element. The function's second half then logs those values. However, the second half, rather than referring to each element by value, does so by reference. It first assigns a pointer to the array, which is the address of the first element. Remember, the & character preceding a variable means it is the variable's address, not its value. The function then increments/moves the pointer by 1, causing the pointer to point to the next element's address in the array. With each loop, the `printf` statement prints the value pointed to by the `expensePointer`. Remember the * character preceding a variable means it is the variable's value, not its address.

C Strings

C *strings* are arrays. They are arrays of the char data type. You can define a character array as an actual array or as a pointer to an implicit array, the second of which is usually referred to as a C string.

```
char firstname[] = {'J', 'A', 'M', 'E', 'S','\0'};
char * lastname = "BRANNAN";
printf("Name:%s %s\n",firstname,lastname);
```

The first line defines a character array. Each letter is an element in the array of six elements. Note the null terminating character, `\0`. Character arrays that are to be used as character strings must end with a terminating null character.

The second line uses a common shortcut by simply declaring a pointer to an array created with the BRANNAN characters. Behind the scenes, the compiler creates a character array from the string and then assigns the pointer to the array's first element's address. For instance, the following code performs the same steps as the preceding code, only manually:

```
char lastnamearray[] = {'B','R','A','N','N','A','N','\0'};
char * plastnamearray = lastnamearray;
printf("Name:%s %s\n",firstname,plastnamearray);
```

Multidimensional Arrays

Arrays need not be linear. You can also define multidimensional arrays when using Objective-C. The following illustrates:

```
int myvalue [4][2];
for(int i = 0; i < 4; i++) {
  for(int ii = 0; ii < 2; ii++) {
    myvalue[i][ii] = i + ii;
  }
}
```

The first statement defines an array of four elements where each element has two elements. The outer for statement loops through the four elements; each time it goes to a new element, it then enters another for loop that loops through the element's two subelements. It assigns the value of the ith + iith iteration to each subelement, writing the following to the debugger console:

```
0,1
1,2
2,3
3,4
4,5
```

The Struct Keyword

Multidimensional arrays are not the only way to store an element that consists of multiple subelements. For instance, suppose you wished to create a song identified by title, artist, and id. A struct is one way you could represent this data type.

```
struct song {
  char * title;
  char * artist;
  long id;
};
```

A song struct consists of a title, an artist, and an id. After defining a struct, you can use it to define other variables as a struct of that type. The following illustrates using the song struct defined previously:

```
struct song asong;
asong.artist = "test artist";
asong.title = "test title";
asong.id = 200;
printf("Artist:%s Title:%s id:%l", asong.artist, asong.title, asong.id);
```

The first line declares that a variable, asong, is of the struct type song. The second, third, and fourth lines assign values to each element in asong. The final line then logs the struct's values.

Try This Using an Array and Structure

1. Open LoopingExample in Xcode. Create a new C header file named **SongDataStructure** (Figure 3-2).

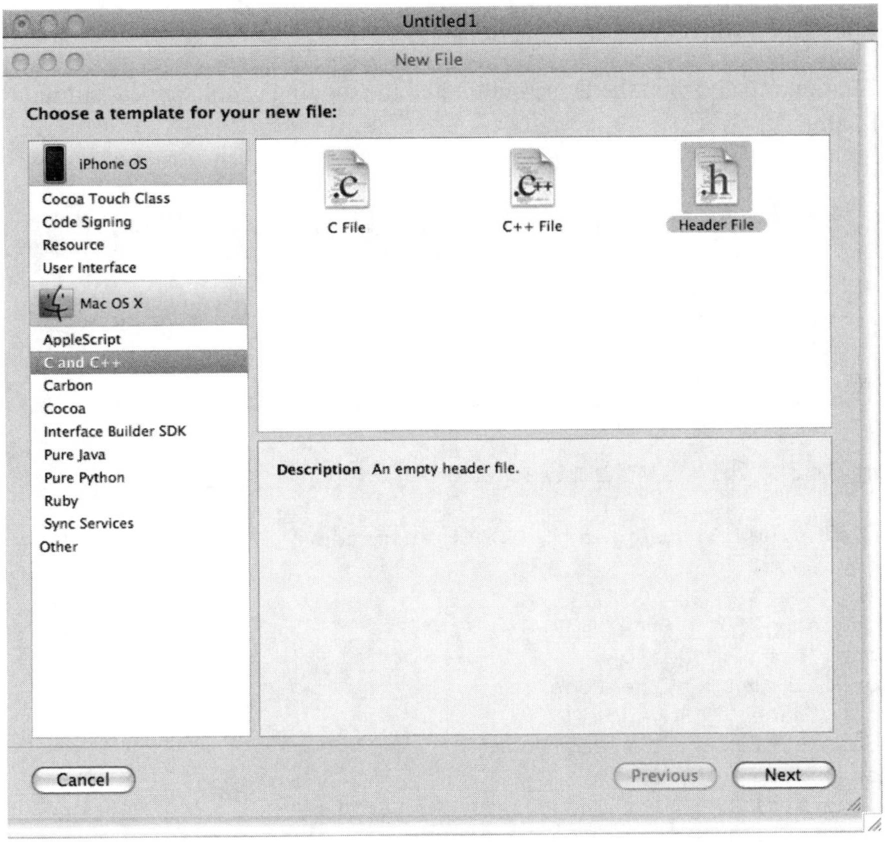

Figure 3-2 Creating a C header file

2. Add the `SongStruct` struct and the `Song` typedef to the header file (Listing 3-12). Notice, like a "real" C programmer, you are doing it in one statement; albeit a C programmer would use pointers rather than passing values around by value, as you do here.

3. Build the application. Open FlipsideViewController.h and import the newly created header file by adding the following to the file's top:

```
#import "SongDataStructure.h"
```

4. Add the `viewWillDisappear` method to FlipsideViewController.m so that it matches Listing 3-13.

(continued)

5. Click Build And Go to run the application.
6. Tap the info and then the Done button and the logging should appear similar to Listing 3-14.

Listing 3-12 The SongDataStructure.h C header file

```
typedef struct SongStruct {
      char * name;
      char * artist;
} Song;
```

Listing 3-13 The `viewWillDisappear` method

```
-(void) viewWillDisappear: (BOOL) animated {
  Song song1;
  Song song2;
  Song song3;
  song1.name = "Hello";
  song1.artist = "The Foos";
  song2.name = "Hey now.";
  song2.artist = "The Hey Nows";
  song3.name = "GoodBye";
  song3.artist = "The Travelling FooBerries";
  Song songsArray[] = {song1, song2, song3};
  for(int i = 0;i < 3; i++) {
    Song curSong = songsArray[i];
    NSLog(@"song: %s artist: %s", curSong.name, curSong.artist);
  }
}
```

Listing 3-14 The debugger console logging

```
first time appearing...
song: Hello artist: The Foos
song: Hey now. artist: The Hey Nows
song: GoodBye artist: The Travelling FooBerries
default
x:2
x:4
x:5
```

The UIViewController's Life-Cycle Methods

Throughout this chapter, without any explanation, you used the Utility Application template. This template creates a simple two-view application. The info button on the application's first view, when pressed, takes the user to the second screen.

The front view is the MainView, and its controller is the UIViewController. The second view is the FlipsideView, and its controller is the FlipsideViewController. The UIView represents a view, while a UIViewController represents a view's controller. Every view has a view controller that handles life-cycle events for the view. When creating a view, you can either accept a view's default view controller by not creating your own, or you can override the default by creating your own view controller for a view. You create your own view controller using something called inheritance, which you will learn in Chapter 6.

Figure 3-3 illustrates how the Utility Application implements its views and view controllers. Note that you can also create a custom view implementation, as Figure 3-3 shows. For now, the important thing to understand from Figure 3-3 is that the MainView and FlipsideView are both UIViews and that the MainViewController and FlipsideViewController are both UIViewControllers. You should also understand that the UIView and the UIViewController work together when displaying a view in an iPhone's window. The UIView handles displaying a view. The UIViewController handles life-cycle methods and other "behind-the-scenes tasks" when displaying a view.

One "behind-the-scenes" job a UIViewController handles is allowing a program to execute custom code when its UIView loads, appears, disappears, and unloads. When a

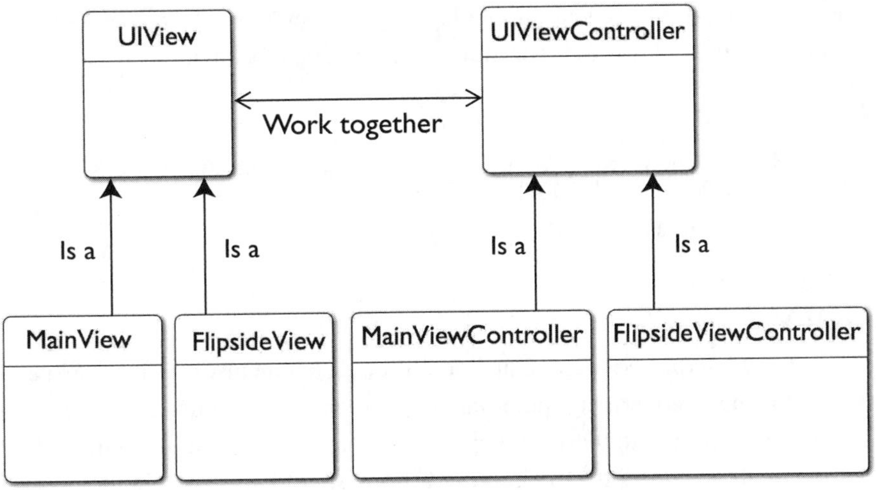

Figure 3-3 UIView, UIViewController, and custom view controllers

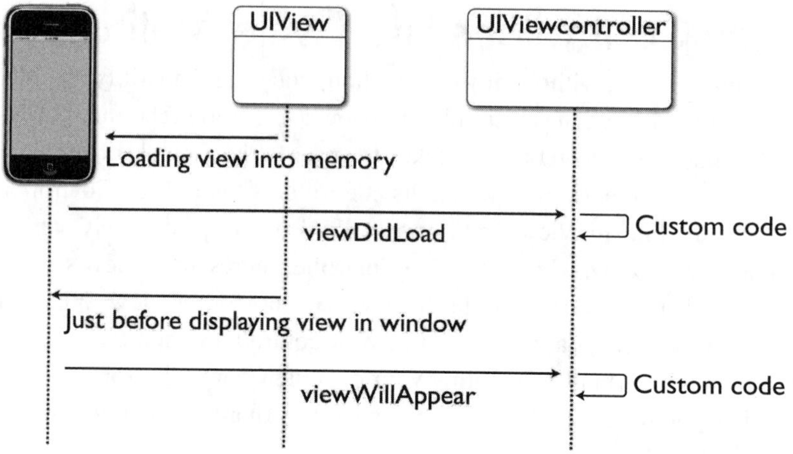

Figure 3-4 Life-cycle methods called when a view loads and is about to be displayed

view is first loaded, or when it is displayed, certain life-cycle methods are called by the application (Figure 3-4).

As Figure 3-4 illustrates, when a view is first loaded into a window by an application, the application fires the "viewDidLoad" event. If the view has a view controller that implements the `viewDidLoad` method, then the `viewDidLoad` method executes its custom code. When a view is first displayed, just before it is displayed the application fires the "viewWillAppear" event. If the associated view controller implements the `viewWillAppear` method, then the custom code written in this method is executed. In this chapter, the custom code was simple looping and conditional statement examples. You can, of course, use these methods for much more practical behavior.

NOTE

For more detail on a UIView, see my book *iPhone SDK Programming: A Beginner's Guide* (McGraw-Hill Professional, 2009).

Summary

In this chapter you explored looping and conditional statements. If you have ever programmed using a modern computer language, then these should have been familiar. If this is your first exposure to these concepts, then you should consult Wikipedia for more information on these concepts. A beginning C book should also contain the necessary information.

You use the for, while, and do while loops constantly when programming using any modern programming language, and Objective-C is no different. These expressions determine how often a program repeats a code block. You also use the `if` and `else` keywords constantly when programming, and so you must understand these keywords and their use too. The if and else if structures determine your program's flow, depending upon different conditions. At any point in time these conditions might be different and your program could take a different path. Conditional statements are what allows programs to be flexible to differing conditions when run.

After exploring looping and conditional statements, you then explored arrays and the struct type. These two concepts, although sort of "tacked on" to this chapter, are important to understand. Arrays are a fundamental computer science concept. Moreover, you will use the NSArray and NSMutableArray Foundation classes throughout this book's second half, and these classes follow the same concept as simple arrays. You will probably rarely use a struct in your code, but understanding them are important, as you will certainly see them used in other programmers' code.

In the next chapter you finally move to classes, objects, and object-oriented programming. These are the exclusive realms of Objective-C. From Chapter 4 forward it will not seem like you are learning C, but rather like you are learning Objective-C.

Chapter 4

Classes, Objects, and Messaging

Key Skills & Concepts

- Understanding Procedural Programming
- Creating Simple Object Models
- Understanding Objects and Classes and Implementing Them Using Objective-C
- Modeling Behavior Using a Sequence Diagram
- Creating a Class Diagram and a Simple Project from a Class Diagram
- Using Convenience Initializers
- Understanding Objective-C Methods

Objective-C is a full-featured object-oriented language. Using Objective-C requires understanding basic object-oriented analysis and design. In this chapter you explore writing classes and using objects created from those classes. Although not a full treatise on object-oriented analysis and design, this chapter should provide more insight on how you progress from object-oriented analysis and design to an Objective-C program. If you understand the thought process behind object orientation, then implementing classes using Objective-C should prove more intuitive; that's this chapter's thesis anyway.

NOTE

This chapter loosely uses a modeling language notation called the Unified Modeling Language to perform object-oriented analysis and design. A good book on UML you might consider purchasing is *UML Demystified* by Paul Kimmel (McGraw-Hill Professional, 2005). It is a small and inexpensive book that makes understanding UML easy. Note that this chapter's UML usage is not formal but rather loosely uses UML's notation to express concepts here. By no means consider this chapter an authoritative UML source.

Object-Oriented Programming vs. Procedural Programming

Object-oriented programming is a programming paradigm that uses objects rather than only functions. This is a profoundly different way of thinking and was a major advance in computer science, but before considering object-oriented programming, consider its predecessor, procedural programming.

Procedural Programming

Computer scientists call programs built from a system of communicating functions procedural programs. The process behind creating these programs is called *procedural programming*. Procedures, or methods, interact with one another to perform computational steps. Figure 4-1 illustrates the execution flow of a typical C program.

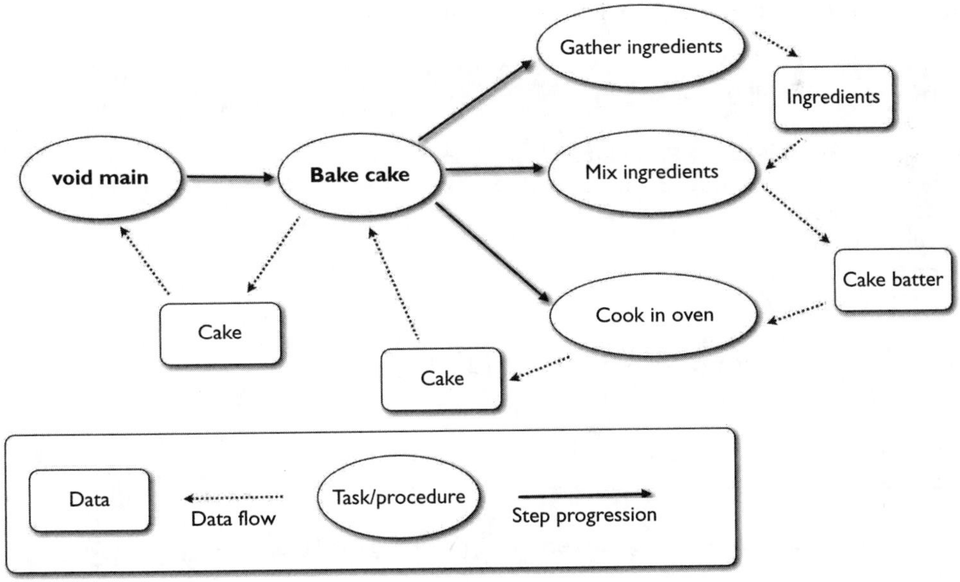

Figure 4-1 Execution flow of a typical C program

TIP

Wikipedia has a good introduction to procedural programming at http://en.wikipedia.org/Procedural_programming.

The program represented in Figure 4-1 simplifies the steps involved in cake baking. First, like all C-based programs, it starts with `main`. Once deciding upon baking a cake, presuming you have bought the ingredients, you set off into the kitchen to bake the cake. However, multiple subtasks compose the "bake cake" task; moreover, you must perform each task in order.

Tasks are not required to produce data, but in Figure 4-1 each task produces, or transforms, data. For instance, gathering ingredients results in the ingredients. Mixing the ingredients results in cake batter. Cooking the batter results in a cake, which is ultimately returned from the overall "baking a cake" task.

Listing 4-1 implements Figure 4-1 using a simple Objective-C program. Although it is an Objective-C program, you should note that it uses no Objective-C principles such as classes. Instead it mixes C into the Objective-C to implement the program. Listing 4-2 is the debugger console's output when running the program.

Listing 4-1 Baking a cake

```
#import <Foundation/Foundation.h>
typedef struct ingredient_struct {
  BOOL mixed;
} ingredients;
typedef struct cake_struct {
  BOOL cooked;
} cake;
ingredients gather_ingredients(void) {
  NSLog(@"gathering....");
  ingredients myIngredients;
  myIngredients.mixed = NO;
  return myIngredients;
}
void mix_ingredients(ingredients * ptheIngredients) {
  NSLog(@"mixing....");
  ptheIngredients->mixed = YES;
}
cake cook_in_oven(ingredients theIngredients) {
  NSLog(@"cooking....");
  cake theCake;
  theCake.cooked = YES;
  return theCake;
}
```

```
cake bake_cake(void) {
  NSLog(@"baking....");
  ingredients myIngredients = gather_ingredients();
  mix_ingredients(&myIngredients);
  cake myCake = cook_in_oven(myIngredients);
  return myCake;
}
int main (int argc, const char * argv[]) {
  NSAutoreleasePool * pool = [[NSAutoreleasePool alloc] init];
  cake aCake = bake_cake();
  NSLog(@"Baked a cake %@",aCake.cooked?@"YES":@"NO");
  [pool drain];
  return 0;
}
```

Listing 4-2 Debugger console output

```
baking....
gathering....
mixing....
cooking....
Baked a cake YES
```

The program in Listing 4-1 has no classes, objects, or other object-oriented concepts. Instead it is a purely procedural program. The program begins baking a cake by calling the `bake_cake` function. This function in turn calls the `gather_ingredients`, `mix_ingredients`, and `cook_in_oven` functions; there is a one-to-one correspondence between the tasks in Figure 4-1 and the functions in Listing 4-1.

Also notice that structs, further refined as a typedef, define each data item. And finally, notice that in the `mix_ingredients` function, unlike the other C functions used throughout the last few chapters, you use a pointer; real C programmers use pointers.

Object-Oriented Programming: Classes and Objects

Procedural programming was the norm until the 1990s, when object-oriented programming languages such as Smalltalk and C++ became more popular. *Object-oriented* programming, in contrast to procedural programming, uses data structures that interact with each other. These data structures contain both data and methods that can operate on that data. A program's execution flow is from the interaction of these data structures.

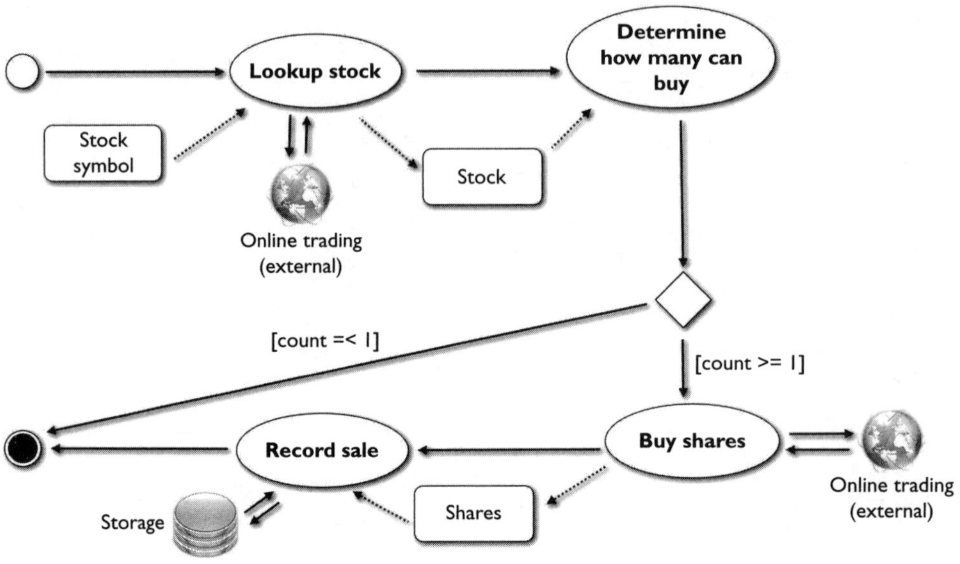

Figure 4-2 Activity diagram for purchasing a stock

Consider the activity diagram in Figure 4-2.

Suppose you wish to purchase a stock. The first task is to obtain a stock. Obtaining a stock is nothing more than using its symbol to look up its name, last price, and last date from an external stock trading system. After obtaining the stock, you determine how many shares you can buy. You then reach a decision point: if you cannot buy at least one share, then you are finished. If you can buy one or more shares, you continue to the next step, buying shares. You then buy shares. After buying shares, you store the purchase in an external data source such as a database, and then you are finished.

Ask the Expert

Q: Shouldn't you explain an activity diagram?

A: An activity diagram analyzes a workflow. The ovals represent activities; the arrows between activities represent transitions. Text labeling the transitions represents guard conditions. A guard condition is something that must be true to progress to the next activity. Figure 4-2 is an activity diagram modeling how I envision the process of buying a stock. For more information on activity diagrams, refer to *UML Demystified,* or refer to Wikipedia's page on the subject (http://en.wikipedia.org/wiki/Activity_diagram).

Notice the data flow through Figure 4-2. Looking up a stock results in a stock, which is the input for determining how many shares you can buy. Determining how many shares you can buy results in a count. If the count is greater than 0, you buy shares. Buying shares results in owned shares, and you record the sale and store it.

Like procedural analysis, object-oriented analysis often begins by reviewing activities and data flow. However, unlike procedural analysis, it does not then implement the activities as functions. Instead, object-oriented analysis first analyzes the objects, or nouns, that compose an activity like Figure 4-2.

NOTE

Another form of analysis, typically performed before activity analysis, is called *use case analysis*. Use case analysis typically occurs after you gather a client's requirements but before conducting activity analysis. Use cases are the basis for transforming written requirements into more formal analysis and design. Refer to *UML Demystified* or Wikipedia's page on the subject (http://en.wikipedia.org/wiki/Use_case_diagram) for more information on use case analysis.

Object-Oriented Analysis

After defining the problem, object-oriented analysis looks at a problem's objects, or its nouns. In Figure 4-2, first consider the broad data types used by defining the nouns. The first noun I see is Stock, and so I know I need a `Stock` class. I also need a `Share`. I can describe the entire activity as "purchasing a stock," and so I surmise that I need a `Purchase` class. Finally, I see two external systems, the trading system and the system used to store the purchase; so I model both of these by creating a `Storage` class and a `TradingSystem` class. Figure 4-3 is a simple model illustrating the classes and their relationship with one another.

NOTE

Notice I use the pronoun "I" rather than "you" when analyzing Figure 4-2 to create Figure 4-3. My pronoun use is intentional. Despite computer scientists' attempts to make object-oriented analysis and design scientific, it remains largely an artistic endeavor. Figure 4-3 models how I see the activity in Figure 4-2, not necessarily how you see the activity. You could do the exact same analysis as I did and derive a very different diagram than Figure 4-3.

TIP

The best book I have read on object-oriented programming and UML is the book *Applying UML and Patterns: An Introduction to Object-Oriented Analysis and Design* by Craig Larman. Prentice Hall published it in 1997, and it is still relevant and in press today. For many years this book was the recommended study guide for IBM's UML certification test (before IBM's acquisition of Rational).

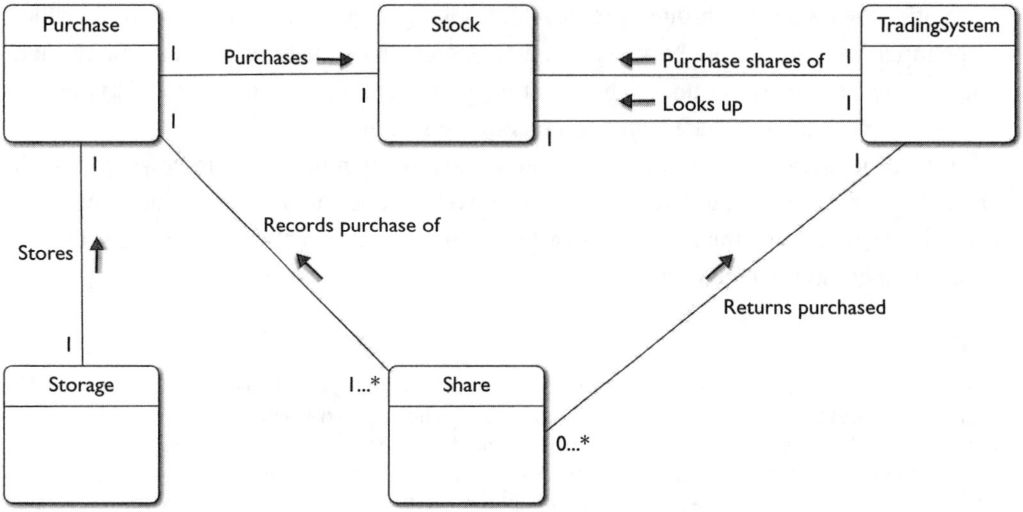

Figure 4-3 A class diagram capturing the objects from Figure 4-2

Classes and Objects

Before continuing, pause to consider the difference between a class and an object. Think of a class as a template for an object. A class is the definition, or a pattern. An object is a physical, live implementation of the pattern. A human being is a class; I am an object, as I am an instance of a human being. Consider the following C typedef:

```
typedef struct stockstruct {
  char * symbol;
  char * name;
  char * lastdate;
  float price;
} stock;
```

CAUTION

A typedef is not a class; I am using a typedef and a struct as a transition to thinking about classes and objects from C data structures. These data structures are in fact the precursors to modern classes and objects.

The type definition of a stock is the "class." Subsequent use of the `stock` typedef is the "object." For instance, the following code creates instances of the `stock` typedef; the `astock` and `mystock` variables are "objects."

```
stock astock = getastock("DFR");
stock  mystock;
```

Like a struct, a human is a class, I am an instance of a class, or an object. Now consider how Objective-C implements classes.

Objective-C Classes

Enough on C structs and typedefs; although helpful for understanding the difference between classes and objects, they are not a class or an object. A true class encapsulates both data and behavior.

Objective-C is an object-oriented language; as such, it relies upon classes and object instances of classes, not structs and typedefs. An Objective-C class consists of an interface, defined in a header file, and an implementation, defined in a source file. The interface contains the class' declarations, while the implementation contains the class' definitions. Figure 4-4 illustrates the sections of an Objective-C interface.

The @interface

An interface declares the class, its data, and its methods. Like a C header file, it does not implement methods but only declares them. At the file's top go any import statements and `@class` directives. The class' declaration begins with the `@interface` directive. This directive signals to the compiler that a class declaration has begun. Immediately following the `@interface` directive is the class' name and its parent type. Instance variables go between the curly braces immediately following the class declaration statement. Methods go after the closing curly brace, but before the @end compiler directive. The class' declaration as a whole starts with the `@interface` compiler directive and ends with the @end compiler directive.

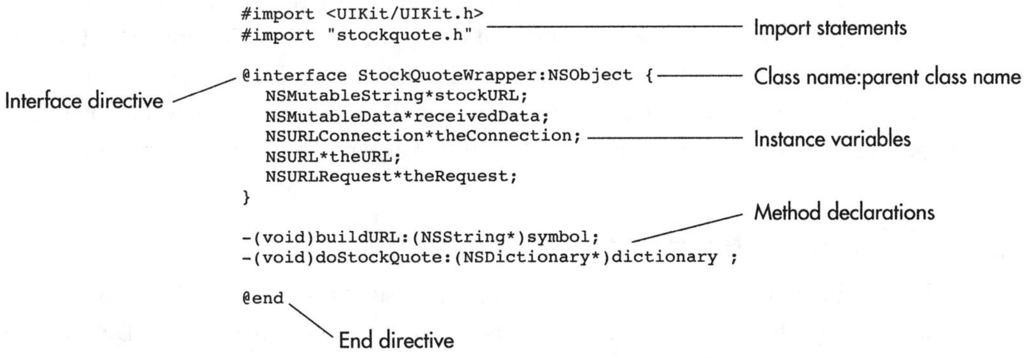
#import <UIKit/UIKit.h>
#import "stockquote.h"
Import statements
@interface StockQuoteWrapper:NSObject {
Class name:parent class name
Interface directive
NSMutableString*stockURL;
NSMutableData*receivedData;
NSURLConnection*theConnection;
Instance variables
NSURL*theURL;
NSURLRequest*theRequest;
}
Method declarations
-(void)buildURL:(NSString*)symbol;
-(void)doStockQuote:(NSDictionary*)dictionary ;
@end
End directive

Figure 4-4 Interface sections

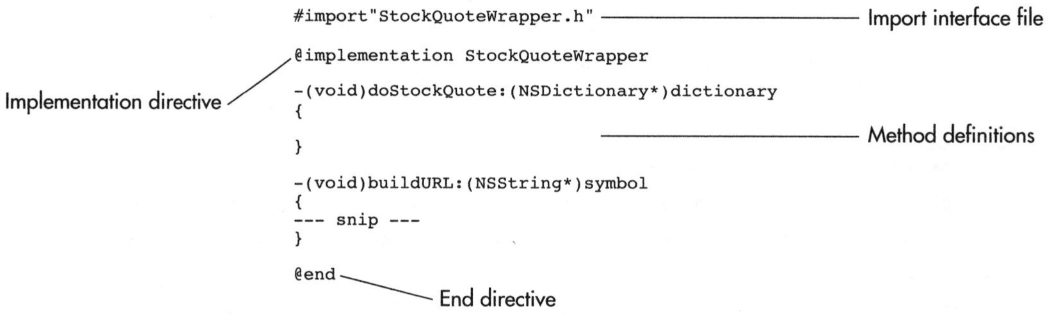

Figure 4-5 Implementation sections

Note in Figure 4-4 that the method declarations look different than C function declarations. Objective-C class methods begin with a minus sign if an instance method and a plus sign if a class method. You learn more on instance and class methods later in this chapter. Also, notice that rather than using parentheses, the method uses a colon and then lists its parameters. You learn more on this different-looking syntax later in this chapter. The important concept to take from this section is that the interface declares a class' structure to the compiler. It lets the compiler know what data variables and methods it will define in its implementation.

The @implementation

An implementation defines a class. It implements the methods declared in the class' corresponding interface. For instance, Figure 4-5 contains the implementation for the interface in Figure 4-4.

An implementation implements a class' interface. For instance, the interface in Figure 4-4 declares the `doStockQuote` and `buildURL` methods. The implementation in Figure 4-5 defines the `doStockQuote` and `buildURL` methods. Method definitions go between the `@implementation` directive and the `@end` directive. For now, don't worry about the method syntax; you examine that later in this chapter. The important concept to take from this section is that the implementation defines a class to the compiler. The implementation is where you write the code that makes the computer do something.

Object-Oriented Programming: Behavior

Now that you better understand an Objective-C class' structure, consider how you determine what methods and instance variables compose an Objective-C class. Determining what instance variables and methods compose an Objective-C class requires you understand that class' behavior. Determining the behavior of classes in a model such as shown earlier in Figure 4-2 is the next step when performing object-oriented analysis and design.

Unlike procedural programming and the C struct, a class can also have behavior. For instance, you are an instance of a Human. You encapsulate the data required as a human; you have a heart, lungs, bones, and muscle. However, you also exhibit behavior; you can run, walk, skip, and jump. Nobody performs these tasks for you; you—the object instance of a Human—perform these tasks. In an object-oriented program, classes are no different than a Human—they encapsulate data and behavior into one construct. Objects are no different than you and I, instances of a human.

After preliminarily analyzing a problem's objects, as in Figure 4-3 earlier, you analyze how those objects interact with one another. This analysis determines each object's behavior during a problem's duration.

Class Interaction

After determining a problem's basic activity (Figure 4-2) and a preliminary conceptual object model (Figure 4-3), you should start analyzing how the objects interact with one another to solve the problem. A good modeling technique/diagram for this analysis is a *sequence diagram.* A sequence diagram models object interactions as a sequence of steps to accomplish some larger task. Figure 4-6 models how I envision object instances from the classes in Figure 4-3 interacting.

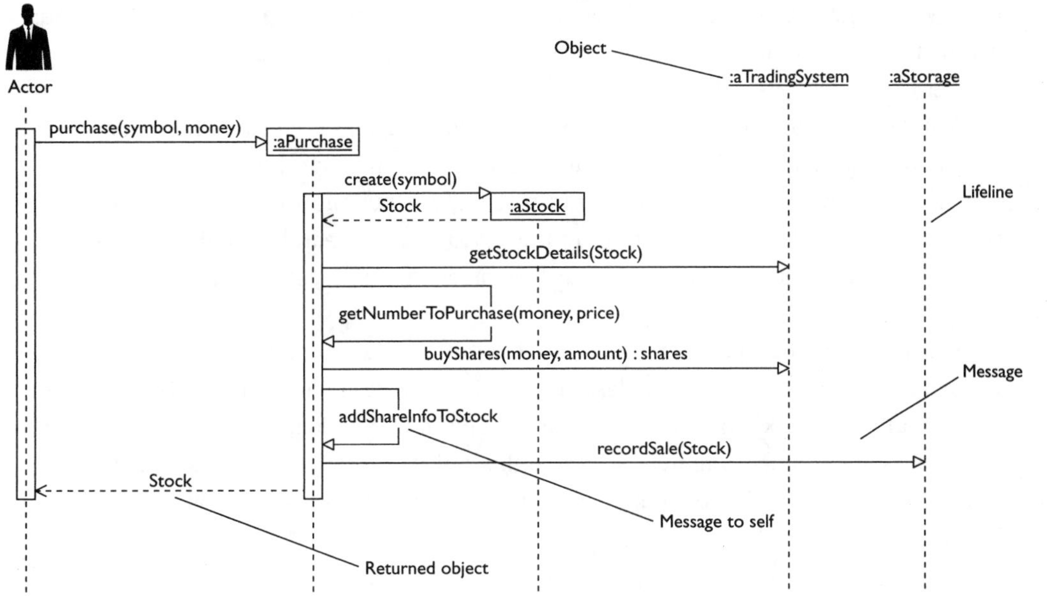

Figure 4-6 A sequence diagram capturing the classes' interactions

A user first initializes a purchase with a string containing the stock symbol and an amount he or she has budgeted for purchasing stocks. This first interaction creates a `Purchase`. The `Purchase` then calls the `TradingSystem` to get the `Stock`'s information. The `StockPurchase` then determines how many stocks it can buy. If zero, it returns immediately with no further processing. If not zero, it calls `TradingSystem` to buy shares of the stock.

NOTE

Do not be alarmed at the slight variance between the activity diagram in Figure 4-2 and the sequence diagram in Figure 4-6. When performing object-oriented analysis and design, your understanding of a problem often matures as you progress through analysis and design.

After purchasing the stock, the `TradingSystem` returns how many shares were purchased. Notice that since the number of purchased shares is actually just a count, the sequence diagram does away with the `Share` class and instead makes it a property of the `Stock` class. After recording the sale, the system returns the `Stock` to the initiator and the sequence terminates.

The sequence diagram in Figure 4-6 captures the interaction of specific object instances of your model's classes. For instance, a `Purchase` instance gets a `Stock` instance's information by asking a `TradingSystem` instance to get information on the stock. Together, these interactions, modeled in a sequence diagram, provide a more complete understanding of the methods needed, and their sequence, to complete a problem.

You use the interactions in a sequence diagram to create each class' methods. When creating methods, be certain you assign them to the appropriate class. For instance, `Purchase` is asking `TradingSystem` for stock information. Therefore, the `getStockDetails` method belongs to the `TradingSystem` class and not `Purchase`. Going through all the interactions in the sequence diagram creates a class model like Figure 4-7.

Unlike a sequence diagram or activity diagram, a class diagram is static and models a class, not an object instance of a class. Think of this diagram as a blueprint for how you will actually write code rather than a diagram helping you understand a problem better.

A class diagram like Figure 4-7, although similar to a conceptual class diagram like Figure 4-3, is much more detailed. It captures a class, its instance variables, and its methods.

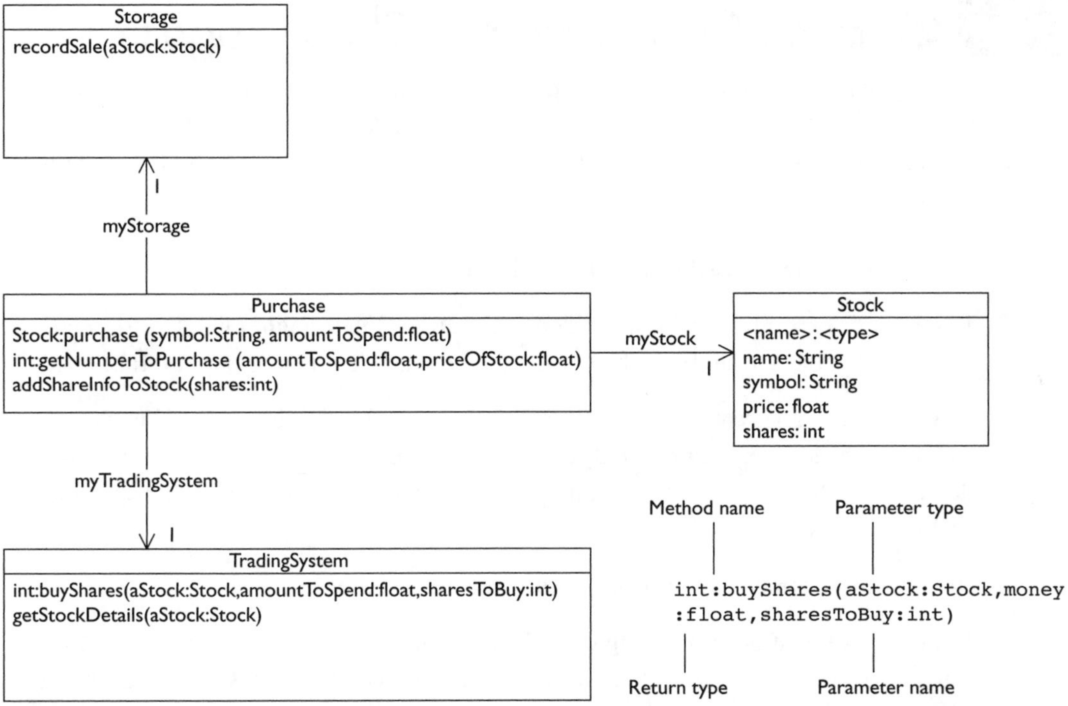

Figure 4-7 A class diagram modeling purchasing a stock

In Figure 4-7 a class is a square. The top compartment contains the class name; the next contains the class' instance variables. The bottom compartment contains the class methods. Note that you can omit a middle section if there are no instance variables. The lines between classes are associations; associations model classes "knowing" about each other so that they can solve a problem. Arrows indicate a one-way association; for instance, `Purchase` must know about `Stock`, but `Stock` doesn't require knowing about `Purchase`. Notice that you can also omit a class' middle or bottom section if it has no instance variables or no methods.

With a class diagram completed, you can then begin to write an actual program.

Try This Creating Classes from a Class Diagram

Now that you have a class diagram, complete with methods, you can begin implementing a program from that class model. In this Try This example, as I have not discussed Objective-C methods yet, you only link the classes together. The following is based upon the class diagram in Figure 4-7.

1. Create a new View-based Application called **StockPurchase**.
2. Disclose, or expand, the Classes folder in Groups & Files. Right-click Classes and select Add | New Group from the pop-up menu. Name the new group **model**.
3. Add four new Objective-C `NSObject` subclasses to Model. Name the classes `Purchase`, `Stock`, `TradingSystem`, and `Storage`. Remember, shares was downgraded from an object to an integer primitive that is a property of `Stock` and is no longer a class.
4. Review the interface and implementation generated for each class.
5. Return to the relationships in Figure 4-7. A `Purchase` has a relationship with `Stock`, `Storage`, and `TradingSystem`. To communicate with these classes, it must know about them. To know about them it must import each class' header. Import the `Stock` and `Storage` classes into Purchase.h (Listing 4-1).
6. For `TradingSystem`, rather than importing `TradingSystem` in Purchase.h, use the `@class` directive.
7. The arrows in Figure 4-7 are labeled. You turn those labels into object variables in the class having the relationship with the other class. `Purchase` has a relationship with `Stock`, `Storage`, and `TradingSystem`. `Purchase`'s relationship with `Stock` is through an object instance of `Stock` called `myStock`. The diagram tells us there is only one `Stock` instance `Modify Purchase` to have three instance variables: `myStock`, `myTradingSystem`, and `myStorage`.
8. Now, although there is no relationship between `Stock` and `TradingSystem`, note that both the `getStockDetails` and `buyShares` methods require a `Stock`. Therefore, `TradingSystem` must know about `Stock`. Change TradingSystem.h to know about `Stock` using the `@class` directive in its interface (Listing 4-2).

9. Also change `Storage` so that it knows about `Stock` and use the `@class` directive in its interface and import `Stock` in its implementation (Listings 4-3 and 4-4).

10. Build the application and run it if you wish, although it doesn't do anything yet.

Listing 4-1 Purchase.h

```
#import <Foundation/Foundation.h>
#import "Stock.h"
#import "Storage.h"
@class TradingSystem;
@interface Purchase : NSObject {
  Stock * myStock;
  Storage * myStorage;
  TradingSystem * myTradingSystem;
}
@end
```

Listing 4-2 TradingSystem.h

```
#import <Foundation/Foundation.h>
@class Stock;
@interface TradingSystem : NSObject {
}
@end
```

Listing 4-3 Storage.h

```
#import <Foundation/Foundation.h>
@class Stock;
@interface Storage : NSObject {
}
@end
```

Listing 4-4 Storage.m

```
#import "Storage.h"
#import "Stock.h"
@implementation Storage
@end
```

(continued)

A class knowing about another class is no different than a function defined in one C header file knowing about another function defined in a different header file. For the first function to know about the other function, it must include the header file containing the second function. Objective-C classes are no different, for one class to know about another, it must import the second class' interface in its interface.

Notice that one class knowing about another does not require importing the header; instead, you might use a `@class` compiler directive. The next section and subsequent Try This example illustrate how and why you use an `@class` compiler directive. For now, just realize it is another way that one class can know about another.

NOTE

Sometimes class relationships are not a one-to-one relationship such as in Figure 4-7. A class might have a relationship with multiple classes. For instance, an **`AcademicDepartment`** has multiple **`Professors`**; therefore, an **`AcademicDepartment`** aggregates **`Professors`** (Figure 4-8). In this situation you would use a data structure such as an array, NSArray, or NSDictionary to implement the relationship. For more information on aggregation, refer to *UML Demystified*.

The @class Directive

In the previous Try This you used the `@class` directive. The `@class` directive allows you to tell the compiler that a class will be referring to another class by name, but that the class doesn't need to import the other class' header file, Listing 4-1 illustrates using the class directive. `Purchase` needs to "know" about `TradingSystem` so that it can "ask" `TradingSystem` to get a `Stock`'s details and buy shares of a `Stock`. But Listing 4-1 doesn't really require knowing anything about `TradingSystem`'s details, and so it doesn't import `TradingSystem`'s interface.

Now, although the `@class` directive allows `Purchase` to refer to the `TradingSystem` class in its class interface, it does not allow `Purchase` to use `TradingSystem` in its class implementation. For instance, `Purchase` refers to `TradingSystem` in Listing 4-1, but to actually use `TradingSystem` in its implementation, the implementation must import `TradingSystem`.

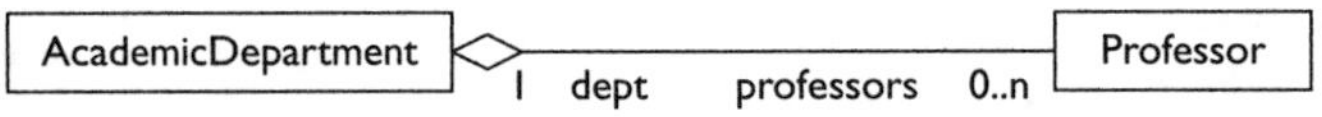

Figure 4-8 An aggregation example

If you must still import the used class' interface in a class' implementation to use the class, this begs the question, why should you use the `@class` directive instead of the `#import` directive? Most texts will tell you to avoid needless compilation. Their reasoning, although correct, is rarely going to be an issue when programming an iPhone App. However, there is a more practical reason for using the `@class` directive. You use the `@class` directive to mitigate circular dependencies.

A circular dependency is when two classes are both dependent upon each other. For instance, `Foo` might need `Bar` to print "foobar" to the debugger console. `Bar` might need `Foo` to print "barfoo" to the debugger console. Because they both rely upon one another, they would normally need to import each other's header file. But to build `Foo`, Bar.h must be included in Foo.h, To build `Bar`, Foo.h must be included in Bar.h, and so the compiler gets confused and refuses to compile. The `@class` directive mitigates this circular dependency; the following Try This illustrates.

Try This Mitigating a Circular Dependency Using the @class Directive

Suppose you had two classes that both refer to one another, as in Figure 4-9, where both classes must "know" about one another to do their jobs. In this Try This you mitigate the problem of a circular dependency such as that in Figure 4-9 by using the `@class` directive.

NOTE

Notice in Figure 4-9 that there are arrows on both ends of the line connecting **`Foo`** with **`Bar`**. Arrows indicate directionality in a relationship. For example, in Figure 4-7 **`Purchase`** must communicate with **`Stock`**, but **`Stock`** does not need to communicate with **`Purchase`**, and so an arrow is added to the line end connecting to **`Stock`**. When both classes must communicate with one another, arrows are either omitted or arrows are added to both line ends. Figure 4-8 is an example of arrows having been omitted; both **`AcademicDepartment`** and **`Professor`** must know about each other. In Figure 4-9, the arrows are both included, indicating a bidirectional relationship.

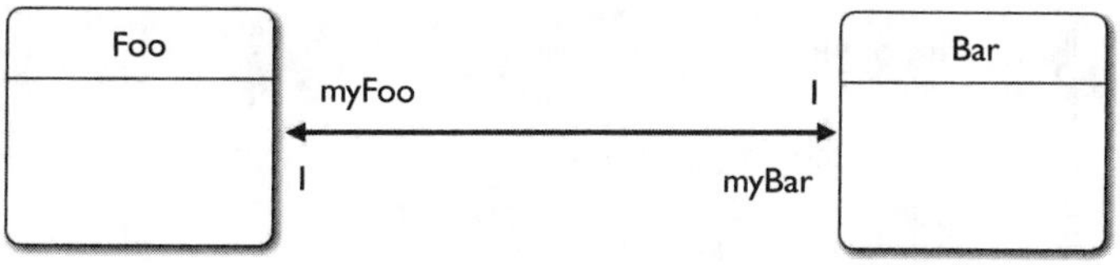

Figure 4-9 Two classes in a circular dependency

(continued)

1. Create a new View-based Application named **Circular**.
2. Create two new Objective-C `NSObject` subclasses named `Foo` and `Bar` (Listings 4-5, 4-6, 4-7, and 4-8).
3. Import `Foo` in `Bar` and `Bar` in `Foo`, and then implement both classes as in Listings 4-5 through 4-8.
4. Try building the application and note that the application does not compile.

Listing 4-5 Foo.h (incorrect)

```
#import <Foundation/Foundation.h>
#import "Bar.h"
@interface Foo : NSObject {
  Bar * myBar;
}
- (void) sayFooBar;
- (NSString *) sayBarFoo;
@end
```

Listing 4-6 Foo.m (incorrect)

```
#import "Foo.h"
@implementation Foo
- (void) sayFooBar {
  myBar = [[Bar alloc] init];
  NSLog(@"sayFooBar:%@", [myBar sayBarFoo]);
}
- (NSString *) sayBarFoo {
  return @"sayBarFoo";
}
@end
```

Listing 4-7 Bar.h (incorrect)

```
#import <Foundation/Foundation.h>
#import "Foo.h";
@interface Bar : NSObject {
  Foo * myFoo;
}
- (NSString *) sayBarFoo;
@end
```

Listing 4-8 Bar.m (incorrect)

```
#import "Bar.h"
@implementation Bar
- (NSString *) sayBarFoo {
  myFoo = [[Foo alloc] init];
  return [myFoo sayBarFoo];
}
@end
```

1. Modify Foo.h to refer to `Bar` using the `@class` directive and not import Bar.h (Listings 4-9 and 4-10).
2. Modify Bar.h to refer to `Foo` using the `@class` directive and not import Foo.h (Listings 4-11 and 4-12).
3. Try building the application and note that it compiles and runs, but notice the warning received in both classes' implementation (Figure 4-10).
4. Modify both implementations so that they import each other; Foo.m should import Bar.h and Bar.m should import Foo.h.
5. Click Build And Debug and the application builds and runs, only this time the compiler generates no warnings.

Listing 4-9 Foo.h (correct)

```
#import <Foundation/Foundation.h>
@class Bar;
@interface Foo : NSObject {
--- snip ---
@end
```

Listing 4-10 Foo.m (correct)

```
#import "Foo.h"
#import "Bar.h"
@implementation Foo
--- snip ---
@end
```

(continued)

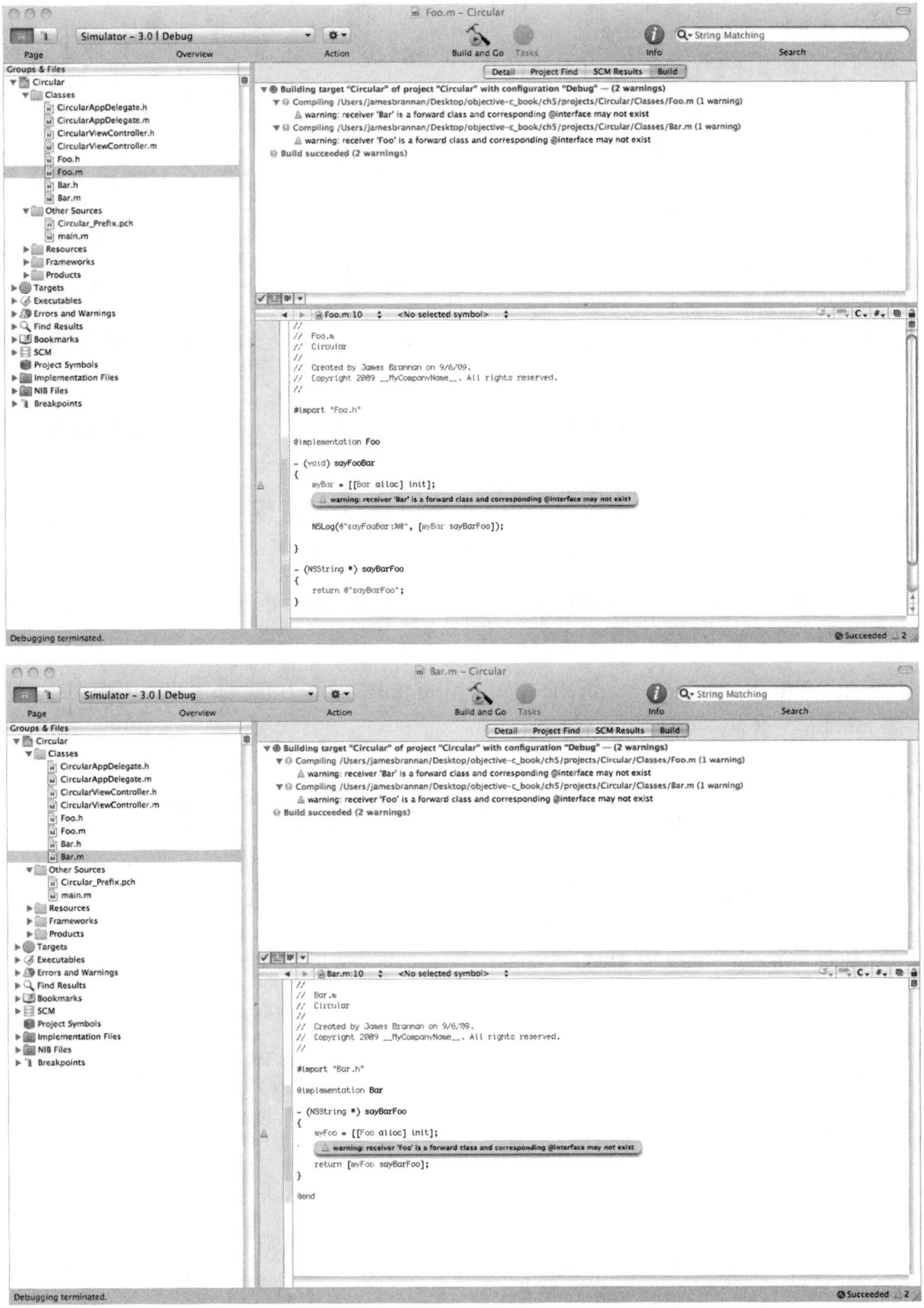

Figure 4-10 Compiler warning

Listing 4-11 Bar.h (correct)

```
#import <Foundation/Foundation.h>
@class Foo;
@interface Bar : NSObject {
--- snip ---
@end
```

Listing 4-12 Bar.m (correct)

```
#import "Bar.h"
#import "Foo.h"
@implementation Bar
--- snip ---
@end
```

Methods and Messaging

Up to now, I have glossed over Objective-C's strange syntax. However, this strange syntax is actually quite elegant. Figure 4-11 illustrates a typical method declaration in Objective-C.

A method declaration begins with a + or – sign. As you learn in the next section, this indicates whether the method is a class method or instance method. The declaration then specifies the method's return type. For instance, in Figure 4-11 the method returns an NSMutableString. Note that if a method does not return anything, you write `void` in the parentheses, as the following code illustrates:

```
-(void) buildHelloString:(NSString *) personName;
```

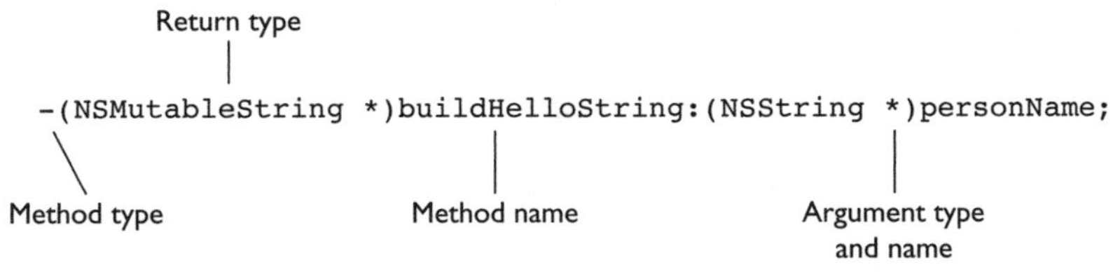

Figure 4-11 An Objective-C method

Methods taking a parameter follow its name with a colon. Methods without a parameter omit the colon. This distinction is important, as the colon becomes part of the method's name.

NOTE

Objective-C methods that take a parameter use a colon. That colon is part of the method's name. For instance, the method's name in Figure 4-11 is not **`buildHelloString`**, but rather, **`buildHelloString:`**—this is an important distinction.

If a method has a colon, then the parameter's type, in parentheses, follows the colon. Following the parameter's type is the parameter's name, followed by a semicolon, which ends the declaration.

An Objective-C class' methods, when called by other objects, appear very different than code calling C functions. This difference is because Objective-C uses something called infix notation. Infix notation mixes operands and operators. Figure 4-12 illustrates an Objective-C message.

An Objective-C message from one object to another begins with an opening square brace and ends with a closing square brace. The message begins with an opening square brace, followed by the object's name (the receiver). The receiver is followed by a space, and then the object's method being called (the message). If a message takes a parameter, then the method's name includes a colon and a parameter value.

Class and Instance Methods

Instance methods begin with a minus sign, while class methods begin with a plus sign. If you are familiar with Java, note that a class method is the same as a Java static method. A class method occurs at the class level and does not apply to an object instance of the class.

Using a class method does not require first creating a class instance before using it. As you saw earlier, `alloc` is a class method. You do not instantiate an instance and then call `alloc`, but rather, use `alloc` to instantiate an instance of an instance.

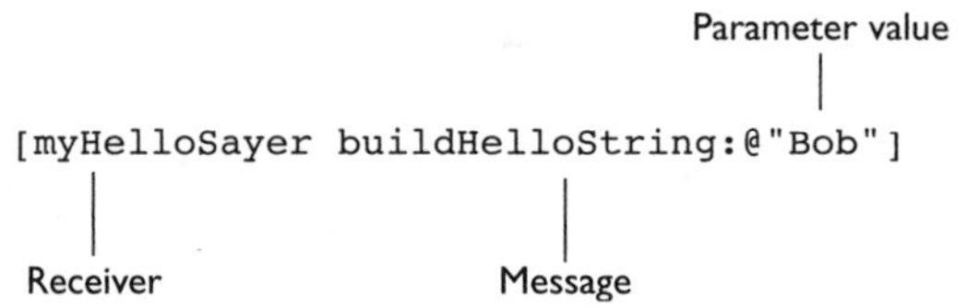

Figure 4-12 An Objective-C message

While class methods operate at the class level, instance methods are tied to particular instances of a class. Instance methods rely upon a class instance's state. Instance methods, unlike class methods, can refer to an object's instance variables and the object itself.

Try This Creating a Simple Class Method and Instance Method

1. Create a new View-based application named **ClassInstanceExample** in Xcode.
2. Create a new Objective-C `NSObject` subclass in Classes named `MyClass`. In MyClass.h add declarations for an instance method named `sayHelloInstance` and a method named `sayHelloClass` (Listing 4-13). Also add a variable named `myName`.
3. Implement the methods as in Listing 4-14. Try placing the same NSLog statement from `sayHelloInstance` in `sayHelloClass`.
4. Add the class and call the methods in main.m (Listing 4-15).
5. Build and Debug to run the application. The application crashes. Notice the compiler warning "instance variable 'myName' accessed in class method."
6. Change `sayHelloClass` so that it no longer refers to the `myName` instance variable but instead simply logs "Hello." Build and Debug and the application runs fine.

Listing 4-13 MyClass.h

```
#import <Foundation/Foundation.h>
@interface MyClass : NSObject {
  NSString * myName;
}
-(void) sayHelloInstance;
+(void) sayHelloClass;
@end
```

Listing 4-14 MyClass.m

```
#import "MyClass.h"
@implementation MyClass
- (id) init {
```

(continued)

```
  if([super init] == nil) return nil;
  myName = [[NSString alloc] initWithString:@"Hello"];
  return self;
}
-(void) sayHelloInstance {
  NSLog(myName);
}
+(void) sayHelloClass {
  //NSLog(myName);
  NSLog(@"Hello");
}
-(void) dealloc {
  [myName release];
  [super dealloc];
}
@end
```

Listing 4-15 The main.m file

```
#import <UIKit/UIKit.h>
#import "MyClass.h"
int main(int argc, char *argv[]) {
  NSAutoreleasePool * pool = [[NSAutoreleasePool alloc] init];
  MyClass * objMyClass = [[MyClass alloc] init];
  [objMyClass sayHelloInstance];
  [MyClass sayHelloClass];
  [objMyClass release];
  int retVal = UIApplicationMain(argc, argv, nil, nil);
  [pool release];
  return retVal;
}
```

In this application you used both an instance method and a class method. Originally, in Step 5, you tried accessing an instance variable in the class method. But this resulted in a compiler error, as class methods cannot refer to any of a class' properties or methods, only other class methods. This restriction is logical, as you are not required to instantiate an object instance of a class to use its class methods, and if there is no object instance, then you cannot refer to properties or methods belonging to an object.

Allocating and Initializing Objects

Remember, a class is a template, while an object is an instance of that template. For instance, an architect's drawing tells a builder how to create an instance of a house defined by the architect's drawing. Moreover, a builder can create multiple instances of houses based upon the drawing. Think of the architect's drawing as the class and the houses as objects that implement the drawing.

Creating a house from a drawing is considerable work; the builders must construct the house to create an instance of it. Same with Objective-C, or any object-oriented program: to create an object instance of a class, a running program must instantiate the object.

But before the builders can even begin, they must allocate land to build the house upon. Again, same with an Objective-C program: it must first allocate memory to build the object in. After allocating memory, the running program can then build the object.

Allocating Memory and Constructing

If you are familiar with Java or C++, note that unlike these languages, there is no `new` keyword in Objective-C. In C++ and Java you use the `new` keyword to create a new object instance of a class. For instance, the following Java creates a new object from a `Foo` class:

```
Foo myFoo = new Foo( );
In C++ this line would be written
Foo *myFoo = new Foo();
```

This statement both allocates space and constructs and initializes the new object in one statement. But Objective-C requires two steps to create an object instance. You allocate an object and build a generic instance of the object using the `alloc` keyword. Here is how `alloc` works. Every Objective-C class ultimately inherits from a base object called `NSObject` (more on inheritance later). `NSObject` has a class method called `alloc` (more on class methods later). The `alloc` method allocates the necessary space in memory for the object. It also builds a generic instance of the object according to the class template. The following code allocates space and builds a `Foo` instance:

```
Foo * myFoo = [Foo alloc];
```

Allocating memory instructs a running program to create space for an object instance and construct a generic instance of a class.

Initializing Objects

Constructing identical object instances has limited value. In the real world, usually no two instances of something are truly identical. Return to the house building analogy. Once the house is built and sold, the owners usually modify it prior to moving in. This modification, or initialization, makes the house the owners' own unique house version. Although all houses built using the same drawing are initially identical, owners initialize the house. Same with Objective-C: after allocating space and building an object, you then initialize it.

You initialize a class using the `init` method. Just like `alloc`, every Objective-C class inherits `NSObject`'s `init` method. However, `init` is an instance method rather than a class method (more on instance methods later). You call a class' `init` method immediately after allocating the class. For instance, the following code allocates an object and then initializes it:

```
Foo * myFoo = [Foo alloc];
[myFoo init];
```

NOTE

As you shall notice throughout this book, you usually see an object's allocation and initialization written in a single line. The following line first allocates space for a **`Foo`** instance, it then initializes that instance and returns an id. That id is assigned to **`myFoo`**.

```
Foo * myFoo = [[Foo alloc] init];
```

Writing Custom Initializers

Look through Apple's documentation on Foundation classes and you will see numerous methods like the following:

```
initWith<qualifier>
```

These initializers are called convenience initializers. For instance, `NSString` has over 15 custom `init` methods. If you wish to create an `NSString` from a C string, you might write the following:

```
char * test = "Hello James";
NSString * myTest = [[NSString alloc] initWithUTF8String:test];
```

You can create custom initializers for your classes too; the following Try This illustrates.

Try This Using a Convenience Initializer

1. Open ClassInstanceExample in Xcode. Modify MyClass.m so that it has a convenience initializer rather than `init` (Listing 4-16).
2. Modify main.m so that it matches Listing 4-17.
3. Click Build And Debug and the application uses the convenience initializer.

Listing 4-16 MyClass.m modified to contain a convenience initializer

```
#import "MyClass.h"
@implementation MyClass
- (id) initWithString: (NSString *) inputString {
  self = [super init];
  if(self != nil) {
    myName = inputString;
    [myName retain];
  }
  return self;
}
- (void) sayHelloInstance {
  NSLog(myName);
}
+ (void) sayHelloClass {
  NSLog(@"hello");
}
- (void) dealloc {
  [myName release];
  [super dealloc];
}
@end
```

Listing 4-17 The main.m file modified to use the convenience initializer

```
#import <UIKit/UIKit.h>
#import "MyClass.h"
int main(int argc, char *argv[]) {
  NSAutoreleasePool * pool = [[NSAutoreleasePool alloc] init];
  MyClass * objMyClass = [[MyClass alloc] initWithString:@"This is hello."];
  [objMyClass sayHelloInstance];
```

(continued)

```
  [objMyClass release];
  int retVal = UIApplicationMain(argc, argv, nil, nil);
  [pool release];
  return retVal;
}
```

The `initWithString:` method in Listing 4-16 takes an `NSString` as a parameter. It then calls its superclass' `init` method. If `init` doesn't return a null value, it initializes its `myName` instance variable to `inputString`. Do not worry about the keyword `retain` for now; you learn about that in Chapter 5. All it does is ensure that the pointer to `inputString` remains valid. Remember, Objective-C passes around objects by reference, not value, so `myName` is not a unique instance of an `NSString`, but rather a pointer to the `NSString` `inputString`. As you will see in Chapter 5, `retain` ensures that reference remains valid. The initializer ends by returning itself as an id.

CAUTION

Be certain you read the section on designated initializers in Chapter 7. Notice that if you used either **`Foo`**'s or **`Bar`**'s **`init`** method (not **`initWithString`**), then the string would be a null value and nothing would print to the debugger console. A designated initializer avoids this problem.

Ask the Expert

Q: You talk about a superclass in the previous Try This. What is a superclass?

A: I haven't discussed inheritance yet, but a superclass is a parent of a subclass. In object-oriented programming languages classes can inherit the methods and instance variables of a parent class. For instance, a `Car` class might inherit from a `Vehicle` class. A `Vehicle` class might have a `move` method. The `Car` class, as a child of `Vehicle`, inherits the `move` method. Parent classes can in turn inherit from a parent class, just as your parents inherit from your grandparents. Every class you write will ultimately inherit from `NSObject` as its base parent class. `NSObject` defines an `init` method, and so every child class of `NSObject` is guaranteed to have an `init` method. You will learn more on inheritance in Chapter 6.

Multiple Argument Methods

Methods can have more than one argument. Multiple argument methods are where Objective-C really shines. Although at first confusing, Objective-C's multiple argument syntax makes it easier to read and maintain than other languages such as Java and C++.

NOTE

Parameter and argument are synonyms. They both refer to a value passed between methods.

Consider the following C function being called, what exactly do the parameters mean?

```
doIt("Bill Cosby", "Leonard Part 6", 37);
```

Now consider the same function as an Objective-C message.

```
[myMultiple doIt:@"Bill Cosby" movieName:@"Leonard Part 6" timesSeen:37];
```

You know exactly what the last two methods mean, and you can infer what the first method means. You are calling the method `doIt` with an actor name, a movie name, and the number of times the movie was seen.

Objective-C methods that have more than one parameter use a space between arguments. For instance, you might implement the preceding `doIt` method as follows:

```
- (void) doIt:(NSString *) actorName movieName: (NSString*) value timesSeen:
(int)times {
  NSLog(@"%@ is my favorite actor in the movie %@, I saw it %i times.",
actorName, value, times);
}
```

An Objective-C method's first parameter is not named, while the remaining parameters are named. This allows you to know exactly what the remaining parameters mean. After the first argument, you specify each subsequent argument by an argument name, a colon, the argument's type, and the actual argument's name referred to internally by the implementing method. Figure 4-13 illustrates. Although this convention is initially confusing, you will use multiargument methods so frequently when using Foundation classes such as `NSString`, they will soon become second nature.

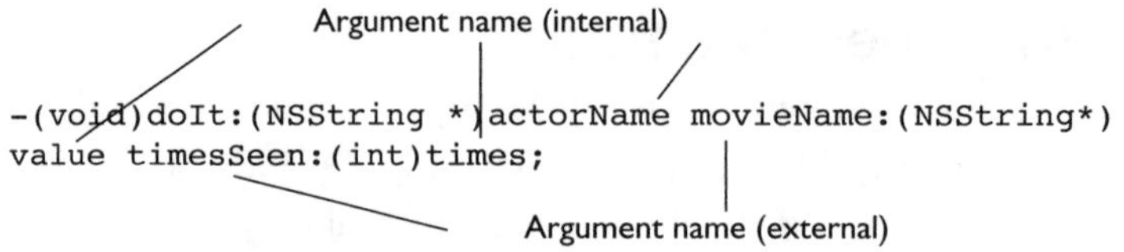

Figure 4-13 Multiple argument method declaration

Try This Implementing the StockPurchase Program in Objective-C

You haven't learned about properties, inheritance, and many other object-oriented principles yet, so any example is going to be contrived. For this Try This example, suspend disbelief and implement the methods as presented in this example. Although contrived, the methods do illustrate going from earlier Figures 4-7 and 4-8 to code.

1. Open StockPurchase in Xcode.
2. Refer to Figures 4-7 and 4-8 and begin with the `Stock` class. This class has four instance variables, but no methods. Add the variables to `Stock` (Listing 4-18). Also add a method called `logStockInformation` to `Stock` (Listings 4-18 and 4-19). Also, as you have not learned about Objective-C's properties yet, add accessor methods for price and shares.
3. Now refer to Figure 4-7 and notice that the `Purchase` class creates a `Stock` instance by passing a stock symbol. To implement this behavior, you add an `initWithSymbol` method, as in Listing 4-19.
4. Now refer to `Storage`. This class has the `recordSale` method, and so you add it to `Storage`'s interface and implementation (Listings 4-20 and 4-21).
5. Refer to the `TradingSystem` class. This class has the `buyShares` and `getStockDetails` methods. Implement both methods as in Listings 4-22 and 4-23. Note that `buyShares` takes multiple arguments (parameters). The modeled argument names in Figure 4-8 become the external argument names; this is why you made these argument names descriptive in Figure 4-8.
6. Move to the `Purchase` class. This class drives the overall program flow. Implement the `purchase`, `getNumberToPurchase`, and `addShareInfoToStock` methods to `Purchase` (Listings 4-24 and 4-25).

7. Now notice in Figure 4-7 that the actor calls only the purchase method. All other method calls are messages from `Purchase` to other objects. Open StockPurchaseAppDelegate.h (Listing 4-26) and import the `Purchase` class. Then modify the `applicationDidFinishLaunching:` method in StockPurchaseAppDelegate.m (Listing 4-27) so that it instantiates `Purchase` and sends the purchase message to the `Purchase` instance.

8. Click Build And Debug and the application compiles and runs.

Listing 4-18 Stock.h

```
#import <Foundation/Foundation.h>
@interface Stock : NSObject {
  NSString * name;
  NSString * symbol;
  float price;
  int shares;
}
- (id) initWithSymbol: (NSString *) aSymbol;
- (void) logStockInformation;
- (float) getPrice;
- (int) getShares;
@end
```

Listing 4-19 Stock.m

```
#import "Stock.h"
@implementation Stock
- (id) initWithSymbol: (NSString *) aSymbol {
  if([super init] == nil) return nil;
  symbol = aSymbol;
  [symbol retain];
  return self;
}
- (void) logStockInformation {
  NSLog(@"The stock:%@ price:%f shares:%i", symbol, price, shares);
}
- (float) getPrice {
  return 39.99F;
}
```

(continued)

```
- (int) getShares {
  return 22;
}
@end
```

Listing 4-20 Storage.h

```
#import <Foundation/Foundation.h>
@class Stock;
@interface Storage : NSObject {
}
-(void) recordSale: (Stock *) aStock;
@end
```

Listing 4-21 Storage.m

```
#import "Storage.h"
#import "Stock.h"
@implementation Storage
-(void) recordSale: (Stock *) aStock {
  NSLog(@"recording sale for stock.");
  [aStock logStockInformation];
}
@end
```

Listing 4-22 TradingSystem.h

```
#import <Foundation/Foundation.h>
@class Stock;
@interface TradingSystem : NSObject {
}
- (int) buyShares: (Stock *) aStock amountToSpend: (float) money sharesToBuy:
(int) shares;
- (void) getStockDetails: (Stock *) aStock;
@end
```

Listing 4-23 TradingSystem.m

```
#import "TradingSystem.h"
@implementation TradingSystem
- (int) buyShares: (Stock *) aStock amountToSpend: (float) money sharesToBuy:
```

```
(int) shares {
  NSLog(@"simulating buying shares with amount:%f to buy %i shares.", money,
shares);
  return 2;
}
- (void) getStockDetails: (Stock *) aStock {
  NSLog(@"simulating getStockDetails...");
}
@end
```

Listing 4-24 Purchase.h

```
#import <Foundation/Foundation.h>
#import "Stock.h"
#import "Storage.h"
@class TradingSystem;
@interface Purchase : NSObject {
  Stock * myStock;
  Storage * myStorage;
  TradingSystem * myTradingSystem;
}
-(Stock *) purchase: (NSString *) symbol amountToSpend: (float) money;
-(int) getNumberToPurchase: (float) amountToSpend priceOfStock: (float) price;
-(void) addShareInfoToStock: (int) shares;
@end
```

Listing 4-25 Purchase.m

```
#import "Purchase.h"
#import "Stock.h"
#import "TradingSystem.h"
@implementation Purchase
-(Stock *) purchase: (NSString *) symbol amountToSpend: (float) money {
  NSLog(@"purchase in Purchase...Symbol:%@ amountToSpend:%f", symbol, money);
  myStorage = [[Storage alloc] init];
  myTradingSystem = [[TradingSystem alloc] init];
  myStock = [[Stock alloc] initWithSymbol: @"IAG"];
  [myTradingSystem getStockDetails:myStock];
  int amountToBuy = [self getNumberToPurchase:money priceOfStock:[myStock
getPrice]];
  [myTradingSystem buyShares:myStock amountToSpend:money sharesToBuy:amountToBuy];
  [self addShareInfoToStock:[myStock getShares]];
```

(continued)

```
    [myStorage recordSale:myStock];
    [myStorage release];
    [myTradingSystem release];
    return myStock;
}
-(int) getNumberToPurchase: (float) amountToSpend priceOfStock: (float) price {
    NSLog(@"amountToSpend:%f and prices:%f", amountToSpend, price);
    return 2;
}
-(void) addShareInfoToStock: (int) shares {
    NSLog(@"addShareInfoToStock with shares:%i", shares);
}
@end
```

Listing 4-26 StockPurchaseAppDelegate.h

```
#import <UIKit/UIKit.h>
@class StockPurchaseViewController;
@interface StockPurchaseAppDelegate : NSObject <UIApplicationDelegate> {
    UIWindow *window;
    StockPurchaseViewController *viewController;
}
@property (nonatomic, retain) IBOutlet UIWindow *window;
@property (nonatomic, retain) IBOutlet StockPurchaseViewController
*viewController;
@end
```

Listing 4-27 StockPurchaseAppDelegate.m

```
#import "StockPurchaseAppDelegate.h"
#import "StockPurchaseViewController.h"
#import "Purchase.h"
@implementation StockPurchaseAppDelegate
@synthesize window;
@synthesize viewController;
- (void)applicationDidFinishLaunching:(UIApplication *)application {
    Purchase * myPurchase = [[Purchase alloc] init];
    [myPurchase purchase:@"AIG" amountToSpend:55.37F];
    [myPurchase release];
    [window addSubview:viewController.view];
    [window makeKeyAndVisible];
}
```

```
- (void)dealloc {
  [viewController release];
  [window release];
  [super dealloc];
}
@end
```

The interaction in Figure 4-7 begins when the external actor, StockPurchaseApp Delegate, sends the purchase message to its Purchase instance, myPurchase. The interaction ends when myPurchase is finished purchasing the stock. Purchase creates a Stock instance; however, in doing so it passes the symbol of the stock to create, and so you implemented a convenience initializer that takes a stock's symbol. Purchase then gets the stock's details from its TradingSystem instance, myTradingSystem. After getting the stock's details, it determines how many it can purchase. Note that you created accessor methods in Stock so that you can obtain the values of its price and symbol instance variables; this is contrived. In Chapter 5 you learn about properties and how these make accessing a class' instance variables trivial.

After determining how many shares it can purchase, myPurchase sends the buyShares message to myTradingSystem. After buying shares, myPurchase adds the number of shares purchased to the stock and then has myStorage record the sale. After completing, myPurchase returns control to StockPurchaseAppDelegate.

Summary

In this chapter you explored classes and objects in Objective-C and in the process learned a little about object-oriented analysis and design. Objective-C classes consist of an interface and an implementation. The interface is declared in a header file, while the implementation is defined in a source file. Remember, unlike a C source file, an Objective-C file uses a .m extension rather than a .c extension.

Classes consist of data and behavior. A class encapsulates data as instance variables while behavior is encapsulated as methods. Objective-C methods, although different in appearance than C++ and Java methods, are elegant and descriptive, particularly when passing multiple arguments to a method.

Notice that the instance variables in this chapter are not accessible to other classes unless you use a method to get the value. Moreover, other classes cannot set a value in another class unless you use a method to set the value. You call these getter and setter methods accessor methods. There are particular nuances when getting and setting a class' instance variables not covered in this chapter. This omission is intentional. In Chapter 5 you learn about Objective-C's properties; properties make getting and setting a class' instance variables trivial.

Chapter 5

Memory Management and Properties

Key Skills & Concepts

- Understanding Manual Memory Management
- Understanding Encapsulation
- Using Properties
- Understanding "Ownership"
- Understanding Memory Management Using Autorelease
- Using IBOutlet

If your experience lies with a language such as Java, Visual Basic, or a scripting language, and not a language such as C++ or C, then Objective-C's memory management might seem confusing at first. However, it will quickly seem intuitive. Problem is, once you start coding—and more important, debugging—Objective-C's memory management will seem mystifying once again as you track down elusive memory-related errors. But then, as you gain experience, it will start to seem more natural. In this chapter you explore how you manage memory when programming using Objective-C on the iPhone.

After learning about managing memory, you learn about properties. Properties are new to Objective-C 2.0 and simplify using instance variables in your classes. Properties also simplify managing memory considerably. From this chapter on, you use properties extensively, and so you must understand them. Properties are also used with the `IBOutlet` keyword for connecting controls in Interface Builder with instance variables in a class. For instance, you might have a label on a view that is connected to a label property in a class. By using the `IBOutlet` keyword, you can have changes in code correspond to changes in an associated view's appearance.

Memory Management

Beginning with Mac OS X version 10.5, Cocoa offers automatic memory management using something called garbage collection. Garbage collection makes memory management trivial when developing applications or Mac OS X. Problem is the iPhone, as its resources are more constrained, has no garbage collection. Instead you must manage memory manually or use something called autorelease pools.

Manual Memory Management

Cocoa classes and Objective-C classes you create are subclasses of `NSObject`. `NSObject` has several methods used for memory management. The class method `alloc` allocates memory space for an object. The instance method `dealloc` deallocates an object's memory. But you should never call `dealloc` in your code, though, as the runtime does that for you. Instead you use something called reference counting.

Along with `alloc` and `dealloc`, every object that inherits from `NSObject` also has `retain` and `release` methods. The `retain` method increases an object's `retainCount` variable by 1. The `release` method decreases an object's `retainCount` by 1.

When memory is allocated for an object using the `alloc` keyword, the runtime increases an object's `retainCount` variable by 1. During the object's lifetime, you might create other reference variables you wish to point to the same underlying object. When you do that, you explicitly call `retain`, so the runtime knows the new reference is pointing to the object and has a stake in the object's existence. This is commonly referred to as "ownership" by Objective-C developers.

```
Foo * myFooOne = [[Foo alloc] init];  //retain count is 1
Foo * myFooTwo = myFooOne;  //myFooTwo points to original Foo

                            //retain count remains 1
[myFooTwo retain];  //runtime now knows myFooTwo points to Foo,

                    //retain count is 2
```

In the preceding code snippet, by calling `retain`, `myFooTwo` is expressing to the runtime that it has an ownership stake in the original `Foo`. During an object's lifetime, many different reference variables might retain the object. However, reference variables can also relinquish their ownership stake through the `release` method. The `release` method tells the runtime that the reference variable is finished with the object and no longer needs it, and so the object's `retainCount` is decremented by one.

While an object has a `retainCount` of one or more, the runtime persists the object. When an object's `retainCount` is zero, the runtime deallocates the object and reclaims its memory space.

Figure 5-1 illustrates a `Foo` object's lifetime. The `Foo` object is first allocated in memory by a `myFooOne` reference variable. At this point the `Foo` object's retain count is 1.

```
Foo * myFooOne = [[Foo alloc] init];
```

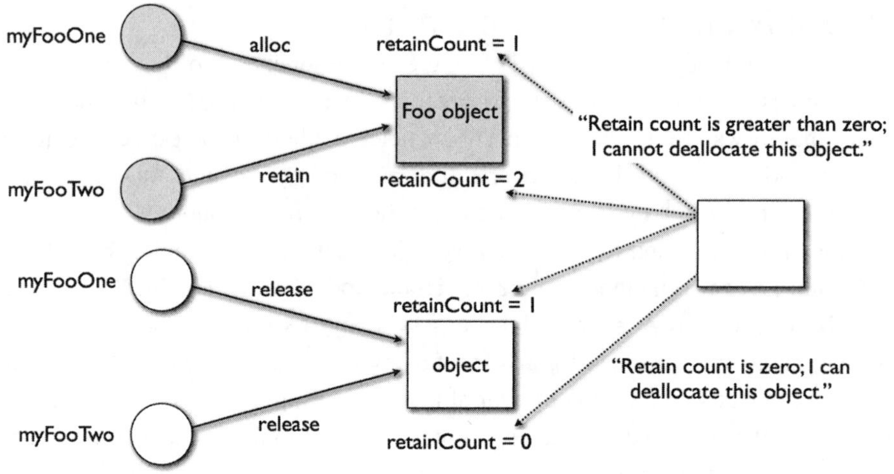

Figure 5-1 Objective-C manual memory management

A second reference variable is created that refers (points) to the Foo object. The reference is then sent the retain message, which of course is the same as sending it to the actual Foo object, and so the Foo object's retain count is 2.

```
Foo * myFooTwo = myFooOne;
[myFooTwo retain];
```

Later, when myFooOne is no longer needed, myFooOne is sent the release message and the Foo object's retain count becomes 1 again.

```
[myFooOne release];
```

When myFooTwo is no longer needed, it too is sent the release message and the Foo object's retain count is zero. When the object's retain count is zero, the runtime knows it can destroy the Foo object and reclaim the memory used by Foo.

Memory Management Within a Method

It is helpful to consider memory management in two separate contexts. Within a method, there are local variables, and you must manage those local variables. There are also instance variables whose scope persists as long as a class persists. In this section you consider memory management of local variables within a single method.

You often declare and use objects within a method. For instance, consider the following (incorrect) method:

```
-(void) myMethod {

  //incorrect method
  NSString * myString = [[NSString alloc] init];  //retainCount = 1
  Foo * myFoo = [[Foo alloc] initWithName:myString]; //retainCount = 1
  NSLog(@"Foo's Name:%@", [myFoo getName]);
}
```

In this method you allocate space for both `myString` and `myFoo`. At the method's end, both local variables are out of scope and the reference variables, `myString` and `myFoo`, are no longer valid. However, the method never releases the objects, and so the runtime never deallocates the space reserved for the objects. That memory is unavailable until your program terminates. This is called a memory leak, because your program is "leaking" memory.

To prevent a memory leak, whenever you allocate a new object or create a copy of an object, you must explicitly send a release message to the object.

```
-(void) myMethod {
  NSString * myString = [[NSString alloc] init]; //retainCount=1
  Foo * myFoo = [[Foo alloc] initWithName:myString]; //retainCount=1
  NSLog("Foo's Name:%@", [myFoo getName]);

  [myFoo release]; //retainCount=0 so deallocate
  [myString release]; //retainCount=0 so deallocate
}
```

I cannot stress enough, when you allocate an object, you must release that object. If you do not, your application will leak memory. When your application leaks memory, your application will usually begin to slow. Ultimately, the iPhone's runtime, sensing it is running dangerously low on memory, will abruptly terminate your application.

Weak References and Retaining

Besides inheriting memory management methods such as retain and release from `NSObject`, every object that traces its lineage to `NSObject` also has a `retainCount` instance variable. The retain count is how the runtime determines if an object can be destroyed. Unlike when writing C, you never explicitly destroy, or deallocate in Objective-C terminology, an object. Instead you release it. Releasing an object decrements the object's `retainCount`. When the `retainCount` is zero, the runtime knows there are no more owners and it deallocates the object.

Notice the word ownership in the previous paragraph. Ownership is important to understanding Objective-C memory management. When you create a new reference to an object instance, you must send the retain message to the object. Consider a method that doesn't call retain after obtaining a reference to an object.

```
-(void) myMethod {

  //an incorrect method

  Foo * myFooOne = [[Foo alloc] initWithName:@"James"]; //retainCount=1
  Foo * myFooTwo = myFooOne;  //retainCount still 1
  [myFooOne release];  //retaincount=0 so deallocated
  NSLog("Name:%@", [myFooTwo printOutName]); //runtime error
}
```

In the preceding code, the myFooTwo reference variable is what's termed a "weak reference." It's called a weak reference because myFooTwo is never officially declared a partial owner of the underlying Foo object by being sent a retain message. Figure 5-2 illustrates.

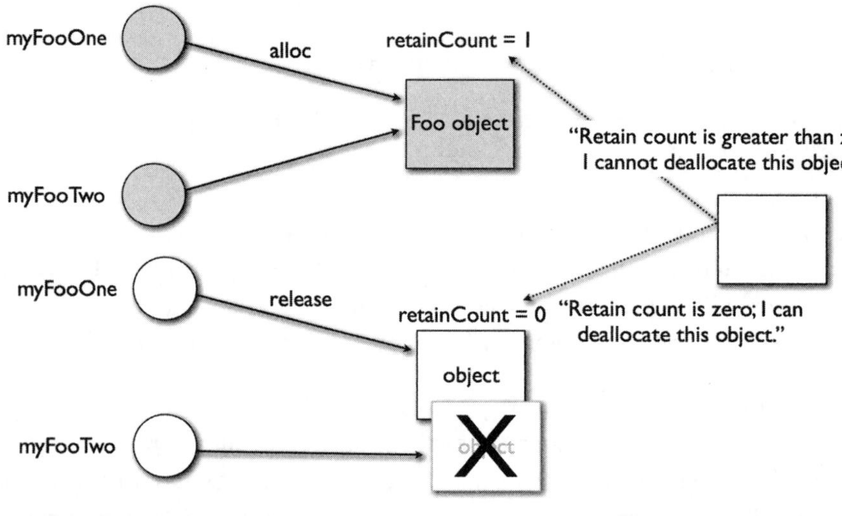

Figure 5-2 A weak reference

A new reference variable pointing to an object must specifically send a retain message to the underlying object if it wishes to have a stake in the object's life cycle. The following code fixes the previous incorrect code:

```
-(void) myMethod {

  Foo * myFooOne = [[Foo alloc] initWithName:@"James"]; //retainCount=1
  Foo * myFooTwo = myFooOne;  //retainCount still 1

  [myFooTwo retain]; //retain count=2
  [myFooOne release];  //retaincount=1
  NSLog("Name:%@", [myFooTwo printOutName]);
}
```

However, you should note that the preceding code is somewhat contrived, as you never do something like that when writing production code. But it does illustrate using `retain`. Just realize that creating a reference to an object does not cause an object's `retainCount` to be incremented; you must call `retain` to increase an object's `retainCount`.

Try This Exploring an Object's Retain Count

1. Create a new command-line project using the Foundation Tool project template (Figure 5-3). Name the project ExploreRetainCount.
2. Create a new Objective-C class named Foo. Implement it as in Listings 5-1 and 5-2.
3. Modify ExploreRetainCount.m to match Listing 5-3.
4. Click Build And Debug to run the application and your debug log should print the same retain counts as Listing 5-4.

Listing 5-1 Foo.h

```
#import <Foundation/Foundation.h>
@interface Foo : NSObject {
}
-(void) sayHello: (NSString *) personName;
@end
```

(continued)

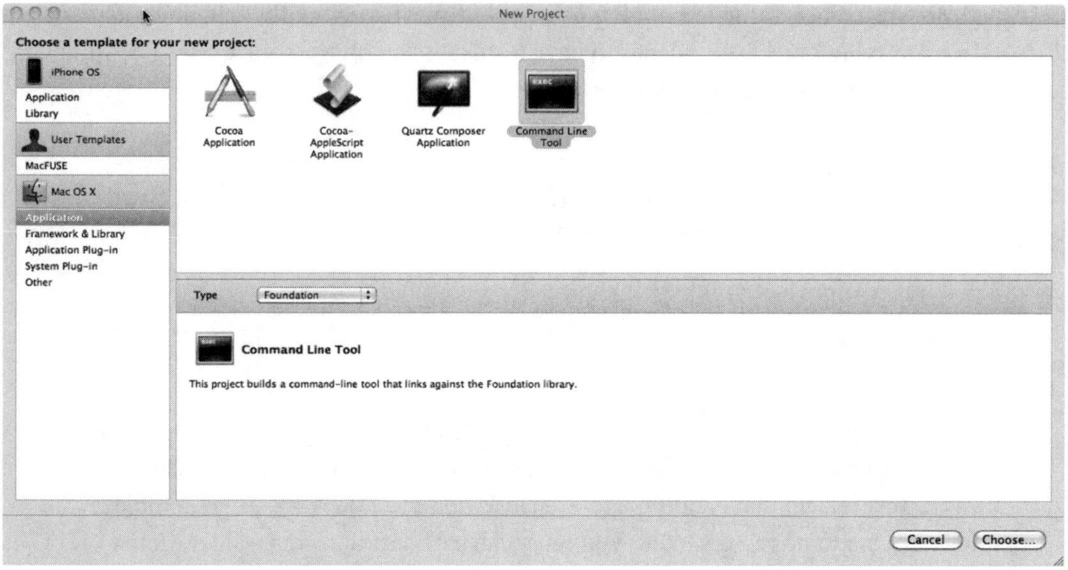

Figure 5-3 Foundation Tool project template

Listing 5-2 Foo.m

```
#import "Foo.h"
@implementation Foo
-(void) sayHello: (NSString *) personName {
  NSMutableString * myHelloString = [[NSMutableString alloc]
initWithString:@"Hello "];
  [myHelloString appendString:personName];

  NSLog(@"Hello %@", myHelloString);
  NSLog(@"retain count of myHelloString:%i", [myHelloString retainCount]);
  [myHelloString release];
}
@end
```

Listing 5-3 ExploreRetainCount.m

```
#import <Foundation/Foundation.h>
#import "Foo.h"
int main (int argc, const char * argv[]) {
```

```
    NSAutoreleasePool * pool = [[NSAutoreleasePool alloc] init];
    Foo * myFooOne = [[Foo alloc] init];
    NSLog(@"Foo retainCount at time t1:%i", [myFooOne retainCount]);
    Foo * myFooTwo = myFooOne;
    NSLog(@"Foo retainCount at time t2:%i", [myFooOne retainCount]);
    NSLog(@"Foo retainCount at time t2:%i", [myFooTwo retainCount]);
    [myFooOne sayHello:@"Tom"];
    [myFooTwo retain];
    NSLog(@"Foo retainCount at time t3:%i", [myFooOne retainCount]);
    NSLog(@"Foo retainCount at time t3:%i", [myFooTwo retainCount]);
    [myFooOne release];
    NSLog(@"Foo retainCount at time t3:%i", [myFooTwo retainCount]);
    [myFooTwo release];

    [pool drain];
    return 0;
}
```

Listing 5-4 Debugger console logging

```
Foo retainCount at time t1:1
Foo retainCount at time t2:1
Foo retainCount at time t2:1
Hello Hello Tom
retain count of myHelloString:1
Foo retainCount at time t3:2
Foo retainCount at time t3:2
Foo retainCount at time t3:1
```

The `sayHello:` method in Foo.m illustrates using release. The `myHelloString` allocates an `NSMutableString` instance, which results in a `retainCount` of 1. When finished, the method sends the release message to `myHelloString`, which results in a `retainCount` of zero, and the runtime deallocates the underlying object.

In ExploreRetainCount.m the `main` method instantiates a `Foo` instance, setting the reference `myFooOne` to the new object. At this point the debug console prints out a `retainCount` of 1. The `myFooTwo` reference variable is then set to point to the same object `myFooOne` points to. Note that the `retainCount` of the underlying `Foo` object remains 1. After `myFooTwo` is sent the retain message, the object's retain count becomes 2.

After `myFooOne` is released, the underlying object's `retainCount` becomes 1. Then, after `myFooTwo` is released, the `retainCount` becomes zero and the runtime can release the underlying `Foo` object.

(continued)

5. Just for fun, add the following line just before the end of the main method:

```
[myFooOne sayHello:@"Terry"];
```

6. Build and Debug, and the application crashes.

```
objc[412]: FREED(id): message sayHello: sent to freed object=0x103330
```

7. Replace the line you just added with the following two lines:

```
Foo * myFooThree;
[myFooThree sayHello:@"James"];
```

8. Build and Debug, and the application crashes with a very cryptic error.

```
The Debugger has exited due to signal 11 (SIGSEGV). The Debugger
has exited due to signal 11 (SIGSEGV).
```

9. Change myFooThree to initialize the object to nil, and also release myFooThree.

```
Foo * myFooThree = nil;
[myFooThree sayHello:@"James"];
[myFooThree release];
```

10. Build and Debug and the application runs fine, although myFooThree's sayHello never executes.

The first error occurred because myFooOne was already released. Now consider the second error. This is one of the more confusing errors for new developers. Creating a variable, but not initializing it, and then sending a message to it is an error. However, if you initialize it to nil, sending a message to it is not an error. In Objective-C it is perfectly acceptable to send a message to nil. Also notice you can release it too, although you aren't truly releasing anything.

Ask the Expert

Q: What is the keyword nil and how do you use it?

A: The nil keyword is an Objective-C type that represents an object's absence. Do not confuse it with NULL, though; that is a C keyword. Moreover, you use nil with objects, NULL with primitives or C-style pointers.

Encapsulation and Memory Management

In previous sections you examined memory management within a method using local variables. In this section you explore memory management using an object's instance variables. Remember, an instance variable's scope is the same as the object's, and they are declared in an object's interface. Now, good object-oriented programmers never reference these variables externally, instead using something called accessor methods. To understand accessor methods better, first consider an object-oriented concept called encapsulation.

Encapsulation is an object-oriented programming design tenet stating that instance variables should be encapsulated from the outside world. In a nutshell, never access a class's instance variables directly. Instead you should set or get a class's instance variables using methods termed *accessor* methods. These methods are for getting and setting an instance variable properly, and allow things such as validation to occur prior to setting an object's instance variable.

Accessor methods are also further loosely referred to as "getter" and "setter" methods. A getter is for getting an instance variable from an object, while a setter is for setting an instance variable in an object. Getters and setters take on increased importance in an Objective-C program when you consider memory management and retain counts.

Try This Creating Accessor Methods for an Object and a Primitive

1. Create a new Command Line Utility using the Foundation Tool template. Name the project Accessors.
2. Create a new class called `Bar` and implement it as in Listings 5-5 and 5-6.
3. Create a new class called `Foo` and implement it as in Listings 5-7 and 5-8.
4. Modify Accessors.m to match Listing 5-9.
5. Build and run the application.

Listing 5-5 Bar.h

```
#import <Foundation/Foundation.h>
@interface Bar : NSObject {
```

(continued)

```
    int myAge;
    NSString * myName;
}
- (void) setMyAge: (int) theAge;
- (int) getMyAge;
-(void) setMyName: (NSString *) theName;
-(NSString *) getMyName;
- (void) sayNameAndAge;
@end
```

Listing 5-6 Bar.m

```
#import "Bar.h"
@implementation Bar
- (void) setMyAge: (int) theAge {
    myAge = theAge;
}
- (int) getMyAge {

    return myAge;
}
-(void) setMyName: (NSString *) theName {
    [myName release];
    myName = [theName copy];
}
-(NSString *) getMyName {


return myName;
}
- (void) sayNameAndAge {
    NSLog(@"My name is:%@ and my age is:%i", myName, myAge);
}
-(void) dealloc {
    [myName release];
    [super dealloc];
}
@end
```

Listing 5-7 Foo.h

```
#import <Foundation/Foundation.h>
@class Bar;
@interface Foo : NSObject {
```

```
  Bar * myBar;
}
- (void) setMyBar: (Bar *) theBar;
- (Bar *) getMyBar;
@end
```

Listing 5-8 Foo.m

```
#import "Foo.h"
#import "Bar.h"
@implementation Foo
- (void) setMyBar: (Bar *) theBar {
  [theBar retain];
  [myBar release];
  myBar = theBar;
}
- (Bar *) getMyBar {
  return myBar;
}
- (void) dealloc {
  [myBar release];
  [super dealloc];
}
@end
```

Listing 5-9 Accessors.m

```
#import <Foundation/Foundation.h>
#import "Foo.h"
#import "Bar.h"
int main (int argc, const char * argv[]) {
  NSAutoreleasePool * pool = [[NSAutoreleasePool alloc] init];
  Foo * myFoo = [[Foo alloc] init];
  Bar * myBar = [[Bar alloc] init];
  [myBar setMyAge:40];
  [myBar setMyName:@"James"];
  [myFoo setMyBar:myBar];
  [[myFoo getMyBar] sayNameAndAge];
  [myFoo release];
  [myBar release];
  [pool drain];
 return 0;
}
```

The Bar class is a simple class with two instance variables, myAge and myName. The myAge variable is an integer, which is a primitive data type, and so there is no required memory management. The setMyAge: method uses assignment to assign myAge to the parameter theAge. Name, in contrast, is an object. In the setMyName: method you create a copy of the theName variable passed as a parameter.

```
[myName release];

myName = [theName copy];
```

Creating a copy of an object creates a new object instance, and so myName references a distinct object. Because you are creating a copy, you do not call retain, as copying automatically sets the myName retainCount to 1.

Notice that you release myName before assigning the new value; if you did not, a memory leak would occur. Remember, myName points to an actual object; switching the address myName points to without releasing the underlying object would fail to decrement the object's retainCount.

Copying an object, like the myName variable, is not something you do frequently. You only make an object copy when you wish to ensure that nobody else has a reference to the object. You wish to have a unique object instance. More often, you simply create a new reference to an object. Foo's setMyBar illustrates how you typically accomplish this task.

```
[theBar retain];
[myBar release];
myBar = theBar;
```

First you retain the passed parameter, theBar. Remember, once you set myBar to theBar, it points to the same underlying Bar object; increasing theBar's retainCount is equivalent to increasing myBar's retainCount. After retaining, you release myBar so that if it points to another object instance, the runtime knows to decrement the object's retainCount. The method then sets myBar to refer to theBar, which refers to the underlying object instance.

Notice that both getter methods, getMyName and getMyBar, return weak references to each class's respective instance variable. If you wished to persist a variable obtained via one of these getters, then you would have to explicitly retain them.

Properties

Beginning with Objective-C 2.0, Apple introduced something called *properties* to the language. Properties greatly simplify using class instance methods, removing the tedium of writing accessor methods. Moreover, properties can handle retaining and releasing instance variables for you. Like all Objective-C's extensions to C, properties are implemented using compiler directives.

Declaring Properties

Properties are declared in a class's interface and defined in a class's implementation. A property's declaration begins with the @property compiler directive. Immediately following the @property directive is an optional list of attributes enclosed in parentheses. The instance variable's type and name then follows. Listing 5-10 illustrates a typical property declaration.

Listing 5-10 A typical property declaration

```
#import <Foundation/Foundation.h>
@interface FooBar : NSObject {
  NSString * myName;
}
@property (nonatomic,retain) NSString * myName;
@end
```

After declaring a property, you define the property in a class's implementation. The @synthesize directive goes in a class's implementation (Listing 5-11). Defining a property is trivial when using the @synthesize compiler directive. The @synthesize compiler directive tells the compiler to create accessor methods for a property.

Listing 5-11 A typical @synthesize directive

```
#import "FooBar.h"
@implementation FooBar
@synthesize myName;
@end
```

The default getters and setters generated for a property are <propertyname> for the getter and set<propertyname> for the setter. Note that if a property's first letter is lowercase, the method changes it to uppercase.

```
FooBar * myFooBar;
```

would capitalize the setter and getter as follows:

```
-(void) setMyFooBar: (FooBar*) aFooBar;
-(FooBar*) getMyFooBar;
```

For instance, you might write the code shown in Listing 5-12 in a `main` method to refer to myName.

Listing 5-12 Using a property via its accessor methods

```
#import <Foundation/Foundation.h>
#import "FooBar.h"
int main (int argc, const char * argv[]) {
  NSAutoreleasePool * pool = [[NSAutoreleasePool alloc] init];
  FooBar * myFooBar = [[FooBar alloc] init];
  [myFooBar setMyName:@"James"];
  NSLog(@"Name:%@", [myFooBar myName]);
  [myFooBar release];
  [pool drain];
  return 0;
}
```

Listing 5-12 illustrates using a setter and a getter. The `@synthesize` directive tells the compiler to generate setter and getter methods for the myName property. Because the compiler generates these methods at compile time, you can refer to the setter and getter as in Listing 5-12.

You usually do not refer to an object's properties using its accessor methods; instead, you access properties using dot notation. Dot notation allows you to refer to a property's getter and setter directly using the property's name.

Dot Notation

Objective-C has a dot operator that makes it easier to refer to a property. Depending upon the context, the compiler knows you are actually accessing the property's generated getter or setter accessor method. The following code illustrates accessing a property's setter method:

```
self.myFoo = tempFoo;
```

The next code snippet illustrates getting a property using dot notation:

```
Foo * aFoo = myObject.myFoo;
```

This snippet accesses an object's myFoo instance variable using the myFoo property's getter method.

Property Attributes

Properties usually have one or more attributes further specifying to the compiler how to generate accessor methods for the property. Attributes are placed in parentheses immediately following the @property declaration. For instance, consider the following property declaration:

```
@property (nonatomic, retain) Foo * myFoo;
```

This line first declares that it is declaring a property. It then declares that the property is nonatomic and that the setter for the property should call retain on the object. Essentially, it is telling the compiler to generate the following setter:

```
-(void) setFoo : (Foo *) aFoo {
  [aFoo retain];
  [myFoo release];
  myFoo = aFoo;
}
```

Table 5-1 shows a list of property attributes you may use when declaring a property.

Attribute	Description
Read/Write attributes. The default setting for a property is readwrite.	
readwrite	Tells the compiler the property may be read and written to.
readonly	Tells the compiler that the property may only be read.
Setter attributes. The default setting for a property is assign.	
assign	Tells the compiler that the property uses assignment in the property's setter.
retain	Tells the compiler that the property's setter should call retain on the property when setting it.
copy	Tells the compiler that the property's setter should create a new copy of the object.
Other property attributes.	
nonatomic	Tells the compiler that the property's accessor methods are not thread safe.
setter=	Tells the compiler that you wish specifying a setter of your own name.
getter=	Tells the compiler that you wish specifying a getter of your own name.

Table 5-1 Property Attributes You May Use When Declaring a Property

Writability

Not all properties need a setter. Moreover, some properties, such as primitive data types, should use simple assignment, while other properties, such as objects, should either be retained or have a new copy created. The `readwrite` and `readonly` properties tell the compiler whether it should generate a setter or not. If not provided, the default behavior is to generate a setter. If `readonly`, the compiler generates only a getter for the property, making the property read-only. The following code snippet illustrates two read/write property declarations and one read-only property declaration:

```
@property Foo * myFoo;  //the default - read/write
@property (readwrite, retain) Foo * myFoo;
@property (readonly) Foo * myFoo;
```

Setter Attributes

The `assign`, `retain`, and `copy` attributes direct how the compiler generates setter methods for a property. The `assign` attribute is for simple assignment and should only be used with primitives. Note that `assign` is a property's default behavior; therefore, you should almost always specify a setter attribute. For instance, you might have an `int` property that you specify uses simple assignment.

```
@property (assign) int myFooCount;
```

While `assign` is useful for primitives, the `retain` property is the attribute you specify more often. The `retain` property tells the compiler that the setter should release the old reference and retain the new reference. Remember, every object derived from `NSObject` has an associated retain count that the runtime uses to decide if an object should be released or not. When setting a property, the old reference must be released; otherwise, a memory leak occurs. Consider the following property declaration (ignore the `nonatomic` property for now):

```
@property (nonatomic, retain) Foo * myFoo;
```

When compiling, the compiler generates the following setter method:

```
-(void) setFoo : (Foo *) aFoo {
  [aFoo retain];
  [myFoo release];
  myFoo = aFoo;
}
```

This method first calls `retain` on the `Foo` instance passed to the method, increasing its retain count by 1. It then releases its reference to the old `Foo` instance, decreasing its retain count by 1. It then changes its `myFoo` reference to point to the `Foo` instance referenced by `aFoo`.

The `copy` attribute specifies that a setter should make a bona fide object copy. It is a unique object instance. The behavior is to release the previous object instance, create a copy of the new object, and assign the instance variable the new copy. You can only use `copy` with objects that implement the NSCopying protocol. As you haven't learned inheritance or how to copy an object yet, you will revisit the `copy` property attribute at the end of Chapter 7.

Other Property Attributes

The `nonatomic` attribute tells the compiler not to generate locks in a property's getter and setter methods. Discussing threading, multithreaded programs, and mutexes (locks) is beyond this chapter's scope. But think of your computer's hardware. Chances are you have a dual-core processor. This means your computer can do more than one thing at the same instance in time. As your skills progress, you can write programs that do more than one thing at the same time—these different "things" are different threads in the same program. These multiple threads can access a property using its accessor methods at the same exact instance in time. A lock allows only one thread to access the variable at a time and forces the others to wait their turn. Realize this is a simplification, however, it gives you a general idea of how threading works. Until you start writing multithreaded iPhone applications, just use `nonatomic`.

Try This Exploring Properties and Property Attributes

1. Create a new Foundation command-line project named ExploringProperties.
2. Create a new class called `FooBar`.
3. Implement `FooBar` as in Listings 5-13 and 5-14.
4. Implement ExploringProperties.m as in Listing 5-15.
5. Click Build And Debug to build and run the application.

(continued)

Listing 5-13 FooBar.h

```
#import <Foundation/Foundation.h>
@interface FooBar : NSObject {
  NSString * myName;
  int myAge;
  NSNumber * myHeight;
  NSString * myGreeting;
}
@property (nonatomic, copy) NSString * myName;
@property (nonatomic, assign) int myAge;
@property (nonatomic, retain) NSNumber * myHeight;
@property (nonatomic,retain) NSString * myGreeting;
@end
```

Listing 5-14 FooBar.m

```
#import "FooBar.h"
@implementation FooBar
@synthesize myName;
@synthesize myAge;
@synthesize myHeight;
@synthesize myGreeting;
-(void) setMyGreeting: (NSString *) theGreeting {
  NSLog(@"in the custom greeting....");
  [theGreeting retain];
  [myGreeting release];
  myGreeting = theGreeting;
}
-(void) dealloc {
  [myName release];
  [myHeight release];
  [myGreeting release];
  [super dealloc];
}
@end
```

Listing 5-15 ExploringProperties.m

```
#import <Foundation/Foundation.h>
#import "FooBar.h"
int main (int argc, const char * argv[]) {
  //NOTE NO POOL CREATED
  //NSAutoreleasePool * pool = [[NSAutoreleasePool alloc] init];
```

```
  FooBar * myFooBar = [[FooBar alloc] init];
  myFooBar.myAge = 40;
  NSNumber * tempNumber = [[NSNumber alloc] initWithFloat:5.9];
  myFooBar.myHeight = tempNumber;
  NSString * tempString = [[NSString alloc] initWithString:@"James"];
  myFooBar.myName = tempString;
  myFooBar.myGreeting = @"Hello World";
  NSLog(myFooBar.myGreeting);
  NSLog(@"Name:%@ and age:%i and height:%f", myFooBar.myName,
myFooBar.myAge, [myFooBar.myHeight floatValue] );
  [myFooBar release];
  [tempString release];
  [tempNumber release];
  //[pool drain];
  return 0;
}
```

Listing 5-16 shows the debugger console output. The `FooBar` object has three instance variables: myName, myAge, and `myHeight`. The myAge is an integer, a primitive, and so the property is set to `assign`. The myName property uses copy, and so myName is always given its own `NSString` object. The `NSNumber` uses `retain`, and so it creates a new reference to an underlying object.

Notice the `sayMyGreeting:` method in `FooBar`; `synthesize` is flexible, if the compiler sees that you already created a setter or getter, it will use that accessor method rather than generating it. Here, you created the setter method, and so the compiler does not generate a setter but uses yours instead.

Listing 5-16 The debugger console

```
in the custom greeting....
Hello World
Name:James and age:40 and height:5.900000
```

Ownership and Properties Revisited

Two sections ago, you were presented the following code as an example illustrating a property's getter accessor.

```
Foo * aFoo = myObject.myFoo;
```

The code, though valid and not unusual, appears as if it should cause problems, as you are not calling `retain` as you would expect. But it does not cause problems because behind the scenes `myFoo` is retained by the accessor method before being returned to `aFoo`.

Now, had you called an instance variable directly, without calling `retain`, you obtain a weak reference. For instance, the following code results in a runtime error because you are calling `release` on the "real" `Foo` instance, without having first called `retain`.

```
Foo * aFoo = myFoo;

[aFoo release]; //this is incorrect
NSLog("%i", [myObject.myFoo retainCount]);
```

The reason for this runtime error is that the `aFoo` instance variable does not "own" the underlying `Foo` instance; it is merely obtaining a weak reference to `myFoo`.

Avoiding weak references is another reason for using properties to get and set an object's instance variables. Properties generate code similar to the following for a property's getter method:

```
- (Foo *) myFoo {
  return [myFoo retain];
}
```

Autorelease and Pools

Objective-C offers an alternative to manually managing memory. If you wish, you can use autorelease to manage memory. Even if you never explicitly use autorelease with your own custom objects, you still use autorelease if you use a Cocoa object's convenience method. For instance, the following convenience method uses autorelease behind the scenes:

```
NSString * myString = [NSString stringWithString:@"This is my
string."];
```

Notice that `myString` is a weak reference, as `myString` does not control its underlying string's lifetime. To persist the actual string `myString` points to, you would need to explicitly retain it.

Also notice that the `main` method in the previous example (Listing 5-15) begins and ends by referring to something named "pool." The `pool` variable refers to something called an NSAutoreleasePool. An autorelease pool is a pool for objects that are released automatically by the runtime, freeing you from having to worry about managing the objects yourself.

Autorelease and Custom Classes

When you wish an original object to use autorelease, you send it an autorelease message. Listing 5-17 is Listing 5-15 rewritten to use autorelease.

Listing 5-17 ExploringProperties.m rewritten to use NSAutoreleasePool

```
#import <Foundation/Foundation.h>
#import "FooBar.h"
int main (int argc, const char * argv[]) {
  NSAutoreleasePool * pool = [[NSAutoreleasePool alloc] init];
  FooBar * myFooBar = [[[FooBar alloc] init] autorelease];
  myFooBar.myAge = 40;
  NSNumber * tempNumber = [[[NSNumber alloc] initWithFloat:5.9]
autorelease];
  myFooBar.myHeight = tempNumber;
  NSString * tempString = [[[NSString alloc] initWithString:@"James"]
autorelease];
  myFooBar.myName = tempString';
  myFooBar.myGreeting = @"Hello World";
  NSLog(myFooBar.myGreeting);
  NSLog(@"Name:%@ and age:%i and height:%f", myFooBar.myName,
myFooBar.myAge,
[myFooBar.myHeight floatValue] );
  [pool drain];
  return 0;
}
```

The first thing main does is create a new autorelease pool. As this is a simple Foundation command-line application, any objects created and sent the autorelease message are added to the pool. At the end of main, the pool is drained and any object added to the pool is released and cleaned up.

Try This Using Autorelease in a Method

1. Create a new Foundation command-line tool named AutoRelease.
2. Create a new NSObject named Bar and implement it like Listings 5-18 and 5-19.
3. Create a new NSObject named Foo and implement it like Listings 5-20 and 5-21.

(continued)

4. Modify AutoRelease.m's `main` method (Listing 5-22).
5. Click Build And Debug to compile and run the application.

Listing 5-18 Bar.h

```
#import <Foundation/Foundation.h>
@interface Bar : NSObject {
}
- (void) sayHello;
@end
```

Listing 5-19 Bar.m

```
#import "Bar.h"
@implementation Bar
- (void) sayHello {
  NSLog(@"Say Hello");
}
@end
```

Listing 5-20 Foo.h

```
#import <Foundation/Foundation.h>
#import "Bar.h"
@interface Foo : NSObject {
}
-(Bar *) giveMeABar;
@end
```

Listing 5-21 Foo.m

```
#import "Foo.h"
@implementation Foo
- (Bar *) giveMeABar {
  Bar * tempBar = [[[Bar alloc] init] autorelease];
  return tempBar;
}
@end
```

Listing 5-22 AutoRelease.m

```
#import <Foundation/Foundation.h>
#import "Foo.h"
int main (int argc, const char * argv[]) {
  NSAutoreleasePool * pool = [[NSAutoreleasePool alloc] init];
  Foo * myFoo = [[[Foo alloc] init] autorelease];''''

  [[myFoo giveMeABar] sayHello];
  [pool drain];
  return 0;
}
```

The Foo giveMeABar method illustrates a common use of autorelease. Notice the following line in AutoRelease.m:

```
[[myFoo giveMeABar] sayHello];
```

Nowhere are you releasing the Bar object reference returned by the giveMeABar method; without using autorelease in giveMeABar, a memory leak would occur. Without using autorelease in giveMeABar, you would have to replace the one-line call in main with three lines.

```
Bar * myTempBar = [myFoo giveMeABar];
[myTempBar sayHello];
[myTempBar release];
```

Using autorelease avoids this and allows you to conveniently not worry about memory management. Note that in this chapter you only used the auto-generated autorelease pools. You find this autorelease pool in the project's main method. In iPhone applications, the runtime manages an autorelease pool for each runtime loop. Do not worry about the details of that, just realize the iPhone handles the autorelease pools for you.

You should not rely upon autorelease too much. Instead, you should manually manage your own retain count for your custom objects. And be careful when using convenience methods. Although it is contrived, consider the following code snippet in Listing 5-23 and its object allocation in Figure 5-4.

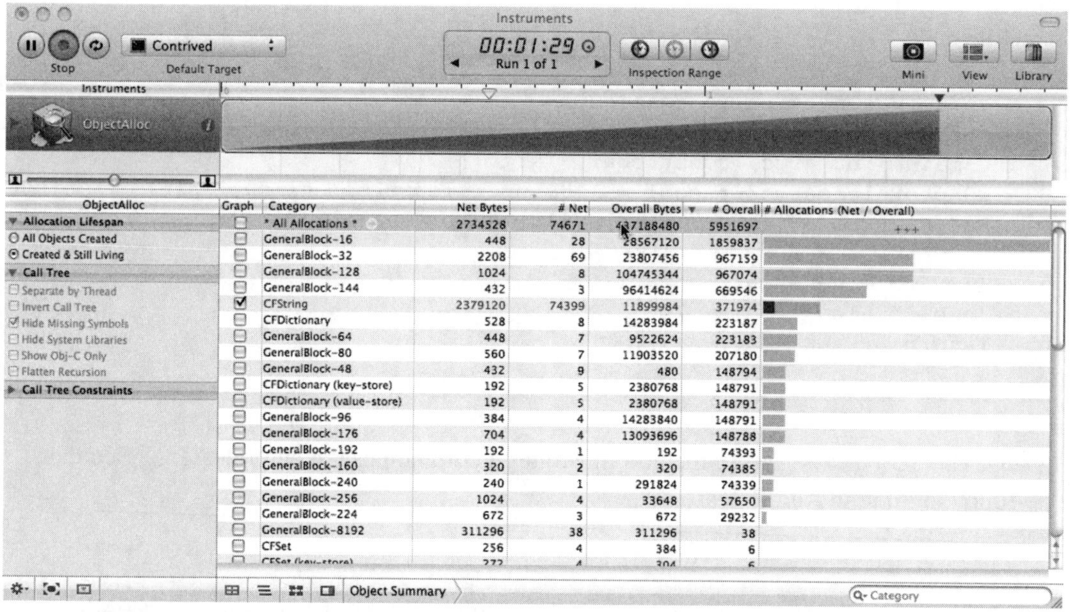

Figure 5-4 The object allocation

Listing 5-23 A memory-gobbling `main`

```
#import <Foundation/Foundation.h>
int main (int argc, const char * argv[]) {
  NSAutoreleasePool * pool = [[NSAutoreleasePool alloc] init];
  int count = 0;
  while(count++ < 1000000000) {
    NSString * tempString = [NSString stringWithFormat:@"Test%i",count];
    NSLog(tempString);
  }
  [pool drain];
  return 0;
}
```

Figure 5-4 is the simple program in Listing 5-23 running using the Object Allocations tool in Instruments. Notice the Net Bytes column value for CFString. The number of objects created but not released steadily climbs. If you tried something like this in an iPhone application, your application would become sluggish and would then be abruptly terminated by the iPhone's operating system.

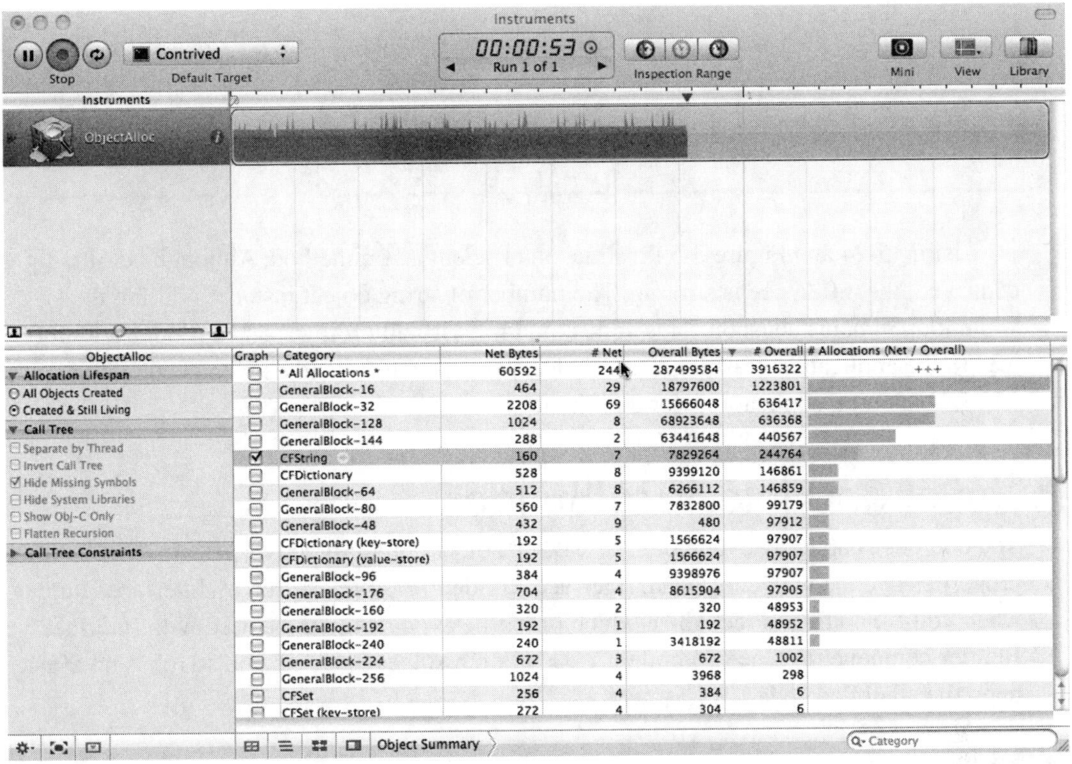

Figure 5-5 Object allocations of an efficient `main`

The reason for this behavior is you are relying upon autorelease but an autorelease pool doesn't release its constituents until the pool is drained. Here the pool is not drained until after the while loop, and so the temporary strings are not released and the memory grows with each loop. Compare this with Listing 5-24 and Figure 5-5.

Listing 5-24 An efficient `main`

```
#import <Foundation/Foundation.h>
int main (int argc, const char * argv[]) {
  NSAutoreleasePool * pool = [[NSAutoreleasePool alloc] init];
  int count = 0;
  while(count++ < 1000000000) {
    NSString * tempString = [[NSString alloc] initWithFormat:@"Test%i",count];
```

```
      NSLog(tempString);
      [tempString release];
    }
    [pool drain];
    return 0;
}
```

Listing 5-24 and Figure 5-5 illustrate an efficient `main` method. Although admittedly contrived, the difference is striking. The number of string object instances during the while loop remains constant. This code could run virtually forever on an iPhone and not lead to the application crashing. Be very leery of autorelease and convenience methods when developing applications for an iPhone.

IBOutlet and Interface Builder

You end this chapter by examining the `IBOutlet` compiler directive. `IBOutlet` connects properties in code with controls in Interface Builder. IBOutlet is used by Interface Builder when you are coding to recognize which properties you intend to be used with Interface Builder components. Once compiled, `IBOutlet` resolves to `void`, and so it has no effect upon the compiled code.

Try This Using IBOutlet

1. Create a new View-based application named OutletProgram.
2. Modify OutletProgramViewController.h and OutletProgramViewController.m to use a `UILabel` property called `myGreetingLabel` (Listings 5-25 and 5-26). Ensure you use the `IBOutlet` keyword before the variable's declaration.
3. Implement `viewDidLoad` in OutletProgramViewController.m as in Listing 5-26.
4. Compile, but do not run the application.
5. Open OutletProgramViewController.xib in Interface Builder.
6. Drag a UILabel from the Library to the view's canvas (Figure 5-6).
7. Resize the label (Figure 5-7).

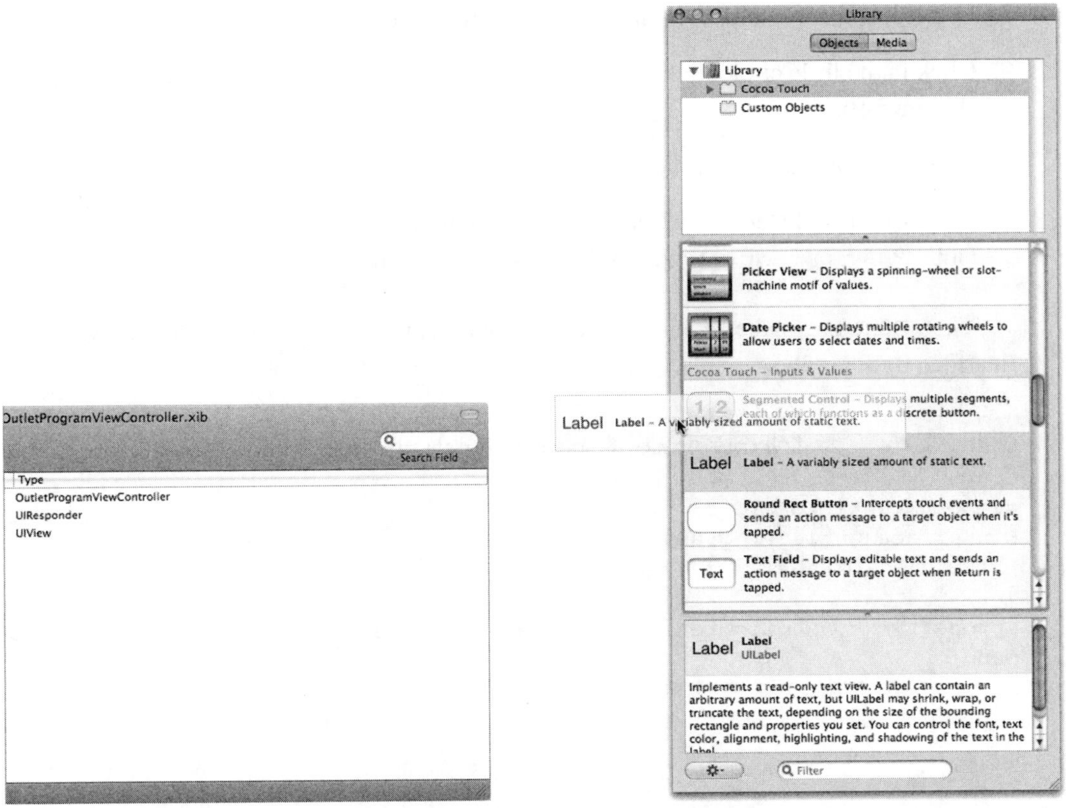

Figure 5-6 Adding a UILabel to a view's canvas

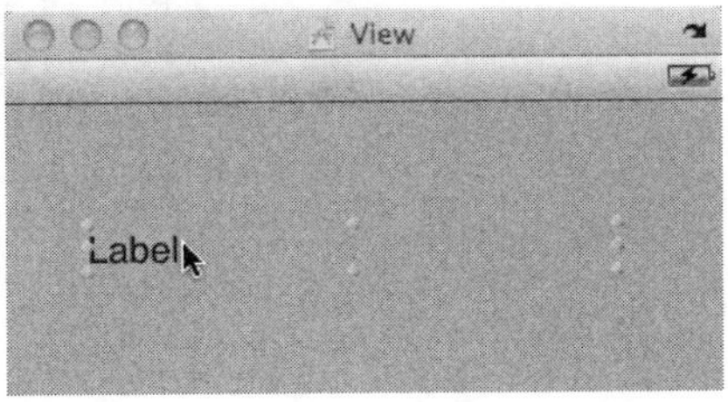

Figure 5-7 Resizing the UILabel

(continued)

8. In the document window, right-click File's Owner (Figure 5-8).
9. Click in the little circle to the right of myGreetingLabel and drag and drop on the label (Figure 5-9).
10. Save and exit Interface Builder.
11. Click Build And Debug and the application runs. The text set in OutletProgramViewController.m displays in the simulator (Figure 5-10).

The `IBOutlet` makes connecting code in your Xcode methods to controls in your Interface Builder xib.

Listing 5-25 OutletProgramViewControllerProgram.h

```
#import <UIKit/UIKit.h>
@interface OutletProgramViewController : UIViewController {
  IBOutlet UILabel * myGreetingLabel;
}
@property (nonatomic,retain) UILabel * myGreetingLabel;
@end
```

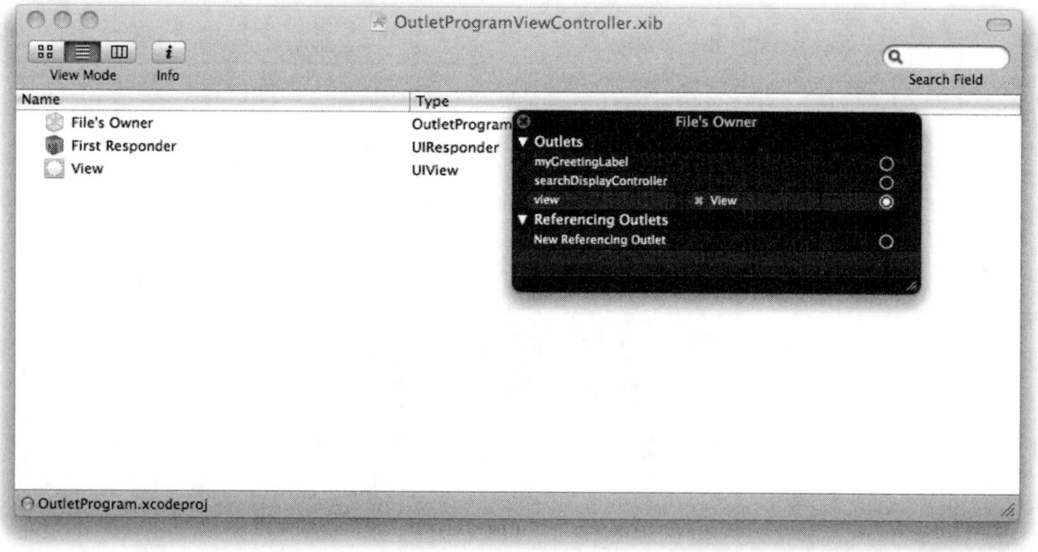

Figure 5-8 Right-clicking on File's Owner

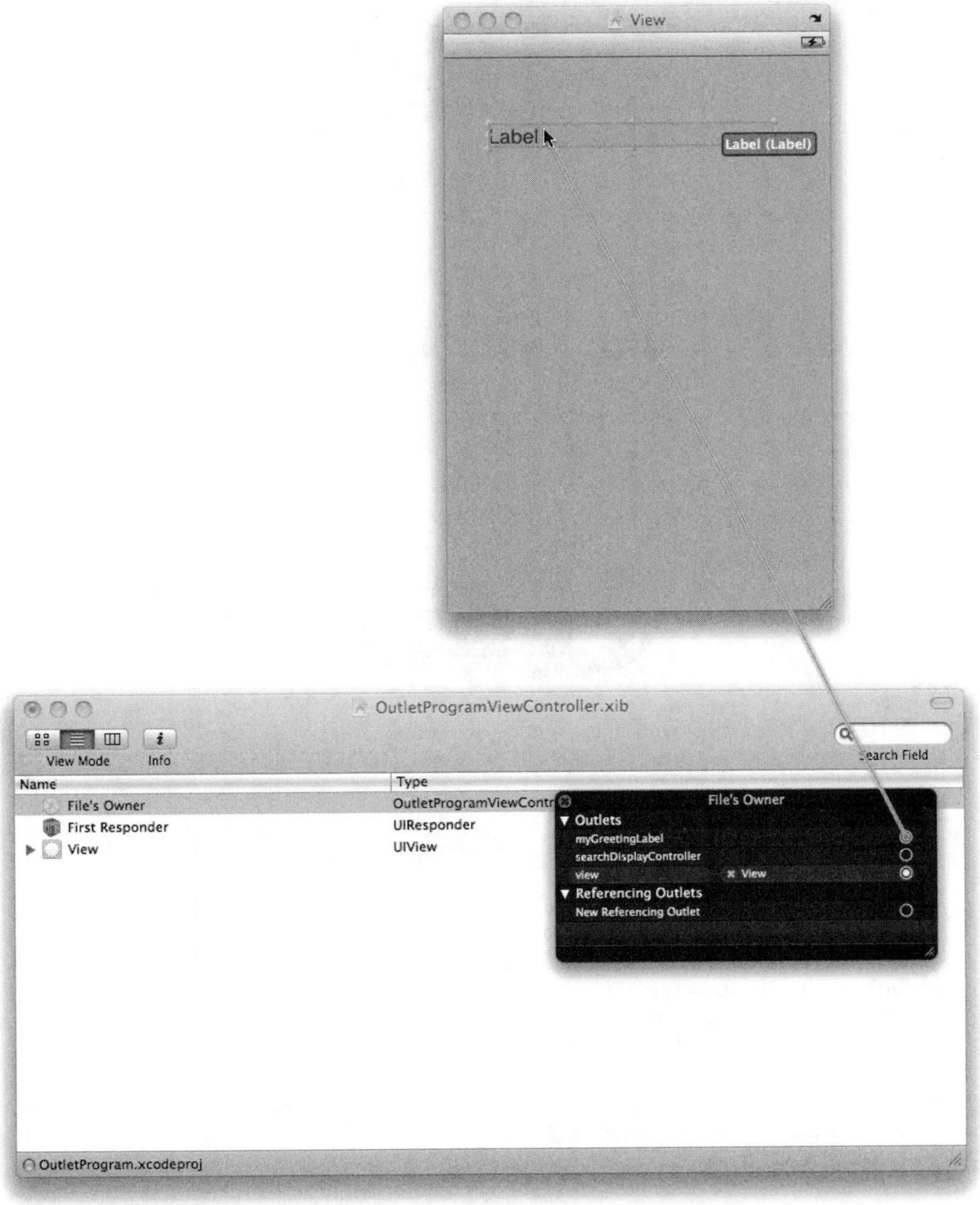

Figure 5-9 Dragging and dropping on the view's canvas

(continued)

Figure 5-10 The label displayed in the iPhone simulator

Listing 5-26 OutletProgramViewControllerProgram.m

```
#import "OutletProgramViewController.h"
@implementation OutletProgramViewController
@synthesize myGreetingLabel;
- (void) viewDidLoad {
  myGreetingLabel.text = @"Hello World";
  [super viewDidLoad];
}
- (void)dealloc {
  [myGreetingLabel release];
  [super dealloc];
}
@end
```

Deallocating and Nil Revisited

Before ending the chapter, there is one final thing to cover using properties and deallocating an object. Throughout this chapter, and throughout this book in fact, all examples assume that a class's properties are set. For instance, consider the class in Listing 5-27.

Listing 5-27 Foo.m assuming properties are set

```
#import "Foo.h"
@implementation Foo
@synthesize myBar;
-(void) dealloc {
  [super dealloc];
  [self.myBar release];
}
@end
```

The code in Listing 5-27 appears sound, but if `myBar` is never allocated and initialized, a runtime error results because you are trying to release an unallocated object. When using properties, there are two easy ways to deal with this potential problem. The first way is by implementing your own `init` method, where you initialize the class's objects to `nil` (Listing 5-28). Remember, sending a message such as `release` to `nil` is valid.

Listing 5-28 Foo.m initializing its property

```
#import "Foo.h"
@implementation Foo
@synthesize myBar;
-(void) init {
  self = [super init];
  self.myBar = nil;
}
-(void) dealloc {
  [super dealloc];
  [self.myBar release];
}
@end
```

However, a more common technique many developers use is to not release a property at all but to instead assign it a nil value in the class's dealloc method (Listing 5-29).

Listing 5-29 Foo.m assuming properties are set

```
#import "Foo.h"
@implementation Foo
@synthesize myBar;
-(void) dealloc {
  [super dealloc];
  self.myBar=nil;
}
@end
```

Remember, when setting a class's property, the generated setter first releases the property and then assigns the property the new value. After assigning the new value, the setter retains the object. When you set a property with nil, the setter releases the old value, assigns nil as the new value, and then sends retain to nil. Thus the property is released, but at the same time, if the property is never allocated, no error is thrown. Of the two techniques, the second is more popular because it is an easy way to ensure you release all of an object's properties without risking that the properties were never allocated.

Summary

In this chapter you explored memory management, properties, and IBOutlet. Properties simplify respecting a class's instance variable encapsulation by automatically creating accessor methods. Always respect a class's encapsulation by accessing an instance variable through the property; avoid creating your own accessor methods and let Objective-C do its job by making things easier for you through properties. Properties simplify your code, make your programs less prone to memory leaks, and help reduce program crashes.

IBOutlets are a directive to Interface Builder that connects controls in your Interface Builder GUI to properties in your classes. IBOutlet compiles to void and so they are meaningless when compiled. You use IBOutlets extensively when using Interface Builder.

Chapter 6

Inheritance

Key Skills & Concepts

- Understanding Inheritance
- Modeling Inheritance
- Understanding Inheritance Syntax
- Understanding NSObject and Cocoa Classes
- Extending Classes with New Variables and Methods
- Overriding Parent Methods with Child Methods
- Understanding the `dealloc` Method and `super` Keyword

Inheritance

Inheritance is a powerful object-oriented concept for extending a class' functionality. As you have already seen in previous chapters, Objective-C uses inheritance extensively. In this chapter you explore how Objective-C implements inheritance. You first learn Objective-C's inheritance syntax and how you can model inheritance. You then explore how inheritance facilitates extending an ancestor class and also facilitates redefining an ancestor class.

Inheritance Explained

Inheritance is an object-oriented principle that allows reusing existing code with less modification. How it works is that a *child* class extends a *base* class. A base class is also often referred to as the child class' *parent*. The child class can then use the base class' instance variables and methods. This reuse is called inheritance because child classes inherit the methods and instance variables of its ancestor classes.

A child classes can extend a parent class' functionality. And a child class can replace a parent class' functionality. For instance, all fruit have certain shared characteristics. However, different fruit can have different characteristics that specialize a Fruit. All fruits have skin, but apple, orange, and pear skins are all a little different. Or consider a living organism. Both plants and animals are living organisms and both breathe. However, a plant breathes carbon dioxide and animals breathe oxygen. You can model both these examples using a diagram called a *class diagram.*

Modeling Inheritance

The Unified Modeling Language (UML) offers a convenient syntax for modeling inheritance. Figure 6-1 illustrates a simple class diagram.

A child class' relationship with a parent class is modeled using an arrow with an open arrow. The arrow points from the child to the parent. In Figure 6-1, a `Pear`, `Orange`, and `Apple` are all children of `Fruit`. You can also, of course, create a more detailed class diagram, much as you did in Chapter 5 (Figure 6-2).

In Figure 6-2, a `LivingOrganism` is the parent, while `Animal` and `Plant` are children of `LivingOrganism`. A class is modeled as a rectangle. The rectangle's top compartment contains the class' name. The second compartment contains the class' instance variables. The third compartment contains the class' methods.

Figure 6-3 illustrates another inheritance principle. A child class inherits not only from its immediate parent; it also inherits from every ancestor to its root class.

In Figure 6-3, a `Fuji`'s parent is `Apple`. An `Apple`'s parent is `Fruit`. A `Fruit`'s parent is `NSObject`. `NSObject` is the root class. A `Fuji` inherits from `Apple`, `Fruit`, and `NSObject`.

NOTE

A parent class is also often referred to as a superclass, and a child class is often referred to as a subclass.

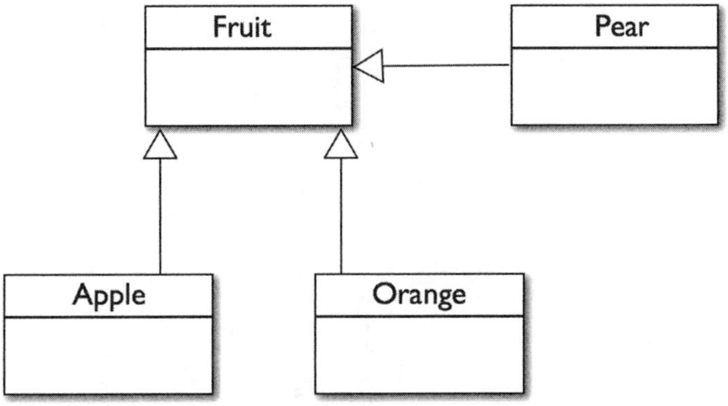

Figure 6-1 A UML class diagram modeling inheritance

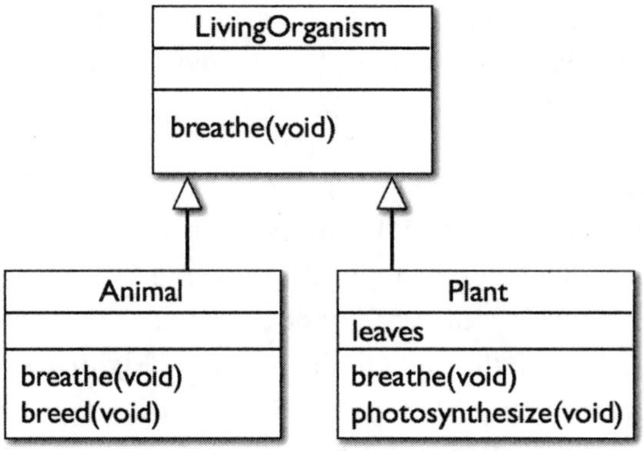

Figure 6-2 A more detailed UML class diagram modeling inheritance

Inheritance Syntax

Objective-C implements inheritance in an object's interface. The following code illustrates:

```
#import <Foundation/Foundation.h>
#import "MyParent.h"
@interface MyChild : MyParent {
  int state;
}
```

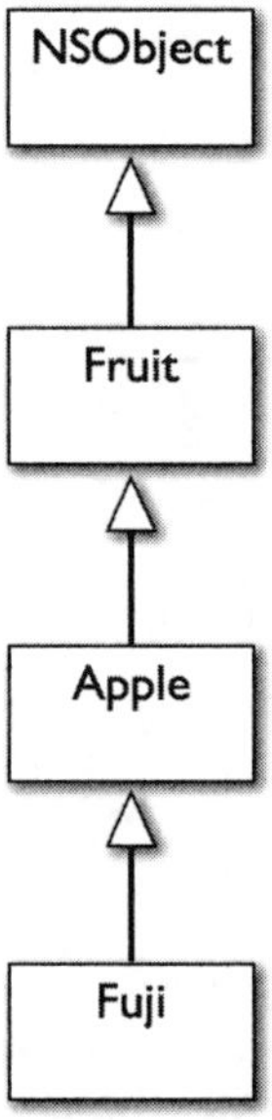

Figure 6-3 A class inheritance hierarchy

You import the parent, and then you place a colon followed by the parent class on the line with the `@interface` compiler declaration. Essentially the line containing the `@interface` declaration tells the compiler that it is declaring a `MyChild` class that inherits from `MyParent`. The following Try This illustrates Objective-C's inheritance syntax.

Try This Examining Simple Inheritance

1. Create a new View-based Application named **SimpleInheritance**.
2. Create three new Objective-C classes named `Fruit`, `Apple`, and `Orange`. Have `Apple` and `Orange` inherit from `Fruit` (Listings 6-1 through 6-6). Note that creating a subclass requires you first create an Objective-C `NSObject` subclass. In the created class, import the parent class header file and change the newly created object's parent from `NSObject` to the desired superclass.
3. Create an integer as an instance variable, and name the variable `state`.
4. Create two methods named `getState` and `ripen`, as in Listings 6-1 and 6-2.
5. Create a class named `Environment` (Listings 6-7 and 6-8). Add an `Apple` and `Orange` as properties and create two methods, `handleTimeSecond` and `startTime`. Also, add an `NSTimer` to `Environment`.
6. Implement the `init` and `dealloc` methods in `Environment`, as in Listing 6-8.
7. Modify SimpleInheritanceViewController.h so that it imports the `Environment` class and declares an `Environment` property named `myEnvironment` (Listing 6-9).
8. Modify SimpleInheritanceViewController.m so that it creates and initializes a new `Environment` instance in the `applicationDidFinishLaunching:` method (Listing 6-10). Be certain to release `myEnvironment` in `SimpleInheritanceView Controller`'s `dealloc` method.
9. Click Build And Debug to run the application. You should see the debug statements in Listing 6-11 print to the debugger console.

(continued)

Listing 6-1 Fruit.h

```
#import <Foundation/Foundation.h>
#define UNRIPE 0
#define RIPE 1
#define VERY_RIPE 2
#define ROTTEN 3
#define VERY_ROTTEN 4
#define PUTRID 5
@interface Fruit : NSObject {
  int state;
}
- (NSString *) getState;
- (void) ripen;
@end
```

Listing 6-2 Fruit.m

```
#import "Fruit.h"
@implementation Fruit
- (void) ripen {
  state++;
}
- (NSString *) getState {
  switch (state) {
    case 0:
      return @"unripe";
    case 1:
      return @"ripe";
    case 2:
      return @"very ripe";
    case 3:
      return @"rotten";
    case 4:
      return @"very rotten";
    case 5:
      return @"putrid";
    default:
      return nil;
}
}
@end
```

Listing 6-3 Apple.h

```
#import <Foundation/Foundation.h>
#import "Fruit.h"
@interface Apple : Fruit {
}
@end
```

Listing 6-4 Apple.m

```
#import "Apple.h"
@implementation Apple
@end
```

Listing 6-5 Orange.h

```
#import <Foundation/Foundation.h>
#import "Fruit.h"
@interface Orange : Fruit {
}
@end
```

Listing 6-6 Orange.m

```
#import "Orange.h"
@implementation Orange
@end
```

Listing 6-7 Environment.h

```
#import <Foundation/Foundation.h>
@class "Fruit.h"
@class "Apple.h"
@class "Orange.h"
@interface Environment : NSObject {
  NSTimer * myTimer;
  Apple * myApple;
  Orange * myOrange;
}
```

(continued)

```
@property (nonatomic,retain) Apple * myApple;
@property (nonatomic,retain) Orange * myOrange;
- (void) handleTimeSecond;
- (void) startTime;
@end
```

Listing 6-8 Environment.m

```
#import "Environment.h"
#import "Apple.h"
#import "Orange.h"
#import "Fruit.h"
@implementation Environment
@synthesize myOrange;
@synthesize myApple;
- (id) init {
  if([super init] == nil) return nil;
  Apple * tempApple = [[Apple alloc] init];
  self.myApple = tempApple;
  [tempApple release];
  Orange * tempOrange = [[Orange alloc] init];
  self.myOrange = tempOrange;
  [tempOrange release];
  [self startTime];
  NSLog(@"is a kind of Fruit:%i", [self.myApple isKindOfClass:
[Fruit class]]);
  NSLog(@"is a subclass of Fruit:%i", [[Orange class] isSubclassOfClass:
[Fruit class]]);
  NSLog(@"does orange respond to ripen:%i", [self.myOrange
respondsToSelector:@selector(ripen)]);
  NSLog(@"does orange respond to foo:%i", [self.myOrange
respondsToSelector:@selector(foo)]);
  return self;
}
- (void) startTime {
  myTimer = [NSTimer scheduledTimerWithTimeInterval:1.0 target:self
selector:@selector(handleTimeSecond) userInfo:nil repeats:YES];
}
- (void) handleTimeSecond {
  [self.myApple ripen];
  NSLog(@"apple's state:%@", [self.myApple getState]);
  [self.myOrange ripen];
  NSLog(@"orange's state:%@", [self.myOrange getState]);
  if([[self.myApple getState] isEqualToString:@"putrid"] &&
[[self.myOrange getState] isEqualToString:@"putrid"]) {
```

```
    [myTimer invalidate];
  }
}
- (void) dealloc {
  [self.myApple release];
  [self.myOrange release];
  [super dealloc];
}
@end
```

Listing 6-9 SimpleInheritanceAppDelegate.h

```
#import <UIKit/UIKit.h>
#import "Environment.h"
@class SimpleInheritanceViewController;
@interface SimpleInheritanceAppDelegate : NSObject
<UIApplicationDelegate> {
  UIWindow *window;
  SimpleInheritanceViewController *viewController;
  Environment * myEnvironment;
}
@property (nonatomic, retain) IBOutlet UIWindow *window;
@property (nonatomic, retain) IBOutlet SimpleInheritanceViewController
*viewController;
@property (nonatomic, retain) Environment * myEnvironment;
@end
```

Listing 6-10 SimpleInheritanceAppDelegate.m

```
#import "SimpleInheritanceAppDelegate.h"
#import "SimpleInheritanceViewController.h"
@implementation SimpleInheritanceAppDelegate
@synthesize window;
@synthesize viewController;
@synthesize myEnvironment;
- (void)applicationDidFinishLaunching:(UIApplication *)application {
  Environment * tempE = [[Environment alloc] init];
 self.myEnvironment = tempE;
  [tempE release];
  [window addSubview:viewController.view];
  [window makeKeyAndVisible];
}
```

(continued)

```
- (void)dealloc {
  [viewController release];
  [window release];
  [myEnvironment release];
  [super dealloc];
}
@end
```

Listing 6-11 Debugger console logging

```
is a kind of Fruit:1
is a subclass of Fruit:1
does orange respond to ripen:1
does orange respond to foo:0
apple's state:ripe
orange's state:ripe
apple's state:very ripe
orange's state:very ripe
apple's state:rotten
orange's state:rotten
apple's state:very rotten
orange's state:very rotten
apple's state:putrid
orange's state:putrid
```

In this example, you created a base class of type `Fruit` (Listings 6-1 and 6-2). You then created `Apple` and `Orange` child classes (Listings 6-3 through 6-6). You specified each inherited from `Fruit`.

```
@interface Orange : Fruit {
@interface Apple : Fruit {
```

Due to the environment, all fruit eventually ripen. You modeled this natural process as a method in the `Fruit` class, naming the method "ripen." You also created the `state` instance variable in `Fruit` to represent the fruit's state of decay. Fruits progress from unripened to putrid, and these states are defined as constants in `Fruit`'s header.

```
#define UNRIPE 0
#define RIPE 1
#define VERY_RIPE 2
#define ROTTEN 3
#define VERY_ROTTEN 4
#define PUTRID 5
```

Because both Apple and Orange inherit from Fruit, they both have the ripen and getState methods and they both have the state variable available to them.

The Environment class models time using an NSTimer. When initialized, the Environment class starts keeping the time. Time is represented using an NSTimer class. A new timer is created that fires the handleTimeSecond method every one second.

```
myTimer = [NSTimer scheduledTimerWithTimeInterval:1.0 target:self
selector:@selector(handleTimeSecond) userInfo:nil repeats:YES];
```

Every second, the timer fires the handleTimeSecond method. The handleTimeSecond method then sends a ripen message to Apple and Orange. Behind the scenes, the runtime sees if myApple or myOrange can respond to the ripen message sent by myEnvironment. Neither can, and so the runtime checks each class' parent class for the method, finds it, and calls it instead. It does the same with the getState method. Figure 6-4 illustrates how the runtime handles inherited methods.

When an Orange instance is sent a ripen message, the runtime first checks to see if Orange can respond to the message. If it cannot, then it checks Orange's parent. The runtime continues checking Orange's ancestor hierarchy until it either finds a class that can respond to the message or it reaches NSObject. If no ancestor class can react to the message, then a runtime error occurs.

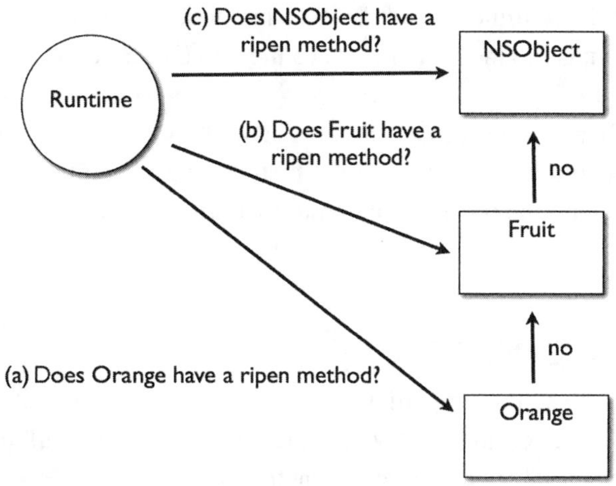

Figure 6-4 Runtime's behavior handling inheritance

(continued)

NOTE

The official terminology for the runtime behavior in Figure 6-4 is "message dispatching."

Notice that just for fun, you threw in the `isKindOfClass`, `isSubclassOfClass`, and `respondsToSelector` methods in Listing 6-9. The `isKindOfClass` method checks if an object is an instance of a class or an instance of one of a class' child classes. The `isSubclassOfClass` checks if a class is a subclass of another class. The `respondsToSelector` method checks if a class can respond to a method sent to it. In this example, all three return 1, or YES. Note that neither `Orange` nor `Fruit` implements a `foo` method, and so the `respondsToSelector` for `foo` returns 0, or NO.

The important concept to take from this example is how inheritance works. Child classes inherit the instance variables and methods of their parent. They also inherit from every one of their ancestors.

Ancestry Inheritance

If you haven't surmised by now, child classes inherit the instance variables and methods from every class in their ancestor hierarchy. Moreover, when a message is dispatched to a child class, if the runtime doesn't find the method, it searches the class' inheritance hierarchy until it finds the method or reaches the child's root class. For instance, consider Figure 6-5.

Suppose you had an object that sent the `isKindOfClass:` message to a `Fuji` instance. When the runtime fails to find the method in `Fuji`, it then checks `Apple`. It then continues searching up the inheritance hierarchy until it finds the method in `NSObject` and calls it.

Inheriting Properties

Before discussing inheriting properties, note that in reality, a child class inherits its parent's instance variables and methods, not its properties. After all, properties are nothing more than instance variables and accessor methods.

Good object-oriented programming dictates that you practice encapsulation even between parent and child classes. You should not access a parent's instance variables directly. Instead, you should access them through accessor methods. Properties are the easiest way to generate accessor methods for instance variables, and so the next example illustrates using properties between classes.

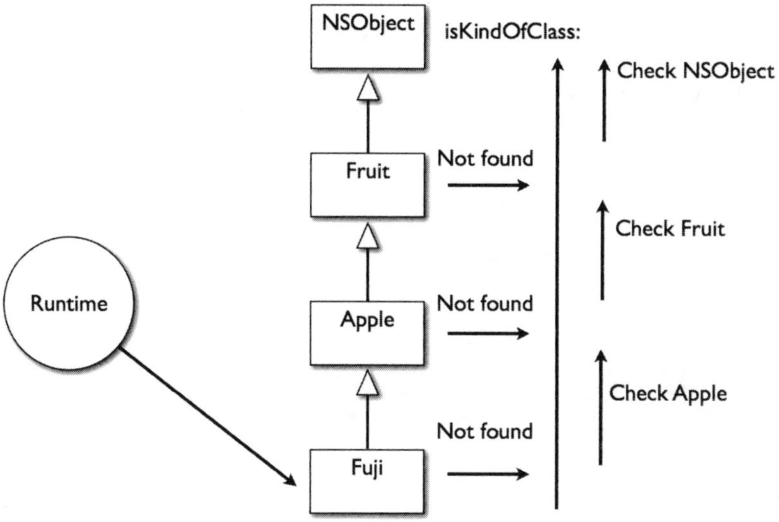

Figure 6-5 Inheritance hierarchy

Try This Adding Properties Through Inheritance

1. Create a new Command Line Foundation Tool called **BirdCall**.
2. Create a `Bird` class and a `Seagull` class (Listings 6-12 through 6-15). Make `Seagull` a child of `Bird`.
3. Add a property named call to `Bird`. Also add a custom `init` method to `Seagull`.
4. Modify BirdCall.m as in Listing 6-16.
5. Click Build And Go and run the application (Listing 6-17).

Listing 6-12 Bird.h

```
#import <Foundation/Foundation.h>
@interface Bird : NSObject {
  NSString * call;
}
@property (nonatomic, retain) NSString * call;
@end
```

(continued)

Listing 6-13 Bird.m

```
#import "Bird.h"
@implementation Bird
@synthesize call;
- (void) dealloc {
  self.call = nil;
  [super dealloc];
}
@end
```

Listing 6-14 Seagull.h

```
#import <Foundation/Foundation.h>
#import "Bird.h"
@interface Seagull : Bird {
}
@end
```

Listing 6-15 Seagull.m

```
#import "Seagull.h"
@implementation Seagull
- (id) init {
  if([super init]==nil) return nil;
  self.call = @"seagull call...";
  return self;
}
@end
```

Listing 6-16 BirdCall.m

```
#import <Foundation/Foundation.h>
#import "Bird.h"
#import "Seagull.h"
int main (int argc, const char * argv[]) {
  NSAutoreleasePool * pool = [[NSAutoreleasePool alloc] init];
  Seagull * aSeagull = [[[Seagull alloc] init] autorelease];

NSLog([aSeagull call]);
  [pool drain];
  return 0;
}
```

Listing 6-17 Debugger log

```
seagull call...
```

In this example you created a `Bird` parent class and the `Seagull` child class. You suspended disbelief and assumed all birds have a "call." Because all birds have a call, you created the `call` property in `Bird`. Because `Seagull` inherits `Bird`'s instance variables and methods, you can say that `Seagull` essentially inherits `Bird`'s properties, even though it is really inheriting the instance variable and the accessor methods.

Extension

A child class can extend its parent class by adding additional methods and instance variables to its parent. In this section you consider extending a class using methods. There really is not much to explain; this section is only illustrating that you often define new methods and instance variables to child classes that further refine a parent class. The following Try This example illustrates.

Try This Extending a Parent

1. Create a new Command Line Tool project. Name the project **DroidSimulation**.
2. Create a `Droid` superclass and two subclasses named `HousekeeperDroid` and `WarriorDroid` (Listings 6-18 through 6-23).
3. Create a `speak` method in `Droid`, a `fireLaserCannon` method in `WarriorDroid`, and a `mopFloor` method in `HousekeeperDroid`.
4. Change DroidSimulation.m to match Listing 6-24.
5. Click Build And Go to run the application. Listing 6-25 illustrates the debugger console logging.

(continued)

Listing 6-18 Droid.h

```
#import <Foundation/Foundation.h>
@interface Droid : NSObject {
}
- (void) speak;
@end
```

Listing 6-19 Droid.m

```
#import "Droid.h"
@implementation Droid
- (void) speak {
  NSLog(@"hello, I'm speaking...");
}
@end
```

Listing 6-20 WarriorDroid.h

```
#import <Foundation/Foundation.h>
#import "Droid.h"
@interface WarriorDroid : Droid {
}
- (void) fireLaserCannon;
@end
```

Listing 6-21 WarriorDroid.m

```
#import "WarriorDroid.h"
@implementation WarriorDroid
- (void) fireLaserCannon {
  NSLog(@"firing lasers...");
}
@end
```

Listing 6-22 HouseKeeperDroid.h

```
#import <Foundation/Foundation.h>
#import "Droid.h"
@interface HouseKeeperDroid : Droid {
}
```

```
- (void) mopFloor;
@end
```

Listing 6-23 HouseKeeperDroid.m

```
#import "HouseKeeperDroid.h"
@implementation HouseKeeperDroid
- (void) mopFloor {
  NSLog(@"mopping floor...");
}
@end
```

Listing 6-24 DroidSimulation.m

```
#import <Foundation/Foundation.h>
#import "Droid.h"
#import "WarriorDroid.h"
#import "HouseKeeperDroid.h"
int main (int argc, const char * argv[]) {
  NSAutoreleasePool * pool = [[NSAutoreleasePool alloc] init];
  WarriorDroid * myWarriorDroid = [[[WarriorDroid alloc] init] autorelease];
  HouseKeeperDroid * myHouseKeeperDroid = [[[HouseKeeperDroid alloc] init]
autorelease];
  [myWarriorDroid speak];
  [myWarriorDroid fireLaserCannon];
  [myHouseKeeperDroid speak];
  [myHouseKeeperDroid mopFloor];
  [pool drain];
  return 0;
}
```

Listing 6-25 Debugger console logging

```
hello, I'm speaking...
firing lasers...
hello, I'm speaking...
mopping floor...
```

This example doesn't do anything new or dramatic, but it nicely illustrates adding new functionality in a child class. In this example you created two `Droids`, a `WarriorDroid`,

(continued)

and a HouseKeeperDroid. The parent class, Droid, has a speak method, as all droids speak. But a warrior droid's other behavior is very different than a housekeeper's. Only warrior droids have laser cannons, and so you added a method to fire a cannon to the warrior droid only. Only housekeeper droids have embedded mops, and so you added a method for mopping a floor to housekeeper droid only.

This Try This is simply repeating what you learned in this chapter's first few sections. Inheritance is for sharing common attributes and behavior among different classes. HousekeeperDroid and WarriorDroid both add new methods to their parent, Droid. But because they both share the speak method, rather than repeating that code in each class, you had both inherit from Droid and use Droid's speak method.

Overriding Methods

A child object can also specialize a parent's methods by overriding them. Child classes can either replace a parent's method outright or extend a parent method's functionality. You can redefine a parent's method by re-implementing it in a child class. When another object sends a message to the child, it sends the message to the child's implementation rather than its parent's. If a child replaces its parent's method, then the calling object only invokes the child's method. If a child extends its parent's method, then the calling object invokes the child's method, which in turn invokes its parent's method.

Replacing a Parent's Method

You replace a parent's method by implementing the same method in a child. For instance, a Ball might have Football and Basketball child classes. Moreover, Ball might implement a flyThroughAir method. That method could be replaced by Football and Basketball. Listings 6-26 through 6-28 contain all three classes' implementation.

Listing 6-26 Ball.m

```
#import "Ball.h"
@implementation Ball
- (void) flyThroughAir {
  NSLog(@"ball's flythroughair...");
}
@end
```

Listing 6-27 Basketball.m

```
#import "Basketball.h"
@implementation Basketball
-(void) flyThroughAir {
  NSLog(@"basketball's flythroughair...");
}
@end
```

Listing 6-28 Football.m

```
#import "Football.h"
@implementation Football
- (void) flyThroughAir {
  NSLog(@"flying through air football...");
}
@end
```

When an object sends a `flyThroughAir` message to `Football`, the runtime calls `Football`'s `flyThroughAir` method. When a `flyThroughAir` message is sent to `Basketball`, the runtime calls `Basketball`'s `flyThroughAir` method. Because neither `Football`'s nor `Basketball`'s `flyThroughAir` method explicitly call `Ball`'s `flyThroughAir` method, they replace `Ball`'s `flyThroughAir` method.

Extending a Parent's Method

Although replacing a parent's method with a child's is useful, you more often extend a parent's method by adding additional functionality in a child rather than replacing a parent's method. A custom `init` method is a good illustration of extending functionality.

```
-(id) init {
  if([super init]==nil) return nil;
  //additional functionality here
  return self;
}
```

The `init` tries to first initialize its parent. If it returns `nil`, then the child returns `nil`. If it doesn't, then the child's method performs additional initialization.

You can add additional functionality to your own custom methods, as Listing 6-29 illustrates.

Listing 6-29 Football's `flyThroughAir` method reimplemented

```
#import "Football.h"
@implementation Football
- (void) flyThroughAir {
  NSLog(@"flying through air football...");
  [super flyThroughAir];
}
@end
```

The `flyThroughAir` method in Listing 6-29 adds additional functionality rather than replacing `Ball`'s `flyThroughAir` method. When an object invokes a `Football` instance's `flyThroughAir` method, the `Football` instance performs its own custom processing. After finishing, it then invokes its parent's `flyThroughAir` method.

Try This Overriding Methods Through Inheritance

1. Create a new Command Line Foundation Tool and name it **OverridingMethods**.
2. Create an `Animal` class and two children, `Fish` and `Cat` (Listings 6-30 through 6-35).
3. Define a `breathe` method in all three classes. Have `Fish` replace `Animal`'s `breathe` method and have `Cat` enhance `Animal`'s `breathe` method.
4. Implement OverridingMethods.m as in Listing 6-36.
5. Click Build And Go to run the application.

Listing 6-30 Animal.h

```
#import <Foundation/Foundation.h>
@interface Animal : NSObject {
}
- (void) breathe;
@end
```

Listing 6-31 Animal.m

```
#import <Foundation/Foundation.h>
#import "Animal.h"
```

```
@implementation Animal : NSObject {
}
- (void) breathe {
  NSLog(@"animal breathing....");
}
@end
```

Listing 6-32 Fish.h

```
#import <Foundation/Foundation.h>
#import "Animal.h"
@interface Fish : Animal {
}
- (void) breathe;
@end
```

Listing 6-33 Fish.m

```
#import "Fish.h"
@implementation Fish
- (void) breathe {
  NSLog(@"fish breathing....");
}
@end
```

Listing 6-34 Cat.h

```
#import <Foundation/Foundation.h>
#import "Animal.h"
@interface Cat : Animal {
}
- (void) breathe;
@end
```

Listing 6-35 Cat.m

```
#import "Cat.h"
@implementation Cat
- (void) breathe {
  NSLog(@"cat breathing...");
```

(continued)

```
  [super breathe];
}
@end
```

Listing 6-36 OverridingMethods.m

```
#import <Foundation/Foundation.h>
#import "Animal.h"
#import "Fish.h"
#import "Cat.h"
int main (int argc, const char * argv[]) {
  NSAutoreleasePool * pool = [[NSAutoreleasePool alloc] init];
  Fish * myFish = [[Fish alloc] init];
  Cat * myCat = [[Cat alloc] init];
  [myFish breathe];
  [myCat breathe];
  [myCat release];
  [myFish release];
  [pool drain];
  return 0;
}
```

Listing 6-37 Debugger console logging

```
fish breathing....
cat breathing...
animal breathing...
```

In this simple example, `Fish` replaced `Animal`'s `breathe` method, while `Cat` added additional functionality to it by extending it. After `Cat` completes its own processing in `breathe`, it then invokes its parent, `Animal`, so that `Animal` can complete its processing.

No Overriding Instance Variables and No Overloading

You cannot override instance variables and you cannot overload methods when using Objective-C.

No Overriding Instance Variables

Remember, properties are nothing more than instance variables with accessor methods. Although you can override accessor methods, you cannot override instance variables. For instance, if you tried to create a count variable in `Ball`, `Football`, or `Basketball`, you would obtain the following compiler error: "error: duplicate member 'myCount'." You cannot redefine a parent's instance variables with a child class' instance variables.

No Method Overloading

In a language such as Java, you have an object-oriented principle called overloading. Overloading allows creating a method of the same name, but with different parameters. For instance, you might have the following two methods in a Java class:

```
public void playSound(String soundURL);
public void playSound(int soundID);
```

Although languages such as Java allow creating two methods with the same name, Objective-C does not allow overloading methods. You cannot, for instance, have the following two methods in the same Objective-C class.

```
-(void) playSound:(NSString*) soundURL;
-(void) playSound:(int) soundID;
```

Instead, you follow a loose convention that incorporates the parameter's type into the name. For instance, the `playsound` methods would be modified to incorporate the parameters.

```
-(void) playSoundFromURL:(NSString*) soundURL;
-(void) playSoundFromInt:(int) soundID;
```

You see this pattern in the Foundation framework classes, particularly the `init` method. For instance, the `NSString`'s `initWithFormat:` and `initWithString:` are examples of this convention. Now, before you hold up a method such as `NSString`'s `initWithFormat:` as an example of method overloading, recall the discussion on method syntax from Chapter 5. `NSString` actually only has one `initWithFormat` method; the other methods' names are `initWithFormat:arguments:`, `initWithFormat:locale:`, and `initWithFormat:locale:arguments:`. Each of these is a distinct method name.

Inheritance and UIViewController

In this chapter you learned about Objective-C inheritance using plain `NSObject` classes. When you write an iPhone application, you use inheritance extensively. For instance, every control, such as a `UIButton`, `UIBarButtonItem`, or `UIWebView`, traces its lineage to `UIView`.

You can see an object's inheritance hierarchy when accessing its documentation as Figure 6-6 illustrates.

A `UIView` is descended from `UIResponder`, which is descended from its root class, `NSObject`.

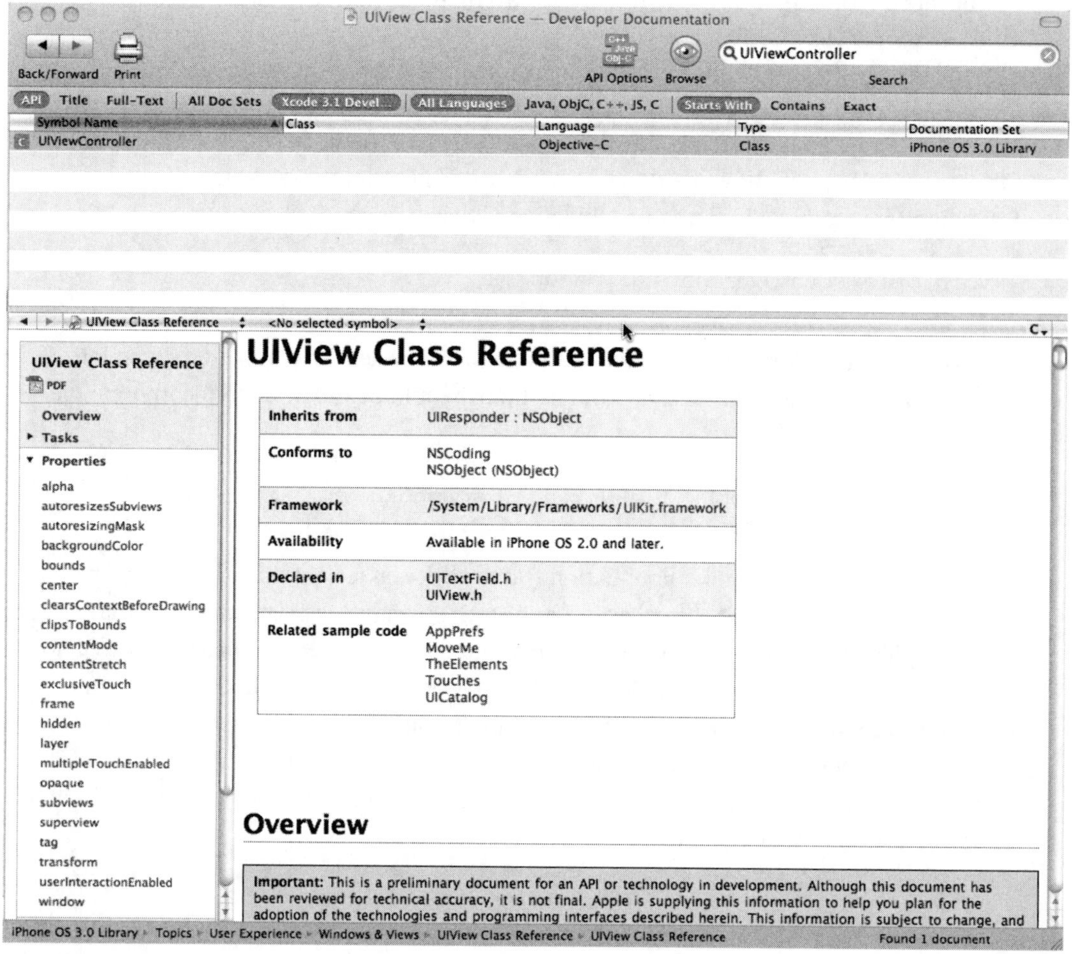

Figure 6-6 `UIView`'s Class Reference

You can use inheritance to simplify creating iPhone application views as well as your model classes. The following Try This illustrates.

Try This Extending a UIViewController

1. Create a new Utility Application named **GreenView**.
2. Expand both MainViewController.h and FlipsideViewController.h; notice both are children of `UIViewController`.
3. Create a new `UIViewController` class called `GreenViewController`. Xcode should generate a GreenViewController.h and a GreenViewController.m file. Be certain that the check box to generate an XIB is not selected.
4. Modify GreenViewController.h and GreenViewController.m so that it has a `myColor` property, as in Listings 6-38 and 6-39.
5. Change MainViewController.h so that it is a child of `GreenViewController` (Listing 6-40).
6. Implement the `viewDidLoad` method in MainViewController.m (Listing 6-41).
7. Click Build And Go to run the application; MainView's background color is green.

Listing 6-38 GreenViewController.h

```
#import <UIKit/UIKit.h>
@interface GreenViewController : UIViewController {
  UIColor * myColor;
}
@property (nonatomic,retain) UIColor * myColor;
@end
```

Listing 6-39 GreenViewController.m

```
#import "GreenViewController.h"
@implementation GreenViewController
@synthesize myColor;
- (void)viewDidLoad {
  self.myColor = [UIColor greenColor];
```

(continued)

```
    [super viewDidLoad];
}
- (void)dealloc {
    [myColor release];
    [super dealloc];
}
@end
```

Listing 6-40 MainViewController.h

```
#import "FlipsideViewController.h"
#import "GreenViewController.h"
@interface MainViewController : GreenViewController
<FlipsideViewControllerDelegate> {
}
- (IBAction)showInfo;
@end
```

Listing 6-41 MainViewController.m's `viewDidLoad` method

```
- (void)viewDidLoad {
    [super viewDidLoad];
   self.view.backgroundColor = self.myColor;
 }
```

The `MainViewController` is a child of `GreenViewController` rather than `UIViewController`. Instead, `UIViewController` is `MainViewController`'s "grandparent." When the `UIViewController` first loads its associated view, it calls `viewDidLoad`. Its `viewDidLoad` method first calls `GreenViewController`'s `viewDidLoad` method. After `GreenViewController` is finished, control is returned to `MainViewController`'s `viewDidLoad` method, which sets its view's background color to its `myColor` value. The `myColor` property, although declared and defined in `GreenViewController`, is recognized as a property of `MainViewController`.

Admittedly, this is a trivial example; however, it does have real-world implications. Suppose you were creating a large application with many views. Moreover, suppose a back-end content management system drove the application's appearance, and that different "divisions" had different color schemes. By creating a parent `UIViewController` with a `myColor` property, you only have to change the color once—presuming every other

`UIViewController` in your application inherits from the view controller implementing the color property. You can use this inheritance to great effect when creating non-trivial user interfaces.

Summary

In this chapter you explored how Objective-C implements inheritance. A child class inherits its parent class' instance variables and methods. Moreover, it inherits every ancestor's instance variables and methods. This allows efficient code reuse and makes your applications less prone to error because it has less duplicated code.

A child class can both extend a parent and override a parent's functionality. When extending a parent, a child adds new functionality to a parent. When overriding a parent's functionality, it can either replace a parent's functionality or add to it. But remember, you can only replace a parent's methods and not its instance variables.

You will use inheritance extensively when developing iPhone applications. All `UIKit` graphical controls ultimately inherit from the `UIView` class. Moreover, when you create a view's view controller, you almost always create a `UIViewController` subclass. In fact, when using the Foundation framework or the `UIKit`, unless working directly with `NSObject`, you are always using a child class. Understanding inheritance is fundamental to understanding Objective-C.

Chapter 7

Protocols and Categories

Key Skills & Concepts

- Understanding Protocols
- Modeling Protocols Using UML
- Adopting Protocols
- Using Protocols
- Understanding Categories
- Using Categories

If you know anything about Java's interfaces, then you already have a reasonable understanding of Objective-C's protocols. A *protocol* is a contract that specifies methods that an adopting class must implement if it is to properly adopt the protocol. Protocols are an important Objective-C programming concept that you must understand to successfully write iPhone applications. In this chapter you learn about protocols.

Protocols

Protocols declare the behavior an object can exhibit or what other objects can do to an object. For instance, suppose you had `Bumblebee`, `Jet`, and `Bird` classes. All three, although unrelated, implement the flying behavior, and so you could say they are each a `Flyer`. Also notice that you could shoot all three with a gun, and so you could also say they are `Shootable`. In both situations you are using a concept to group unrelated objects based upon behaviors. Protocols model these types of situations.

A class that wishes to adopt a protocol must implement the methods declared by the protocol. By requiring the adopting class to implement methods, a protocol forms a contract. That contract ensures the runtime that a class that adopts a protocol implements the methods declared by the protocol.

NOTE

If you come from a Java background, you are accustomed to classes implementing interfaces. In Objective-C terminology classes do not implement protocols, but rather they adopt them. But in reality adopt and implement have the same meaning.

Modeling Protocols

The UML class diagram has a convenient notation for modeling protocols (Figure 7-1).

In Figure 7-1 the `Bird`, `Jet`, and `Bumblebee` all adopt the `Flyer` protocol and so you draw a dashed arrow with a white point from the adopter to the adopted. The `Flyer`, being a protocol, is added the «`protocol`» stereotype. Don't worry about a stereotype's definition; all that it means here is that you are using a symbol normally used for a class to represent a protocol.

Syntax

A protocol's syntax is similar to a class' interface. But unlike when writing a class, you only create a header file and do not create an implementation. A protocol begins with the `@protocol` compiler directive and ends with the @end compiler directive. Between the two compiler directives go any method declarations you wish an adopting class to implement.

```
@protocol Hopper
- (void) hop;
- (BOOL) setHopDistance: (long long) distance
@end
```

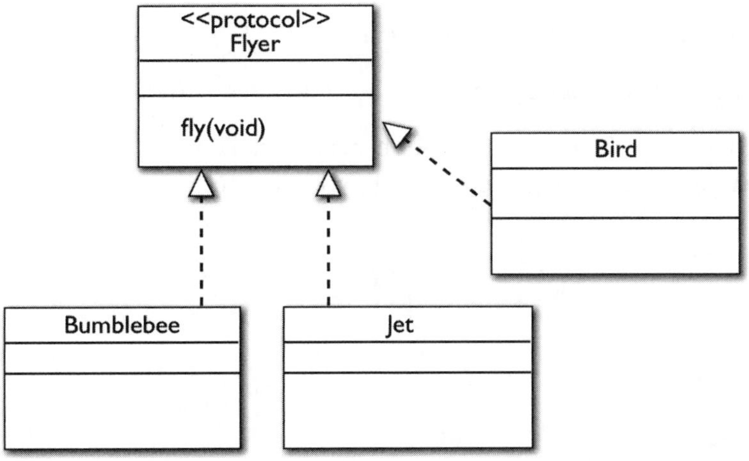

Figure 7-1 Modeling a protocol

Here you are declaring a Hopper that declares the hop and setHopDistance methods. Classes that wish to adopt a Hopper must implement the hop and setHopDistance methods.

NOTE

In this chapter I focus on using protocols to model behavior. You can also use protocols to model what you can do to an object. For instance, you can hunt, roast, and eat a duck, and so you could have a **Duck** class adopt the **Huntable**, **Roastable**, and **Eatable** protocols.

Adopting a Protocol

Classes adopt protocols. For instance, a Frog class might implement the Hopper protocol. For Frog to adopt Hopper, it must first import the Hopper.h header file. It then includes Hopper in its @interface compiler directive.

```
@interface Frog: Amphibian <Hopper>
```

A frog is an amphibian, and so it inherits from its Amphibian parent class. Following the parent class is the protocol the frog adopts. The protocol's name is surrounded by angle brackets. The following Try This illustrates adopting a protocol.

Try This Creating and Adopting a Simple Protocol

1. Create a View-based application named **SimpleFlyer**.
2. Create a new C header file called **Flyer.h** (Figure 7-2).
3. Modify Flyer.h to be a Flyer protocol that declares a "fly" method (Listing 7-1).
4. Create three new Objective-C classes named Bumblebee, Bird, and Jet. Change all three so that they adopt the Flyer protocol (Listings 7-2 through 7-7).

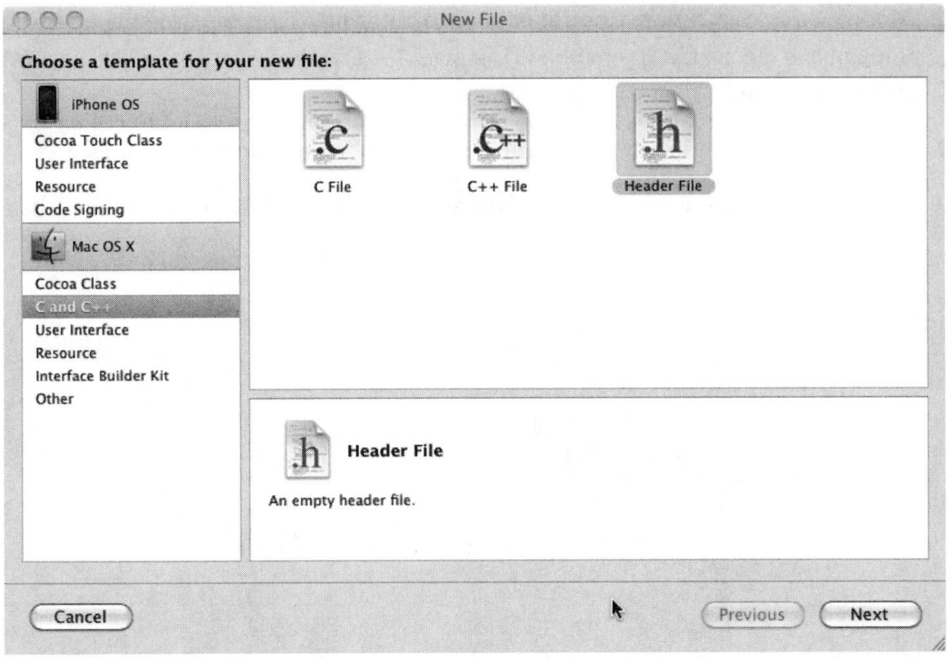

Figure 7-2 Creating a C header file

5. Modify SimpleFlyerViewController.h so that it knows about all three classes and the protocol by using the `@class` and `@protocol` precompiler directives. Also declare a `callFly` method and create three properties for each of the three classes (Listing 7-8). Also create a `changeLabel` method and be certain you precede the method with the `IBAction` keyword rather than `void`.

6. Create an `IBOutlet` for a `UILabel` and name the property `myLabel`.

(continued)

7. Modify SimpleFlyerViewController.m so that it synthesizes the properties and implements the `callFly` method (Listing 7-9). Do not forget to import the classes from the interface.

8. Double-click SimpleFlyerViewController.xib to open it in Interface Builder.

9. Add a button to the view's canvas (Figure 7-3). Double-click the button and change its title to **Fly**.

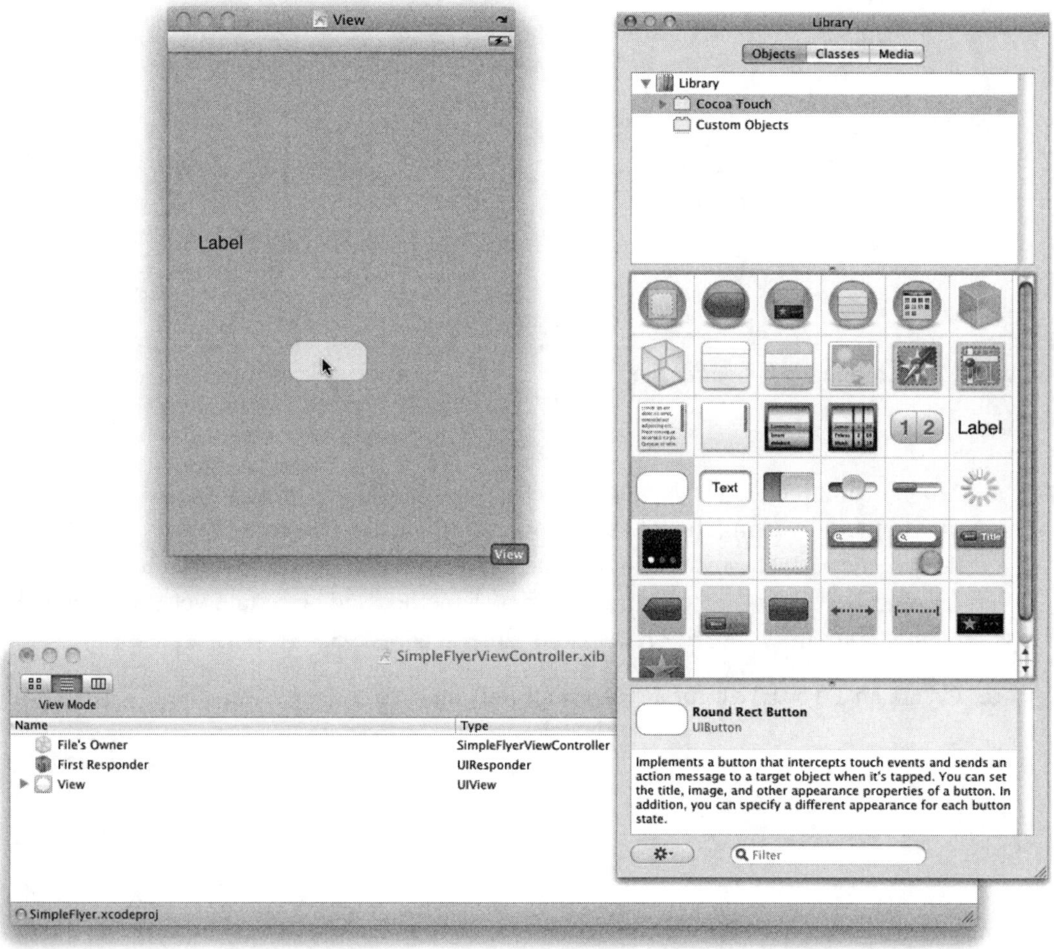

Figure 7-3 Adding a button to a view

10. Add a label to the view's canvas and resize the label (Figure 7-4).
11. Connect the File's Owner `myLabel` outlet to the label (Figure 7-5). Remember, the "outlet" term is simply shorthand for referring to the `IBOutlet`.

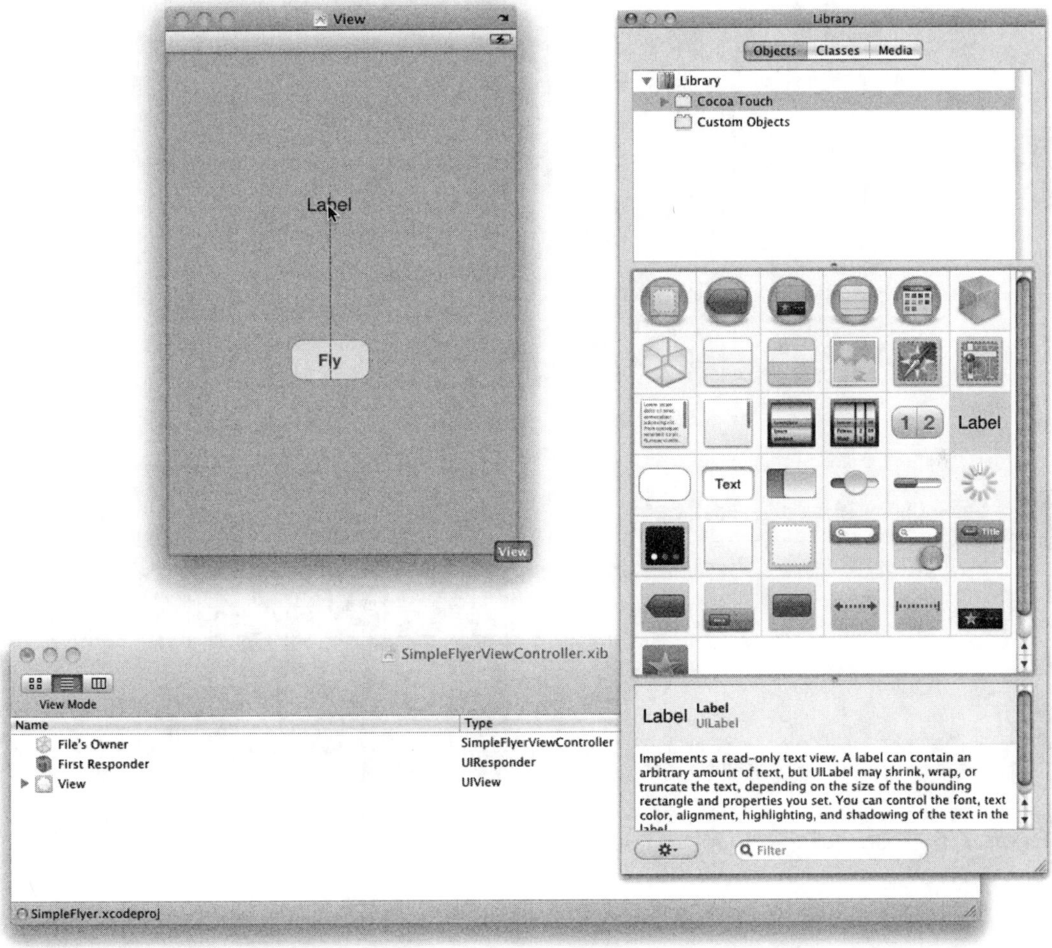

Figure 7-4 Adding a label to a view

(continued)

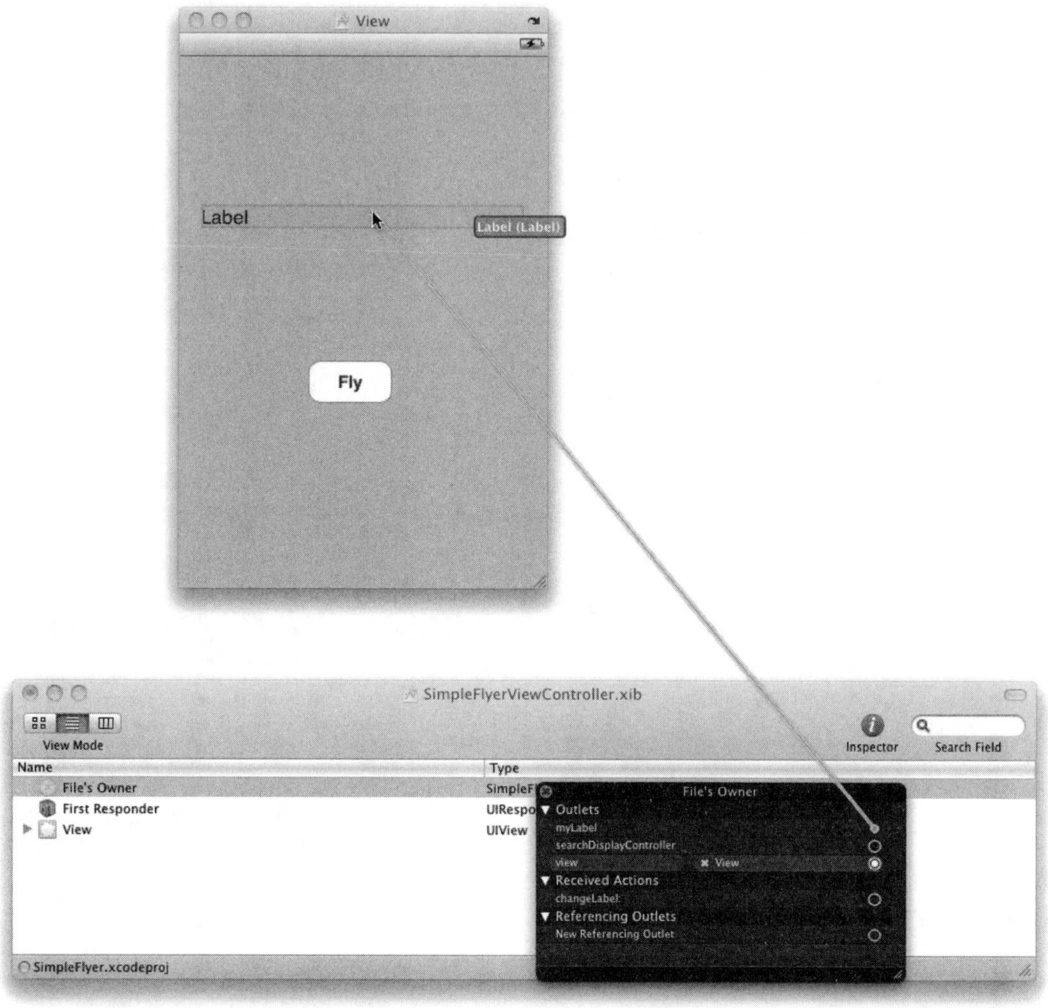

Figure 7-5 Connecting a label to an outlet

12. Connect the File's Owner `callFly:` action to the button's Touch Up Inside event (Figure 7-6).
13. Save and exit Interface Builder.

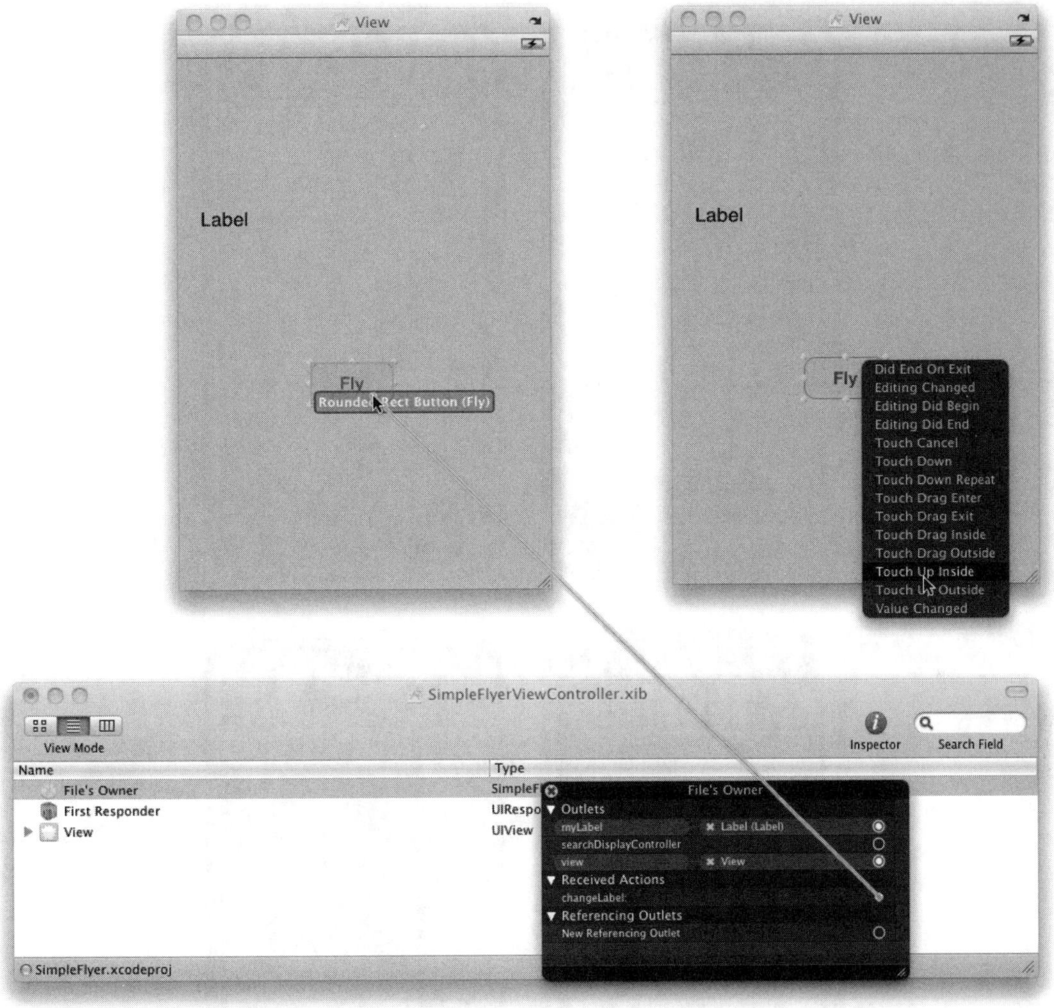

Figure 7-6 Connecting a button to an action

14. Click Build And Run to run the application. Remember, the button might say Build And Debug. Or, if you have an older XCode version, it might even say Build And Go.

15. Tap the button three times, and each time the application displays the relevant text from each class' `fly` method (Figure 7-7).

(continued)

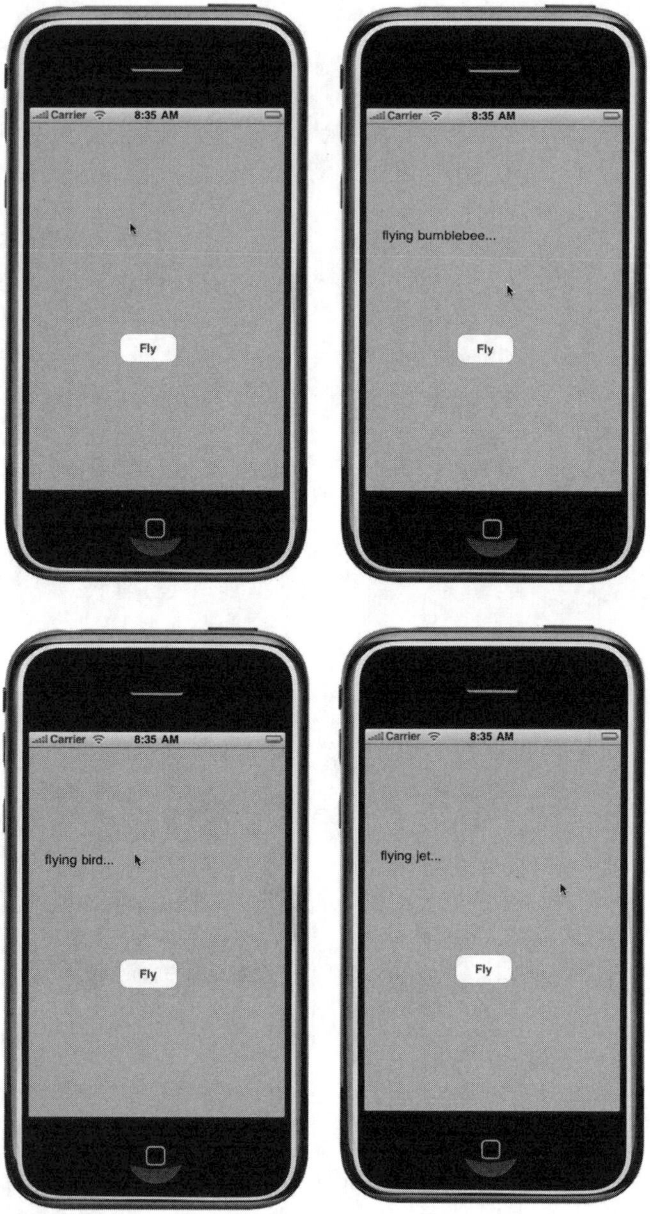

Figure 7-7 The application running in iPhone simulator

Listing 7-1 Flyer.h

```
@protocol Flyer
- (NSString *) fly;
@end
```

Listing 7-2 Bumblebee.h

```
#import <Foundation/Foundation.h>
#import "Flyer.h"
@interface Bumblebee : NSObject <Flyer> {
}
@end
```

Listing 7-3 Bumblebee.m

```
#import "Bumblebee.h"
@implementation Bumblebee
- (NSString *) fly {
  return @"flying bumblebee...";
}
@end
```

Listing 7-4 Bird.h

```
#import <Foundation/Foundation.h>
#import "Flyer.h"
@interface Bird : NSObject <Flyer> {
}
@end
```

Listing 7-5 Bird.m

```
#import "Bird.h"
@implementation Bird
- (NSString *) fly {
  return @"flying bird...";
}
@end
```

(continued)

Listing 7-6 Jet.h

```
#import <Foundation/Foundation.h>
#import "Flyer.h"
@interface Jet : NSObject <Flyer> {
}
@end
```

Listing 7-7 Jet.m

```
#import "Jet.h"
@implementation Jet
- (NSString*) fly {
  return @"flying jet...";
}
@end
```

Listing 7-8 SimpleFlyerViewController.h

```
#import <UIKit/UIKit.h>
@protocol Flyer;
@class Jet;
@class Bird;
@class Bumblebee
@interface SimpleFlyerViewController : UIViewController {
  Bumblebee * myBee;
  Bird * myBird;
  Jet * myJet;
  IBOutlet UILabel * myLabel;
}
@property (nonatomic,retain) Bumblebee * myBee;
@property (nonatomic,retain) Bird * myBird;
@property (nonatomic,retain) Jet * myJet;
@property (nonatomic,retain) UILabel * myLabel;
- (IBAction) changeLabel: (id) sender;
- (NSString*) callFly: (id <Flyer>) aFlyer;
@end
```

Listing 7-9 SimpleFlyerViewController.m

```
#import "SimpleFlyerViewController.h"
#import "Flyer.h"
```

```
#import "Bumblebee.h"
#import "Bird.h"
#import "Jet.h"
@implementation SimpleFlyerViewController
@synthesize myBee;
@synthesize myBird;
@synthesize myJet;
@synthesize myLabel;
static int clicks = 0;
- (IBAction) changeLabel: (id) sender {
  if(clicks == 0) {
    self.myLabel.text = [self callFly:self.myBee];
  }
  else if(clicks == 1) {
    self.myLabel.text = [self callFly:self.myBird];
  }
  else {
    self.myLabel.text = [self callFly:self.myJet];
  }
  clicks++;
}
- (NSString *) callFly: (id <Flyer>) aFlyer {
  return [aFlyer fly];
}
- (void) viewDidLoad {
  [super viewDidLoad];
  self.myBee = [[Bumblebee alloc] init];
  self.myBird = [[Bird alloc] init];
  self.myJet = [[Jet alloc] init];
}
- (void)dealloc {
  [self.myJet release];
  [self.myLabel release];
  [self.myBee release];
  [self.myBird release];
  [super dealloc];
}
@end
```

This application illustrates how you adopt a protocol. `Bumblebee`, `Bird`, and `Jet` are all very different, but all three fly. Because they all fly, you created a `Flyer` protocol that declared the `fly` method. All three implemented the `fly` method.

(continued)

Rather than taking a concrete class as a parameter, the `callFly:` method takes a `Flyer` protocol as a parameter. Because `Flyer` specifies that an adopter must implement a `fly` method, the `callFly:` method is assured that regardless of the underlying class, because the object implements the `Flyer` protocol, it has a `fly` method.

Notice the `IBAction` in Listings 7-8 and 7-9. An `IBAction` is how you connect methods in your custom code to events that are fired by Interface Builder components. Chapter 11 explains the `IBAction` keyword further. For now, just note how you used it so that when a user clicks and releases the button, it calls the `callFly:` method in the `SimpleFlyerViewController`.

Also notice the `callFly:` method takes a `Flyer` as a parameter (Listing 7-9).

```
-(IBAction) callFly: (id <Flyer>) aFlyer;
```

Remember, `id` is a generic pointer to any Objective-C class. Specifying `id` as a parameter's type allows passing any class as the parameter. However, in Listing 7-9 you are limiting the `id` to only accept classes that adopt the `Flyer` protocol. Any class may be passed as a parameter to the method, but only if it adopts the `Flyer` protocol.

Finally, notice that nowhere in the three class' interface do you declare the `fly` method. When using a protocol-declared method, you are not required to, as the method is declared in the protocol.

Properties and Protocols

You can declare properties in a protocol. Any classes that then wish to adopt the protocol either must implement custom accessor methods or must synthesize the property. A property's syntax in a protocol is similar to an interface, only you do not declare an instance variable.

```
@protocol Countable
@property (nonatomic, retain) NSNumber * maximumDigit;
@end
```

By declaring a property in a protocol, you are informing the compiler that implementing classes must either synthesize the property or create custom accessor methods. But note, any class implementing the protocol must synthesize the property and declare the property as an instance variable in the class' header. The following Try This illustrates.

Try This Using Properties with Protocols

1. Create a new Command Line Foundation program. Name the application **SingingFool**.
2. Create a protocol named `Singer` and declare a method called `sing` and a property called `singerName` (Listing 7-10).
3. Create a `Tenor` class and have it adopt the `Singer` protocol (Listing 7-11). Have `Tenor` adopt the `sing` method (Listing 7-12).
4. Declare a `singerName` instance variable in `Tenor`'s interface.
5. Synthesize the `singerName` property in `Tenor`'s implementation.
6. Modify `main` in SingingFool.m to match Listing 7-13.
7. Build and Run the application.

Listing 7-10 Singer.h

```
@protocol Singer
@property (nonatomic,retain) NSString * singerName;
- (void) sing;
@end
```

Listing 7-11 Tenor.h

```
#import <Foundation/Foundation.h>
#import "Singer.h"
@interface Tenor : NSObject <Singer> {
  NSString * singerName;
}
@end
```

Listing 7-12 Tenor.m

```
#import "Tenor.h"
@implementation Tenor
@synthesize singerName;
```

(continued)

```
- (void) sing {
  NSLog(@"%@, the singing tenor...", self.singerName);
}
@end
```

Listing 7-13 SingingFool.m

```
#import <Foundation/Foundation.h>
#import "Tenor.h"
#import "Singer.h"
int main (int argc, const char * argv[]) {
  NSAutoreleasePool * pool = [[NSAutoreleasePool alloc] init];
  Tenor * myTenor = [[[Tenor alloc] init] autorelease];
  myTenor.singerName = @"Jameserotti";
  [myTenor sing];
  [pool drain];
  return 0;
}
```

In this example you declared a property in a Singer protocol. You then declared the `singerName` as an instance variable and synthesized the property (added accessor methods) in the `Tenor` class, which adopted the protocol. Upon running the application, the runtime calls the `sing` method and the following is logged to the debugger console:

```
Jameserotti, the singing tenor...
```

Note that, same as a normal class, you can implement the accessor methods yourself and the compiler realizes that you are replacing the auto-generated accessor method.

Optional Methods

Objective-C allows developers considerable flexibility. Protocols can also declare optional methods that adopters are not required to implement. The following protocol illustrates:

```
@protocol Fighter
@required
  -(void) punch;
  -(void) kick;
@optional
  - (void) cry;
@end
```

An object that adopts `Fighter` must punch and kick. Because these methods are required, they are preceded by the `@required` compiler directive. Any methods declared after this compiler directive, but before any `@optional` compiler directive, must be implemented by an adopting class. The `@required` compiler directive is the default; methods without a preceding compiler directive are assumed required.

A `Fighter` doesn't have to cry; this method declaration is preceded by the `@optional` compiler directive. By using the `@optional` compiler directive, you can add method declarations that are optional to adopting classes.

Optional methods require more thought than required methods. When trying to send a message to a class adopting a protocol, you must now ensure the class adopting the protocol implements the optional method. For instance, I might wish to implement the following method in a class:

```
- (void) hitInFace: (id <Fighter>) aFighter;
```

When hit in the face, some `Fighters` might cry, while others might not. For instance, the famous American fighter, Butterbean, would definitely not cry. The author, however, would cry like a baby. The problem is, both Author and Butterbean adopt the `Fighter` protocol, but only Author implements the `cry` method. If you wish to call an optional protocol method in another method such as `hitInFace`, you must check for the method's existence in the adopting class.

```
- (void) hitInFace: (id <Fighter>) aFighter {
  if([aFighter respondsToSelector:@selector(cry)]) {
    [aFighter cry];
  }
```

The easiest way to ensure a class responds to an optional protocol method is through the `respondsToSelector:` method. Notice you are using a compiler directive `@selector` in this method. You haven't learned about selectors yet, but you will in Chapter 11. For now, simply realize you are telling the compiler to ensure the `Fighter` passed to the method does in fact implement the `cry` method. As an aside, note that had `cry` taken a parameter, you would have written the preceding line containing the selector with a colon as part of the `@selector` compiler directive.

```
if([aFighter respondsToSelector:@selector(cry:)])
```

Try This Exploring Optional Methods

1. Create a new Command Line Foundation Tool named **EatingExample**.
2. Create a protocol named `Eater` (Listing 7-14).
3. Create two classes that adopt the `Eater` protocol. Name one class `Glutton` and the other `Socialite` (Listings 7-15 through 7-18).
4. Have `Glutton` implement the `belch` method.
5. Implement the `main` method in EatingExample.m as in Listing 7-19.
6. Build and Run the application.

Listing 7-14 Eater.h

```
@protocol Eater
@required //default
- (void) eat;
@optional
- (void) belch;
@end
```

Listing 7-15 Glutton.h

```
#import <Foundation/Foundation.h>
#import "Eater.h"
@interface Glutton : NSObject <Eater> {
}
@end
```

Listing 7-16 Glutton.m

```
#import "Glutton.h"
@implementation Glutton
- (void) eat {
  NSLog(@"glutton eating...");
}
- (void) belch {
  NSLog(@"glutton belching...");
}
@end
```

Listing 7-17 Socialite.h

```
#import <Foundation/Foundation.h>
#import "Eater.h"
@interface Socialite : NSObject <Eater> {
}
@end
```

Listing 7-18 Socialite.m

```
#import "Socialite.h"
@implementation Socialite
- (void) eat {
  NSLog(@"socialite is eating...");
}
@end
```

Listing 7-19 EatingExample.m

```
#import <Foundation/Foundation.h>
#import "Glutton.h"
#import "Socialite.h"
int main (int argc, const char * argv[]) {
  NSAutoreleasePool * pool = [[NSAutoreleasePool alloc] init];
  Glutton * myGlutton = [[[Glutton alloc] init] autorelease];
  Socialite * mySocialite = [[[Socialite alloc] init] autorelease];
  [myGlutton eat];
  [mySocialite eat];
  if([myGlutton respondsToSelector:@selector(belch)]) {
    [myGlutton belch];
  }
  if([mySocialite respondsToSelector:@selector(belch)]) {
    [mySocialite belch];
  }
  [pool drain];
  return 0;
}
```

Protocols and id

In Listing 7-9 you used a protocol as a method's parameter. Although this is valid, you often see methods that only take an id. In this section you learn three different syntaxes you might use when declaring a method that accepts a protocol as a parameter. The following three method declarations illustrate the syntax you might see:

```
- (void) doAttach: (id) aFloater;
- (void) detach: (<Floater>) aFloater;
- (void) sinkAFloater: (id <Floater>) aFloater;
```

The first method takes an id only, the second a protocol only, and the third an id and a protocol. In reality, method declarations two and three are equivalent. Consider all three in turn.

Using id Only

One way you can use a protocol as a method parameter is by using the `id` keyword. The `id` type is a generic pointer that can point to any object.

```
- (void) doAttach: (id) aFloater {
  if([aFloater conformsToProtocol:@protocol(Floater)]) {
    [aFloater attach];
  }
}
```

In the `doAttach:` method the `id` points to an object adopting the `Floater` protocol. Because any object could be sent to `doAttach:`, it first ensures the object adopts the required protocol by using the `conformsToProtocol:` method. The `conformsToProtocol:` method is inherited from `NSObject` and does exactly what its name says it does: it checks if an object conforms to a protocol provided as a parameter, returning YES or NO.

Using id with a Protocol Restriction

When writing your own custom classes, you will probably want your methods to accept parameters more strongly typed than `id`. You can restrict a method's parameter so that it can still take an `id`, but only if that `id`'s object adopts the specified protocol. The following `detach` method illustrates.

```
- (void) detach: (<Floater>) aFloater {
  [aFloater detach];
}
```

In `detach` the `id` parameter is implicit. The method takes any object provided the object implements the `Floater` protocol. You can also make the `id` explicit, as the following `sinkAFloater` method illustrates.

```
- (void) sinkAFloater: (id <Floater>) aFloater {
  [aFloater sink];
}
```

Specifying a protocol as a parameter's type forces the `id` to be an adopter of the protocol.

Adopting Multiple Protocols

Sometimes you might wish to create a class that adopts multiple protocols. Consider ducks. Ducks can fly and so they should adopt the `Flyer` protocol you declared earlier. But ducks can also swim. Swimming, like flying, is a behavior shared by many unrelated entities, and so you should probably create a `Swimmer` protocol with a `swim` method declaration.

`Duck` should adopt both protocols. Objective-C allows objects to adopt more than one protocol. When a class adopts more than one protocol, you list the protocols as a comma-separated list.

```
@interface Duck : NSObject <Flyer, Swimmer>
```

The `Duck` class adopts the `Flyer` and `Swimmer` protocols in the preceding code snippet. A class is unlimited in how many protocols it can adopt. For instance, you might have the following interface declaration for a `Duck`:

```
@interface Duck : NSObject <Flyer, Swimmer, Quacker, Roastable, Diver,
Eatable>
```

Try This Adopting Multiple Protocols

1. Open the SimpleFlyer project completed previously in Xcode.
2. Add the `Swimmer` protocol to the project (Listing 7-20).
3. Create and implement `Duck` so that it adopts the `Swimmer` protocol (Listings 7-21 and 7-22).
4. Modify `SimpleFlyerViewController` so that it matches Listings 7-23 and 7-24.
5. Build and Run.

(continued)

Listing 7-20 Swimmer.h

```
@protocol Swimmer
- (NSString *) swim;
@end
```

Listing 7-21 Duck.h

```
#import <Foundation/Foundation.h>
#import "Flyer.h"
#import "Swimmer.h"
@interface Duck : NSObject <Flyer, Swimmer> {
}
@end
```

Listing 7-22 Duck.m

```
#import "Duck.h"
@implementation Duck
- (NSString *) fly {
  return @"flying duck...";
}
- (NSString *) swim {
  return @"swimming duck...";
}
@end
```

Listing 7-23 SimpleFlyerViewController.h

```
#import <UIKit/UIKit.h>
@class Duck;
@class Jet;
@class Bumblebee;
@class Bird;

@interface SimpleFlyerViewController : UIViewController {
  Bumblebee * myBee;
  Bird * myBird;
  Jet * myJet;
  Duck * myDuck;
  IBOutlet UILabel * myLabel;
}
```

```
@property (nonatomic,retain) Bumblebee * myBee;
@property (nonatomic,retain) Bird * myBird;
@property (nonatomic,retain) Jet * myJet;
@property (nonatomic,retain) Duck * myDuck;
@property (nonatomic,retain) UILabel * myLabel;
- (IBAction) changeLabel: (id) sender;
- (NSString*) callFly: (id <Flyer>) aFlyer;
- (void) callSwim: (id) aFlyer;
@end
```

Listing 7-24 SimpleFlyerViewController.m

```
#import "SimpleFlyerViewController.h"
#import "Flyer.h"
#import "Bumblebee.h"
#import "Bird.h"
#import "Jet.h"
#import "Duck.h"
@implementation SimpleFlyerViewController
@synthesize myBee;
@synthesize myBird;
@synthesize myJet;
@synthesize myLabel;
@synthesize myDuck;
static int clicks = 0;
- (IBAction) changeLabel: (id) sender {
  id myObject = nil;
  if(clicks == 0) {
    self.myLabel.text = [self callFly:self.myBee];
    myObject = self.myBee;
  }
  else if(clicks == 1) {
    self.myLabel.text = [self callFly:self.myBird];
    myObject = self.myBird;
  }
  else if(clicks == 2) {
    self.myLabel.text = [self callFly:self.myJet];
    myObject = self.myJet;
  }
  else {
    self.myLabel.text = [self callFly:self.myDuck];
    myObject = self.myDuck;
  }
  [self callSwim:myObject];
  clicks++;
}
```

(continued)

```
- (NSString *) callFly: (id <Flyer>) aFlyer {
  return [aFlyer fly];
}
- (void) callSwim: (id) aFlyer {
  if ( [aFlyer conformsToProtocol:@protocol(Swimmer)]  ) {
    NSLog([aFlyer swim]);
  }
}
- (void) viewDidLoad {
  [super viewDidLoad];
  self.myBee = [[[Bumblebee alloc] init] autorelease];
  self.myBird = [[[Bird alloc] init] autorelease];
  self.myJet = [[[Jet alloc] init] autorelease];
  self.myDuck = [[[Duck alloc] init] autorelease];
}
- (void)dealloc {
  [self.myJet release];
  [self.myBee release];
  [self.myBird release];
  [self.myDuck release];
  [self.mylabel release];
  [super dealloc];
}
@end
```

Bumblebee, Jet, Bird, and Duck all fly, and so they adopt the Flyer protocol. However, only Duck swims, and so only Duck adopts the Swimmer protocol. The Duck is treated as a Flyer and as a Swimmer. When a user taps the button, the first four taps calls the Bee, Bird, Jet, and Duck fly method. This method is declared in the Flyer protocol so all four classes have a fly method. SimpleFlyerViewController treats Duck as a Flyer. But on the fifth tap, SimpleFlyerViewController treats Duck as a Swimmer and invokes Duck's swim method.

Notice that the callSwim method in Listing 7-24 takes an id as a parameter; however, rather than using the respondsToSelector: method, it uses the conformsToProtocol: method.

```
if ( [aFlyer conformsToProtocol:@protocol(Swimmer)]  ) {
```

The conformsToProtocol method is another way you might ensure a class implementing a protocol has a method prior to calling the method (unless the method is optional in the protocol).

Extending Protocols

You can also have protocols adopt other protocols. Suppose you had driftwood and a duck. Both are buoyant, and so each adopts the "Floater" protocol. But only the duck implements the swimming behavior. Now, it seems reasonable that a `Swimmer` must be a `Floater`, otherwise how could a swimmer swim? And so you have the `Swimmer` protocol adopt the `Floater` protocol.

The syntax for a protocol extending another protocol is as follows:

```
@protocol Swimmer <Floater>
```

You declare the protocol and then declare that it adopts the protocol you wish extending. In the preceding code snippet you are declaring a `Swimmer` protocol that adopts the `Floater` protocol. A class that adopts a child protocol automatically adopts the parent protocol. This means the class must implement both protocol's methods. Note that you are not allowed to redefine methods in a protocol as you do with inherited classes.

Try This Extending a Protocol

1. Create a new Command Line Foundation Tool named **DriftwoodDuck**.
2. Create a new protocol named `Sinkable` (Listing 7-25).
3. Create a protocol named `Floater` (Listing 7-26). Import `Sinkable` and have `Floater` adopt the `Sinkable` protocol.
4. Create a new protocol named `Swimmer` (Listing 7-27). Import `Floater` and have `Swimmer` adopt the `Floater` protocol.
5. Create a class called `Driftwood` and a class called `Duck` (Listings 7-28 through 7-31).
6. Have `Driftwood` adopt the `Floater` protocol and `Duck` adopt the `Swimmer` protocol.
7. Be certain to implement the `swim`, `sink`, and `floatMe` methods in `Duck`. Be certain to implement the `sink` and `floatMe` methods in `Driftwood`.
8. Create a third class named `LeadWeight` (Listings 7-32 and 7-33). Create a method named `sinkASinkable` and have it take a `Sinkable` as a parameter.

(continued)

9. Modify `main` in DriftwoodDuck.m to match Listing 7-34.
10. Build and Run. Listing 7-35 contains the debugger console logging.

Listing 7-25 Sinkable.h

```
@protocol Sinkable
- (void) sink;
@end
```

Listing 7-26 Floater.h

```
#import "Sinkable.h"
@protocol Floater <Sinkable>
- (void) floatMe;
@end
```

Listing 7-27 Swimmer.h

```
#import "Floater.h"
@protocol Swimmer <Floater>
-(void) swim;
@end
```

Listing 7-28 Driftwood.h

```
#import <Foundation/Foundation.h>
#import "Floater.h"
@interface Driftwood : NSObject <Floater> {
}
@end
```

Listing 7-29 Driftwood.m

```
#import "Driftwood.h"
@implementation Driftwood
-(void) floatMe {
  NSLog(@"driftwood floating...");
}
```

```
-(void) sink {
  NSLog(@"driftwood sinking....");
}
@end
```

Listing 7-30 Duck.h

```
#import <Foundation/Foundation.h>
#import "Swimmer.h"
@interface Duck : NSObject  <Swimmer>{
}
@end
```

Listing 7-31 Duck.m

```
#import "Duck.h"
@implementation Duck
- (void) swim {
  NSLog(@"duck swimming...");
}
-(void) floatMe {
  NSLog(@"duck floating....");
}
- (void) sink {
  NSLog(@"duck sinking....");
}
@end
```

Listing 7-32 LeadWeight.h

```
#import <Foundation/Foundation.h>
#import "Floater.h"
@interface LeadWeight : NSObject {
}
- (void) sinkASinkable: (id <Sinkable>) aSinkable;
@end
```

(continued)

Listing 7-33 LeadWeight.m

```
#import "LeadWeight.h"
@implementation LeadWeight
- (void) sinkASinkable: (id <Sinkable>) aSinkable; {
  [aSinkable sink];
}
@end
```

Listing 7-34 DriftwoodDuck.m

```
#import <Foundation/Foundation.h>
#import "Duck.h"
#import "Driftwood.h"
#import "LeadWeight.h"
int main (int argc, const char * argv[]) {
  NSAutoreleasePool * pool = [[NSAutoreleasePool alloc] init];
  Duck * myDuck = [[[Duck alloc] init] autorelease];
  [myDuck floatMe];
  [myDuck swim];
  Driftwood * myDriftwood = [[[Driftwood alloc] init] autorelease];
  [myDriftwood floatMe];
  LeadWeight * myWeight = [[[LeadWeight alloc] init] autorelease];
  [myWeight sinkASinkable:myDriftwood];
  [myWeight sinkASinkable:myDuck];
  [pool drain];
  return 0;
}
```

Listing 7-35 Debugger console logging

```
duck floating....
duck swimming...
driftwood floating...
driftwood sinking....
duck sinking....
```

In main you treat Duck as a Swimmer and a Floater. In LeadWeight's sinkASinkable: method you treat Duck as a Sinkable. But notice that nowhere in Duck's interface or implementation do you specify Duck adopts the Sinkable or Floater protocol. The same is true for Driftwood; nowhere do you specify that Driftwood adopts the Sinkable protocol.

Because Swimmer adopts the Floater protocol, which adopts the Sinkable protocol, the compiler understands that Duck adopts the Floater and Sinkable protocols in addition to the Swimmer protocol. Because Driftwood adopts the Floater protocol, the compiler understands that Driftwood also adopts the Sinkable protocol.

Protocols and Delegates in UIKit

Enough about Ducks, Floaters, Swimmers, and Sinkables; you will use much more pragmatic protocols extensively when developing iPhone applications. The UIKit uses protocols to implement something called delegates.

A *delegate* is an object whose purpose is to help another object. The UIKit implements these helpers as protocols and allows you to define the custom class implementing the helper. There are many protocols that are predefined by the Foundation framework and the UIKit framework. For instance, most delegates in the UIKit are protocols.

A UIWebView is for loading web pages and uses a delegate called a UIWebViewDelegate. The UIWebView handles the layout and all the technical aspects of making the page appear in your application. It does not handle events such as a page beginning to load, loading, and then finishing loading. Instead, the UIKit provides the UIWebViewDelegate protocol. Developers are responsible for implementing that protocol should he or she wish to respond to page loading events. They then register the specific protocol implementation with the UIWebView. In the following Try This you implement a simple view that loads a webpage. You accomplish it by creating a GuideViewController, which inherits from UIViewController and adopts the UIWebViewDelegate (Figure 7-8).

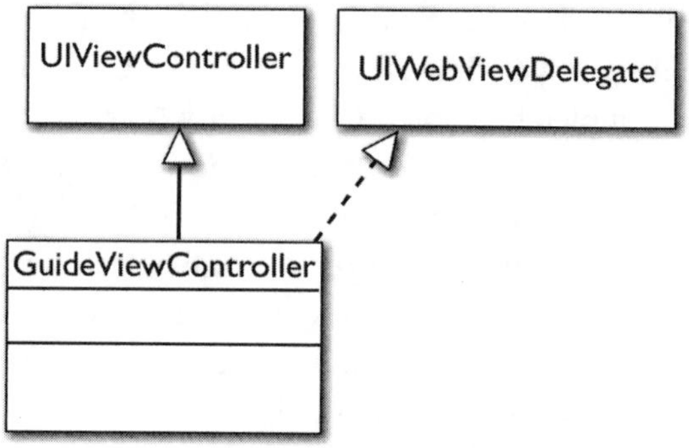

Figure 7-8 A view controller that adopts the `UIWebViewDelegate` protocol

Try This Adopting the UIWebViewDelegate

1. Create a new View-based application and name the application **Guide**.
2. Expand Classes and notice that the template created GuideViewController.h and GuideViewController.m for you.
3. Open GuideViewController.h in the editor and notice that the template also extended `UIViewController` for you.
4. Modify GuideViewController.h so that it adopts the `UIWebViewDelegate` (Listing 7-36). Also add a property declaration for the `UIWebView` that you will add as an `IBOutlet`.
5. Build the project, but do not run. Alternatively, you can save GuideViewController.h. You need to be certain that the newly added `IBOutlet` appears in Interface Builder.
6. Open GuideViewController.xib in Interface Builder.
7. Add a `UIWebView` from the library to the view's canvas (Figure 7-9).

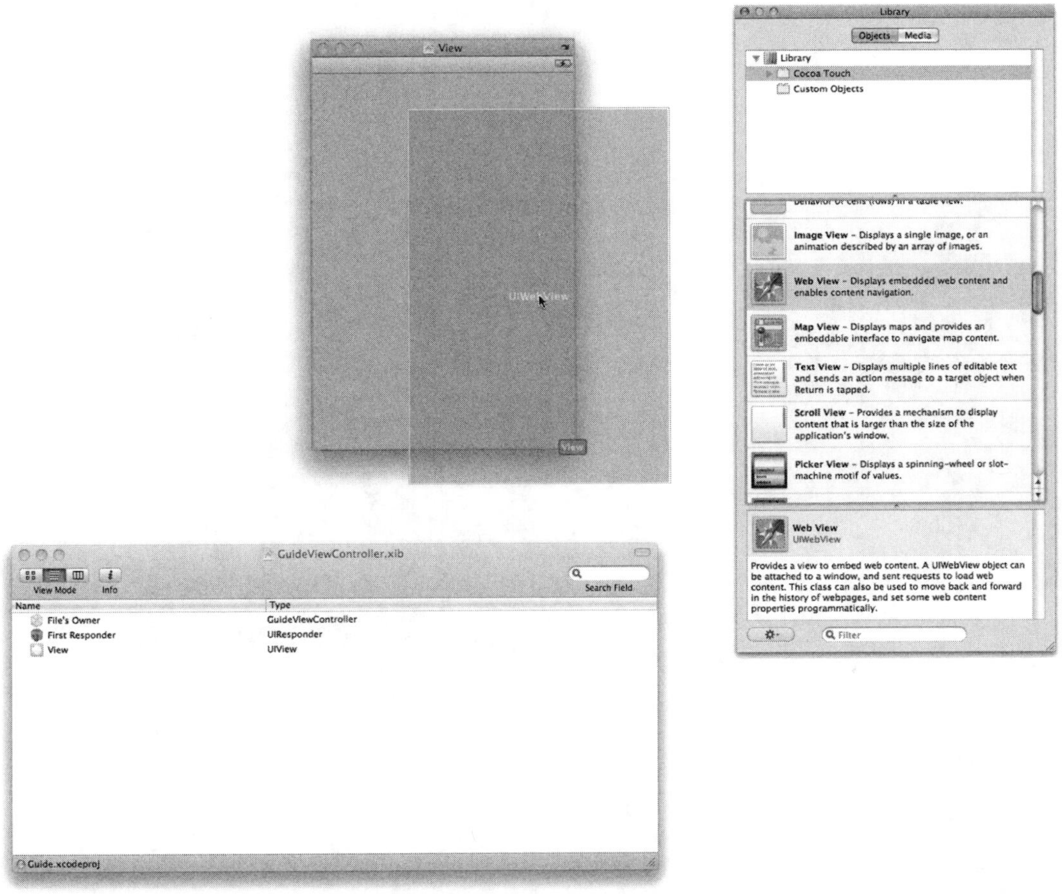

Figure 7-9 Adding a `UIWebView` to a view's canvas

8. Connect the File's Owner `myWebView` outlet to the `UIWebView` you just added to the canvas (Figure 7-10).
9. Connect the `UIWebView`'s `delegate` property to the File's Owner (Figure 7-11).
10. Save and exit Interface Builder.

(continued)

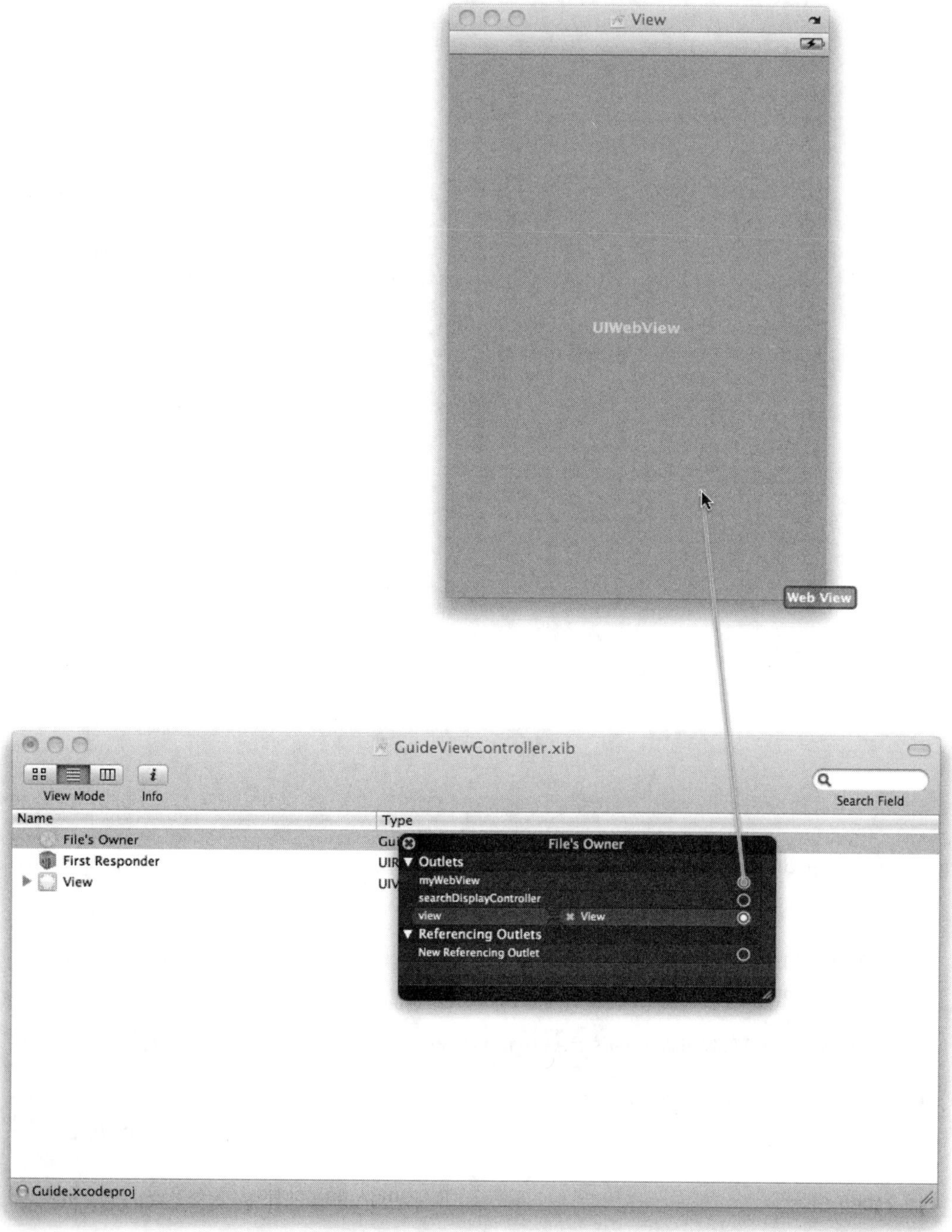

Figure 7-10 Connecting a `UIWebView`'s outlet to a `UIWebView`

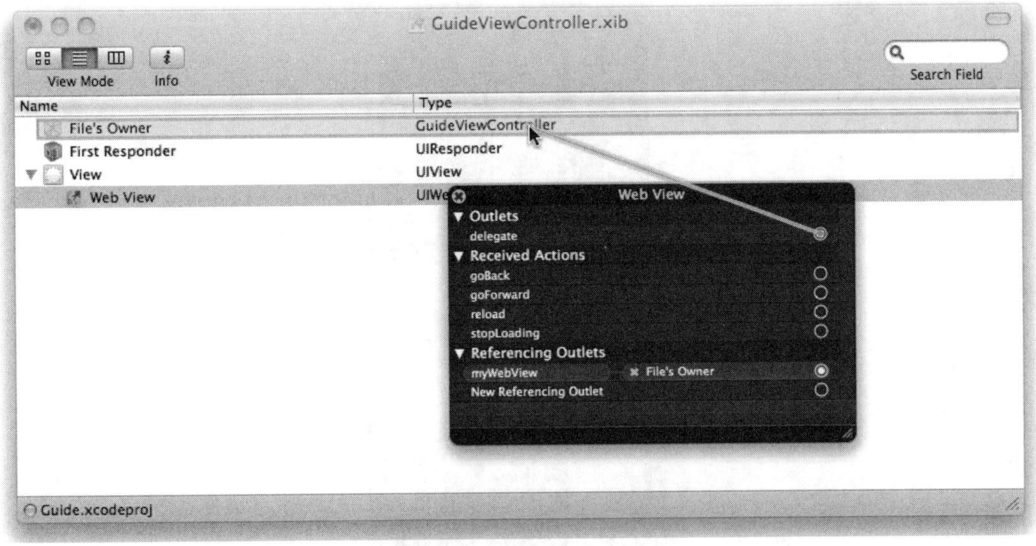

Figure 7-11 Connecting a `UIWebView`'s `delegate` property

11. Implement GuideViewController.m as in Listing 7-37.
12. Click Build And Go to run the application. If you are connected to the Internet, your application should appear similar to Figure 7-12. The debugger console logging should appear like Listing 7-38.

Listing 7-36 GuideViewController.h

```
#import <UIKit/UIKit.h>
@interface GuideViewController : UIViewController <UIWebViewDelegate> {
  IBOutlet UIWebView * myWebView;
}
@property (nonatomic, retain) UIWebView * myWebView;
@end
```

(continued)

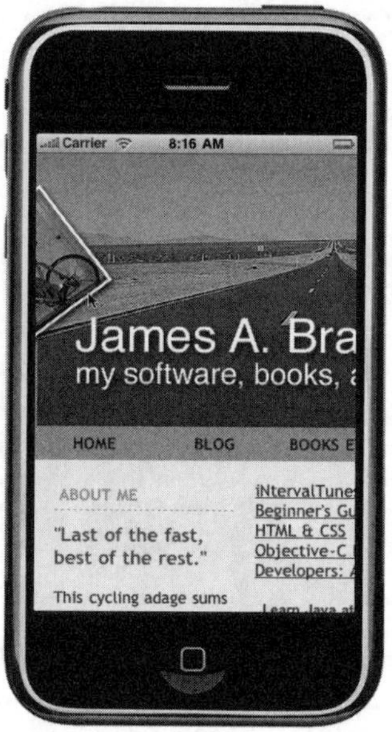

Figure 7-12 The application loading www.jamesabrannan.com

Listing 7-37 GuideViewController.m

```
#import "GuideViewController.h"
@implementation GuideViewController
@synthesize myWebView;
- (void)viewDidLoad {
  [super viewDidLoad];
  NSURL * url = [NSURL URLWithString:@"http://www.jamesabrannan.com"];
  NSURLRequest * req = [NSURLRequest requestWithURL:url];
  [self.myWebView loadRequest:req];
}
- (void)webViewDidStartLoad:(UIWebView *) webView {
  NSLog(@"I Started loading...");
}
- (void)webView:(UIWebView *) webView didFailLoadWithError:(NSError *) error {
  NSLog(@"I FAILED TO LOAD");
}
- (void) webViewDidFinishLoad: (UIWebView *) webView {
  NSLog(@"Finished Loading....");
}
```

```
- (void)dealloc {
  [myWebView release];
  [super dealloc];
}
@end
```

Listing 7-38 Debugger console logging

```
I Started loading...
I Started loading...
I Started loading...
I Started loading...
I Started loading...
Finished Loading....
Finished Loading....
Finished Loading....
Finished Loading....
Finished Loading....
```

In this example you used a `UIWebView` and had it load a URL. You had `GuideViewController` adopt the `UIWebViewDelegate` protocol.

```
@interface GuideViewController : UIViewController <UIWebViewDelegate>
```

You then connected the `UIWebView`'s delegate to `GuideViewController` in Interface Builder. The web view, as it starts loading and finishes loading resources, sends messages to its delegate's `webDidStartLoad:` and `webDidFinishLoad:` methods. Because `GuideViewController` adopts the protocol and was set as the web view's delegate, `GuideViewController` gets these messages. And so you can handle them in your custom code.

Categories

Categories allow extending a class' functionality without extending a class. Recall in Chapter 6 when you learned that a child class can have methods in addition to its parent's methods; a child can extend its parent. If you wish, rather than using inheritance, you can also use a category to add methods to another class.

Categories Explained

Listing 7-39 illustrates a simple category that adds additional functionality to the NSMutableString Foundation framework class.

Listing 7-39 NSMutableString+FooBar.h

```
#import <Foundation/Foundation.h>
@interface NSMutableString (FooBar)
- (void) addFooBar;
@end
```

A category declares an interface of the same name it wishes to add to. For instance, in Listing 7-39 the category declares an `NSMutableString`. It puts the name of the category in parentheses following the original class. By convention, developers typically name the header file the original class' name + the category's name. Listing 7-39 has a filename of NSMutableString+FooBar.h, for instance.

The category's implementation also uses the original class' name followed by the category's name in parentheses (Listing 7-40).

Listing 7-40 NSMutableString+FooBar.m

```
#import "NSMutableString+FooBar.h"
@implementation NSMutableString (FooBar)
- (void) addFooBar {
  [self appendString:@" FooBar"];
}
@end
```

The category implements the new method, but at the same time "inherits" the original class' method. For instance, in Listing 7-41 you first import the header file declaring the category. You then work with the original class by name, but because you imported the category, the compiler is smart enough to add the additional functionality to the name. The `main` method treats `NSMutableString` as an `NSMutableString`, but behind the scenes, it knows that it is a `FooBar` category and adds the additional method.

Listing 7-41 CategoryExample.m

```
#import <Foundation/Foundation.h>
#import "NSMutableString+FooBar.h"
int main (int argc, const char * argv[]) {
  NSAutoreleasePool * pool = [[NSAutoreleasePool alloc] init];
  NSMutableString * myMutString = [NSMutableString
stringWithString:@"This is a string"];
  [myMutString addFooBar];
  NSLog(myMutString);
  [pool drain];
  return 0;
}
```

Try This Extending a Duck with a Better Duck

1. Open the DriftwoodDuck project in Xcode.
2. Create a new class named `BetterDuck+Duck`; Xcode generates BetterDuck+Duck.h and BetterDuck+Duck.m files.
3. Open BetterDuck+Duck.h and change the interface declaration to match Listing 7-42.
4. Also change the implementation to match Listing 7-43.
5. Modify `main` in DriftwoodDuck.m so that it imports BetterDuck+Duck.h rather than the Duck.h header file (Listing 7-44).
6. Also modify `main` so that it sends a message to the duck telling it to quack.
7. Build and Run.

Listing 7-42 BetterDuck+Duck.h

```
#import <Foundation/Foundation.h>
#import "Duck.h"
@interface Duck (BetterDuck)
  -(void) quack;
@end
```

(continued)

Listing 7-43 BetterDuck+Duck.m

```
#import "BetterDuck+Duck.h"
@implementation Duck (BetterDuck)
- (void) quack {
  NSLog(@"quack...");
}
@end
```

Listing 7-44 DriftwoodDuck.m

```
#import <Foundation/Foundation.h>
//#import "Duck.h"
#import "Driftwood.h"
#import "LeadWeight.h"
#import "BetterDuck+Duck.h"
int main (int argc, const char * argv[]) {
  NSAutoreleasePool * pool = [[NSAutoreleasePool alloc] init];
  Duck * myDuck = [[[Duck alloc] init] autorelease];
  [myDuck float];
  [myDuck swim];
  Driftwood * myDriftwood = [[[Driftwood alloc] init] autorelease];
  [myDriftwood float];
  LeadWeight * myWeight = [[[LeadWeight alloc] init] autorelease];

  [myWeight sinkASinkable:myDriftwood];
  [myWeight sinkASinkable:myDuck];
  Duck * myBetterDuck = [[[Duck alloc] init] autorelease];
  [myBetterDuck float];
  [myBetterDuck swim];
  [myBetterDuck quack];
  [pool drain];
  return 0;
}
```

Changing from `Duck` to `BetterDuck` does not change the preexisting code's behavior. A `BetterDuck` is seen as a `Duck`, only now you have the additional `quack` method.

Notice what this example also illustrates: poor design. Categories allow ad hoc additions to classes; but ad hoc additions are a poor substitute for correctly designing your application. In a real project you should return to the original class and add the `quack` method to `Duck`. But sometimes this isn't an option, for instance, when using the `NSMutableString` Foundation class. When changing the original class isn't an option, you can either extend the original class with a new child class or you can use a category.

Summary

In this chapter you explored protocols and categories. Protocols are an important object-oriented concept that allows grouping related and unrelated objects based upon their behavior. In this chapter you used simplistic, real-world examples; however, you will see protocols used extensively when programming iPhone applications.

The `UIWebView` and its `UIWebViewDelegate` is just one example of an iPhone application using a protocol to implement a class' delegate. A `UIWebView` has a delegate property. When certain life-cycle methods occur, such as a page loading, it invokes the applicable delegate's method. Because the class assigned to the delegate property adopts the `UIWebViewDelegate` protocol, it implements the delegate methods called by the `UIWebView`.

Categories are a way you might add functionality to an existing class. When developing your application, you should not rely upon categories. For instance, if during a project, you find that you require a "BetterDuck," as in the Try This example, then you are better off modifying `Duck` than using a `BetterDuck` category. Categories should not be a license to add additional functionality to poorly thought-out classes.

Where categories are useful, though, is when extending preexisting classes, such as Foundation framework classes. Often you do not wish to create a subclass of a class such as `NSString`. Instead, you only wish to add one or two additional methods. In this situation, you might consider using a category.

Chapter 8

Some Foundation Framework Classes

Key Skills & Concepts

- Understanding Mutable and Nonmutable Objects
- Using `NSString` and `NSMutableString`
- Understanding Objective-C Numbers
- Using Dates in Objective-C
- Using `NSArray` and `NSMutableArray`
- Using `NSDictionary` and `NSMutableDictionary`

The Foundation framework is a collection of Objective-C classes that make working with primitive data elements and data structures such as arrays easier by wrapping them in an Objective-C class. The Foundation framework contains many classes that you can use when developing your application. In this chapter you explore several of the Foundation framework classes that you will use most often when developing an iPhone application. But this chapter cannot possibly do the Foundation framework justice, and you should at least skim the Foundation framework's online documentation at Apple's web site so that you have a better understanding of everything the Foundation framework has to offer. You cannot be a good iPhone developer unless you understand this framework.

Although there are many Foundation framework classes available, in this chapter you only explore a few of those classes; namely the `NSString`, `NSMutableString`, `NSNumber`, `NSDate`, `NSArray`, `NSMutableArray`, `NSDictionary`, and `NSMutableDictionary` classes. These classes all make working with data easier. For instance, the `NSNumber` class wraps numeric primitives and provides many functions for manipulating its underlying primitive value. The `NSString` makes working with C character arrays much easier by providing many data manipulation functions. And the `NSArray` and `NSDictionary` classes make handling an Objective-C object collection easier. These eight classes are arguably the most important Foundation framework classes, and you should understand them all.

NOTE

Using any of the Foundation framework classes only requires that you import the Foundation framework header file. You have already done this throughout this book.

```
#import <Foundation/Foundation.h>
```

You also must ensure you link against the framework, but Xcode does this for you when developing an iPhone project.

NSString and NSMutableString

The `NSString` and `NSMutableString` classes store string values. The `NSString` class is immutable, meaning you cannot change its value once initialized. The `NSMutableString` class is mutable, meaning you can change it after initialized. Each of these classes has many methods for modifying its values. In this section you explore both these classes and several of their methods.

TIP

If you OPTION-CLICK an Objective-C class in Xcode, you will get a pop-up window that summarizes the class (Figure 8-1). If you then click the icon that looks like an open book in the window's upper-right corner, the documentation on your computer opens (Figure 8-2).

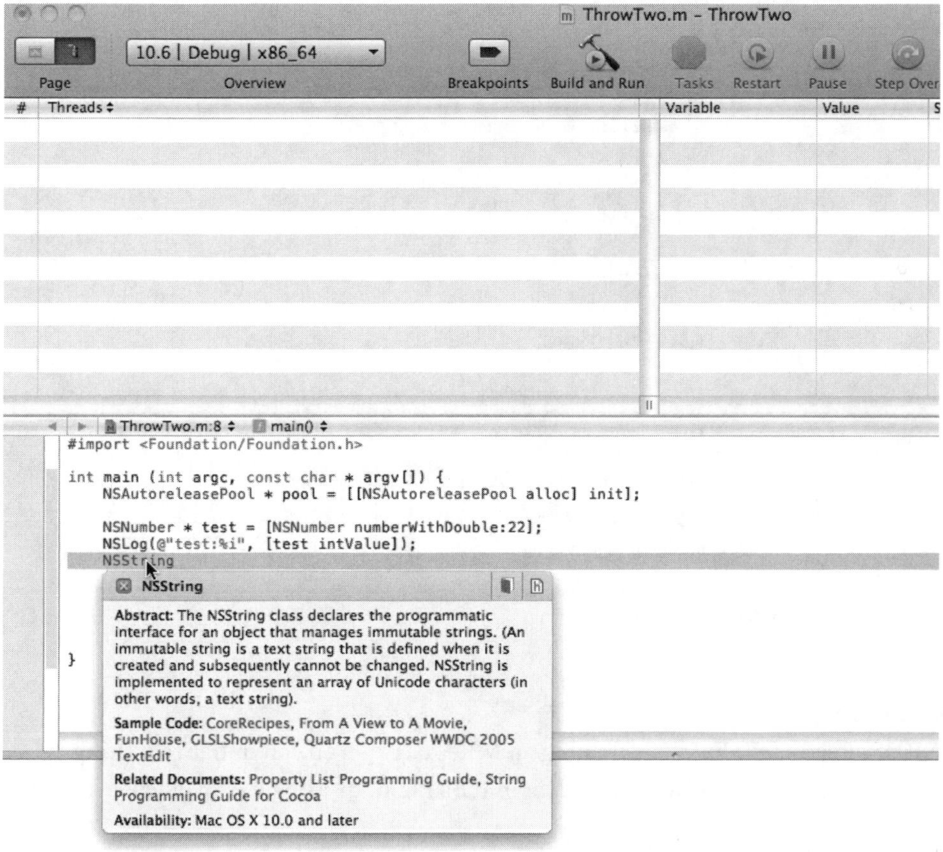

Figure 8-1 OPTION-CLICKING an Objective-C class

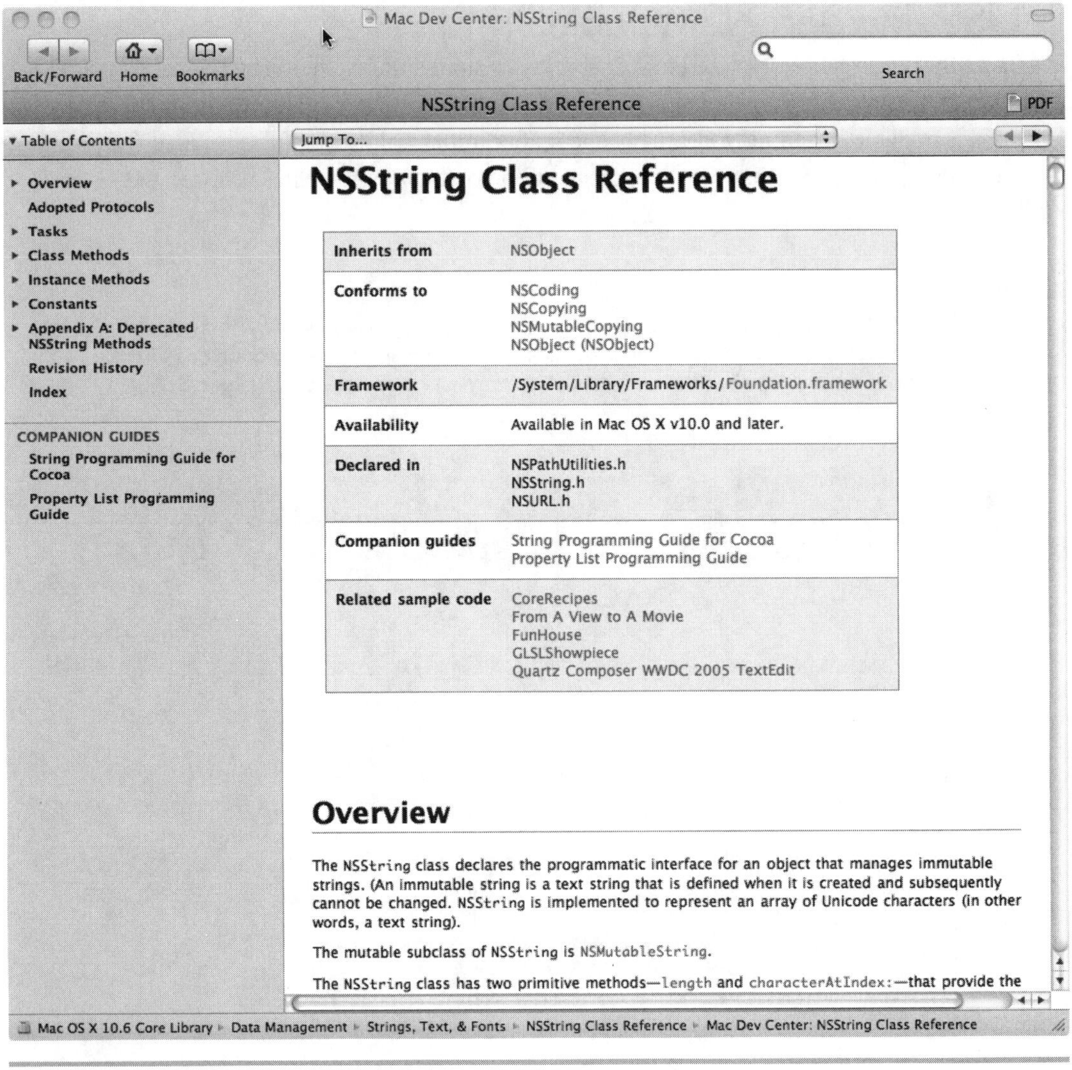

Figure 8-2 Documentation for `NSString`

NSString

You are already familiar with creating an `NSString`. You can initialize a string by simply assigning it a value, allocating and then initializing it, or using a convenience constructor.

```
NSString * myString = @"My String.";
NSString * myString2 = [[NSString alloc] initWithString:@"My String."];
NSString * myString3 = [NSString stringWithString:@"My String."];
```

TIP

When using a convenience constructor, always be certain you call `retain` if you wish to persist the object.

```
NSString * myString = @"My String.";
```

The `myString` variable is a weak reference to the underlying string.

You can also initialize a string with a C string. For instance, the following initializes a UTF8-encoded C string.

```
char * myCString = "This is a test.";
NSString * myString = [NSString stringWithUTF8String:myCString];
```

You can covert an `NSString` to a C string.

```
NSString * myString = @"This is my string.";
char * myCString = [myString getUTF8String];
```

NOTE

UTF-8 encoding is a Unicode character encoding. This encoding allows using languages such as Japanese. Don't worry too much about it; just realize that all your strings use this encoding.

You might also initialize a string with the contents of a URL or the contents of a file. You will see an example of initializing an `NSString` with a file's content in Chapter 9, when you explore file handling.

Yet another commonly used string initialization is `stringWithFormat`.

```
NSString * myString = [[NSString alloc] initWithFormat:@"I am %i years old.",41];
```

This method allows you to easily add a number or some other value to a string, much like you would when using the `NSLog` method. For those with prior C/C++ experience, it's a lot like `printf`.

NOTE

See "String Format Specifiers" in Apple's "String Programming Guide for Cocoa" for a complete listing of formats.

Once you have a string, there are many things you might do with it. For instance, if the string contains a string representation of a double, you can convert the string to a double.

```
NSString * myString = @"33.4444";
double mydouble = [myString doubleValue];
```

Or if your string contains an integer, you can convert the string to an integer.

```
NSString * myString = [NSString stringWithString:@"41"];
int myage = [myString intValue];
```

You can also compare two strings.

```
NSString * myStringOne = [[NSString alloc] initWithString:@"James"];
NSString * myStringTwo = [NSString stringWithString:@"James"];
if( [myStringOne equalsString:myStringTwo] == YES) {
NSLog(@"They are the same.");
```

You can also create a new string by appending a string.

```
NSString * myStringOne = @"My name is ";
NSString * myStringTwo = [myStringOne stringByAppendingString:@"James"];
```

NOTE

There are many string functions related to file paths. You explore these methods in Chapter 9.

NSString: Obtaining Substrings

Obtaining substrings is a little more involved than in other string methods. The methods you use are the `substringFromIndex:`, `substringToIndex:`, and `substringWithRange:` methods. The `substringToIndex:` method starts at a string's beginning and gets the characters to the index value. For instance, the following copies the first five characters from the string, creating the string `"James"`. Note that strings begin with an index of zero, so the fifth character is at position 4.

```
NSString * myName = @"James Brannan";
NSString * myFirstName = [myName substringToIndex:4];
```

The `substringFromIndex:` begins at the index and goes to the string's end. For instance, the following example's substring is `"Brannan"`.

```
NSString * myName = @"James Brannan";
NSString * myLastName = [myName substringFromIndex:5];
```

Notice that the substring starts at the next character after the index. But in the preceding example, that character is a blank, so you specify 5 so that the substring begins at the sixth index and does not include the blank.

Often you want to get a substring from the middle of a string. To do this, you must use another data type called an `NSRange`. An `NSRange`, although named like a class, is a structure that has a location and a length. You use `NSRange`, combined with `NSString`, to locate and extract a substring from a string. The following code illustrates:

```
NSString * myName = @"James A. Brannan";
NSRange myRange = [myName rangeOfString:@"A."];
if (myRange.location != NSNotFound) {
  NSString * myInitial = [myName substringWithRange:myRange];
}
```

The `NSString` class has a method called `rangeOfString` that returns the range of a substring that matches the string passed as a parameter. The range returned in the preceding code snipped has a location of 6 and a length of 2, which obtains the substring `"A."`. If the string fails to find the string, it returns an `NSNotFound` as the range's location. If the substring is found, then you use the range to create a new string from the original string, as in the proceeding code.

NSMutableString

Oftentimes you wish to manipulate a string and change its value depending upon differing circumstances. To accomplish this functionality, you should use the `NSMutableString` class rather than `NSString`. The `NSMutableString` is a subclass of `NSString`; it inherits all of `NSString`'s methods, but it also adds several methods for appending strings to itself without requiring you to declare a new string. You initialize it the same way you would a regular string, only you use the mutable version.

```
NSMutableString * myFullName = [[NSMutableString alloc] initWithString
:@"James"];
```

Because you created a mutable rather than immutable string, you can modify the original string without creating a new string. The following code illustrates the difference:

```
NSMutableString * myFullName = [[NSMutableString alloc] initWithString:@"James"];
[myFullName appendString:@" A. Brannan"];  //James A. Brannan

NSString * myFirstName = [[NSString alloc] initWithString:@"James"];
NSString * fullName = [myFirstName stringByAppendingString:@"Brannan"];
//James A. Brannan
```

You can also append a format to a mutable string:

```
[myFullName appendFormat:@" and my age is:%i", 41];  //James A. Brannan and
my age is:41
```

When using a string that you will modify, you should use the `NSMutableString` class rather than `NSString`.

NSNumber

The `NSNumber` class is a Cocoa wrapper around numeric primitives. Wrapping a numeric primitive with an Objective-C class allows you to send messages to the number. You typically create an `NSNumber` instance by using a `numberWith<type>:` convenience constructor. For instance, if wrapping a float, you would write the following.

```
NSNumber * myNumber = [NSNumber numberWithFloat:5.2];
```

You would then access that primitive value using an accessor method.

```
float myfloat = [myNumber floatValue];
```

Table 8-1 lists `NSNumber` convenience constructors. Note that each method in Table 8-1 also has a corresponding `init` method. For instance, rather than using the convenience method to create the `myNumber` value in the previous code fragment, you could have allocated the number and then initialized it using the `initWithFloat:` method.

```
NSNumber * myNumber = [[NSNumber alloc] initWithFloat:5.2]];
```

Like the convenience constructors, every primitive numeric type has its own `init` method in `NSNumber`.

You compare two `NSNumbers` using the `compare:` or `isEqualToNumber:` method. The `compare:` method compares if a number is less than, greater than, or equal to another number.

```
NSNumber * myNumber1 = [NSNumber numberWithInt:10];
NSNumber * myNumber2 = [[NSNumber alloc] initWithInt:20];
if ([myNumber1 compare:myNumber2) == NSOrderedAscending) {
NSLog(@"%i is < "%i", [myNumber1 intValue], [myNumber2 intValue]);
```

When comparing two numbers, there are three possible results: `NSOrderedAscending`, `NSOrderedSame`, and `NSOrderedDescending`. If the message sender is less than the message receiver, the result is `NSOrderedAscending`. If the message sender is

NSNumber Convenience Constructors	NSNumber init Methods
numberWithBool:	initWithBool:
numberWithChar:	initWithChar:
numberWithDouble:	initWithDouble:
numberWithFloat:	initWithFloat:
numberWithInt:	initWithInt:
numberWithInteger:	initWithInteger:
numberWithLong:	initWithLong:
numberWithLongLong:	initWithLongLong:
numberWithShort:	initWithShort:
numberWithUnsignedChar:	initWithUnsignedChar:
numberWithUnsignedInt:	initWithUnsignedInt:
numberWithUnsignedInteger:	initWithUnsignedInteger:
numberWithUnsignedLong:	initWithUnsignedLong:
numberWithUnsignedLongLong:	initWithUnsignedLongLong:
numberWithUnsignedShort:	initWithUnsignedShort:

Table 8-1 NSNumber Convenience Constructors and init Methods

greater than the message receiver, the result is NSOrderedDescending. If both are the same, the result is NSOrderedSame.

Sometimes you only wish to check if two numbers are equal. For this, NSNumber provides the isEqualToNumber: method. This method return YES if the two numbers are equal and NO if they are not.

```
if([myNumber1 isEqualToNumber:myNumber2] == YES) {
NSLog(@"They are equal.");
```

Besides initializing an NSNumber with a primitive value, you can also obtain that primitive value from the NSNumber.

```
NSNumber * myNumber1 = [NSNumber numberWithInt:10];
NSLog("int Value:%i", [myNumber1 intValue];
NSNumber * myNumber2 = [NSNumber numberWithFloat:33.45];
NSLog("int value:%f", [myNumber2 floatValue];
```

Table 8-2 lists the methods for obtaining primitives from NSNumber.

Accessor Methods
boolValue
charValue
decimalValue
floatValue
intValue
integerValue
longLongValue
longValue
shortValue
unsignedCharValue
unsignedIntegerValue
unsignedIntValue
unsignedLongLongValue
unsignedLongValue
unsignedShortValue

Table 8-2 Methods to Obtain Primitives from `NSNumber`

Ask the Expert

Q: Say I have an `NSNumber` that stores an int and I ask for a double—what happens?

A: You obtain a the number cast as a double value; `NSNumber` casts its primitive values appropriately.

NSDate and NSDateFormatter

The `NSDate` class encapsulates a date and time. It has several convenience methods, including the `date` and `dateWithString:` methods. As with other Foundation framework classes, you can allocate and initialize dates using `init` methods.

```
NSDate * today1 = [NSDate date];
NSDate * today2 = [[NSDate alloc] init];
```

The `NSDateFormatter` formats a date and time for displaying it. For instance, the following code formats a string before logging it.

```
NSDate * today1 = [NSDate date];
NSDateFormatter * myFormat = [[NSDateFormatter alloc] init];
[myFormat setDateFormat:"yyyy-MM-dd"];
NSString * myValue = [myFormat stringFromDate:myDate];
NSLog(@"the date:%@", myValue);
```

NOTE

Refer to the Unicode Technical Standard #35, Locale Data Markup Language (LDML), for a complete listing of date format patterns. This resource is available online at The Unicode Technical Reports web site (www.unicode.org/reports).

Try This Using an NSDate and NSDateFormatter to Display a Date

1. Create a new Command Line Foundation Tool named **DatePrinter**.
2. Open DatePrinter.m and modify the main method as in Listing 8-1.
3. Build and Run. Listing 8-2 is the debugger's logging.

Listing 8-1 DatePrinter.m

```
#import <Foundation/Foundation.h>
int main (int argc, const char * argv[]) {
  NSAutoreleasePool * pool = [[NSAutoreleasePool alloc] init];
  NSDate * now = [[NSDate alloc] init];
  NSDateFormatter * formatOne = [[NSDateFormatter alloc] init];
  [formatOne setDateFormat:@"yy/MM/dd"];
  NSLog(@"First date: %@", [formatOne stringFromDate:now]);
  [formatOne setDateFormat:@"EEEE MMMM d','yyyy"];
  NSLog(@"Second date: %@", [formatOne stringFromDate:now]);
  [formatOne setDateFormat:@"yyyy-MM-dd HH:mm"];
  NSLog(@"Third date: %@", [formatOne stringFromDate:now]);
  [formatOne setDateFormat:@"hh:mm a"];
  NSLog(@"Fourth date: %@", [formatOne stringFromDate:now]);
```

(continued)

```
    [now release];
    [pool drain];
    return 0;
}
```

Listing 8-2 Debugger console logging

```
First date: 09/10/18
Second date: Sunday October 18,2009
Third date: 2009-10-18 20:29
Fourth date: 08:29 PM
```

Listing 8-1 illustrates four different ways you might format a date. Each of these formats uses the Unicode technical standard. For instance, the first format formatted the date so it printed yy/mm/dd.

```
[formatOne setDateFormat:@"yy/MM/dd"];
```

After setting the format, you applied it to the date, which returns an `NSString`.

```
NSLog(@"First date: %@", [formatOne stringFromDate:now]);
```

Collections

Wikipedia defines a collection as "a grouping of some variable number of data items (possibly zero) that have some shared significance to the problem being solved and need to be operated upon together in some controlled fashion." An array is a collection, for instance, as it is an ordered grouping of some values with the same data type. Typical collections in most programming languages include sets, arrays, and dictionaries. In this section you explore the `NSArray`, `NSMutableArray`, `NSDictionary`, and `NSMutableDictionary` classes. These four classes, although not all the Objective-C collections classes, are the most important, as you will use them in almost every application you write.

NSArray and NSMutableArray

The `NSArray` and `NSMutableArray` are collection classes for holding an ordered collection of Objective-C objects. The `NSArray` is immutable, meaning it cannot be changed, while the `NSMutableArray` is mutable and can be changed.

The NSArray and NSMutableArray can only hold Objective-C objects, and cannot hold C primitives, or C constructs such as structs. But that is where the Objective-C wrapper classes are useful. If you wish to store a primitive in an NSArray or NSMutableArray, simply store the primitive in the wrapper class before adding it to the array.

```
NSNumber * myAge = [[NSNumber alloc] initWithInt:41];
[myFamilyAgesArray addObject:myAge];
```

Initializing an Array

Arrays provide several convenience constructors for creating an NSArray. One convenience constructor that you use often is the arrayWithObjects: method.

```
NSArray * myArray = [NSArray arrayWithObjects: @"A", @"B", @"C",nil];
```

This method takes an object list, terminated by nil, and creates a new array that contains the objects. The nil value indicates the array's end; however, it is not included as part of the array. In the preceding code snippet, the array's length is 3; nil is excluded.

Rather than using the arrayWithObjects: convenience method, you could have allocated the array and then initialized it.

```
NSArray * myArray = [[NSArray alloc] initWithObjects: @"A", @"B", @"C", nil];
```

Other convenience constructors you might use to create an array include the arrayWithArray:, arrayWithContentsOfFile:, arrayWithContentsOfURL:, arrayWithObject:, arrayWithObjects:, and arrayWithObjects:count: methods. As with most other Foundation framework classes, each of these convenience constructors have a corresponding init method if you prefer to manage memory yourself by allocating the array and then initializing it.

NOTE

Remember, if you use a convenience constructor, the convenience constructor adds the object instance created to the autorelease pool. The runtime, not you, manages these objects' life cycle. If you allocate and then initialize the object, you must manage the object's life cycle. If you wish to manage an object's lifetime that was created using a convenience constructor, then you must explicitly call retain on the object. But note, if you set a property to an object created using a convenience constructor you are calling retain, making this note moot. For instance, the following line retains the string even though you use a convenience constructor, assuming myString is a property with the retain attribute in its @property compiler directive.

```
foo.myString = [NSString stringWithString:"A Test"];
```

Initializing a Mutable Array

The `NSArray` is immutable. Once initialized, you cannot modify it. In contrast, the `NSMutableArray` allows modifying an array after creating it. Because it allows adding and removing objects from the array, the `NSMutableArray` has another convenience method named `arrayWithCapacity:`. This method allows creating a mutable array and allocating space in advance for a given number of objects to be added to the array.

```
NSMutableArray * myArray = [NSMutableArray arrayWithCapacity:3];
```

Note that the array in the preceding code snippet is not limited to three objects. The `arrayWithCapacity:` method allocates enough space for three objects; however, you can add more objects if needed. Moreover, note that you are not required to use the `arrayWithCapacity:` method when creating an `NSMutableArray` instance; any of the other `NSArray` convenience constructors or `init` methods work. The `arrayWithCapacity:` method is simply more efficient by allocating the needed space when created. When adding objects later, the runtime isn't required to allocate the space for the objects.

Adding, Removing, and Replacing Objects

When using an `NSMutableArray`, you can add, remove, and replace objects that are in the array. For instance, the `addObject:` and `insertObject:atIndex:` methods allow adding an object, the `removeObjectAtIndex:` method allows removing an object at a location in an array, and the `replaceObject:atIndex:` method allows replacing an object.

Try This Using an NSMutableArray

1. Create a new Command Line Foundation Tool unnamed **MutableArrayExample**.
2. Create a new class called `Foo` and add an `NSString` as a property (Listings 8-3 and 8-4).
3. Modify MutableArrayExample.m as in Listing 8-5.
4. Build and Run the application. Listing 8-6 contains the debugger console logging.

Listing 8-3 Foo.h

```
#import <Foundation/Foundation.h>
@interface Foo : NSObject {
```

```
  NSString * myName;
}
@property (nonatomic, retain) NSString * myName;
@end
```

Listing 8-4 Foo.m

```
#import "Foo.h"
@implementation Foo
@synthesize myName;
- (void) dealloc {
  [self.myName release];
  [super dealloc];
}
@end
```

Listing 8-5 MutableArrayExample.m

```
#import <Foundation/Foundation.h>
#import "Foo.h"
#define FOOS_MAX 5
int main (int argc, const char * argv[]) {
  NSAutoreleasePool * pool = [[NSAutoreleasePool alloc] init];
  NSMutableArray * myMutableArray = [[NSMutableArray alloc]
initWithCapacity:FOOS_MAX];
  for (int i = 0; i < FOOS_MAX; i++) {
    Foo * tempFoo = [[Foo alloc] init];
    tempFoo.myName = [NSString stringWithFormat:@"Sam%i", i];
    [myMutableArray addObject:tempFoo];
    [tempFoo release];
  }
  NSLog(@"There are %i Foo objects in the array.", [myMutableArray count]);
  for (int i = 0; i < [myMutableArray count]; i++) {
    NSLog(@"Foo's name:%@ at index:%i", ((Foo*)[myMutableArray
objectAtIndex:i]).myName, i);
  }
  [myMutableArray removeObjectAtIndex:FOOS_MAX-2];
  Foo * objRalph = [[Foo alloc] init];
  objRalph.myName = @"Ralph";
  [myMutableArray replaceObjectAtIndex:1 withObject:objRalph];
  [objRalph release];
  NSLog(@"There are %i Foo objects in the array.", [myMutableArray count]);
  for (int i = 0; i < [myMutableArray count]; i++) {
```

(continued)

```
    NSLog(@"Foo's name:%@ at index:%i", ((Foo*)[myMutableArray
objectAtIndex:i]).myName, i);
  }
  [myMutableArray release];
  [pool drain];
  return 0;
}
```

Listing 8-6 Debugger console logging

```
There are 5 Foo objects in the array.
Foo's name:Sam0 at index:0
Foo's name:Sam1 at index:1
Foo's name:Sam2 at index:2
Foo's name:Sam3 at index:3
Foo's name:Sam4 at index:4
There are 4 Foo objects in the array.
Foo's name:Sam0 at index:0
Foo's name:Ralph at index:1'
Foo's name:Sam2 at index:2
Foo's name:Sam4 at index:3
```

In this example you first create a mutable array. You initialize it with the number of objects you wish to add to the array. After adding the objects, a second loop prints each object's `myName` property. Rather than using the `FOOS_MAX` constant for the loop's upper bound, it uses the array's `count` method. This method returns the array's object count.

```
[myMutableArray count]);
```

The `objectAtIndex:` method returns the object in the array at the specified index. Because an array can store any object, the method returns an `id`. To use the object and call its methods, you cast it to the appropriate class first.

```
((Foo*)[myMutableArray objectAtIndex:i]).myName
```

After casting the object, you use it as a `Foo` instance.

NSEnumerator and Fast Enumeration

In previous code in this chapter you used a for loop to iterate through an array. Another way, arguably better, is using the `NSEnumerator` Foundation framework class. The `NSEnumerator` class is what is called an enumerator. An *enumerator* is for iterating through an array's elements. In this section you explore enumeration, and a related technique called *fast enumeration.*

NSEnumerator

The `NSArray` and `NSMutableArray` both have an `objectEnumerator` property that holds an `NSEnumerator`. You obtain an array's enumerator by getting this property.

```
NSEnumerator * myEnumerator = myArray.myEnumerator;
```

After obtaining the enumerator, you then iterate through each value in the array. For instance, in Listing 8-5 you used a for loop to iterate through the array's values.

```
for (int i = 0; i < [myMutableArray count]; i++) {
  NSLog(@"Foo's name:%@ at index:%i", ((Foo*)[myMutableArray
objectAtIndex:i]).myName, i);
}
```

Instead, you could use an enumerator.

```
NSEnumerator * myEnumerator = myMutableArray.objectEnumerator;
id object;
while(object = [myEnumerator nextObject]) {
  NSLog(@"Foo's name:%@", ((Foo*)object).myName);
}
```

Note that in the preceding code snippet the enumerator's `nextObject` method returns an `id`, so you declare an `id` to refer to the object. To use the object as a `Foo`, you first cast it to a `Foo` type before accessing the `myName` property.

Fast Enumeration

Fast enumeration is another way you can enumerate through an array's objects. Any class that adopts the `NSFastEnumeration` protocol can be enumerated over using fast enumeration. For instance, both `NSNumber` and `NSString` adopt the `NSFastEnumeration` protocol. Consider the program in Listing 8-7.

Listing 8-7 Program using fast enumeration

```
#import <Foundation/Foundation.h>
int main (int argc, const char * argv[]) {
  NSAutoreleasePool * pool = [[NSAutoreleasePool alloc] init];
  NSMutableArray * myArray = [[NSMutableArray alloc] init];
  for(int i = 0; i < 10; i++) {
    NSNumber * temp = [[NSNumber alloc] initWithInt:i];
```

```
      [myArray addObject:temp];
      [temp release];
    }
    for(NSNumber * myNumber in myArray) {
      NSLog(@"Value:%i", [myNumber intValue]);
    }
  [pool drain];
return 0;
}
```

The NSNumber method implements the NSFastEnumeration protocol, and so you can use it to iterate through the NSNumbers in the array.

Fast enumeration also works with any object, provided you use id rather than a typed value. For instance, in Listing 8-7 you strongly typed the enumerator as an NSNumber. You are not required to strongly type the enumerator; instead, you can use an id. You can rewrite the loop in Listing 8-7 as the following:

```
id myValue;
for(myValue in myArray) {
     NSLog(@"Value:%i", [((NSNumber*)myNumber) intValue]);
   }
```

When you use an id rather than a typed value, you can use fast enumeration with any object, as the following Try This illustrates.

Try This Iterating Through an NSMutableArray Using Fast Enumeration

1. Create a new Command Line Foundation Tool application named **Iterating**.
2. Create a new class named Foo and add an integer as a property (Listings 8-8 and 8-9).
3. Implement Iterating.m as in Listing 8-10.
4. Build and Run the application and the debugger console logs ten Foo values.

Listing 8-8 Foo.h

```
#import <Foundation/Foundation.h>
@interface Foo : NSObject {
```

```
  int value;
}
@property (nonatomic,assign) int value;
@end
```

Listing 8-9 Foo.m

```
#import "Foo.h"
@implementation Foo
@synthesize value;
@end
```

Listing 8-10 Iterating.m

```
#import <Foundation/Foundation.h>
#import "Foo.h"
int main (int argc, const char * argv[]) {
  NSAutoreleasePool * pool = [[NSAutoreleasePool alloc] init];
  NSMutableArray * myArray = [[NSMutableArray alloc] init];
  for(int i = 0; i < 10; i++) {
    Foo * temp = [[Foo alloc] init];
    temp.value = i;
    [myArray addObject:temp];
    [temp release];
  }
  id myValue;
  for(myValue in myArray) {
    NSLog(@"Value:%i", ((Foo*)myValue).value);
  }
  [pool drain];
  return 0;
}
```

NSDictionary and NSMutableDictionary

The `NSDictionary` and `NSMutableDictionary` store data sorted by keys. If familiar with Java, then you have probably heard of a hashmap; an `NSDictionary` is the Foundation framework's equivalent to a hashmap. If you haven't heard of a hashmap, then think of a dictionary. A dictionary has a definition and a keyword. A dictionary orders its words alphabetically. Moreover, it has helpful things like lettered tabs that make finding a word easier. Once you find the value, you read its definition.

Now, imagine a dictionary where its definitions are in random order, much as they would be if you randomly placed objects in an NSArray. Finding a word would require you to iterate through every value until you found the word you were searching for. Real dictionaries, in contrast, let you thumb to the letter, and then let you thumb to the first few letters of a word. You can then scan the page and find the exact word.

A dictionary, or hashmap, lets your application do the same thing. Using some underlying search algorithms, the NSDictionary can search for a particular value more efficiently than you could by iterating through an array. This efficiency results in less wasted resources and quicker applications.

Dictionary Keys

In an NSDictionary, for each entry there are two objects stored, the key and the value. The key is how you find an object stored in the dictionary; it is the "word." For instance, the following code fragment searches a dictionary for a Foo object with the NSString key having a value "firstFoo". Because the objectForKey: method returns an id, you cast the value before setting it to a concrete class type.

```
NSString * myKey = @"firstFoo";
Foo * myFoo = (Foo*)[myDictionary objectForKey:myKey];
```

A key does not require its class to be an NSString. Any class that inherits from NSObject can be a key. The NSObject class implements a method called isEqual:. This method checks if two objects are equivalent. The NSDictionary will call the object's isEqual: method to see if the object is equal to the key.

```
- (BOOL)isEqual:(id)anObject
```

For instance, the NSNumber class checks to see if another number is the same value as it, not if both NSNumbers point to the same underlying object.

```
NSNumber * myNumber1 = [NSNumber numberWithInt:2];
NSNumber * myNumber2 = [NSNumber numberWithInt:2];
if([myNumber2 isEqual:myNumber1];
```

Using another Foundation framework object as a key is straightforward. For instance, the following code snippet uses an NSNumber that contains an integer as a key:

```
NSNumber * myNumberKey = [NSNumber numberWithInt:22];
Foo * myFoo = (Foo*)[myDictionary objectForKey:myNumberKey];
```

NOTE

If you wish to use a custom object as a key, you must adopt the `NSCopying` protocol. This means that any class you use as a key must implement the `copyWithZone:zone:` method. You must also override the `isEqual:` and `hash` methods in `NSObject`. For more information, refer to Apple's documentation on the `NSCopying` protocol. It is much easier to just use a primitive value in a Foundation framework class as your key, though, and it will be sufficient for 99 percent of the code you write.

Creating a Dictionary

There are several ways to create an `NSDictionary`. Using the `dictionaryWithObjects:forKeys:` is one way you might create a dictionary. For instance, the following code fragment declares an array of values and an array of keys. It then uses them to create a dictionary.

```
NSArray * myKeys = [NSArray arrayWithObjects: @"firstkey", @"secondkey",
@"thirdkey", nil];
NSArray * myObjects = [NSArray arrayWithObjects: @"valueone", @"valuetwo",
@"valuethree", nil];
NSDictionary * myDictionary = [NSDictionary dictionaryWithObjects:myObjects
forKeys:myKeys];
```

You can also create an `NSMutableDictionary` using the `dictionaryWithCapacity:` method. Like the `NSMutableArray`'s `arrayWithCapacity:` method, the `dictionaryWithCapacity:` method creates a dictionary and allocates memory for the dictionary.

```
NSMutableDictionary * myDictionary = [NSMutableDictionary
dictionaryWithCapacity:3];
```

You can then add objects to the dictionary as needed.

```
[myDictionary setObject:@"valueone" forKey:@"firstkey"];
[myDictionary setObject:@"valuetwo" forKey:@"secondkey"];
[myDictionary setObject:@"valuethree" forKey:@"thirdkey"];
```

As when working with other Foundation framework classes, rather than using a convenience method, you can allocate and initialize an `NSDictionary`.

```
NSDictionary * myDictionary = [[NSDictionary alloc] initWithObjects:myObjects
forKeys:myKeys];
```

Besides obtaining objects using the `objectForKey:` method, you can also remove a single object, or multiple objects, as needed.

```
[myDictionary removeObjectForKey:"@firstkey"];
NSArray * keysToRemove = [NSArray arrayWithObjects:@"secondkey", @"thirdkey"];
[myDictionary removeObjectsForKey:keysToRemove];
```

When you need to store objects and then later obtain them based upon some key, such as an ID (not to be confused with an Objective-C `id`), you should consider using an `NSDictionary` or `NSMutableDictionary`.

Try This Creating a Mutable Dictionary and Accessing the Values

1. Create a new Command Line Foundation Tool application named **Dictionary**.
2. Create a new class called `Foo` and implement it the same as you did previously in Listings 8-8 and 8-9.
3. Implement Dictionary.m as in Listing 8-11.
4. Build and Run the application. Listing 8-12 contains the debugger console logging.

Listing 8-11 Dictionary.m

```
#import <Foundation/Foundation.h>
#import "Foo.h"
int main (int argc, const char * argv[]) {
  NSAutoreleasePool * pool = [[NSAutoreleasePool alloc] init];
  NSMutableDictionary * myDictionary = [[NSMutableDictionary alloc] init];
  for (int i = 0; i < 5; i++) {
    Foo * temp = [[Foo alloc] init];
    temp.value = i + 10;
    [myDictionary setObject:temp forKey:[NSNumber numberWithInt:i]];
    [temp release] ;
  }
  NSLog(@"The value for key:3 is %i", ((Foo*)[myDictionary objectForKey:
[NSNumber numberWithInt:3]]).value);
  NSEnumerator * myKeyEnumerator = [myDictionary keyEnumerator];
  id curKey;
  while (curKey = [myKeyEnumerator nextObject]) {
```

```
      Foo * temp = (Foo *)[myDictionary objectForKey:curKey];
      NSLog(@"key:%@ Value:%i", curKey, temp.value);
    }
    [myDictionary release];
    [pool drain];
    return 0;
}
```

Listing 8-12 Debugger console logging

```
The value for key:3 is 13
key:0 Value:10
key:3 Value:13
key:2 Value:12
key:1 Value:11
key:4 Value:14
```

In this example you create a mutable dictionary that contains `Foo` class instances as the objects and integers, wrapped in the `NSNumber` class, as the keys. After creating the dictionary, you access the value stored with the key having the value of 3.

```
NSLog(@"The value for key:3 is %i", ((Foo*)[myDictionary objectForKey:
[NSNumber numberWithInt:3]]).value);
```

But note, 3 is the key and does not imply any index location in the dictionary. For instance, after obtaining the value, you then get all the keys as an enumerator and then loop through the keys. In the loop's body you fetch the value from the original dictionary by key. But as you can see in Listing 8-12, the values are not stored in order of the key's value.

Summary

In this chapter you explored several Objective-C Foundation framework classes. These classes all wrapped primitive data objects or more basic C constructs such as arrays. `NSString` and `NSMutableString` make working with strings easier. `NSNumber` wraps primitive numeric values and makes working with numbers easier. `NSDate` allows working with dates. The `NSArray`, `NSMutableArray`, `NSDictionary`, and

NSMutableDictionary classes are for storing Objective-C classes. Arrays store objects as an ordered set of objects. Dictionaries store objects by a key.

All classes covered in this chapter are Foundation framework classes that you will use frequently when developing iPhone applications. However, this chapter was not a comprehensive discussion of the Foundation framework classes. There are many more Foundation framework classes. For instance, NSSet and NSMutableSet are collection classes that implement a set. NSData, which you will see used in Chapter 10, wraps binary data. For more complete Foundation framework coverage, refer to Apple's "Foundation Framework Reference," available online.

Chapter 9

File Handling

Key Skills & Concepts

- Understanding an iPhone App's Directories
- Handling Directories and Files with the `NSFileManager` Class
- Understanding the `NSBundle`
- Using the `NSString`'s File Handling Methods
- Using `NSData` and `UIImage`
- Reading and Writing a Binary File

In this chapter you explore file handling. As with most topics in this book, there are far too many topics to adequately cover in a beginner's book. However, you do explore the file handling aspects most relevant to getting started as an iPhone developer. Like the wrapper classes in Chapter 8, the Foundation framework makes working with files much easier than if you used lower-level C file handling functions.

You first explore the directories you may write to when writing an iPhone application. You then learn basic path manipulation using the `NSFileManager` class. After that you learn several of `NSString`'s methods for working with paths and files. You also explore `NSData` and using it to read and write binary data. Again, although not a comprehensive treatise on any single file handling subject, the chapter is enough to get you started.

iPhone Directories

The iPhone operating system limits applications to only accessing files in its own directories. These directories are part of an application's sandbox. It is called a sandbox because the operating system isolates the application and its files from the rest of the operating system. Things inside the sandbox cannot interact with things outside the sandbox, except through Apple-crafted APIs.

When installed, an application is placed in its own root directory. Under this directory are the Documents, Preferences, Caches, and tmp directories. These are the directories available to you as a developer:

```
<Application Root>/Documents
<Application Root>/Preferences
```

```
<Application Root>/Caches
<Application Root>/tmp
```

You write your application's preferences to the Preferences folder. You write temporary files to the tmp folder. Data written to the tmp folder is not persisted between application invocations and is not backed up by iTunes on a user's desktop. You write your application's data to the Documents directory. This directory's content is persisted between invocations and is backed up by iTunes on a user's desktop or laptop.

NSHomeDirectory

Every iPhone application has a home directory. The home directory is your application's root directory. The following code illustrates how you obtain the path to your root directory.

```
NSString * pathToHome = NSHomeDirectory(void);
```

But obtaining your application's home directory isn't very useful, though, as you do not write to this directory. Moreover, resources such as images and text files that you place in your Xcode project's Resources group are placed in your application's bundle and are more easily accessed using the `NSBundle`, as you will see in a couple sections. It is also not very useful for obtaining your application's temporary, cache, or documents directory, as the easiest and most robust way to obtain one of these subdirectories is through the `NSSearchPathForDirectoriesInDomains` C function.

NSSearchPathForDirectoriesInDomains

Obtain your application's documents or caches directory using the `NSSearchPathForDirectoriesInDomains` method. This method takes three parameters: the directory to begin the search, the search path domain mask, and a flag indicating if tildes should be converted to actual paths. The method returns an array of `NSStrings` for all found paths. Although on a desktop computer the method returns more than one path in the array, on the iPhone the method always returns an array with only one element. The following code snippet illustrates using the `NSSearchPathForDirectoriesInDomains` method to obtain an application's documents directory:

```
NSArray * myPaths = NSSearchPathForDirectoriesInDomains (NSDocumentDirectory,
NSUserDomainMask, YES);
NSString * myDocPath = [myPaths objectAtIndex:0];
```

Other values you might use for the directory parameter include `NSApplicationDirectory`, `NSCachesDirectory`, and `NSApplicationSupportDirectory`.

NSTemporaryDirectory

Obtaining your application's temporary directory is straightforward. You use the `NSTemporaryDirectory` method.

```
NSString * myTempDirector = NSTemporaryDirectory(void);
```

This method returns the path to your application's temporary directory. You use this directory to store temporary data that does not require persisting between application invocations. This directory is also not backed up by iTunes when synchronizing a device.

NSBundle

When you develop your app, you add resources to the Resources group in your iPhone project (Figure 9-1). These files are part of your application's bundle. iPhone applications are bundled in a directory with a <filename>.app name. Although it appears and acts like a standard executable, it is actually a directory storing the application and resources.

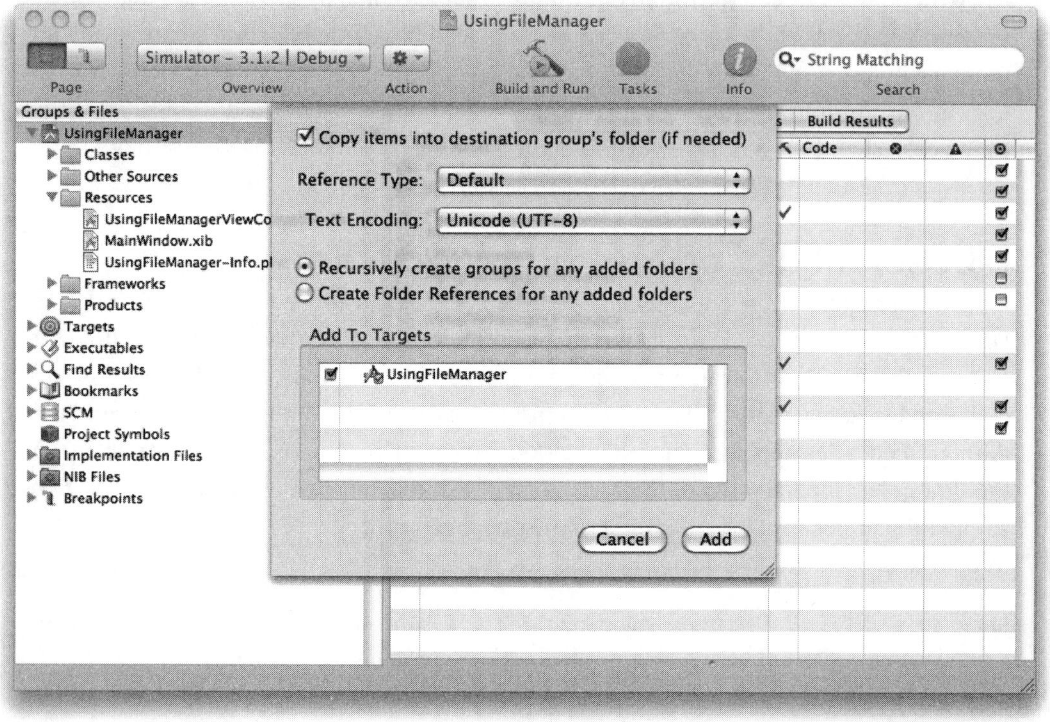

Figure 9-1 You store resources in your project's Resources group.

The easiest way to obtain resources stored in an application's bundle is through the NSBundle class. The following code snippet illustrates obtaining a file path from an application's bundle.

```
NSString * pathToMyFile = [[NSBundle mainBundle] pathForResource:@"winesales"
 ofType:@"csv"];
```

Although this is useful for obtaining a resource in your application's bundle, note that you must move the resource to another directory before modifying it. An application's bundle is read only.

File Handling

Once you obtain a path to a file, you usually wish to manipulate it in some way. The NSFileManager class has many methods you can use to manipulate both directories and files.

NSFileManager

The NSFileManager class has many methods for manipulating files. Table 9-1 summarizes several of NSFileManager's methods. For more complete NSFileManager coverage, and a listing of all methods, you should refer to Apple's NSFileManager Class Reference.

Method Name	Description
fileExistsAtPath:	Determines if the path specified exists.
fileExistsAtPath:isDirectory:	Determines if the path specified exists and if it is a directory.
contentsOfDirectoryAtPath:error:	Returns directories and files of the directory passed as a parameter.
enumeratorAtPath:	Returns an NSDirectoryEnumerator to enumerate a directory's content.
moveItemAtPath:toPath:error:	Moves the directory or file to a different location.
copyItemAtPath:toPath:error:	Copies a directory or file to a different location.
removeItemAtPath:error:	Deletes a directory or file.
currentDirectoryPath	Returns the current directory path.
changeCurrentDirectoryPath:	Changes the current directory path to the path specified in parameter.

Table 9-1 Several NSFileManager Methods

NOTE

Remember, to access `NSFileManager`, just open Xcode, open Help, and type **NSFileManager** in the Search field at the help screen's upper right.

Determining if a File Exists

Determine if a file exists by using the `fileExistsAtPath:` or `fileExistsAtPath:isDirectory:` method. The first checks if the provided path specifies a file or directory, while the second checks that the provided path both exists and is a directory.

```
NSString * myFile = [NSTemporaryDirectory() stringByAppendingPathComponent:
@"test.xml"
BOOL hasFile = [[NSFileManager defaultManager] fileExistsAtPath:myFile];
```

The code snippet first creates a path to the file you wish to determine exists, test .xml, in the application's temporary directory. If the file exists, it returns YES; otherwise, it returns NO. Note the `stringByAppendingPathComponent:` method. This is an `NSString` method discussed later in this chapter; however, the method's name is intuitive.

You can also check if the path is to a directory, as the following code illustrates:

```
BOOL isDir;
BOOL isADirectory = [[NSFileManager defaultManager] fileExistsAtPath:
NSTemporaryDirectory() isDirectory:&isDir];
if(isADirectory && isDir) {
  NSLog(@"yes is a directory");
}
```

This code checks if the path to a file exists and is also a directory. Notice that you are not passing a BOOL, but rather an address of a BOOL, which is admittedly strange. You then check that the method returns YES and that the `isDir` is YES. If both are true, then the path exists and is a directory.

Listing a Directory's Content

`NSFileManager` also has techniques for listing a directory's contents. Listing 9-1 illustrates using the `contentsOfDirectoryAtPath:error:` method, and Listing 9-2 illustrates using an `NSDirectoryEnumerator` class.

Listing 9-1 Using the `contentsOfDirectoryAtPath:error:` method

```
- (void) viewDidLoad {
  [super viewDidLoad];
  NSString * bundleDir = [[NSBundle mainBundle] resourcePath];
```

```
  NSError * myError = nil;
  NSArray * myContents = [[NSFileManager defaultManager]
contentsOfDirectoryAtPath:bundleDir error:&myError];
  id myiter;
  for(myiter in myContents) {
    NSLog(@"name:%@", myiter);
  }
}
```

Listing 9-2 Using the `NSDirectoryEnumerator`

```
- (void) viewDidLoad {
  NSString * homeDir = NSHomeDirectory();
  NSLog(@"the home directory:%@", homeDir);
  NSDirectoryEnumerator * dEnum;
  dEnum = [[NSFileManager defaultManager] enumeratorAtPath:homeDir];
  id curItem;
  while (curItem = [dEnum nextObject]) {
    NSLog(@"path:%@", curItem);
  }
}
```

The `contentsOfDirectoryAtPath:error:` method returns an `NSArray` containing the directory's content as an `NSString`. It does not return the items' paths, only the name. For instance, the following is the output from Listing 9-1, if run in an application named CheckIfWritable. As an aside, notice the .nib and absence of a .xib. Once compiled, the application's .xib file becomes a .nib file, which is why you see the Interface Builder file referred to as both "the xib" and "the nib" interchangeably.

```
name:CheckIfWritable
name:CheckIfWritableViewController.nib
name:Info.plist
name:MainWindow.nib
name:PkgInfo
name:test1.txt
```

If you wish to obtain an array of the items as a path, use the `NSDirectoryEnumerator`. This class enumerates through all items in a specified directory. Moreover, it returns each item as a fully qualified path. Listing 9-2 illustrates, while Listing 9-3 lists the output to the debugger console.

Listing 9-3 Debugger console logging from running Listing 9-2

```
the home directory:/Users/jamesbrannan/Library/Application Support/iPhone
Simulator/User/Applications/2BD08609-9C3A-4A72-9B11-0C07C863D402
path:CheckIfWritable.app
path:CheckIfWritable.app/CheckIfWritable
path:CheckIfWritable.app/CheckIfWritableViewController.nib
path:CheckIfWritable.app/Info.plist
path:CheckIfWritable.app/MainWindow.nib
path:CheckIfWritable.app/PkgInfo
path:CheckIfWritable.app/test1.txt
path:Documents
path:Documents/test.txt
path:Library
Library/.DS_Store
path:Library/Caches
path:Library/Preferences
path:Library/Preferences/.GlobalPreferences.plist
path:Library/Preferences/com.apple.PeoplePicker.plist
path:tmp
```

Moving, Copying, and Deleting Files

You often require moving, copying, and deleting files. The code in Listing 9-4 illustrates accomplishing all three.

Listing 9-4 Code illustrating several file manipulation methods

```
- (void) viewDidLoad {
  NSString * fileDir = [[NSBundle mainBundle] pathForResource:@"test1"
ofType:@"txt"];
  NSError * myError = nil;
  NSArray * myPaths = NSSearchPathForDirectoriesInDomains (NSDocumentDirectory,
NSUserDomainMask, YES);
  NSString * myDocPath = [[myPaths objectAtIndex:0]
stringByAppendingPathComponent:@"test.txt"];
  if([[NSFileManager defaultManager] fileExistsAtPath:myDocPath]) {
    [[NSFileManager defaultManager] removeItemAtPath:myDocPath error:&myError];
  }
  if(myError != nil) {
    NSLog([myError localizedDescription]);
    [myError release];
  }
```

```
  else {
    [[NSFileManager defaultManager] copyItemAtPath:fileDir toPath:myDocPath
error:&myError];
    if(myError != nil) {
      NSLog([myError localizedDescription]);
      [myError release];
    }
    else {
      if([[NSFileManager defaultManager] fileExistsAtPath:myDocPath])
        NSLog(@"file exists");
    }
  }
}
```

The code in Listing 9-4 first checks to see if the file exists by using the `fileExistsAtPath:` method. Trying to copy a file to a location where the file already exists is an error, and so you delete the file if it exists using the `removeItemAtPath:error:` method.

```
if([[NSFileManager defaultManager] fileExistsAtPath:myDocPath]) {
  [[NSFileManager defaultManager] removeItemAtPath:myDocPath error:&myError];
}
```

The code in Listing 9-4 then copies the file to the documents directory.

```
[[NSFileManager defaultManager] copyItemAtPath:fileDir toPath:myDocPath
error:&myError];
```

There is also a `moveItemAtPath:toPath:error:` method if you wish to move an item rather than copy it. The following Try This illustrates moving and copying a file.

Try This Moving and Copying a File from the Bundle to Documents Directory

1. Create a new View-based application. Name the application **UsingFileManager**.
2. Add two text files, named **test1.txt** and **test2.txt**, to the Resources group in your file. Create the files by selecting Other | Empty File from the New File dialog (Figure 9-2).
3. Open UsingFileManagerViewController.m and modify the `viewDidLoad` method so that it moves test1.txt to the application's documents directory (Listing 9-5).

(continued)

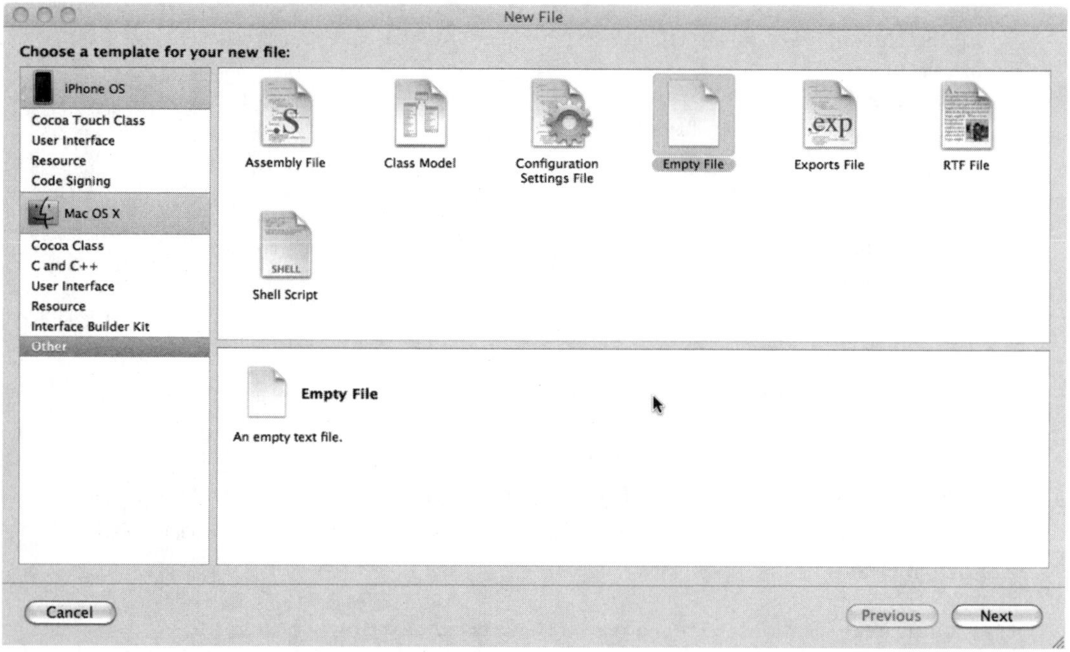

Figure 9-2 Creating a text file

4. Implement the `viewDidAppear:animated:` method so that it moves test2.txt to the documents directory.
5. Build and Run the application. Listing 9-6 contains the debugger console logging.

Listing 9-5 UsingFileManagerViewController.m

```
#import "UsingFileManagerViewController.h"
@implementation UsingFileManagerViewController
- (void) viewDidLoad {
  NSString * pathToFileOne = [[NSBundle mainBundle] pathForResource:@"test1"
ofType:@"txt"];
  NSLog(@"Path to test1.txt in bundle:%@", pathToFileOne);
  NSArray * myPaths =
NSSearchPathForDirectoriesInDomains(NSDocumentDirectory,NSUserDomainMask, YES);
  NSString * pathToDoc = [[myPaths objectAtIndex:0]
stringByAppendingPathComponent:@"test1.txt"];
```

```
  if(![[NSFileManager defaultManager] fileExistsAtPath:pathToDoc]) {
    NSError * myError = nil;
    [[NSFileManager defaultManager] copyItemAtPath:pathToFileOne toPath:pathToDoc
error:&myError];
    if(myError != nil) {
      NSLog([myError localizedDescription]);
      [myError release];
    }
    else {
      BOOL fileExistsInDoc = [[NSFileManager defaultManager]
fileExistsAtPath:[pathToDoc stringByAppendingPathComponent:@"test1.txt"]];
      NSLog(@"Was the file moved successfully:%i", fileExistsInDoc);
    }
  }
}
- (void) viewDidAppear:(BOOL)animated {
  [super viewDidAppear:animated];
  NSString * pathToFileTwo = [[NSBundle mainBundle] pathForResource:@"test2"
ofType:@"txt"];
  NSLog(@"Path to test2.txt in bundle:%@", pathToFileTwo);
  NSArray * myPaths =
NSSearchPathForDirectoriesInDomains(NSDocumentDirectory,NSUserDomainMask, YES);
  NSString * pathToDoc = [[myPaths objectAtIndex:0]
stringByAppendingPathComponent:@"test2.txt"];
  if([[NSFileManager defaultManager] fileExistsAtPath:pathToDoc]==NO &&
[[NSFileManager defaultManager] fileExistsAtPath:pathToFileTwo]==YES) {
    NSError * myError2 = nil;
    [[NSFileManager defaultManager] moveItemAtPath:pathToFileTwo toPath:pathToDoc
error:&myError2];
    if(myError2 != nil) {
      NSLog([myError2 localizedDescription]);
      [myError2 release];
    }
  }
}
- (void)dealloc {
  [super dealloc];
}
@end
```

(continued)

Listing 9-6 Debugger console logging

```
2009-12-05 13:03:36.111 UsingFileManager[567:207] Path to test1.txt in
bundle:/Users/jamesbrannan/Library/Application Support/iPhone
Simulator/User/Applications/00AE5314-B3E7-4D22-B04A-
F197AC851527/UsingFileManager.app/test1.txt
2009-12-05 13:03:36.114 UsingFileManager[567:207] Was the file moved
successfully:0
2009-12-05 13:03:36.116 UsingFileManager[567:207] Path to test2.txt in
bundle:/Users/jamesbrannan/Library/Application Support/iPhone
Simulator/User/Applications/00AE5314-B3E7-4D22-B04A-
F197AC851527/UsingFileManager.app/test2.txt
```

The `viewDidLoad` method copies test1.txt.

```
[[NSFileManager defaultManager] copyItemAtPath:pathToFileOne toPath:pathToDoc
error:&myError];
```

The `viewDidAppear` method moves test2.txt.

```
[[NSFileManager defaultManager] moveItemAtPath:pathToFileTwo toPath:pathToDoc
error:&myError2];
```

Note that the `move` method moves the file, and the file no longer exists in the bundle. The `copy` method, in contrast, makes a file copy, and so it still exists in the bundle.

NSString, Paths, and Text Files

The `NSString` class has many methods that make manipulating paths easier. It also has methods for loading a file's text content into a string. In this section you explore `NSString`'s file-related methods.

NSString from a File

You can initialize a string using the `stringWithContentsOfFile:encoding:error:` convenience constructor or the `initWithContentsOfFile:usedEncoding:error:init` method. The `usedEncoding` parameter specifies the text file's encoding. For more information on this method refer to `NSString`'s reference guide. For most purposes, if not all, on the iPhone you use `NSUTF8StringEncoding`. The following code illustrates using the initializer method.

```
NSString * secondString = [[NSString alloc] initWithContentsOfFile:filePath
encoding:NSUTF8StringEncoding error:&myError];
```

stringByAppendingPathComponent:

You have already used the `stringByAppendingPathComponent:` method. This method safely appends a path component to a preexisting path. If you have ever worked with paths, then you realize this method's importance. For instance, suppose you had a string that contains a path. Does the path end with the last directory name or a forward slash?

```
/Users/James/myfolder
/Users/James/myfolder/
```

If the path ends with a slash, and you wished to add "test.txt" to the path, you would append only "test.txt" to the path. But if the path ends with the directory name, you would append "/test.txt" to the path. You avoid this problem using the `stringByAppendingPathComponent:` method. The following code snippet illustrates a pattern you repeat often when programming iPhone applications.

```
NSArray * myPaths =
NSSearchPathForDirectoriesInDomains(NSDocumentDirectory,NSUserDomainMask, YES);
NSString * pathToDoc = [[myPaths objectAtIndex:0]
stringByAppendingPathComponent:@"test.txt"];
```

The preceding code first gets the path to an application's document directory. It then appends the filename test.txt to the path. You can then access the file using the path.

isAbsolutepath

The `isAbsolutePath` method checks if a string's value is a fully qualified path. The following code illustrates:

```
NSString * homeDir = NSHomeDirectory();
NSLog(@"the home directory:%@", homeDir);
if([pA isAbsolutePath]== YES)
  NSLog(@"It is an absolute path.");
```

lastPathComponent

The `lastPathComponent` method strips the last path component from an `NSString` that contains a path. For instance, the last path component of the following path is Library:

```
/Users/jamesbrannan/Library
```

If an `NSString` contains the string `"/Users/jamesbrannan/Library/"`, then the last path component would be /. Of course this method is most useful for obtaining a filename from a path. The following code snippet would log "test1.txt" to the debugger console:

```
NSString * pathToFile = [[NSBundle mainBundle] pathForResource:|
@"test1" ofType:@"txt"];
NSLog(@"last path comp:%@", [pathToFile lastPathComponent]);
```

pathComponents

You can also obtain the path components of an `NSString` as an `NSArray`. The following code illustrates:

```
NSString * pathToFile = [[NSBundle mainBundle] pathForResource:@"test1"
ofType:@"txt"];
NSArray * components = [pathToFile pathComponents];
NSString * myEnum = nil;
for(myEnum in components) {...}
```

pathExtension

The `pathExtension` method is an `NSString` method for extracting a file extension from a path in an `NSString`. For instance, the following code creates a string with a path to the test1.txt file and then extracts `txt` from the string.

```
NSString * pathToFile = [[NSBundle mainBundle] pathForResource:@"test1"
ofType:@"txt"];
NSLog(@"path extension:%@", [pathToFile pathExtension]);
```

writeToFile:atomically:encoding:error:

`NSString` can write its content directly to a file using the `writeToFile:atomically:encoding:error:` method.

```
[myString writeToFile:filePath atomically:NO encoding:NSUTF8StringEncoding
error:&myError];
```

NOTE

The `atomically` parameter specifies if the string should first write to a temporary file, before moving the data to the specified file. This helps avoid data corruption.

Try This Writing a Simple Text File

1. Create a new View-based application named **FileReader**.
2. Open FileReaderViewController.h and add a `UITextView` as an outlet (Listing 9-7).
3. Save the file and open FileReaderViewController.xib in Interface Builder.
4. Drag a `UITextView` from the library to the view's canvas (Figure 9-3).

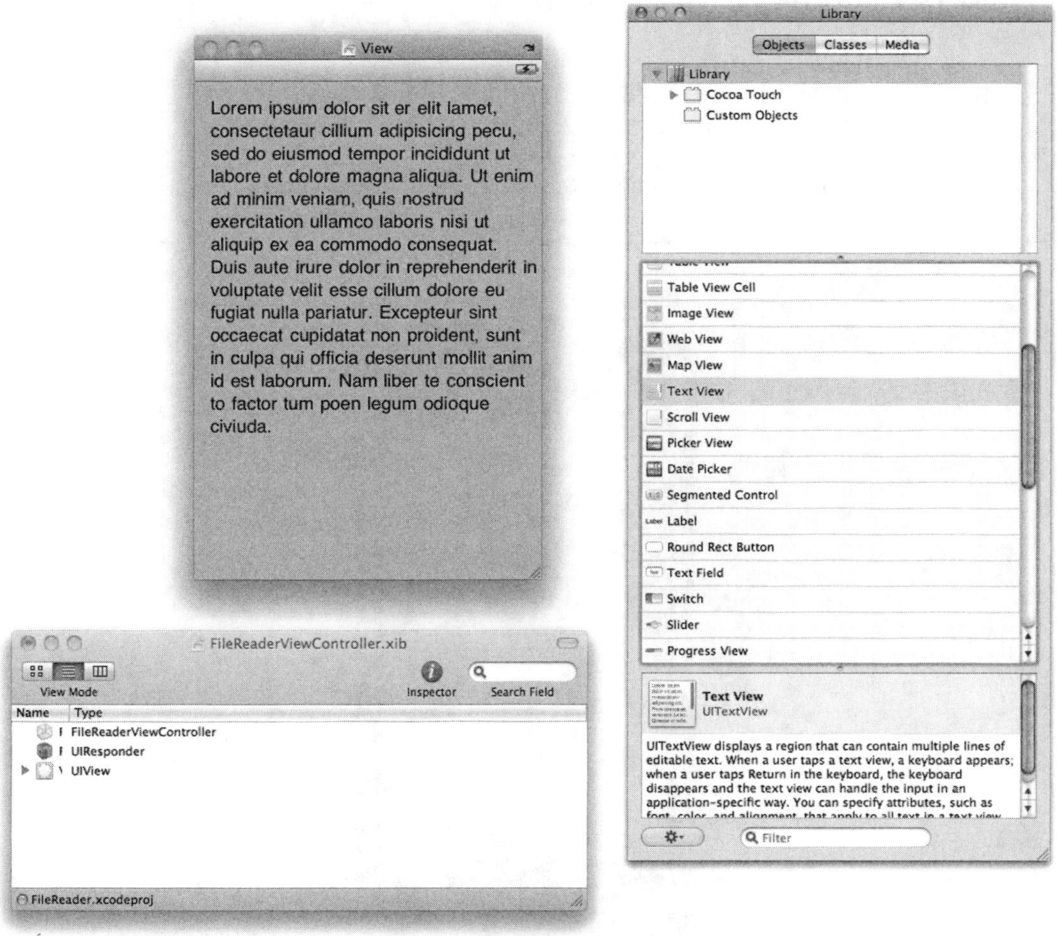

Figure 9-3 Adding a `UITextView`

(continued)

5. Connect File's Owner `myTextView` outlet to the text view just added to the canvas.
6. Save and exit Interface Builder.
7. Open FileReaderViewController.m in Xcode and implement the `viewDidLoad` method (Listing 9-8). Do not forget to synthesize `myTextView`.
8. Build and Run the application. The text in the `UITextView` is the text from the `viewDidLoad` method (Figure 9-4).

Listing 9-7 FileReaderViewController.h

```
#import <UIKit/UIKit.h>
@interface FileReaderViewController : UIViewController {
  IBOutlet UITextView * myTextView;
}
@property (nonatomic, retain) UITextView * myTextView;
@end
```

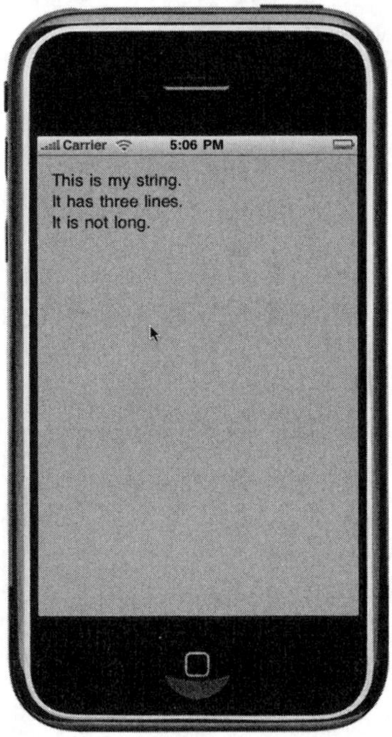

Figure 9-4 The text view containing the text set in `viewDidLoad`

Listing 9-8 FileReaderViewController.m

```
#import "FileReaderViewController.h"
@implementation FileReaderViewController
@synthesize myTextView;
- (void) viewDidLoad {
  [super viewDidLoad];
  NSString * filePath = [NSTemporaryDirectory()
stringByAppendingPathComponent:@"simple.txt"];
  NSString * myString = @"This is my string.\nIt has three lines.\nIt is not
long.";
  NSError * myError = nil;
  [myString writeToFile:filePath atomically:NO encoding:NSUTF8StringEncoding
error:&myError];
  if(myError == nil) {
    NSString * secondString = [[NSString alloc] initWithContentsOfFile:filePath
encoding:NSUTF8StringEncoding error:&myError];
    if(myError == nil) {
      self.myTextView.text = secondString;
    }
  }
}
- (void)dealloc {
  [self.myTextView release];
  [super dealloc];
}
@end
```

Listing 9-8 illustrates several string file–related functions. In the `viewDidLoad` method, the view controller first obtains a path to the temporary directory and then appends a filename to the path.

```
NSString * filePath = [NSTemporaryDirectory()
stringByAppendingPathComponent:@"simple.txt"];
```

After creating a string containing three lines, it writes the file. Note that you do not first check to ensure the file does not exist; the temporary directory is cleared each time you run the application, and so you are guaranteed the file doesn't exist.

```
[myString writeToFile:filePath atomically:NO encoding:NSUTF8StringEncoding
error:&myError];
```

(continued)

After writing the file, it reads the file into another string and then sets the UITextView's text to the newly created string.

```
NSString * secondString = [[NSString alloc] initWithContentsOfFile:filePath
encoding:NSUTF8StringEncoding error:&myError];
```

Not very practical, but it illustrates reading and writing using an NSString.

NSData

The NSData class holds binary data. As with NSString, you can initialize NSData with the contents of a file; only instead of loading the file as text data, it loads the data as binary. Because it loads the file as binary data, you can load any file into NSData. Thus, NSData is useful for working with images and multimedia.

The NSData class has convenience constructors. One you use often is the dataWithContentsOfFile: method. This method creates and initializes an NSData object with the binary content of a file. For instance, the following code snippet obtains the image file, babelfish.png, from an application's bundle and then creates an NSData instance with the file's content.

```
NSData * tempData = [NSData dataWithContentsOfFile:[[NSBundle mainBundle]
pathForResource:@"babelfish" ofType:@"png"]];
```

NOTE

Both NSString and NSData have several methods for working with URLs in addition to files. Refer to both classes' documentation for more detail.

The NSData class can hold anything, as everything is binary. One common development pattern you use when developing an iPhone application is placing your app's images in the bundle. You then dynamically load a UIImageView control with an image obtained from the bundle.

Audio data is something you work with often as binary data. For instance, suppose you wished to play a system sound. You must load the data into an NSData class first. The following Try This illustrates.

NOTE

For more information on Audio handling, refer to *iPhone SDK Programming: A Beginner's Guide* and Apple's online documentation.

Try This Reading and Writing a Binary File

1. Create a new View-based application named **ImageWriting**.
2. Add the AudioToolbox framework to your application's Frameworks group. Right-click Frameworks and choose Add | Existing Frameworks and then select AudioToolbox.framework from the frameworks list (Figure 9-5).
3. Add bug.png and beginworkout.aiff to the application's Resources group.
4. Open ImageWritingViewController.h in Xcode and add a `UIImageView` as a property (Listing 9-9). Also import the audio toolbox header files.
5. Add a declaration for an `IBAction` named `playSound`.
6. Save the file and then open ImageWritingViewController.xib in Interface Builder.

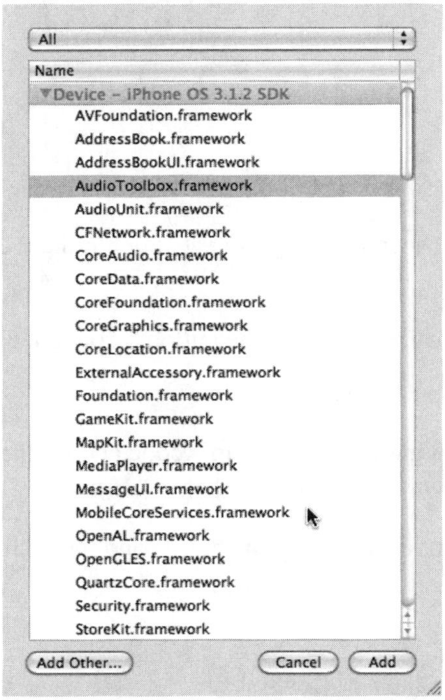

Figure 9-5 Adding the AudioToolbox framework

(continued)

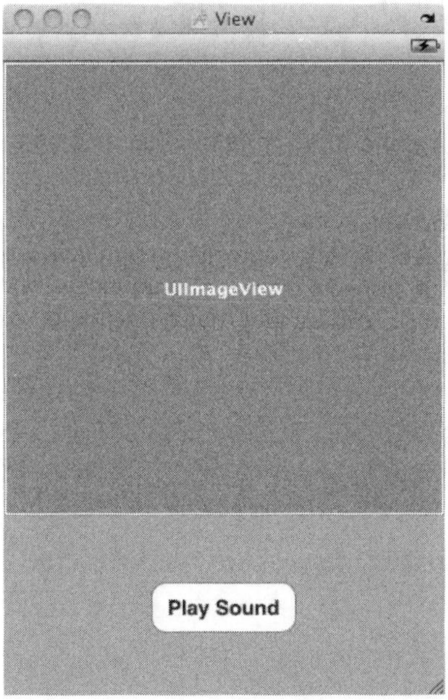

Figure 9-6 The `UIImageView` and button on the view's canvas

7. Add a `UIImageView` and a button to the view's canvas (Figure 9-6).
8. Connect the File's Owner `myImageView` outlet to the `UIImageView` added to the canvas.
9. Connect the `playSound` action to the button's Touch Up Inside event.
10. Save and exit Interface Builder.
11. Open ImageWritingViewController.m in Xcode and synthesize `myImageView`. Also implement the `playSound` method (Listing 9-10).
12. Build and Run the application. Tap the button and the image appears and the sound plays (Figure 9-7).

Listing 9-9 ImageWritingViewController.h

```
#import <UIKit/UIKit.h>
#import <AudioToolbox/AudioToolbox.h>
@interface ImageWritingViewController : UIViewController {
```

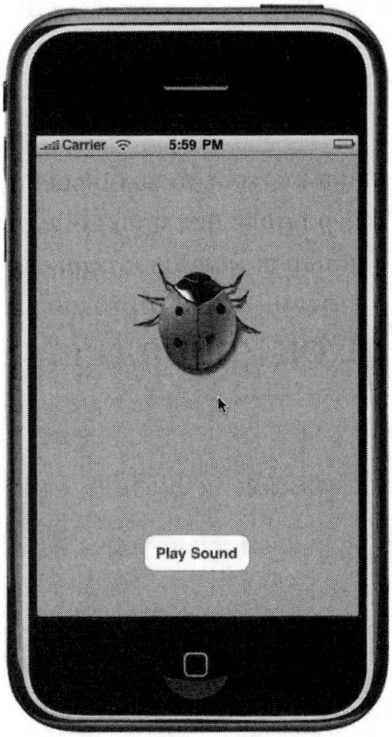

Figure 9-7 Running the application in the simulator

```
  IBOutlet UIImageView * myImageView;
}
@property (nonatomic,retain) UIImageView * myImageView;
- (IBAction) playSound:(id) sender;
@end
```

Listing 9-10 ImageWritingViewController.m

```
#import "ImageWritingViewController.h"
@implementation ImageWritingViewController
@synthesize myImageView;
- (IBAction) playSound:(id) sender {
  NSData * myImage = [NSData dataWithContentsOfFile:[[NSBundle mainBundle]
pathForResource:@"bug" ofType:@"png"]];
  self.myImageView.image = [UIImage imageWithData:myImage];
  NSString *pathBegin = [[NSBundle mainBundle] pathForResource:@"beginworkout"
ofType:@"aiff"];
```

(continued)

```
  NSData * myData = [NSData dataWithContentsOfFile:pathBegin];
  [myData writeToFile:[NSTemporaryDirectory()
stringByAppendingString:@"beginworkout.aiff"] atomically:NO];
  SystemSoundID soundID;
  NSURL *filePath = [NSURL fileURLWithPath:[NSTemporaryDirectory()
stringByAppendingString:@"beginworkout.aiff"] isDirectory:NO];
  AudioServicesCreateSystemSoundID((CFURLRef)filePath, &soundID);
  AudioServicesPlaySystemSound(soundID);
}
- (void)dealloc {
  self.myImageView = nil;
  [super dealloc];
}
@end
```

The NSData class can also load an image into a UIImage using the UIImage's initWithContentsOfFile: method. The following Try This illustrates. However, it also illustrates one of the more confusing things for new iPhone developers; there are multiple ways to do everything. For instance, when you create a UIImage, there are at least three different ways you might initialize the image.

Try This Loading a UIImage Three Different Ways

1. Create a new View-based application named **ImageMoving**.
2. Add the babelfish.png, bug.png, and katuberling.png images to the project's Resources folder.
3. Open ImageMovingViewController.h in Xcode and add a UIImageView as an IBOutlet. Also add a IBAction declaration named changeImage (Listing 9-11).
4. Save the file.
5. Open ImageMovingViewController.xib in Interface Builder.
6. Add a UIImageView to the view's canvas and size it so it takes the top half of the canvas.
7. Select babelfish.png for the UIImageView's image (Figure 9-8).
8. Add a UIButton to the view's bottom half (Figure 9-9).

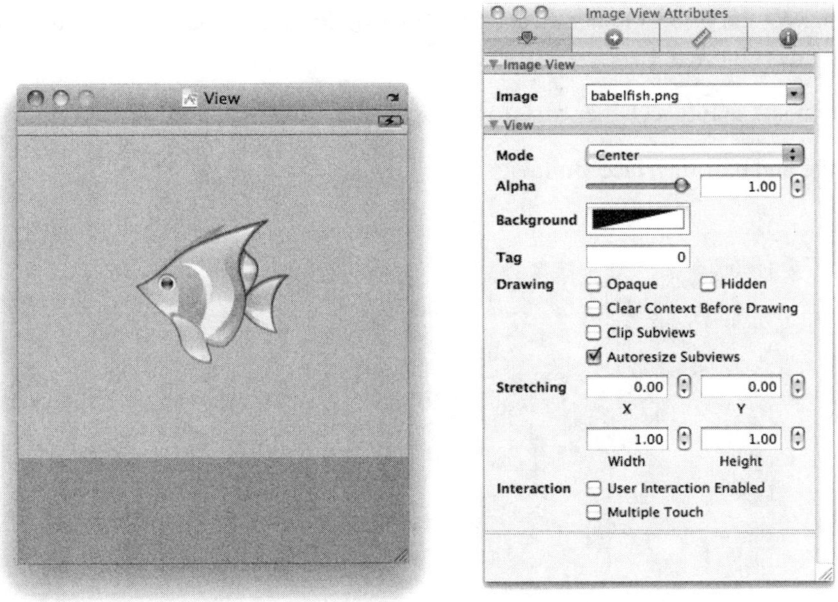

Figure 9-8 Adding a `UIImageView` to a view's canvas

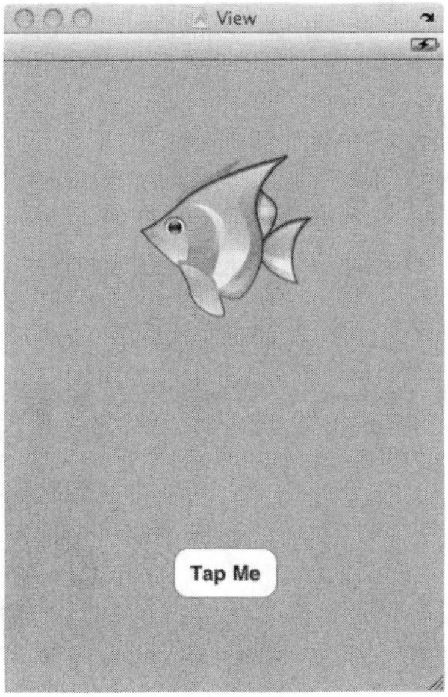

Figure 9-9 Adding a `UIButton`

(continued)

9. Connect the File's Owner `myImageView` outlet to the image view added to the canvas (Figure 9-10).
10. Connect the File's Owner `changeImage` action to the button's Touch Up Inside event.
11. Save and exit Interface Builder.

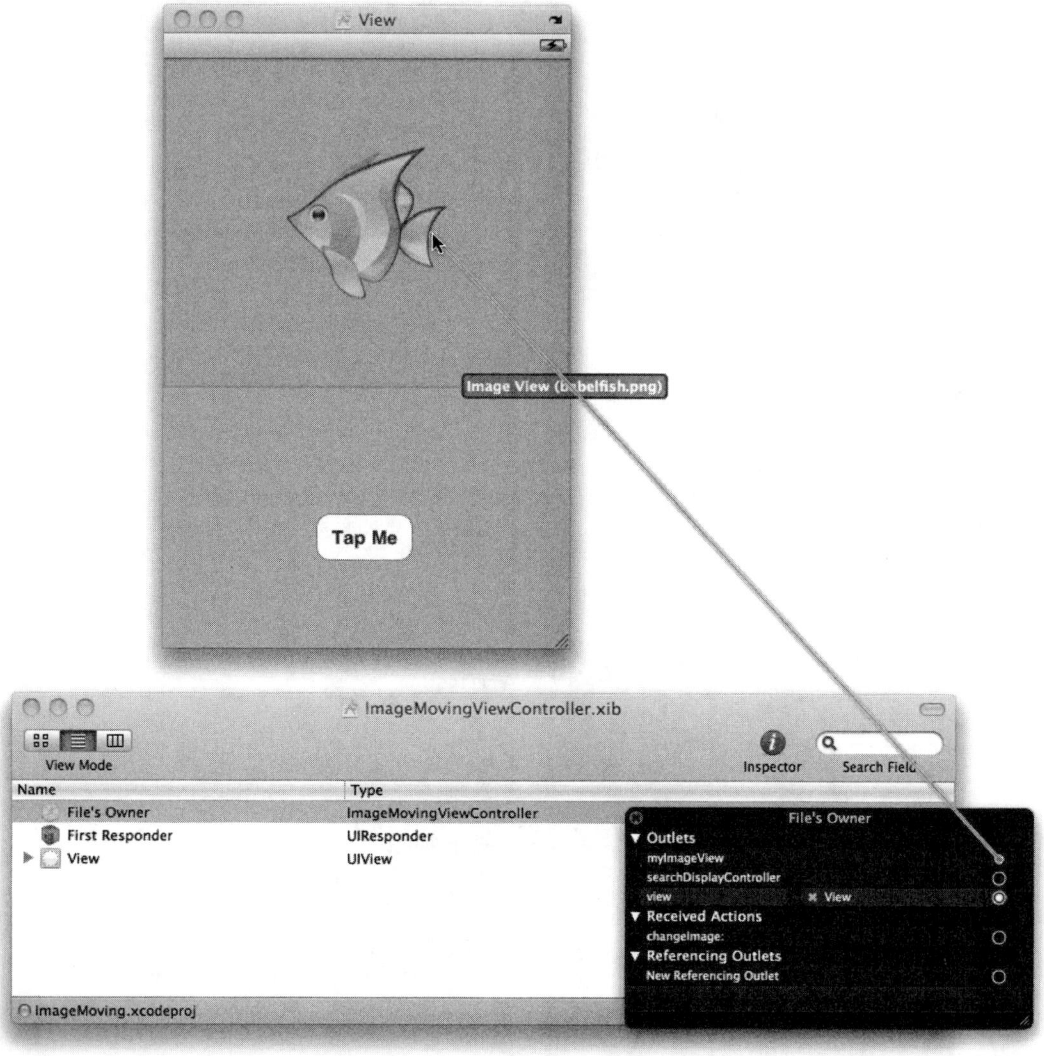

Figure 9-10 Connecting the `myImageView` outlet

12. Open ImageMovingViewController.m and synthesize the `myImageView`. Also implement the `changeImage` method (Listing 9-12).

13. Build and Run. Click the button and notice the application loops through the images (Figure 9-11).

Listing 9-11 ImageMovingViewController.h

```
#import <UIKit/UIKit.h>
@interface ImageMovingViewController : UIViewController {
  IBOutlet UIImageView * myImageView;
}
@property (nonatomic, retain) UIImageView * myImageView;
- (IBAction) changeImage:(id) sender;
@end
```

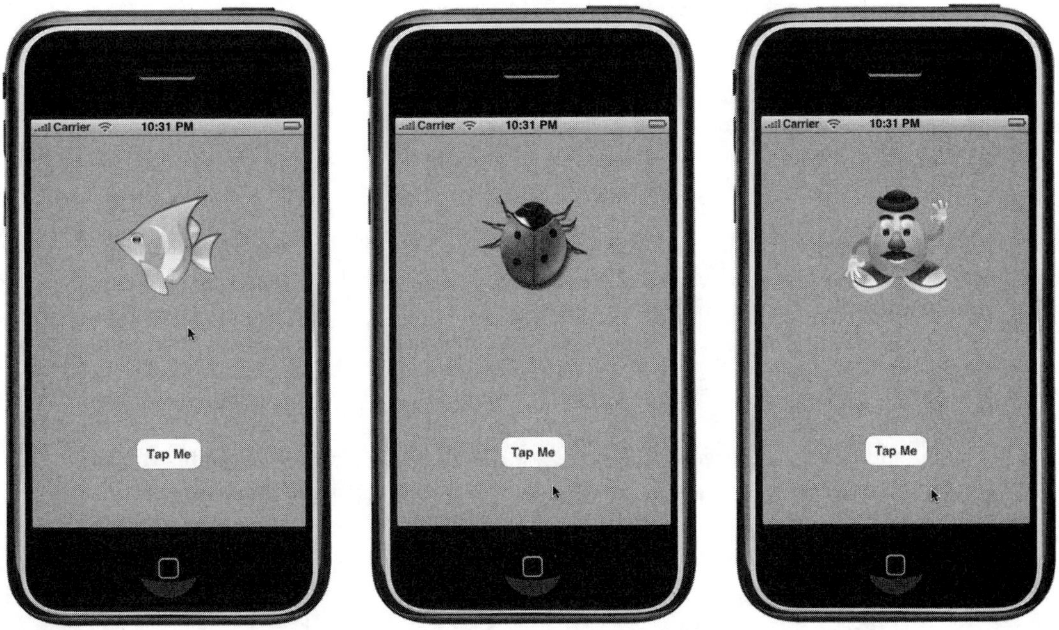

Figure 9-11 The application running in the simulator

(continued)

Listing 9-12 ImageMovingViewController.m

```
#import "ImageMovingViewController.h"
@implementation ImageMovingViewController
@synthesize myImageView;
static int clicks = 0;
- (IBAction) changeImage:(id) sender {
  UIImage * tempImage = nil;
  switch (clicks) {
    case 0:
      tempImage = [UIImage imageNamed:@"bug.png"];
      break;
    case 1:
      tempImage = [[[UIImage alloc] initWithContentsOfFile:[[NSBundle mainBundle]
pathForResource:@"katuberling" ofType:@"png"]] autorelease];
      break;
    case 2: {
      NSData * tempData = [NSData dataWithContentsOfFile:[[NSBundle mainBundle]
pathForResource:@"babelfish" ofType:@"png"]];
      tempImage = [UIImage imageWithData:tempData];
      clicks = -1;
      break;
    }
  }
  clicks++;
  self.myImageView.image = tempImage;
}
- (void)dealloc {
  [myImageView release];
  [super dealloc];
}
@end
```

The code illustrates three different ways to load a `UIImage`. If the image is in the resource bundle, then you can obtain the image directly using the `imageNamed:` method.

```
tempImage = [UIImage imageNamed:@"bug.png"];
```

You can also use the image's convenience initializer.

```
tempImage = [[[UIImage alloc] initWithContentsOfFile:[[NSBundle mainBundle]
pathForResource:@"katuberling" ofType:@"png"]] autorelease];
```

This code snippet loads a path for the image in the resource bundle. It then initializes the `UIImage` by opening the file specified by the path.

If you wished, you might create an image from `NSData`.

```
NSData * tempData = [NSData dataWithContentsOfFile:[[NSBundle mainBundle]
pathForResource:@"babelfish" ofType:@"png"]];
tempImage = [UIImage imageWithData:tempData];
```

There is no single correct way to load an image. Of course, as you gain experience, differing circumstances will dictate using different methods. For instance, the `UIImage imageNamed` method loads an image into a cache that the operating system can then quickly reference the image from, so you should use this method only if you wish the operating system to cache an image while your program is running.

Summary

In this chapter you explored file handling on the iPhone. When you write an iPhone application, you can only write files to directories in your application's sandbox. The `NSFileManager` has many methods for working with files and directories. The `NSString` and `NSData` classes both have methods for working with files and directories also.

An application's bundle is where Xcode places items in the Resources grouping in Xcode. You obtain these resources using the `NSBundle`. But before you can modify a resource in your application's bundle, you must copy or move the resource to another directory such as your documents or tmp directory.

You could, of course, always use the C lower-level file handling functions, but the higher-level Foundation framework classes are easier to work with. You barely scratched the surface of the Foundation framework's many file handling techniques. For more information you should refer to each class' relevant documentation.

Chapter 10

Property Lists, NSCopy, and Archiving

Key Skills & Concepts

- Understanding Property-List Objects
- Serializing Objects Using `writeToFile:atomically:`
- Deserializing Objects Using `readFromFile:atomically:`
- Writing Your Own Serializable Classes

In the last chapter you saw how to easily write data stored in an `NSString` or `NSData` object to a file. As you learn in this chapter, you could do that because these classes are both property-list classes. A property-list object is an instance of a class that you can persist and reconstitute from a property-list file. In this chapter you explore property-list classes. You also learn how to persist several classes together as a single property list. Property lists are an easy means of storing your application's state to a file so that its state can easily be reconstituted the next time a user runs your application.

After learning property lists, you then learn how to persist your own custom objects using archiving. Archiving allows you to persist custom objects that implement the `NSCoding` protocol. You can persist both single objects and also an arbitrary number of objects using archiving. In this chapter you do both.

Property Lists

Mac and iPhone applications often rely heavily upon property lists. A *property list* is an object hierarchy that you can persist and reconstitute from a file for the `NSArray`, `NSDictionary`, `NSString`, `NSData`, `NSDate`, and `NSNumber` classes (or their mutable equivalents). When persisting one of the collection classes, its constituents must also be one of the property-list classes.

When you persist an array or dictionary (i.e., a property list with multiple values), the plist's underlying format is XML. For instance, Listing 10-1 shows an `NSArray` and its corresponding XML file.

Listing 10-1 An array and its plist

```
NSArray * myArray = [[NSArray alloc] initWithObjects:@"first", @"second",
@"third",nil];
```

```
<?xml version="1.0" encoding="UTF-8"?>
<!DOCTYPE plist PUBLIC "-//Apple//DTD PLIST 1.0//EN"
"http://www.apple.com/DTDs/PropertyList-1.0.dtd">
<plist version="1.0">
<array>
  <string>first</string>
  <string>second</string>
  <string>third</string>
</array>
</plist>
```

Because the file is XML, you can modify the file easily using other languages' XML APIs. Table 10-1 lists the Foundation classes that are serializable to a plist and each element's corresponding XML element.

Writing a Property List

Each class listed in Table 10-1 can be serialized to a property list using the class' `writeToFile:atomically:error:` method. Property lists can also be de-serialized into the appropriate property-list object using the `<datatype>WithContentsOfFile:` convenienience constructor or equivalent initializer method.

```
- (BOOL)writeToFile:(NSString *)path atomically:(BOOL)flag
- (id)initWithContentsOfFile:(NSString *)aPath
```

Foundation Class	XML Element
NSArray	<array>
NSDictionary	<dict>
NSData	<data>
NSDate	<date>
NSNumber – storing integer	<integer>
NSNumber – storing float	<real>
NSNumber – storing Boolean	<true/> or <false/>

Table 10-1 Property-List Classes

Note that there is some slight variation in NSString's writeToFile:atomically: method, which is actually the writeToFile:atomically:encoding:error: method, as you must specify the string's encoding.

```
- (BOOL)writeToFile:(NSString *)path atomically:(BOOL)useAuxiliaryFile
encoding:(NSStringEncoding)enc error:(NSError **)error
```

Note that NSNumber and NSDate have no methods for reading and writing to a file. Property lists are meant for preserving lists of values; writing a single numeric value or date to a file doesn't really make sense. Besides, you really should simply use NSString instead.

```
NSString * myValue = [myNumber stringValue];
[myValue writeToFile:"xyz.plist" atomically:NO error:nil];
```

NOTE

You can also write to a URL using a property-list object's writeToURL:atomically: method.

Reading a Property List

You can read the property list back into its representative property-list object(s) using either a convenience constructor or a custom initializer method. For instance, to reconstitute an NSArray from a plist file, you could use either technique.

```
NSArray * myArray = [NSArray arrayWithContentsOfFile:myPathToPlistFile];
NSArray * myArray  = [[NSArray alloc] initWithContentsOfFile:myPathToPlistFile];
```

Remember, though, the convenience constructor doesn't give you ownership of the underlying object. You must explicitly retain it if you wish to persist the object for any time period. Of course, if you set the value to a property, behind the scenes Objective-C handles that for you in the property's setter method.

The following Try This illustrates persisting and reconstituting an NSArray from a property list.

Try This Preserving an NSArray to a Property List

1. Create a new Utility Application named PropertiesExample.

2. Right-click Resources and then select Add | New File and select Property List from the New File dialog (Figure 10-1). Name the file **myproperties**; this creates a file named myproperties.plist.

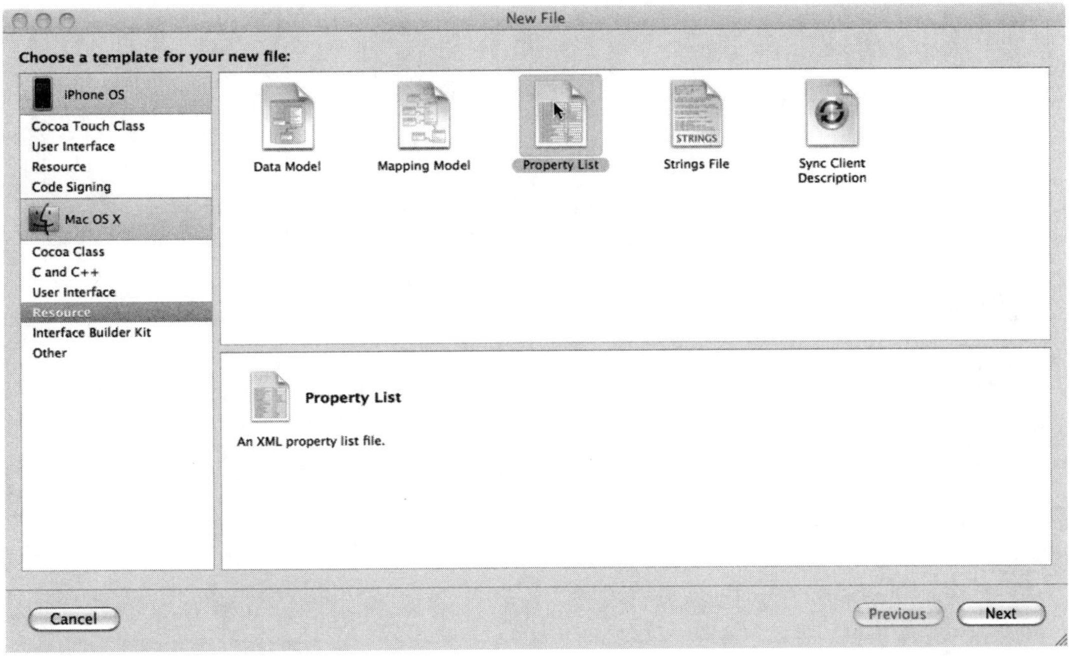

Figure 10-1 Creating a property list in Xcode

3. Open the file in Xcode and click the Root element to highlight it and change its type to Array.
4. Click the button with three small lines that is to the right of the Root row to add a new row.
5. Change the element's value to "Tom" and then add two more rows with "Sue" and "Beth" as the values (Figure 10-2).
6. Open MainViewController.m and implement the `viewDidAppear:` and `viewDidDisappear:` methods so that they read and then write the array to a property list (Listing 10-2).
7. Build and Run the application. Navigate between the two screens and note that the values logged to the debugger console change (Listing 10-3).

(continued)

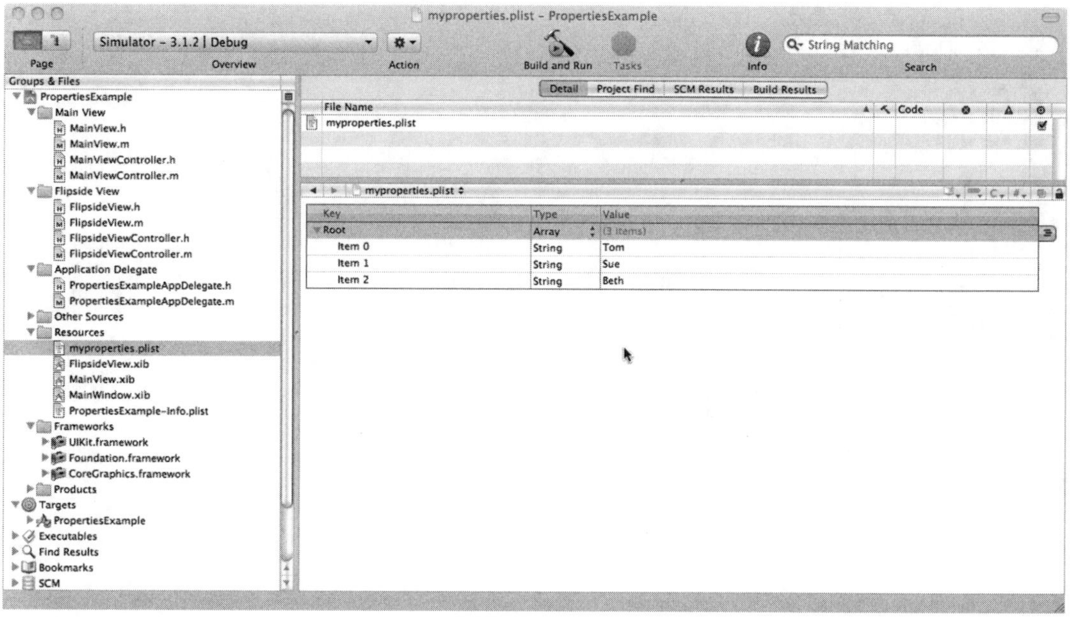

Figure 10-2 Property list in Xcode

Listing 10-2 MainViewController.m

```
#import "MainViewController.h"
#import "MainView.h"
@implementation MainViewController
- (void) viewDidAppear: (BOOL) animated {
  [super viewDidAppear:animated];
  NSString * originalPath = [[NSBundle mainBundle] pathForResource:@"myproperties"
ofType:@"plist"];
  NSString * path = nil;
  path = [(NSString *) [NSSearchPathForDirectoriesInDomains(NSDocumentDirectory,
NSUserDomainMask, YES) objectAtIndex:0]
stringByAppendingPathComponent:@"myproperties.plist"];
  if(![[NSFileManager defaultManager] fileExistsAtPath:path]) {
    [[NSFileManager defaultManager] moveItemAtPath:originalPath toPath:path
error:nil];
  }
  NSString * tempValue;
  NSArray * myArray = [NSArray arrayWithContentsOfFile:path];
  NSEnumerator * myEnum = [myArray objectEnumerator];
```

```
    while(tempValue = [myEnum nextObject]) {
      NSLog(@"The value:%@", tempValue);
    }
}
- (void) viewDidDisappear: (BOOL) animated {
    [super viewDidDisappear:animated];
    NSString * path = nil;
    path = [(NSString *) [NSSearchPathForDirectoriesInDomains(NSDocumentDirectory,
NSUserDomainMask, YES) objectAtIndex:0]
stringByAppendingPathComponent:@"myproperties.plist"];
    NSArray * myArray = [[NSArray alloc] initWithObjects:@"James", @"Roger",
@"Steve", nil];
    [myArray writeToFile:path atomically:NO];
}
- (void)flipsideViewControllerDidFinish:(FlipsideViewController *)controller {
    [self dismissModalViewControllerAnimated:YES];
}
- (IBAction)showInfo {
    FlipsideViewController *controller = [[FlipsideViewController alloc]
initWithNibName:@"FlipsideView" bundle:nil];
    controller.delegate = self;
    controller.modalTransitionStyle = UIModalTransitionStyleFlipHorizontal;
    [self presentModalViewController:controller animated:YES];
    [controller release];
}
- (void)dealloc {
    [super dealloc];
}
@end
```

Listing 10-3 Debugger console logging

```
The value:Tom
The value:Sue
The value:Beth
The value:James
The value:Roger
The value:Steve
```

The first time the view appears, the application copies the plist file from the application's bundle to the Documents directory. Remember, an application's bundle is read-only and so you must copy the file to the application's Documents directory.

```
[[NSFileManager defaultManager] moveItemAtPath:originalPath toPath:path
error:nil];
```

(continued)

The application then initializes an `NSArray` with the file's contents.

```
NSArray * myArray = [NSArray arrayWithContentsOfFile:path];
```

When the main view disappears, the application writes the array's content to the myproperties.plist file. This overwrites the previous plist with the new values.

```
NSArray * myArray = [[NSArray alloc] initWithObjects:@"James", @"Roger",
@"Steve", nil];
[myArray writeToFile:path atomically:NO];
```

Don't take the preceding Try This to suggest that you must create a plist using Xcode. In the next Try This you programmatically create and then reconstitute a dictionary using a property list.

Try This Creating and Reading a Property List Programmatically

1. Create a new View-based application named MyProperties.
2. Open MyPropertiesViewController.h and add `IBOutlets` for a `UIBarButtonItem` and two `UITextFields` (Listing 10-4).
3. Create a method declaration named `loadPersistProperties` and another named `doneEditing`. Make both `IBActions`.
4. Open MyPropertiesViewController.m and synthesize the created properties (Listing 10-5).
5. Save or build the application and then open MyPropertiesViewController.xib in Interface Builder.
6. Add two `UITextFields` and a `UIToolbar` to the view's canvas (Figure 10-3). Double-click the bar button to change its title to "Load Properties."

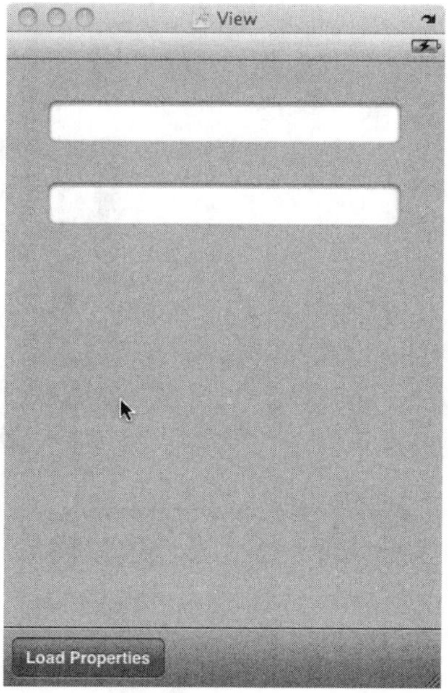

Figure 10-3 Adding two buttons and a toolbar

7. Connect the File's Owner text fields to the text fields on the view's canvas. Do the same for the button.
8. Connect the button to the File's Owner `loadPersistProperties` action.
9. Connect the `doneEditing` action to both text fields and select the "Did End On Exit" option for both fields (Figure 10-4).
10. Build and Run the application. Enter a comma-delimited list of names and jobs (Figure 10-5).
11. Tap the button and nothing happens. Although not acceptable in a real-world application, just tap the button a second time and the application persists the data.
12. Shut down the application and restart it. Click the button and it loads the data from the last time you ran the application.

(continued)

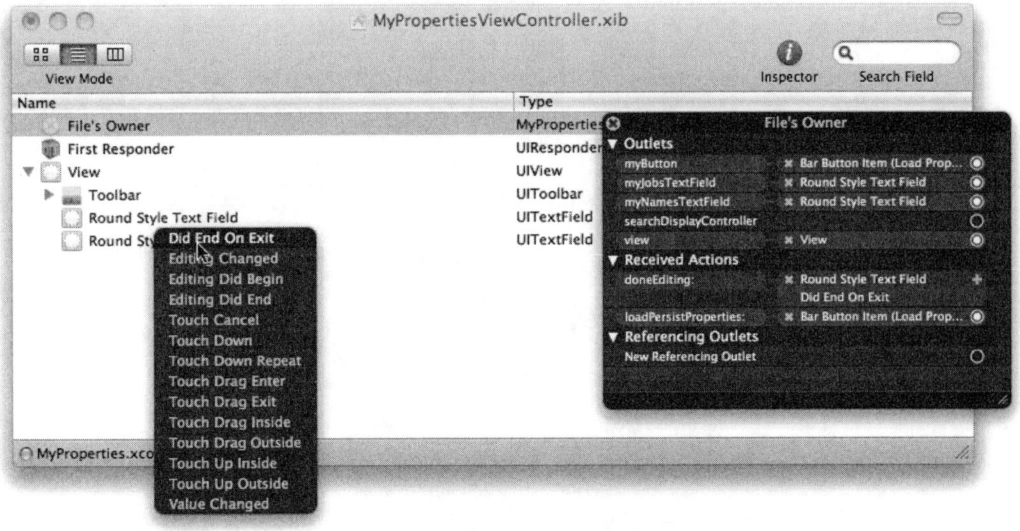

Figure 10-4 Connecting a `UITextField` to the `doneEditing` action

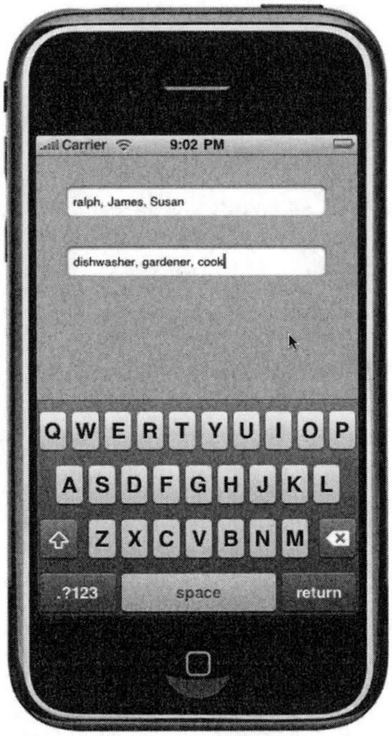

Figure 10-5 Entering text in the text fields

Listing 10-4 MyPropertiesViewController.h

```
#import <UIKit/UIKit.h>
@interface MyPropertiesViewController : UIViewController {
  IBOutlet UITextField * myNamesTextField;
  IBOutlet UITextField * myJobsTextField;
  IBOutlet UIBarButtonItem * myButton;
}
@property (nonatomic, retain) UITextField * myNamesTextField;
@property (nonatomic, retain) UITextField * myJobsTextField;
@property (nonatomic, retain) UIBarButtonItem * myButton;
- (IBAction) loadPersistProperties: (id) sender;
- (IBAction) doneEditing: (id) sender;
@end
```

Listing 10-5 MyPropertiesViewController.m

```
#import "MyPropertiesViewController.h"
#define MY_PROPERTIES @"my_properties"
@implementation MyPropertiesViewController
@synthesize myNamesTextField;
@synthesize myJobsTextField;
@synthesize myButton;
static BOOL loaded;
- (void) persist {
  NSArray * myNames = [self.myNamesTextField.text
componentsSeparatedByString:@","];
  NSArray * myJobs = [self.myJobsTextField.text
componentsSeparatedByString:@","];
  NSDictionary * myDict = [NSDictionary dictionaryWithObjects:[NSArray
arrayWithObjects:myNames,myJobs,nil]
  forKeys:[NSArray arrayWithObjects:@"names",@"jobs",nil]];
  NSString * path = nil;
  path = [(NSString *) [NSSearchPathForDirectoriesInDomains(NSDocumentDirectory,
NSUserDomainMask, YES) objectAtIndex:0]
stringByAppendingPathComponent:MY_PROPERTIES];
  [myDict writeToFile:path atomically:NO];
}
- (void) load {
  NSString * path = nil;
  path = [(NSString *) [NSSearchPathForDirectoriesInDomains(NSDocumentDirectory,
NSUserDomainMask, YES) objectAtIndex:0]
  stringByAppendingPathComponent:MY_PROPERTIES];
```

(continued)

```
  NSDictionary * myProperties = [NSDictionary dictionaryWithContentsOfFile:path];
  if(myProperties) {
    NSArray * myNames = [myProperties valueForKey:@"names"];
    NSArray * myjobs = [myProperties valueForKey:@"jobs"];
    self.myNamesTextField.text = [myNames componentsJoinedByString:@","];
    self.myJobsTextField.text = [myjobs componentsJoinedByString:@","];
  }
}
- (IBAction) loadPersistProperties: (id) sender {
  if(loaded == YES) {
    [self persist];
  }
  else {
    [self load];
    self.myButton.title = @"Persist Properties";
    loaded = YES;
  }
}
- (IBAction) doneEditing: (id) sender {
  [sender resignFirstResponder];
}
-(void) viewDidLoad {
  [super viewDidLoad];
  loaded = NO;
}
- (void)viewDidUnload {
  [super viewDidUnload];
  [self persist];
}
- (void)dealloc {
  self.myJobsTextField = nil;
  self.myNamesTextField = nil;
  self.myButton = nil;
  [super dealloc];
}
@end
```

Writing an application such as the one in Listings 10-4 and 10-5 on the job would likely get you fired. A preferred behavior would, of course, be to have the application load the data automatically when the view appears and persist the data when the view disappears. But suspend disbelief and accept the application.

TIP

Remember, when using `nil` in a class' `dealloc` method, be certain you access the property using its accessor and not directly. The following code releases the object:

```
self.myObject = nil;
```

But the following code does not release the object:

```
myObject = nil;
```

The first time you run the application and tap the button, there is no file containing the dictionary's data and so nothing happens. However, after you enter data and then tap the button, the application serializes the dictionary to a file.

Notice that just for fun you turned the string into an array before storing it in the dictionary.

```
NSArray * myJobs = [self.myJobsTextField.text
componentsSeparatedByString:@", "];
```

You could have simply left the data as an `NSString`, but I thought turning it into an array would be more interesting. Besides, turning an `NSString` into an array is something you will definitely do at some point in your Objective-C career.

After persisting the data, if you open the my_properties file in the TextEdit application you will see that it is XML (Listing 10-6). Note the elements match the elements in Table 10-1.

TIP

Refer to *XML: A Beginner's Guide* by Steven Holzer (McGraw-Hill Professional, 2008) to learn more about XML.

Listing 10-6 The my_properties XML file

```
<?xml version="1.0" encoding="UTF-8"?>
<!DOCTYPE plist PUBLIC "-//Apple//DTD PLIST 1.0//EN"
"http://www.apple.com/DTDs/PropertyList-1.0.dtd">
<plist version="1.0">
<dict>
  <key>jobs</key>
  <array>
    <string>diswasher</string>
    <string>author</string>
    <string>cyclist</string>
    <string>cook</string>
  </array>
  <key>names</key>
```

(continued)

```
  <array>
    <string>James</string>
    <string>Roger</string>
    <string>alan</string>
    <string>Mary</string>
  </array>
</dict>
</plist>
```

The second time you start the application and then tap the button it loads the my_properties file's data. Before setting the text field's value with the data, you turn it into a single string.

```
NSArray * myNames = [myProperties valueForKey:@"names"];
NSArray * myjobs = [myProperties valueForKey:@"jobs"];
self.myNamesTextField.text = [myNames componentsJoinedByString:@", "];
self.myJobsTextField.text = [myjobs componentsJoinedByString:@", "];
```

Persisting a property-list object is straightforward. However, notice what they cannot do; they cannot persist custom classes to a file. For instance, if you had an NSArray of Foo class instances, you could not persist the NSArray as a property list because Foo isn't one of the property-list classes.

Persisting an NSArray containing Foo instances requires using archiving. This chapter's remainder discusses archiving. Archiving is a powerful way to persist custom objects between instances of your application running.

TIP

Refer to Apple's "Property List Programming Guide," available online, for more information on property lists.

Archiving

You can only serialize and deserialize property-list objects when using the writeToFile: atomically: and readFromFile:atomically: methods. But you can serialize and deserialize other objects, including multiple objects, using *archiving.*

The NSKeyedArchiver class creates keyed archives. Each field archived has its own name, or key. When you archive an object, you save its field value with its key. This key/value combination is saved to a file. You can then later reconstitute the object from the file using the NSKeyedUnarchiver class. The NSKeyedUnarchiver class reads archives and reconstitutes objects from the archived objects.

NSCoding Protocol

Archiving an object requires that the object adopt the `NSCoding` protocol. The `NSCoding` protocol requires a class to implement the `encodeWithCoder:` and `initWithCoder:` methods. You encode an object using the `encodeWithCoder:` method, and you decode an object using the `intWithCoder:` method.

```
- (void) encodeWithCoder: (NSCoder*) encoder
-(id) initWithCoder:(NSCoder*) decoder
```

Your class implementing the `NSCoding` protocol encodes other objects that adopt `NSCoding` using the `NSCoder`'s `encodeObject:forKey:` method. It decodes these objects using the `decodeObject:forKey:` method. The `NSCoder` can also encode and decode primitive objects; for instance, to encode and decode a float, you would use the `encodeFloat:forKey:` and `decodeFloat:forKey:` methods.

NSKeyedArchiver and NSKeyedUnarchiver

The `NSKeyedArchiver` and `NSKeyedUnarchiver` classes archive and unarchive objects that adopt the `NSCoding` protocol. The `NSKeyedArchiver` encodes objects into a key/value archive, where you can later retrieve the values based upon the objects' keys. The `NSKeyedUnarchiver` class reconstitutes a class, or classes, from an archive.

You can archive a single class, or you can archive multiple classes. When archiving a single class, you can also archive classes the class has a relationship with, provided those classes also adopt the `NSCoding` protocol.

Archiving a Single Class

When archiving and unarchiving a single object, and its constituents, you can use `NSArchiver`'s `archiveRootObject:toFile:` class method to archive the object and `unarchiveObjectWithFile` class method to unarchive the object. These methods provide an easy means of archiving and unarchiving a single object hierarchy. To archive directly to a file, use the `archiveRootObject:toFile:` method.

```
+ (BOOL)archiveRootObject:(id)rootObject toFile:(NSString *)path
```

To unarchive directly from a file, use the `unarchiveObjectWithFile:` convenience method.

```
+ (id)unarchiveObjectWithFile:(NSString *)path
```

The following Try This first illustrates archiving and unarchiving a single object containing no constituent objects. It then modifies the project so that it archives and unarchives a single object that has relationships with other classes.

Try This Archiving and Unarchiving an Object

1. Create a new Utility Application named **MyArchive**.
2. Create a new class named `Foo`. Have the `Foo` class adopt the `NSCoding` protocol (Listing 10-7).
3. Create an `NSString` and an `NSNumber` as properties.
4. Open Foo.m and synthesize the properties (Listing 10-8).
5. Implement the `encodeWithCoder:` and `initWithCoder:` methods.
6. Open MainViewController.h and add `Foo` and two `UILabels` as properties (Listing 10-9). Make the two `UILabels` `IBOutlets`.
7. Build the application.
8. Open MainView.xib in Interface Builder. Add two `UILabels` to the view's canvas (Figure 10-6). Connect them to the respective outlets in the view's view controller. Change the view's background color to white.
9. Save and exit Interface Builder.
10. Open MainViewController.m and implement the `viewDidLoad:` and `viewDidUnload:` methods as in Listing 10-10.
11. Build and Run the application. Flip between views and each time the first view appears it increments the label's value.

Listing 10-7 Foo.h

```
#import <Foundation/Foundation.h>
@interface Foo : NSObject <NSCoding> {
  NSString * name;
  NSNumber * quantity;
}
@property (nonatomic, retain) NSString * name;
@property (nonatomic, retain) NSNumber * quantity;
@end
```

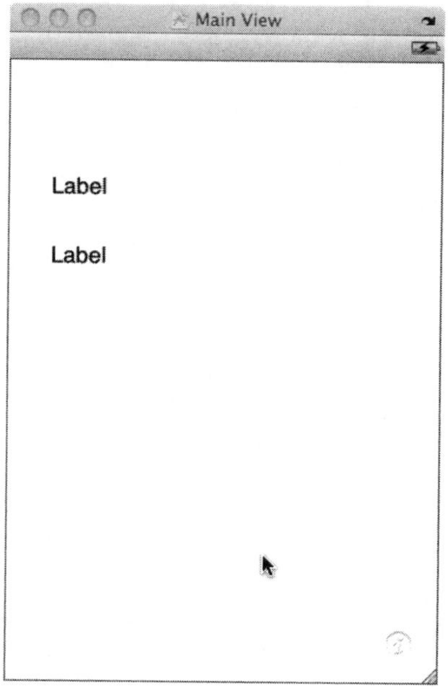

Figure 10-6 Adding two labels to the view's canvas

Listing 10-8 Foo.m

```
#import "Foo.h"
@implementation Foo
@synthesize name;
@synthesize quantity;
- (void) encodeWithCoder:(NSCoder *)aCoder {
  [aCoder encodeObject:name forKey:@"name"];
  [aCoder encodeInt:[quantity intValue] forKey:@"quantity"];
}
-(id) initWithCoder:(NSCoder *)aDecoder {
  if( (self = [super init])!=nil) {
    self.name = [aDecoder decodeObjectForKey:@"name"];
    self.quantity = [NSNumber numberWithInt:[aDecoder
decodeIntForKey:@"quantity"]];
  }
  return self;
}
@end
```

(continued)

Listing 10-9 MainViewController.h

```
#import "FlipsideViewController.h"
@class Foo;
@interface MainViewController : UIViewController
<FlipsideViewControllerDelegate> {
  Foo * myFoo;
  IBOutlet UILabel * name;
  IBOutlet UILabel * quantity;
}
@property (nonatomic, retain) UILabel * name;
@property (nonatomic, retain) UILabel * quantity;
@property (nonatomic,retain) Foo * myFoo;
- (IBAction)showInfo;
@end
```

Listing 10-10 MainViewController.m

```
#import "MainViewController.h"
#import "MainView.h"
#import "Foo.h"
@implementation MainViewController
@synthesize myFoo;
@synthesize name;
@synthesize quantity;
static int incrementer = 0;
- (void) viewDidAppear: (BOOL) animated {
  [super viewDidAppear:animated];
  NSString * path = nil;
  path = [(NSString *) [NSSearchPathForDirectoriesInDomains(NSDocumentDirectory,
NSUserDomainMask, YES) objectAtIndex:0]
stringByAppendingPathComponent:@"foo.archive"];
  self.myFoo = nil;
  self.myFoo = [NSKeyedUnarchiver unarchiveObjectWithFile:path];
  if(self.myFoo == nil) {
    NSLog(@"myFoo had no archive...");
    self.myFoo = [[Foo alloc] init];
    self.myFoo.name = [NSString stringWithFormat:@"Tom %i",incrementer];
    self.myFoo.quantity = [NSNumber numberWithInt:incrementer];
  }
  self.name.text = myFoo.name;
  self.quantity.text = [myFoo.quantity stringValue];
  incrementer = [myFoo.quantity intValue] + 1;
}
- (void) viewDidDisappear: (BOOL) animated {
```

```
  [super viewDidDisappear:animated];
  if(incrementer % 2 == 0) self.myFoo.name = @"Tom";
  else self.myFoo.name = @"Sally";
  self.myFoo.quantity = [NSNumber numberWithInt:incrementer];
  NSString * path = nil;
  path = [(NSString *) [NSSearchPathForDirectoriesInDomains(NSDocumentDirectory,
NSUserDomainMask, YES) objectAtIndex:0]
stringByAppendingPathComponent:@"foo.archive"];
  [NSKeyedArchiver archiveRootObject:self.myFoo toFile:path];
}
- (void)flipsideViewControllerDidFinish:(FlipsideViewController *)controller {
  [self dismissModalViewControllerAnimated:YES];
}
- (IBAction)showInfo {
  FlipsideViewController *controller = [[FlipsideViewController alloc]
initWithNibName:@"FlipsideView" bundle:nil];
  controller.delegate = self;
  controller.modalTransitionStyle = UIModalTransitionStyleFlipHorizontal;
  [self presentModalViewController:controller animated:YES];
  [controller release];
}
- (void)dealloc {
  self.myFoo = nil;
  self.name = nil;
  self.quantity = nil;
  [super dealloc];
}
@end
```

Archiving and unarchiving a single object, although useful, hides archiving's true power. Often a class inherits from parent classes and contains references to other classes. In the following steps you modify the application so that `Foo` inherits from a parent class that implements the `NSCoding` protocol. You also create a new class that `Foo` has a reference to.

1. Create a new class called `SuperFoo` and add an `NSString` as a property (Listing 10-11). Have `SuperFoo` adopt the `NSCoding` protocol.
2. Implement `SuperFoo` (Listing 10-12).
3. Modify Foo.h so that it inherits from `SuperFoo` (Listing 10-13). Be certain you modify the `initWithCoder:` method so that it first calls `SuperFoo`'s `initWithCoder:` method (Listing 10-14). Also be certain to call its superclass' `encodeObject:` method.

(continued)

4. Create a new class called `Bar` that adopts the `NSCoding` protocol and has an `NSString` as a property (Listings 10-15 and 10-16).

5. Add `Bar` to `Foo` as a property and modify `Foo`'s `encodeWithCoder:` and `initWithCoder:` methods so that they encode and decode `Bar`.

6. Modify the `viewDidAppear:` and `viewDidDisappear:` methods so that they log `SuperFoo`'s and `Bar`'s content to the debugger console (Listing 10-17).

7. Click and run the application. If you didn't delete the application from your iPhone simulator, then you will probably see `SuperFoo`'s and `Bar`'s names as null.

8. Stop the application without stopping the iPhone simulator. Just as on a real device, click and hold the MyArchive icon on the simulator's springboard. Click the small *x* to delete the application from the iPhone simulator (Figure 10-7).

9. Build and Run the application. Flip back and forth between the views and the application behaves as expected.

Figure 10-7 Deleting the application from the simulator's springboard

Listing 10-11 SuperFoo.h

```
#import <Foundation/Foundation.h>
@interface SuperFoo : NSObject <NSCoding> {
  NSString * mySuperName;
}
@property (nonatomic,retain) NSString * mySuperName;
@end
```

Listing 10-12 SuperFoo.m

```
#import "SuperFoo.h"
@implementation SuperFoo
@synthesize mySuperName;
- (void) encodeWithCoder:(NSCoder *)aCoder {
  [aCoder encodeObject:mySuperName forKey:@"superName"];
}
-(id) initWithCoder:(NSCoder *)aDecoder {
  if( (self = [super init])!=nil) {
    self.mySuperName = [aDecoder decodeObjectForKey:@"superName"];
  }
  return self;
}
- (void)dealloc {
  [super dealloc];
  [mySuperName release];
}
@end
```

Listing 10-13 Foo.h modified to inherit from `SuperFoo`

```
#import <Foundation/Foundation.h>
#import "SuperFoo.h"
@class Bar;
@interface Foo : SuperFoo <NSCoding> {
  NSString * name;
  NSNumber * quantity;
  Bar * myBar;
}
@property (nonatomic, retain) NSString * name;
@property (nonatomic, retain) NSNumber * quantity;
@property (nonatomic, retain) Bar * myBar;
@end
```

(continued)

Listing 10-14 Foo.m modified to inherit from `SuperFoo` and using `Bar`

```
#import "Foo.h"
#import "Bar.h"
@implementation Foo
@synthesize name;
@synthesize quantity;
@synthesize myBar;
- (void) encodeWithCoder:(NSCoder *)aCoder {
  [super encodeWithCoder:aCoder];
  [aCoder encodeObject:name forKey:@"name"];
  [aCoder encodeInt:[quantity intValue] forKey:@"quantity"];
  [aCoder encodeObject:self.myBar forKey:@"bar"];
}
-(id) initWithCoder:(NSCoder *)aDecoder {
  if( (self = [super initWithCoder:aDecoder])!=nil) {
    self.name = [aDecoder decodeObjectForKey:@"name"];
    self.quantity = [NSNumber numberWithInt:[aDecoder
decodeIntForKey:@"quantity"]];
    self.myBar = [aDecoder decodeObjectForKey:@"bar"];
  }
  return self;
}
- (void)dealloc {
  [name release];
  [quantity release];
  [myBar release];
  [super dealloc];
}
@end
```

Listing 10-15 Bar.h

```
#import <Foundation/Foundation.h>
@interface Bar : NSObject <NSCoding> {
  NSString * barName;
}
@property(nonatomic,retain) NSString * barName;
@end
```

Listing 10-16 Bar.m

```
#import "Bar.h"
@implementation Bar
@synthesize barName;
```

```
- (void) encodeWithCoder:(NSCoder *)aCoder {
  [aCoder encodeObject:barName forKey:@"barName"];
}
-(id) initWithCoder:(NSCoder *)aDecoder {
  if( (self = [super init])!=nil) {
    self.barName = [aDecoder decodeObjectForKey:@"barName"];
  }
  return self;
}
- (void)dealloc {
  [barName release];
  [super dealloc];
}
@end
```

Listing 10-17 MainViewController.m modified

```
#import "MainViewController.h"
#import "MainView.h"
#import "Foo.h"
#import "SuperFoo.h"
#import "Bar.h"
@implementation MainViewController
@synthesize myFoo;
@synthesize name;
@synthesize quantity;
static int incrementer = 0;
- (void) viewDidAppear: (BOOL) animated {
  [super viewDidAppear:animated];
  NSString * path = nil;
  path = [(NSString *) [NSSearchPathForDirectoriesInDomains(NSDocumentDirectory,
NSUserDomainMask, YES) objectAtIndex:0]
stringByAppendingPathComponent:@"foo.archive"];
  self.myFoo = nil;
  self.myFoo = [[NSKeyedUnarchiver unarchiveObjectWithFile:path] retain];
  if(self.myFoo == nil) {
    NSLog(@"myFoo had no archive...");
    self.myFoo = [[Foo alloc] init];
    self.myFoo.name = [[NSString alloc] initWithFormat:@"Tom %i",incrementer];
    self.myFoo.quantity = [[NSNumber alloc] initWithInt:incrementer];
    self.myFoo.mySuperName = [[NSString alloc] initWithString:@"Tom's Dad"];
    Bar * tempBar = [[Bar alloc] init];
    tempBar.barName = [[NSString alloc] initWithString:@"John"];
    self.myFoo.myBar = tempBar;
  }
```

(continued)

```
  else {
    NSLog(@"SuperFoo's Name:%@", self.myFoo.mySuperName);
    NSLog(@"Bar's Name:%@", self.myFoo.myBar.barName);
  }
  self.name.text = myFoo.name;
  self.quantity.text = [myFoo.quantity stringValue];
  incrementer = [myFoo.quantity intValue] + 1;
}
- (void) viewDidDisappear: (BOOL) animated {
  [super viewDidDisappear:animated];
  if(incrementer % 2 == 0) self.myFoo.name = [[NSString alloc]
initWithString:@"Tom"];
  else self.myFoo.name = [[NSString alloc] initWithString:@"Sally"];
  self.myFoo.quantity = [[NSNumber alloc] initWithInt:incrementer];
  NSString * path = nil;
  path = [(NSString *) [NSSearchPathForDirectoriesInDomains(NSDocumentDirectory,
NSUserDomainMask, YES) objectAtIndex:0]
stringByAppendingPathComponent:@"foo.archive"];
  [NSKeyedArchiver archiveRootObject:self.myFoo toFile:path];
}
- (void)flipsideViewControllerDidFinish:(FlipsideViewController *)controller {
  [self dismissModalViewControllerAnimated:YES];
}
- (IBAction)showInfo {
  FlipsideViewController *controller = [[FlipsideViewController alloc]
initWithNibName:@"FlipsideView" bundle:nil];
  controller.delegate = self;
  controller.modalTransitionStyle = UIModalTransitionStyleFlipHorizontal;
  [self presentModalViewController:controller animated:YES];
  [controller release];
}
- (void)dealloc {
  [myFoo release];
  [name release];
  [quantity release];
  [super dealloc];
}
@end
```

As this example illustrates, you can persist other objects the root object has relationships with, provided those objects also implement the `NSCoding` protocol. In `Foo`'s `encodeWithCoder:` method it encodes its `Bar` instance. Doing this invokes `Bar`'s `encodeWithCoder:` method.

```
[aCoder encodeObject:self.myBar forKey:@"bar"];
```

In Foo's `initWithCoder:` method it decodes its `Bar` instance, which invokes `Bar`'s `decodeObjectForKey:` method.

```
self.myBar = [aDecoder decodeObjectForKey:@"bar"];
```

Also notice that if an archivable object inherits from a parent, the `initWithCoder:` method should call the parent's `initWithCoder:` method.

```
if( (self = [super initWithCoder:aDecoder])!=nil)
```

The child object should also invoke its parent's `encodeWithCoder:` method.

```
[super encodeWithCoder:aCoder];
```

Archiving Multiple Classes

Although archiving a single object and the classes it has a relationship with is useful, there are many times when you might wish to archive multiple unrelated objects at the same time. You archive multiple objects at once by using a mutable data buffer and an `NSKeyedArchiver`. What you do is create a data buffer that you can add data to.

```
NSMutableData * theData = [NSMutableData data];
```

You then initialize the `NSKeyedArchiver` with the data buffer.

```
  NSKeyedArchiver * archiver = [[NSKeyedArchiver alloc]
initForWritingWithMutableData:theData];
```

After initializing the archiver, you encode the objects.

```
[archiver encodeObject:myFoos forKey:@"myFoos"];
 [archiver encodeObject:myName forKey:@"myName"];
```

After encoding all the objects you wish to encode, you send a message to the archiver telling it that you are finished encoding. And you then write the data buffer to a file.

```
[archiver finishEncoding];
 [theData writeToFile:pathToFile atomically:NO]
```

Reconstituting the objects from the archive is a similar process. You first read the data into an `NSData` object.

```
NSData * data = [NSData dataWithContentsOfFile:pathToFile];
```

You then create an `NSKeyedUnarchiver` and initialize it with the `NSData` instance.

```
NSKeyedUnarchiver * unarchiver = [[NSKeyedUnarchiver alloc]
initForReadingWithData:data];
```

You then decode the data into the respective classes.

```
myFoos = [unarchiver decodeObjectForKey:@"myFoos"];
myName = [unarchiver decodeObjectForKey:@"myName"];
```

After reconstituting the objects from the `NSData` instance, you then send a message to the unarchiver, telling it that you are finished decoding, and you then release the unarchiver.

```
[unarchiver finishDecoding];
 [unarchiver release];
```

You can archive and unarchive any class that adopts the `NSCoding` protocol using this technique. Moreover, you can archive and unarchive as many of those objects as you wish to a single archive file. This flexibility makes archiving an easy, yet powerful way to persist your application's objects.

NOTE

If you unarchive a nonexistent object, the archiver returns zero for numeric values and nil for objects.

Try This Creating an Archive with Multiple Object Types

1. Create a View-based application named **AdvancedArchive**.
2. Create a new `NSObject` class named `Foo` and implement `name` and `quantity` properties, as in the previous example (Listings 10-18 and 10-19).
3. Open AdvancedArchiveAppDelegate.h and add two properties, an `NSMutableArray` and an `NSString` (Listing 10-20).
4. Open AdvancedArchiveAppDelegate.m, synthesize the two properties, and implement the `applicationDidFinishLaunching:` and `applicationWillResignActive:` methods as in Listing 10-21.

5. Build and Run the application. The application logs its output to the debugger console (Listing 10-22).

Listing 10-18 Foo.h

```
#import <Foundation/Foundation.h>
@interface Foo : NSObject <NSCoding> {
  NSString * name;
  NSNumber * quantity;
}
@property (nonatomic, retain) NSString * name;
@property (nonatomic, retain) NSNumber * quantity;
@end
```

Listing 10-19 Foo.m

```
#import "Foo.h"
@implementation Foo
@synthesize name;
@synthesize quantity;
- (void) encodeWithCoder:(NSCoder *)aCoder {
  [aCoder encodeObject:name forKey:@"name"];
  [aCoder encodeInt:[quantity intValue] forKey:@"quantity"];
}
-(id) initWithCoder:(NSCoder *)aDecoder {
  if( (self = [super init])!=nil) {
    self.name = [aDecoder decodeObjectForKey:@"name"];
    self.quantity = [NSNumber numberWithInt:[aDecoder
decodeIntForKey:@"quantity"]];
  }
  return self;
}
@end
```

Listing 10-20 AdvancedArchiveAppDelegate.h

```
#import <UIKit/UIKit.h>
@class AdvancedArchiveViewController;
@interface AdvancedArchiveAppDelegate : NSObject <UIApplicationDelegate> {
  UIWindow *window;
  AdvancedArchiveViewController *viewController;
```

(continued)

```
  NSMutableArray * myFoos;;
  NSString * myName;;
}
@property (nonatomic, retain) IBOutlet UIWindow *window;
@property (nonatomic, retain) IBOutlet AdvancedArchiveViewController
*viewController;
@property (nonatomic,retain) NSMutableArray * myFoos;
@property (nonatomic,retain) NSString * myName;
@end
```

Listing 10-21 AdvancedArchiveAppDelegate.m

```
#import "AdvancedArchiveAppDelegate.h"
#import "AdvancedArchiveViewController.h"
#import "Foo.h"
@implementation AdvancedArchiveAppDelegate
@synthesize window;
@synthesize viewController;
@synthesize myFoos;
@synthesize myName;
- (void)applicationDidFinishLaunching:(UIApplication *)application {
  self.myFoos = nil;
  self.myName = nil;
  NSString * pathToFile =
[[NSSearchPathForDirectoriesInDomains(NSDocumentDirectory, NSUserDomainMask,
YES) objectAtIndex:0] stringByAppendingPathComponent:@"myarchive.archive"];
  NSData * data = [NSData dataWithContentsOfFile:pathToFile];
  if([data length] > 0) {
    NSKeyedUnarchiver * unarchiver = [[NSKeyedUnarchiver alloc]
initForReadingWithData:data];
    self.myFoos = [unarchiver decodeObjectForKey:@"myFoos"];
    self.myName = [unarchiver decodeObjectForKey:@"myName"];
    [unarchiver finishDecoding];
    [unarchiver release];
  }
  else {
    Foo * aFoo = [[Foo alloc] init];
    aFoo.name = @"widgets";
    aFoo.quantity = [NSNumber numberWithInt:32];
    Foo * aFoo2 = [[Foo alloc] init];
    aFoo2.name = @"plates";
    aFoo2.quantity = [NSNumber numberWithInt:300];
    self.myFoos = [[NSMutableArray alloc]  initWithObjects:aFoo, aFoo2, nil];
    self.myName = @"Bob";
    [aFoo release];
    [aFoo2 release];
  }
```

```
  for(int i = 0; i < [myFoos count]; i++) {
    NSLog(@"There are %i %@ in stock.", [((Foo*)[myFoos objectAtIndex:i])
.quantity intValue], ((Foo*)[self.myFoos objectAtIndex:i]).name);
  }
  NSLog(@"My name is: %@", myName);
  [window addSubview:viewController.view];
  [window makeKeyAndVisible];
}
- (void) applicationWillTerminate:(UIApplication *)application {
  NSString * pathToFile = [[NSSearchPathForDirectoriesInDomains(
NSDocumentDirectory, NSUserDomainMask, YES) objectAtIndex:0]
stringByAppendingPathComponent:@"myarchive.archive"];
  Foo * aFoo = [[Foo alloc] init];
  aFoo.name = @"ipods";
  aFoo.quantity = [NSNumber numberWithInt:44];
  [self.myFoos addObject:aFoo];
  [aFoo release];
  NSMutableData * theData = [NSMutableData data];
  NSKeyedArchiver * archiver = [[NSKeyedArchiver alloc]
initForWritingWithMutableData:theData];
  [archiver encodeObject:myFoos forKey:@"myFoos"];
  [archiver encodeObject:myName forKey:@"myName"];
  [archiver finishEncoding];
  if([theData writeToFile:pathToFile atomically:NO] == NO) {
    NSLog(@"archiving failed...");
  }
  [archiver release];
}
- (void)dealloc {
  [viewController release];
  [window release];
  [self.myFoos release];
  [self.myName release];
  [super dealloc];
}
@end
```

Listing 10-22 Debugger console logging

```
There are 32 widgets in stock.
There are 300 plates in stock.
There are 44 ipods in stock.
My name is: Bob
```

This application illustrates archiving and unarchiving multiple objects. As described earlier, you archive several classes together into a single file. Although the `Foos` are all constituents of `NSArray`, the `NSString` is totally unrelated to the `Foos` in the array. Using this technique allows archiving unrelated objects together in a single archive.

TIP

Refer to Apple's "Archives and Serializations Programming Guide for Cocoa" for more information on archiving.

Summary

Property lists and archiving is an easy way to persist your application's data between users running your application. When using property lists and archives, be certain you persist the data to your Documents directory, as this directory is persisted by iTunes. If you only wish to persist primitive values, use a property list. If you wish to persist objects, then use archiving. Both techniques are easy ways to persist your application's data.

If storing large amounts of data, you should use the SQLite database that comes with the iPhone or you should use Core Data. Both topics are outside this book's scope, but for more information on using both in an iPhone application, refer to *iPhone SDK Programming: A Beginner's Guide.*

Chapter 11

Selectors and Targets

Key Skills & Concepts

- Understanding Selectors
- Using the `performSelector` Methods
- Performing Long-Running Tasks Using a Selector
- Using a Notification with a Selector
- Using a Delegate with a Selector
- Using a Target with a `UIControl`

If you have ever programmed using Cold Fusion, PHP, or Java, then this chapter will seem intuitive. Objective-C allows developers to dynamically invoke a method at runtime. In this chapter you explore an Objective-C concept called selectors. Selectors are arguably one of the most important topics in Objective-C, and allow developers significant flexibility.

Selectors

Objective-C allows varying a message dynamically at runtime. Moreover, rather than invoking a method directly, or in Objective-C speak, sending a message to another object directly, you can use something called a selector to choose which method to invoke dynamically at runtime.

NOTE

If you know C or C++, think of selectors as Objective-C's equivalent to function pointers, only much easier to understand and use—at least to an ex-Java developer like the author.

The `@selector( )` directive is a compiler directive that when compiled replaces the method with a SEL type. A SEL identifies a method and can be used directly in your code. Then, rather than calling a method directly, you can call the selector. The following code illustrates creating a selector:

```
SEL sinkFloatable;
sinkFloatable = @selector(sinkDuck);
```

You are first declaring a selector `sinkFloatable`. You are then setting it to point to the actual method `sinkDuck` by using the `@selector` compiler directive.

Every `NSObject` has seven `performSelector` methods. In this chapter you learn four of those methods: `performSelector:`, `performSelector:withObject:`, `performSelector:withObject:withObject:`, and `performSelector:withObject:afterDelay`. You also learn to use `NSObject`'s `instanceRespondToSelector:` class method.

The `performSelector:` method sends a message to a receiver and returns the method's results as an id. This is an important distinction from regular methods that can return various types—a selector only returns an id. Of course, do not be troubled by this restriction, as an id can be any object, so it really isn't a restriction at all, other than that you cannot return a primitive from a selector.

```
- (id)performSelector:(SEL)aSelector
```

The `performSelector:withObject:` and `performSelector:withObject:withObject:` methods perform the same function as `performSelector:`, only they allow passing objects to the method. The following Try This illustrates using all three `performSelector` variants.

Try This Using a Selector

1. Create a new Command Line Foundation Tool named **SimpleSelector**.
2. Create a new `NSObject` named `Foo` (Listings 11-1 and 11-2).
3. Implement four methods: `run`, `echoNames:`, `testme:nameString:`, and `echoHello` as in Listing 11-2. Have the `run` method call `echoHello` and `echoNames`: using a selector.
4. Modify SimpleSelector.m to match Listing 11-3. Notice that SimpleSelector.m calls Foo's `testme:nameString:` using a selector.
5. Build and Run the application.

Listing 11-1 Foo.h

```
#import <Foundation/Foundation.h>
@interface Foo : NSObject {
}
```

(continued)

```
- (void) run;
-(void) echoNames: (id) objectArray;
- (void) testMe: (id) objectArray nameString: (id) nameString;
- (void) echoHello;
@end
```

Listing 11-2 Foo.m

```
#import "Foo.h"
@implementation Foo
- (void) run {
  [self performSelector:@selector(echoHello)];
  NSArray * myArray = [NSArray arrayWithObjects:@"A",@"B",@"C",@"D",nil];
  [self performSelector:@selector(echoNames:) withObject:myArray];
}
- (void) testMe: (id) objectArray nameString: (id) nameString {
  NSLog(@"The Name:%@", nameString);
  NSLog(@"The count of the array:%i", [objectArray count]);
}
-(void) echoNames: (id) objectArray {
  NSArray * theArray = (NSArray *)objectArray;
  for(int i = 0; i < [theArray count]; i++) {
    NSLog(@"The Name:%@", [theArray objectAtIndex:i]);
  }
}
- (void) echoHello {
  NSLog(@"Hello...");
}
@end
```

Listing 11-3 SimpleSelector.m

```
#import <Foundation/Foundation.h>
#import "Foo.h"
int main (int argc, const char * argv[]) {
  NSAutoreleasePool * pool = [[NSAutoreleasePool alloc] init];
  Foo * myFoo = [[Foo alloc] init];
  [myFoo run];
  NSArray * myArray = [NSArray arrayWithObjects:@"A", @"B", @"C",nil];
  NSString * correctString = @"This is correct.";
  [myFoo performSelector:@selector(testMe:nameString:) withObject:myArray
withObject:correctString];
  [myFoo release];
```

```
  [pool drain];
  return 0;
}
```

Foo's run method calls two methods using a selector. First it calls performSelector, passing only the method's name.

```
[self performSelector:@selector(echoHello)];
```

The run method then creates an array and passes it to the performSelector: withObject: method.

```
NSArray * myArray = [NSArray arrayWithObjects:@"A",@"B",@"C",@"D",nil];
[self performSelector:@selector(echoNames:) withObject:myArray];
```

The echoNames:objectArray: method takes an id, which is actually an NSArray. To help developers pass the correct object type, the method names its parameter objectArray. However, to be safe you should probably test that the parameter is an array before using it.

TIP

Remember, a method without a parameter is the method's name. A method with a parameter has a trailing colon. A method with multiple parameters includes applicable parameter names in its name. The following two lines are not equivalent, as they are two distinct methods:

```
@selector(myMethod);
@selector(myMethod:);
```

The main method in SimpleSelector illustrates another way you can call a selector. However, rather than calling the performSelector method on itself, it calls it on the Foo instance. It also passes two objects, an array and an NSString.

```
[myFoo performSelector:@selector(testMe:nameString:) withObject:myArray
withObject:correctString];
```

The Foo instance, myFoo, is calling the testMe:nameString: method, passing an array and a string to the method.

Delaying a Selector or Running in Background

The `performSelector:withObject:afterDelay:` method allows calling a method after a short delay. Although at first glance, this might seem like a useless method, it allows you to easily accomplish things that might other require multithreading.

Suppose you wished to send a message to an object after a delay, then you could use the `performSelector:withObject:afterDelay:` method. The following code illustrates:

```
[myFoo performSelector:@selector(sayFooName:) withObject:@"Ralph"
afterDelay:20];
```

The preceding code line calls `myFoo`'s `sayFooName:` method after a twenty-second delay. It also passes the string `"Ralph"` as a parameter.

Another method you might use is the `performSelectorInBackground:withObject:` method, which allows calling a method using a different thread, the background thread.

```
SEL mySelector = @selector(sayFooName:);
[myFoo performSelectorInBackground:mySelector withObject:@"Ralph"];
```

The `performSelectorInBackground:withObject:` method calls the selector immediately but does so on a new background thread.

Multithreading

A single-threaded application can only do one thing at a time. Imagine if you could only do one thing at a time—you couldn't drink your morning coffee and read the newspaper at the same time; you would have to wait until you were finished drinking your coffee before reading the paper. A multithreaded application, in contrast, allows you to do multiple things simultaneously; you can drink your coffee and read the newspaper at the same time.

Multithreaded applications are more difficult to write than single-threaded applications, but there are many times when you might need a multithreaded application. For instance, suppose you were loading an iPhone screen's view and part of loading that view required loading a long-running method. The view wouldn't load until the method completed running because the same thread that is running the long-running method is also loading the view, and a single thread can only do one thing at a time.

But using the `performSelectorInBackground:withObject:` method, you can create a new thread and run the method on a different thread than the thread loading the view. You could also mimic the same behavior by using the `performSelector:withObject:afterDelay:` method.

CAUTION

If you use a `performSelector` variant that runs a method on a different thread, note that the thread does not use the application's main autorelease pool. You must either manually manage the memory of all methods called in the new thread or create a new autorelease pool for the thread.

Consider the following code in a `UIViewController`'s `viewWillAppear:` method.

```
[self performSelector:@selector(reallyLongMethod) withObject:nil
afterDelay:.05];
```

In this code, you are using the `performSelector:withObject:afterDelay:` method to perform the selector after a 0.05 second delay. This might seem short to you and me, but to a computer processor, this is a lifetime. The end result is that the long-running method is fired milliseconds after the view-loading code—the view is visible to the user—and the application seems quicker and more responsive. This is a common trick that you will use many times as you develop iPhone applications.

You could also use the `performSelectorInBackground:withObject:` method to perform the selector on a different thread than the thread loading the display.

```
[self performSelectorInBackground:@selector(reallyLongMethod)
withObject:nil];
```

Instead of waiting the 0.05 seconds to begin processing, it processes immediately. But remember, be careful with your memory management when using this method, as your application's autorelease pool is not managing the thread's memory.

But there is a problem using both methods. Suppose the view's display depended upon the `reallyLongMethod` method's results. The problem is that the view is already loaded before the selector completes. What you need to be able to do is somehow communicate to the view that the selector is finished processing and that you can update its display.

Two ways you might accomplish this are by using notifications or by using a delegate. In the next two sections you learn both techniques.

Notifications

A *notification* broadcasts information about events to whoever wishes to receive the notification. For instance, you might register for an e-mail alert when a stock value changes. If you have experience with Java, you might be familiar with its event listeners. Mac and iPhone applications have a similar functionality called *notifications*.

Notifications allow your code to broadcast events, and information about events, to other classes that are registered to listen for those events. It accomplishes this functionality using an `NSNotificationCenter`.

Every application has a notification center called the *default center*. You obtain it using the following code:

```
NSNotificationCenter * tempCenter = [NSNotificationCenter default];
```

After obtaining the notification center, you can send notifications to it. You send notifications using the `NSNotification` class. You might send an "I'm finished performing a long method" notification, for example.

```
[[NSNotification defaultCenter] postNotificationName:@"LongMethodDone"
object:self];
```

The code first obtains the default center and then posts a notification named "LongMethodDone" to the notification center. The object parameter allows you to pass the notification's sender. There is also a method variant that allows posting an `NSDictionary` containing more information you might wish to send along with the notification.

```
NSDictionary * myInfo = [NSDictionary dictionaryWithObject:@"information"
forKey:@"information_key"];
[[NSNotification defaultCenter] postNotificationName:@"LongMethodDone"
object:self userInfo:myInfo];
```

Other classes that wish to receive the "LongMethodDone" notification can register as listeners with the notification center.

```
[[NSNotificationCenter defaultCenter] addObserver: self
selector:@selector(handleLongMethodDone:) name:@"LongMethodDone" object:nil];
```

In this code an object is registering itself as an observer of the "LongMethodDone" notification; it is also specifying that when it receives the notification, the `handleLongMethodDone:` method should be invoked. The object parameter restricts the notification center to only informing the registrant for events in a particular object. For instance, suppose `Foo` and `Bar` both fire the "LongMethodDone" event. Or, suppose you have many `Foo` instances, but you only wish to receive a notification for a particular `Foo` instance. In these situations, you would pass the object to the center. The center would then only inform the registrant of "LongMethodDone" events for the passed `Foo`.

Objects that register as event observers can also deregister themselves as listeners.

```
[[NSNotificationCenter defaultCenter] removeObserver:self];
```

You should always deregister a listener in its `dealloc` method if it is registered as a listener.

NOTE

It is beyond this book's scope to present complete coverage of notifications. There is much you can do with notifications. For complete coverage, refer to Apple's "Notification Programming Topics for Cocoa" document, available online.

Try This: Using a Selector in a Background Thread Using a Notification

1. Create a new View-based application named **SelectorDelay**.
2. Create a new object named `FooBar`.
3. Declare a method named `longMethod` (Listing 11-4) and implement it as in Listing 11-5. Note that the method loops through 5000 values.
4. Open SelectorDelayViewController.h and create a `UIActivityIndicatorView` as an `IBOutlet` (Listings 11-6 and 11-7).
5. Save or build the application and then open SelectorDelayViewController.xib in Interface Builder.
6. Drag a `UIActivityIndicatorView` to the view's canvas (Figure 11-1).
7. Select the activity indicator and in the inspector, change its type to "Large White" and select the Hides When Stopped and Animating check boxes.
8. Connect the File's Owner `myActivity` outlet to the activity indicator on the canvas.
9. Save and exit Interface Builder.
10. Open SelectorDelayViewController.m and implement the `viewWillAppear` method. Have the method invoke `FooBar`'s `longMethod`.
11. Build and Run the application. Note that the view and the activity indicator doesn't appear until after `longMethod` iterates through 5000 loops.

(continued)

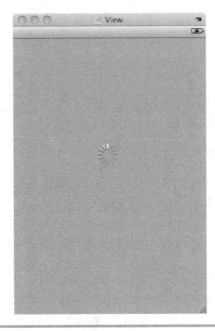

Figure 11-1 A `UIActivityIndicatorView` on a view's canvas

Listing 11-4 FooBar.h

```
#import <Foundation/Foundation.h>
@interface FooBar : NSObject {
}
- (void) longMethod;
@end
```

Listing 11-5 FooBar.m

```
#import "FooBar.h"
@implementation FooBar
- (void) longMethod {
  int x = 0;
  while (x++ < 5000) {
    NSLog(@".");
   }
}
@end
```

Listing 11-6 SelectorDelayViewController.h

```
#import <UIKit/UIKit.h>
@class FooBar;
@interface SelectorDelayViewController : UIViewController {
  IBOutlet UIActivityIndicatorView * myActivity;
  FooBar * fb;
}
@property (nonatomic,retain) UIActivityIndicatorView * myActivity;
@property (nonatomic, retain) FooBar * fb;
@end
```

Listing 11-7 SelectorDelayViewController.m

```
#import "SelectorDelayViewController.h"
#import "FooBar.h"
@implementation SelectorDelayViewController
@synthesize myActivity;
@synthesize fb;
- (void) viewWillAppear:(BOOL)animated {
  [super viewWillAppear:animated];
  self.fb = [[[FooBar alloc] init] autorelease];
  [fb longMethod];
}
- (void)dealloc {
  [fb release];
  [myActivity release];
  [super dealloc];
}
@end
```

12. Modify `viewWillAppear:` so that it uses the `performSelector:afterDelay:` method to invoke `longMethod` (Listing 11-8).

13. Build and Run the application. The view appears before the `longMethod` finishes iterating thorough its values. But notice the activity indicator never disappears from the view's canvas.

(continued)

Listing 11-8 Modifying the `viewWillAppear` method

```
- (void) viewWillAppear:(BOOL)animated {
  [super viewWillAppear:animated];
  self.fb = [[[FooBar alloc] init] autorelease];
  //[fb longMethod];
  [fb performSelectorInBackground:@selector(longMethod) withObject:nil];
}
```

14. Open FooBar.m and modify `longMethod` so that it posts a notification named "longMethodDone" to the application's notification center (Listing 11-9).
15. Open SelectorDelayViewController.m and implement the `viewDidLoad` method so that it registers itself as an observer of the "longMethodDone" notification (Listing 11-10).
16. Modify `SelectorDelayViewController`'s `dealloc` method so that it removes itself as an observer from the application's notification center (Listing 11-11).
17. Build and Run the application and the activity view is removed from the view after the `longMethod` finishes.

Listing 11-9 Modifying `longMethod` to send a notification

```
- (void) longMethod {
  int x = 0;
  while (x++ < 5000) {
    NSLog(@".");
  }
  [[NSNotificationCenter defaultCenter] postNotificationName:@"longMethodDone"
object:nil];
}
```

Listing 11-10 Modifying `viewDidLoad` to register as an observer

```
- (void) viewDidLoad {
  [super viewDidLoad];
  [[NSNotificationCenter defaultCenter] addObserver:self.myActivity
selector:@selector(stopAnimating) name:@"longMethodDone" object:nil];
}
```

Listing 11-11 Modifying `dealloc` to `removeObserver`

```
- (void)dealloc {
  [fb release];
  [[NSNotificationCenter defaultCenter] removeObserver:self.myActivity];
  [myActivity release];
  [super dealloc];
}
```

In this example `SelectorDelayViewController` registers itself as an observer of all "longMethodDone" notifications. When `SelectorDelayViewController's` view appears, it fully loads the view because it runs the `longMethod` on the background thread.

```
[fb performSelectorInBackground:@selector(longMethod) withObject:nil];
```

Notice that the `longMethod` has no memory management needs. It loops through 5000 iterations, logging a period to the debugger console. In the meantime, while it is processing, your application is still responsive. You could have used the `performSelector: withObject:afterDelay:` method to achieve the same results.

Delegates

Notifications are one way you might alert another object that a particularly long method has completed. Another technique, arguably better, is using a *delegate*. How it works is that you have a class adopt a protocol, where the protocol is the delegate. Then in the `performSelector:` method, you pass the delegate as a parameter. The method invoked by the selector then sends a message to the delegate when completed.

Recall how you declare a method that takes a protocol as a parameter.

```
- (void) longMethod: (id<FooBarDelegate>) delegate;
```

You can invoke a method using the `performSelector:` method, then pass the delegate as the object parameter. Because you know the method adopts the `FooBarDelegate` protocol, the invoked method can then invoke one of `FooBarDelegate's` methods, without worrying about the passed object not implementing it. The following Try This illustrates.

Try This Using a Selector with a Delay and a Delegate

1. Copy the preceding Try This project to a new location, as you are modifying this project.
2. Remove the code related to `NSNotification` from `SelectorDelayView Controller` and `FooBar`. The lines you should find and remove are as follows.

```
[[NSNotificationCenter defaultCenter] postNotificationName:@"longMethodDone"
object:nil];
[[NSNotificationCenter defaultCenter] removeObserver:self.myActivity];
[[NSNotificationCenter defaultCenter] addObserver:self.myActivity
selector:@selector(stopAnimating) name:@"longMethodDone" object:nil];
```

3. Build and Run the application. The activity indicator should never disappear.
4. Create a new C header file named FooBarDelegate. Make the file a protocol declaration, as in Listing 11-12.
5. Open FooBar.h and modify `longMethod`'s signature so that it takes a `FooBarDelegate` as a parameter (Listings 11-13 and 11-14).
6. Open SelectorDelayViewController.h and modify it so that it adopts the `FooBarDelegate` protocol (Listing 11-15),
7. Open SelectorDelayViewController.m and implement the `longMethodDone:` in `SelectorDelayViewController`, as in Listing 11-16; also modify `viewWillAppear` so that `SelectorDelayViewController` passes itself as the delegate to `longMethod:`.
8. Build and Run the application. The activity indicator disappears and the dictionary content is logged to the debugger console. But there is a problem: you forgot to manage memory using a different autorelease pool for the `longMethod:` code. Remember, it runs in a different thread. In `longMethod:` you used the `NSDictionary`'s convenience constructor, which uses autorelease, and so the memory leaks because there is no pool in place. You should also see something similar to the warning in Listing 11-17 in the debugger console.
9. To fix this memory leak, you have three main options. You could use the `performSelector:withObject:afterDelay:` method; create your own `NSAutoReleasePool`; or change the code in `FooBar` and `SelectorDelayView Controller` to explicitly allocate, initialize, and release all objects.

10. But in this example, rather than fixing the code's memory handling, simply change the `performSelectorInBackground:withObject` method to use `performSelector:withObject:afterDelay`.

```
//[self.fb performSelectorInBackground:@selector(longMethod:) withObject:self];
[self.fb performSelector:@selector(longMethod:) withObject:self afterDelay:.01];
```

11. Build and Run the application and there are no warnings. Moreover, the end results are the same visually.

Listing 11-12 FooBarDelegate.h

```
@protocol FooBarDelegate
- (void) longMethodDone: (NSDictionary *) data;
@end
```

Listing 11-13 FooBar.h

```
#import <Foundation/Foundation.h>
@protocol FooBarDelegate;
@interface FooBar : NSObject {
}
- (void) longMethod: (id<FooBarDelegate>) delegate;
@end
```

Listing 11-14 FooBar.m

```
#import "FooBar.h"
#import "FooBarDelegate.h"
@implementation FooBar
- (void) longMethod: (id<FooBarDelegate>) delegate {
  int x = 0;
  while (x++ < 5000) {
    NSLog(@".");
  }
  NSDictionary * data = [NSDictionary dictionaryWithObjectsAndKeys:@"5000 loops",
@"msg1", @"while loop",@"msg2",nil];
  [delegate longMethodDone:data];
}
@end
```

(continued)

Listing 11-15 SelectorDelayViewController.h

```
#import <UIKit/UIKit.h>
#import "FooBarDelegate.h"
@class FooBar;
@interface SelectorDelayViewController : UIViewController <FooBarDelegate> {
  IBOutlet UIActivityIndicatorView * myActivity;
  FooBar * fb;
}
@property (nonatomic,retain) UIActivityIndicatorView * myActivity;
@property (nonatomic, retain) FooBar * fb;
@end
```

Listing 11-16 SelectorDelayViewController.m

```
#import "SelectorDelayViewController.h"
#import "FooBar.h"
@implementation SelectorDelayViewController
@synthesize myActivity;
@synthesize fb;
- (void) viewWillAppear:(BOOL)animated {
  [super viewWillAppear:animated];
  self.fb = [[[FooBar alloc] init] autorelease];
  [self.fb performSelectorInBackground:@selector(longMethod:) withObject:self];
}
- (void) longMethodDone: (NSDictionary *) data {
  [self.myActivity stopAnimating];
  NSEnumerator * myKeys = [data keyEnumerator];
  id curKey;
  for (curKey in myKeys)
    NSLog(@"The key:%@ and the value:%@", curKey, [data objectForKey:curKey]);
}
- (void)dealloc {
  [self.fb release];
  [self.myActivity release];
  [super dealloc];
}
@end
```

Listing 11-17 Debugger warning

```
*** _NSAutoreleaseNoPool(): Object 0x3b12890 of class NSCFDictionary autoreleased
with no pool in place - just leaking
```

Target-Action

Throughout this book you graphically connected IBActions in code to events fired by controls in Interface Builder. Although this ability is useful, there are many times when you must dynamically assign an IBAction to a control in your code. You can easily add a target to the control using the addTarget method. For instance, the following code adds the changeMyLabelText: method as an action for a UIButton for the "Touch Up Inside" event.

```
[self.myButtonOne addTarget:self action:@selector(changeMyLabelText:)
forControlEvents:UIControlEventTouchUpInside];
```

All iPhone controls inherit from the UIControl class. This class has a method called addTarget:action:forControlEvents: that allows tying a control event to an action in code.

```
- (void)addTarget:(id)target action:(SEL)action forControlEvents:
(UIControlEvents)controlEvents
```

The target is the object the action that receives the action. The action is a selector identifying the method that should be invoked. The controlEvents are the control's events that should fire the selector. The following Try This illustrates how to programmatically connect an action to a control event using code.

Try This Connecting a Control to an Action Programmatically

1. Create a new View-based application named **TargetAction**.
2. Create a new object named FooBar (Listings 11-18 and 11-19). Have FooBar implement a method named play.
3. Create two buttons and a label as an IBOutlet to TargetActionViewController.h (Listing 11-20). Also add FooBar as a property.
4. Save or build the application and then open TargetActionViewController.xib in Interface Builder.
5. Add two buttons and a label to the canvas (Figure 11-2). Connect them to the outlets in the File's Owner.

(continued)

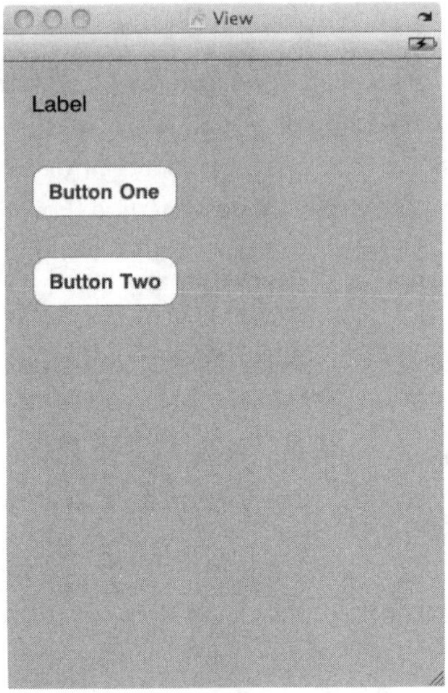

Figure 11-2 Adding two buttons and a label to the canvas

6. Save and exit Interface Builder.
7. Open TargetActionViewController.m and implement the `viewDidLoad` method so that it connects the buttons to the `changeMyLabelText:` and `play` methods (Listing 11-21). Also implement the `changeMyLabelText:` method.
8. Build and Run the application.

Listing 11-18 FooBar.h

```
#import <Foundation/Foundation.h>
@interface FooBar : NSObject {
}
- (void) play;
@end
```

Listing 11-19 FooBar.m

```
#import "FooBar.h"
@implementation FooBar
- (void) play {
  NSLog(@"FooBar play method invoked...");
}
@end
```

Listing 11-20 TargetActionViewController.h

```
#import <UIKit/UIKit.h>
@class FooBar;
@interface TargetActionViewController : UIViewController {
  IBOutlet UIButton * myButtonOne;
  IBOutlet UIButton * myButtonTwo;
  IBOutlet UILabel * myLabel;
  FooBar * myFooBar;
}
@property (nonatomic, retain) UIButton * myButtonOne;
@property (nonatomic,retain) UIButton * myButtonTwo;
@property (nonatomic,retain) UILabel * myLabel;
@property (nonatomic,retain) FooBar * myFooBar;
-(void) changeMyLabelText: (id) sender;
@end
```

Listing 11-21 TargetActionViewController.m

```
#import "TargetActionViewController.h"
#import "FooBar.h"
@implementation TargetActionViewController
@synthesize myButtonOne;
@synthesize myButtonTwo;
@synthesize myLabel;
@synthesize myFooBar;
- (void) viewDidLoad {
  [super viewDidLoad];
  self.myFooBar = [[FooBar alloc] init];
  [self.myButtonOne addTarget:self action:@selector(changeMyLabelText:
)
forControlEvents:UIControlEventTouchUpInside];
```

(continued)

```
  [self.myButtonTwo addTarget:self.myFooBar action:@selector(play)
forControlEvents:UIControlEventTouchUpInside];
}
-(void) changeMyLabelText: (id) sender {
  self.myLabel.text = @"Hello World";
}
- (void)dealloc {
  [self.myFooBar release];
  [myButtonOne release];
  [myButtonTwo release];
  [myLabel release];
  [super dealloc];
}
@end
```

Summary

This chapter touched on several topics normally reserved for more advanced discussions. However, as you progress as an iPhone developer, you will see the topics presented here repeatedly, so it's best to at least get an introduction to them. Using an activity indicator to tell a user to "please wait" or using a progress view to tell a user to "please wait and you have this much time remaining" are typically used when a long-running task is to be performed. Problem is, that task usually blocks the thread loading the view, and the application "freezes" until the task completes. Using the two `performSelector` variants in this chapter avoids this application "freezing."

The easiest method to use is the `performSelector:withObject:afterDelay:` method, as you don't need to worry about memory management. But don't think that this is a substitute for multithreading, as it is not. But it does allow avoiding multithreading for many trivial tasks.

You learned about using both notifications and delegates to inform the class invoking the selector that the selector's method had finished processing. Although both work, in general, you should reserve notifications for general messages to multiple observers, and use delegates for pointed "notifications" to a particular class in a particular point in time. Delegates are the more robust way for a particular class invoking `performSelectorInBackground:withObject:` or `performSelector:withObject:afterDelay:` to be notified that the selector's method has completed.

Chapter 12

The Model-View-Controller Design Pattern

Key Skills & Concepts

- Understanding the Model-View-Controller Design Pattern
- Using Property Lists
- Sharing Data Between Views

Anybody can write a simple program. However, crafting a well-designed program that works well is a much more difficult endeavor. In this chapter you learn about the Model-View-Controller design pattern and how to apply it to your iPhone development efforts using Objective-C. The Model-View-Controller design pattern is arguably one of the biggest advances in computer science, so you would do well by learning it.

The Model-View-Controller Design Pattern

The MVC design pattern separates a program's objects based upon responsibility. The model is responsible for your program's logical objects. These classes hold an application's data and its business logic. Recall the silly classes used in previous chapters. `Duck`, `Driftwood`, and `Glutton` are all examples of model classes. They are logical objects with data and behavior. Their behavior is unrelated to how your application's user interface operates. Instead, logic was related to their business functions; hence the term business logic. Nowhere do these objects define an application's appearance. These are logical objects that reside behind the scenes.

Now consider the `UIView` and `UIViewController` classes that you extended in previous Try This projects. The `UIView` is your view, and the view controller is your application's controller. The view's responsibility is to control the application's appearance. The view controller's responsibility is to handle the view's life cycle methods and serve as a "middleman" between the view and the model. Figure 12-1 illustrates a typical MVC architecture.

The view displays your application's interface to its users. When a user interacts with the view, those events are forwarded to the controller. The controller then updates the state of any related model objects and updates the view. Figure 12-2 illustrates the MVC and an iPhone application.

A `UIView` displays the iPhone application's user interface. A `UIView` has an associated `UIViewController` that responds to a user's interactions with its `UIView`. For instance, suppose you had a simple game where a penguin waddles across a screen.

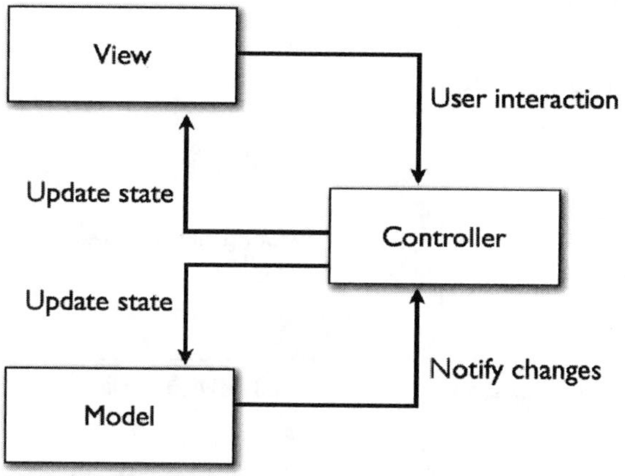

Figure 12-1 Model-View-Controller (MVC) architecture

When a user taps the penguin, it places a large red *X* on the penguin and the penguin stops waddling. When tapped again, the application removes the *X* and the penguin starts waddling again.

A `Penguin` class represents the penguin, which is a model class. In Figure 12-3 a penguin waddles across the screen. When a user clicks the penguin, the view calls the view controller's `shootPenguin:` action. The penguin, a property of the view controller, is "killed" and the penguin's state is updated to dead. The view controller also updates the view's display by stopping the animation and placing a red *X* on the penguin.

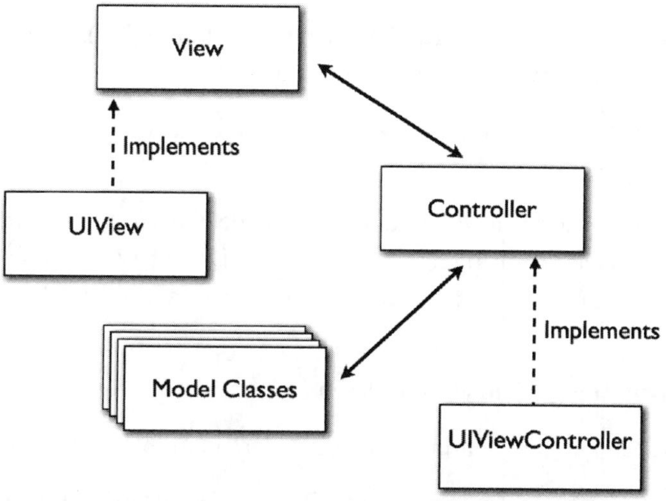

Figure 12-2 MVC architecture and iPhone applications

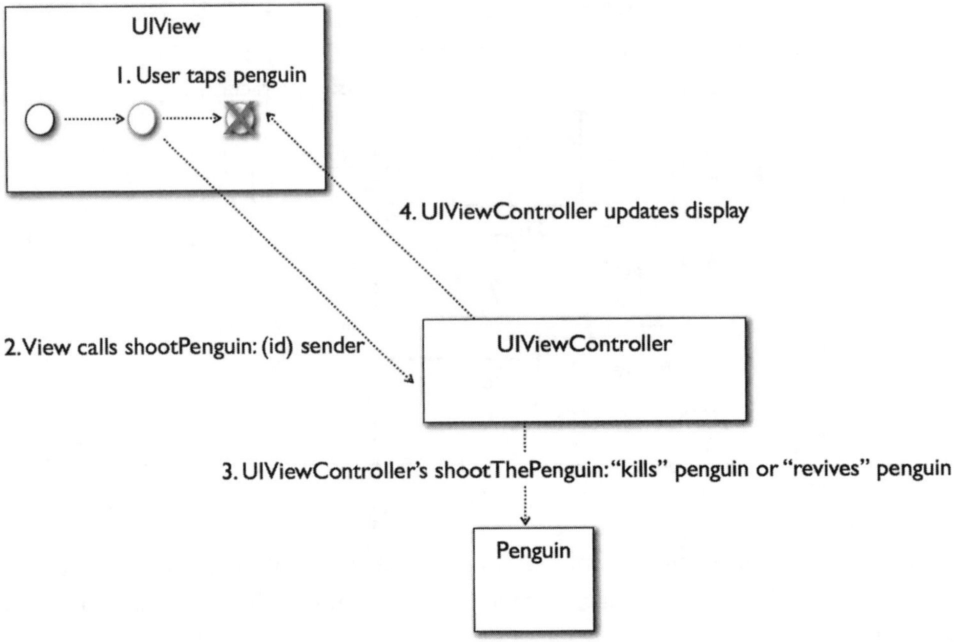

Figure 12-3 Hypothetical penguin game

Try This Creating a Simple MVC Game

1. Create a new View-based application named **PenguinHunting**.
2. Create a new class called `Penguin` (Listings 12-1 and 12-2). Have the `Penguin` implement the `shoot` and `revive` methods.
3. Add a property called `state` to `Penguin` and define two constants, `STATE_ALIVE` and `STATE_DEAD`.
4. Open PenguinHuntingViewController.h in Xcode and add an `IBOutlet` for a `UIButton` named `penguinImageButton` (Listing 12-3). Add an `NSTimer` named `myTimer` and a `Penguin` class named `myPenguin`. Make all three properties.
5. Open PenguinHuntingViewController.m and implement as in Listing 12-4.
6. Save and open PenguinHuntingViewController.xib in Interface Builder.
7. Connect the `penguinImageButton` in File's Owner to a button on the view's canvas.

8. Select the button and change its type to custom and image to tux.png (Figure 12-4).
9. Connect the button's Touch Up Inside event to the `shootThePenguin:` method.
10. Build and Run the application.

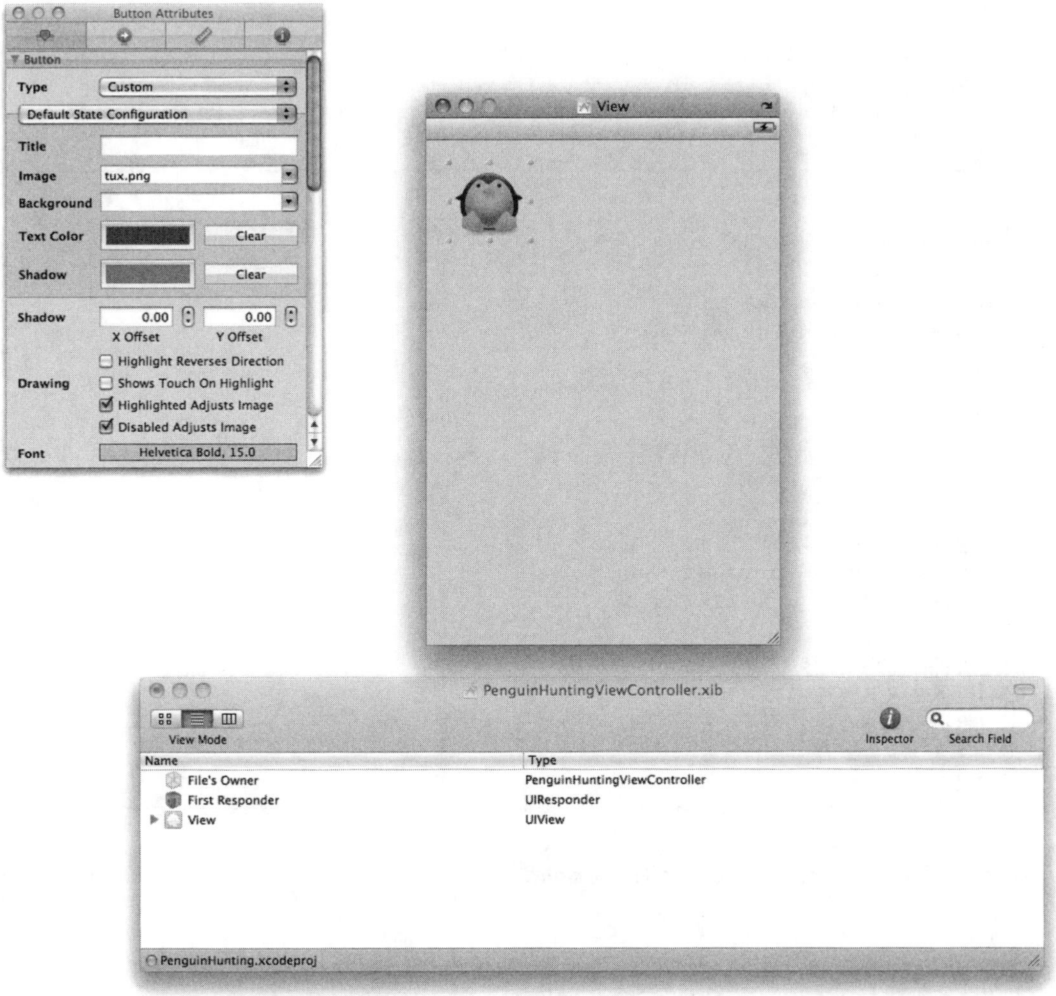

Figure 12-4 Creating a custom button to display the penguin

(continued)

Listing 12-1 Penguin.h

```
#import <Foundation/Foundation.h>
#define STATE_ALIVE 1
#define STATE_DEAD 2
@interface Penguin : NSObject{
  int state;
}
@property (nonatomic, assign) int state;
- (void) shoot;
- (void) revive;
@end
```

Listing 12-2 Penguin.m

```
#import "Penguin.h"
@implementation Penguin
@synthesize state;
- (id) init {
  id toRet = [super init];
  self.state = STATE_ALIVE;
  return toRet;
}
- (void) shoot {
  NSLog(@"penguin is shot...");
'"" self.state = STATE_DEAD;
}
- (void) revive {
  NSLog(@"penguin is revived...");
  self.state = STATE_ALIVE;
}
@end
```

Listing 12-3 PenguinHuntingViewController.h

```
#import <UIKit/UIKit.h>
#import "Penguin.h"
@interface PenguinHuntingViewController : UIViewController {
  IBOutlet UIButton * penguinImageButton;
  NSTimer * myTimer;
  Penguin * myPenguin;
}
@property (nonatomic, retain) Penguin * myPenguin;
```

```
@property (nonatomic,retain) NSTimer * myTimer;
@property (nonatomic,retain) UIButton * penguinImageButton;
- (IBAction) shootThePenguin: (id) sender;
@end
```

Listing 12-4 PenguinHuntingViewController.m

```
#import "PenguinHuntingViewController.h"
@implementation PenguinHuntingViewController
@synthesize penguinImageButton;
@synthesize myTimer;
@synthesize myPenguin;
- (void) viewDidAppear:(BOOL)animated {
  [super viewDidAppear:animated];
  self.myTimer = [NSTimer scheduledTimerWithTimeInterval:.03 target: self
selector:@selector(secondIncrement) userInfo: nil repeats: YES];
  self.myPenguin = [[Penguin alloc] init];
}
static BOOL movingRight = YES;
static BOOL movingDown = YES;
- (void) secondIncrement {
  CGRect frame = self.penguinImageButton.frame;
  if(frame.origin.x > 210) {
    movingRight = NO;
  }
  else if (frame.origin.x < 20) {
    movingRight = YES;
  }
  if(frame.origin.y > 380) {
    movingDown = NO;
  }
  else if(frame.origin.y < 20) {
    movingDown = YES;
  }
  if(movingDown) frame.origin.y += 2;
  else frame.origin.y -= 2;
  if(movingRight) frame.origin.x += 2;
  else frame.origin.x -= 2;
  self.penguinImageButton.frame = frame;
}
- (IBAction) shootThePenguin: (id) sender {
  if(self.myPenguin.state == STATE_ALIVE) {
    [self.myTimer invalidate];
    self.myTimer = nil;
    [self.penguinImageButton setImage:[UIImage imageNamed:@"tux_dead.png"]
forState:UIControlStateNormal];
    [self.myPenguin shoot];
  }
```

(continued)

```
  else {
    self.myTimer = [NSTimer scheduledTimerWithTimeInterval:.03 target: self
selector:@selector(secondIncrement) userInfo: nil repeats: YES];
    [self.penguinImageButton setImage:[UIImage imageNamed:@"tux.png"]
forState:UIControlStateNormal];
    [self.myPenguin revive];
  }
}
- (void)dealloc {
  [penguinImageButton release];
  [self.myPenguin release];
  [self.myTimer release];
  [super dealloc];
}
@end
```

In this application you first build the model class, `Penguin`. `Penguin` has the penguin's state and two methods that change its state. The `PenguinHuntingViewController` is the application's controller and the `UIView` in the PenguinHunting ViewController xib is the view. The view controller coordinates between the view and the model. When the view appears, it sends a message to the view controller's `viewDidAppear` method. The `viewDidAppear` method starts a timer and creates a `Penguin` instance.

The timer in the view controller fires every 0.03 seconds, calling the `secondIncrement` method. Note that this is not an Apple-defined method; you could use any method name provided you assign it as a selector. Assigning a selector to the timer allows the timer to fire the named method every 0.03 seconds.

The `secondIncrement` method moves the button around on the canvas by moving the button's *x* and *y* origins (Figure 12-5). To keep the image from going off the screen, the button's movement changes direction when moving too far in any direction. It is not true animation, but it works. Incidentally, using the `CGRect` as in the `secondIncrement` method is an easy way to move a control on a view programmatically.

When a user taps the button, the view calls the view controller's `shootThePenguin` action. This method changes the penguin's state; if alive, it stops the timer, which causes the penguin to stop moving. It also changes the button's image with a penguin image with an *X* through it (Figure 12-6). When the user taps the button again, the view calls the `shootThePenguin` method, which replaces the button's image with the original image and starts a new timer, so the button starts moving again.

Notice how the application illustrates the quintessential MVC design pattern in an iPhone. The view knows nothing about the penguin. The penguin knows nothing about the view; the penguin actually knows nothing about the controller either.

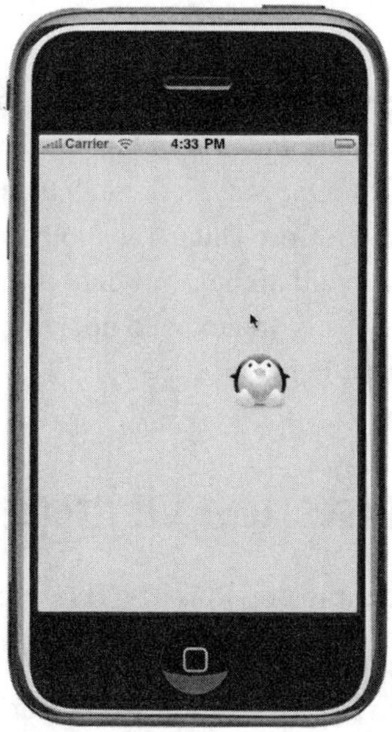

Figure 12-5 The penguin moving on the canvas

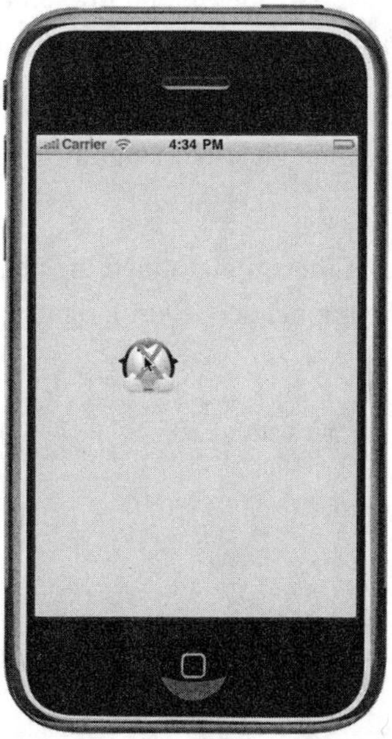

Figure 12-6 The "dead" penguin

Persistence

Models are often persisted between running an application. Typically a model class is persisted and reconstituted as needed. The iPhone offers several different ways you can persist an application's data. One way is through using the iPhone's built-in sqlite database. Another way is through Core Data. Yet another way is through using a property list. The easiest way to persist small amounts of data is through property lists and archiving. In the following Try This you expand upon the model in the last Try This by persisting it between application invocations.

Try This Adding Persistence Using a Property List

1. Open PenguinHunting from the previous Try This application in Xcode.
2. Modify Penguin.h and Penguin.m so that it implements `persistPenguinState:` and `initializePenguinState` methods (Listings 12-5 and 12-6).
3. Modify Penguin's `init` method so that it uses the `initializePenguinState` method to initialize its state.
4. Open PenguinHuntingViewController.m and implement the `viewDidDisappear:` method (Listing 12-7). Also modify the `viewDidAppear:` method so that it initializes the button's behavior depending upon the penguin's state.
5. Build and Run the application. Click the penguin so that it is "dead" and then stop the application in the iPhone simulator.
6. Start the application again in the simulator and the penguin is "dead." Click the penguin to reanimate it and stop the application. Start it again and the penguin is "alive."

Listing 12-5 Penguin.h with persistence

```
#import <Foundation/Foundation.h>
#define STATE_ALIVE 1
#define STATE_DEAD 2
@interface Penguin : NSObject{
  int state;
}
@property (nonatomic, assign) int state;
- (void) shoot;
- (void) revive;
```

```
- (void) persistPenguinState: (int) theState;
- (int) initializePenguinState;
@end
```

Listing 12-6 Penguin.m with persistence

```
#import "Penguin.h"
@implementation Penguin
@synthesize state;
- (id) init {
  id toRet = [super init];
  self.state = [self initializePenguinState];
  return toRet;
}
- (void) shoot {
  NSLog(@"penguin is shot...");
  self.state = STATE_DEAD;
}
- (void) revive {
  NSLog(@"penguin is revived...");
  self.state = STATE_ALIVE;
}
- (void) persistPenguinState: (int) theState {
  NSString *plistPath = [[NSSearchPathForDirectoriesInDomains(
NSDocumentDirectory, NSUserDomainMask, YES) objectAtIndex:0]
stringByAppendingPathComponent:@"properties.plist"];
  NSDictionary *plistDict = [NSDictionary dictionaryWithObjects:
[NSArray arrayWithObjects: [NSNumber numberWithInt:theState], nil]
forKeys:[NSArray arrayWithObjects: @"state", nil]];
  NSData *plistData = [NSPropertyListSerialization dataFromPropertyList:
plistDict format:NSPropertyListXMLFormat_v1_0 errorDescription:nil];
 [plistData writeToFile:plistPath atomically:YES];
}
- (int) initializePenguinState {
  NSPropertyListFormat format;
  NSString *plistPath = [[NSSearchPathForDirectoriesInDomains(
NSDocumentDirectory, NSUserDomainMask, YES) objectAtIndex:0]
stringByAppendingPathComponent:@"properties.plist"];
  if([[NSFileManager defaultManager] fileExistsAtPath:plistPath] == NO) {
    return 1;
  }
  else {
    NSData * plistData = [NSData dataWithContentsOfFile:plistPath];
    NSDictionary * props = (NSDictionary *)[NSPropertyListSerialization
propertyListFromData:plistData mutabilityOption:NSPropertyListImmutable
format:&format errorDescription:nil];
```

(continued)

```
    return [((NSNumber*)[props objectForKey:@"state"]) intValue];
  }
}
@end
```

Listing 12-7 PenguinHuntingViewController.h

```
#import "PenguinHuntingViewController.h"
@implementation PenguinHuntingViewController
@synthesize penguinImageButton;
@synthesize myTimer;
@synthesize myPenguin;
- (void) viewDidAppear:(BOOL)animated {
  self.myPenguin = [[Penguin alloc] init];
  if(self.myPenguin.state == STATE_DEAD) {
  [self.penguinImageButton setImage:[UIImage imageNamed:@"tux_dead.png"]
forState:UIControlStateNormal];
  }
  else {
    self.myTimer = [NSTimer scheduledTimerWithTimeInterval:.03 target: self
selector:@selector(secondIncrement) userInfo: nil repeats: YES];
  }
}
- (void) viewDidDisappear: (BOOL) animated {
  [self.myPenguin persistPenguinState:self.myPenguin.state];
  [super viewDidDisappear:animated];
}
static BOOL movingRight = YES;
static BOOL movingDown = YES;
- (void) secondIncrement {
  CGRect frame = self.penguinImageButton.frame;
  if(frame.origin.x > 210) {
    movingRight = NO;
  }
  else if (frame.origin.x < 20) {
    movingRight = YES;
  }
  if(frame.origin.y > 380) {
    movingDown = NO;
  }
  else if(frame.origin.y < 20) {
    movingDown = YES;
  }
  if(movingDown) frame.origin.y += 2;
  else frame.origin.y -= 2;
  if(movingRight) frame.origin.x += 2;
  else frame.origin.x -= 2;
  self.penguinImageButton.frame = frame;
}
```

```
- (IBAction) shootThePenguin: (id) sender {
  if(self.myPenguin.state == STATE_ALIVE) {
    [self.myTimer invalidate];
    self.myTimer = nil;
    [self.penguinImageButton setImage:[UIImage imageNamed:@"tux_dead.png"]
forState:UIControlStateNormal];
    [self.myPenguin shoot];
  }
  else {
    self.myTimer = [NSTimer scheduledTimerWithTimeInterval:.03 target: self
selector:@selector(secondIncrement) userInfo: nil repeats: YES];
    [self.penguinImageButton setImage:[UIImage imageNamed:@"tux.png"]
forState:UIControlStateNormal];
    [self.myPenguin revive];
  }
}
- (void)dealloc {
  [self.penguinImageButton release];
  [self.myTimer release];
  [self.myPenguin release];
  [super dealloc];
}
@end
```

The `Penguin` class persists itself to a property list named properties.plist. Because you specified NSPropertyListXMLFormat_v1_0 as the file's format, it persists the data as an XML text document (Listing 12-8).

Listing 12-8 Persisting the data as XML

```
<?xml version="1.0" encoding="UTF-8"?>
<!DOCTYPE plist PUBLIC "-//Apple//DTD PLIST 1.0//EN"
"http://www.apple.com/DTDs/PropertyList-1.0.dtd">
<plist version="1.0">
<dict>
  <key>state</key>
  <integer>2</integer>
</dict>
</plist>
```

Notice the controller knows nothing about how the penguin persists itself; it merely sends a message to the penguin to persist itself. The view, of course, is oblivious to the model's persistence. There is a strict separation between the model, view, and controller.

Multiple Xibs

Most iPhone applications consist of multiple xibs. Each xib contains a single view. As a user navigates through an application, each xib is loaded as needed and displays its view. This saves memory, as your application only loads the xib's content as needed. If all views were in one xib, then all views are loaded regardless of whether they are needed.

Try This Sharing Data Between Xibs

1. Create a new Tab Bar application named **TabsMultiple** (Figure 12-7).
2. Create a new class named `MyAnswers` (Listings 12-9 and 12-10).
3. Open FirstViewController.h and import `MyAnswers`.
4. Create two `IBOutlets` for `UITextFields` and one `IBOutlet` for `MyAnswers` (Listings 12-11 and 12-12). Also create an `IBAction` named `getAnswer`.
5. Create a new `UIViewController` named `SecondViewController` (Listings 12-13 and 12-14).

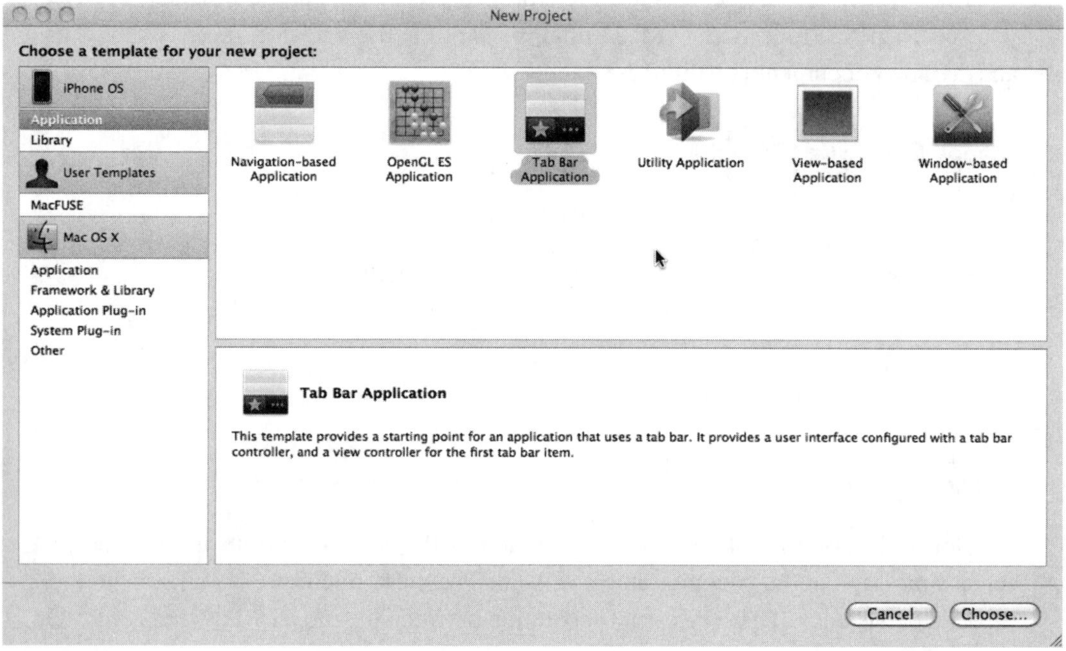

Figure 12-7 Creating a Tab Bar application

6. Be certain that you do not check the "With XIB for user interface" check box. Instead you will use this controller for the template-created SecondView.xib file.
7. Open `SecondViewController` and add two `UILabels` as `IBOutlets`. Also add an `IBOutlet` for the `MyAnswers` class.
8. Create another class named `MyTabBarController` that implements the `UITabBarController` (Listings 12-15 and 12-16). Add a property for the `MyAnswers` class named `myMyAnswers`.
9. Build and then open MainWindow.xib in Interface Builder.
10. Drag an object from the Library to the project's main window and change the object's class to `MyAnswers` (Figure 12-8).

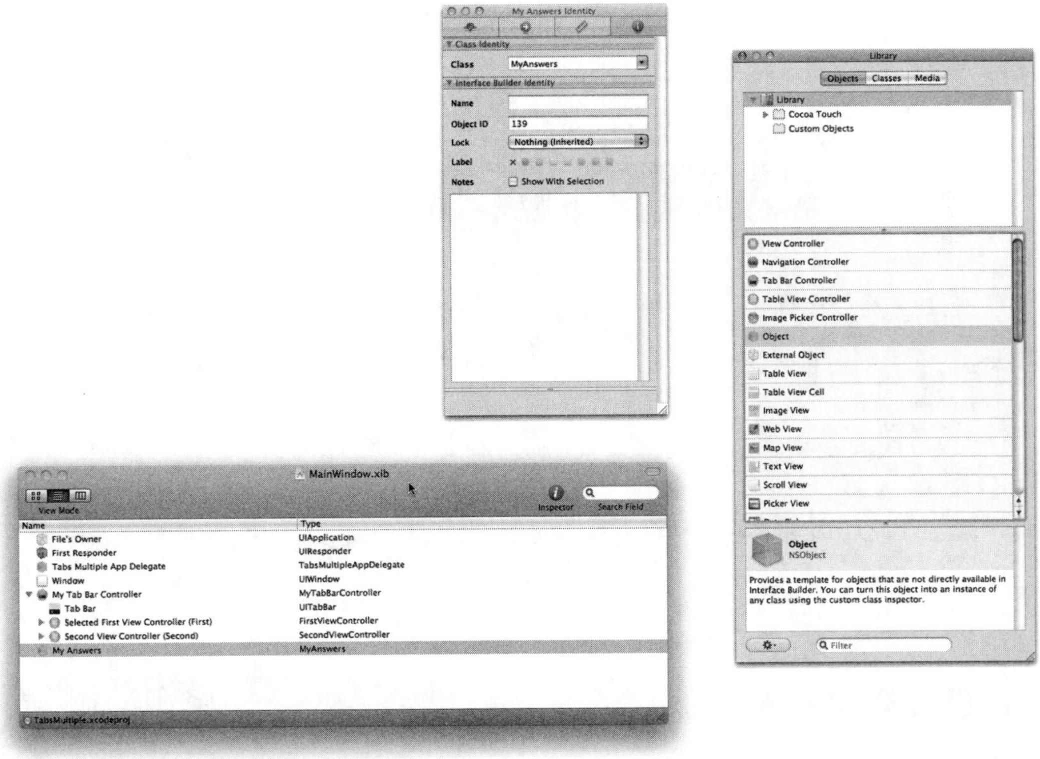

Figure 12-8 Adding an object to main window

(continued)

11. Add two `UITextFields` to the first view's canvas (Figure 12-9.). Change the topmost text field's tag value to 1 in the text field's inspector.

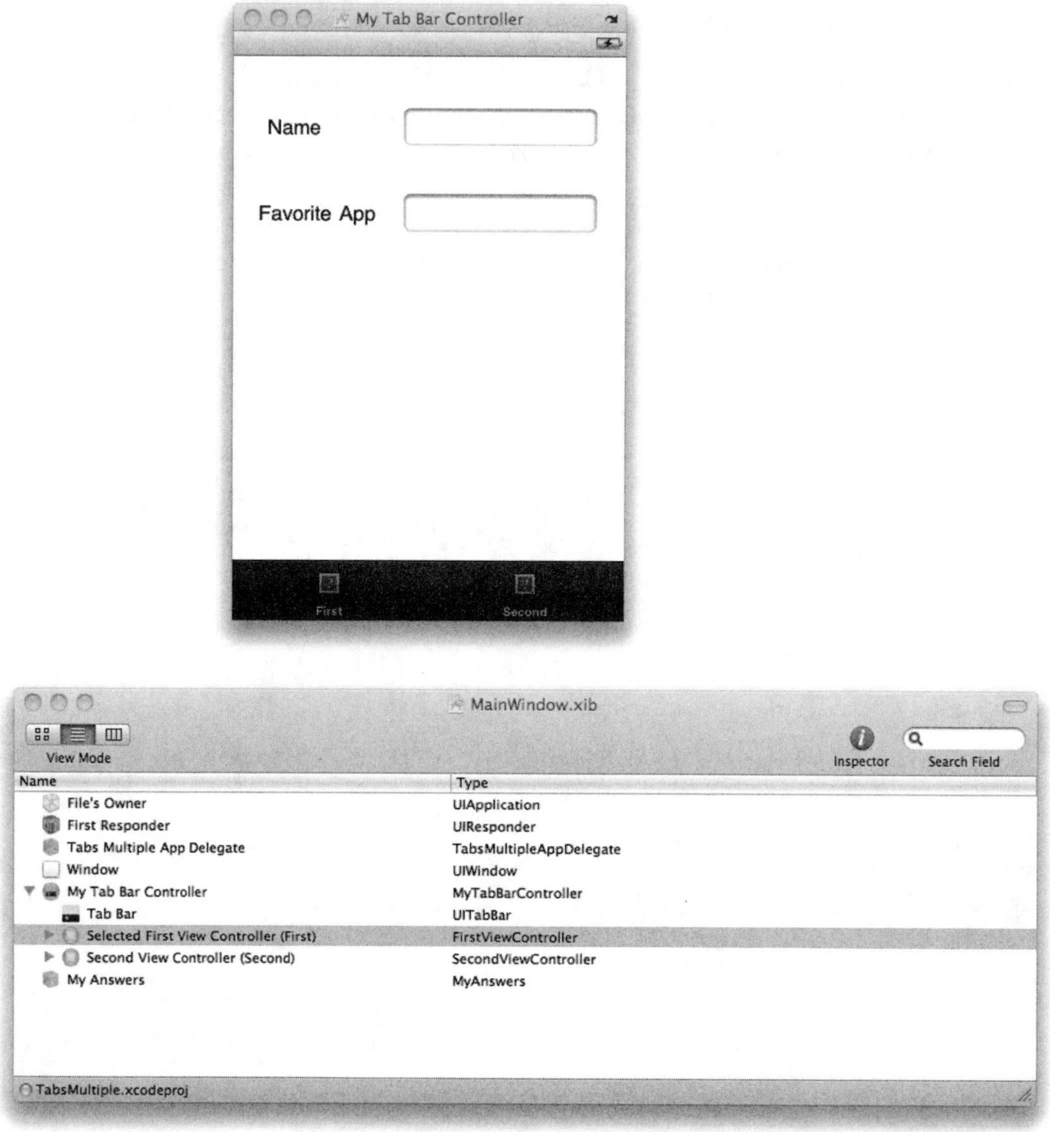

Figure 12-9 Adding two text fields to the canvas

12. Connect the two `IBOutlets` in `FirstViewController` to the `UITextFields` on the canvas (Figure 12-10).

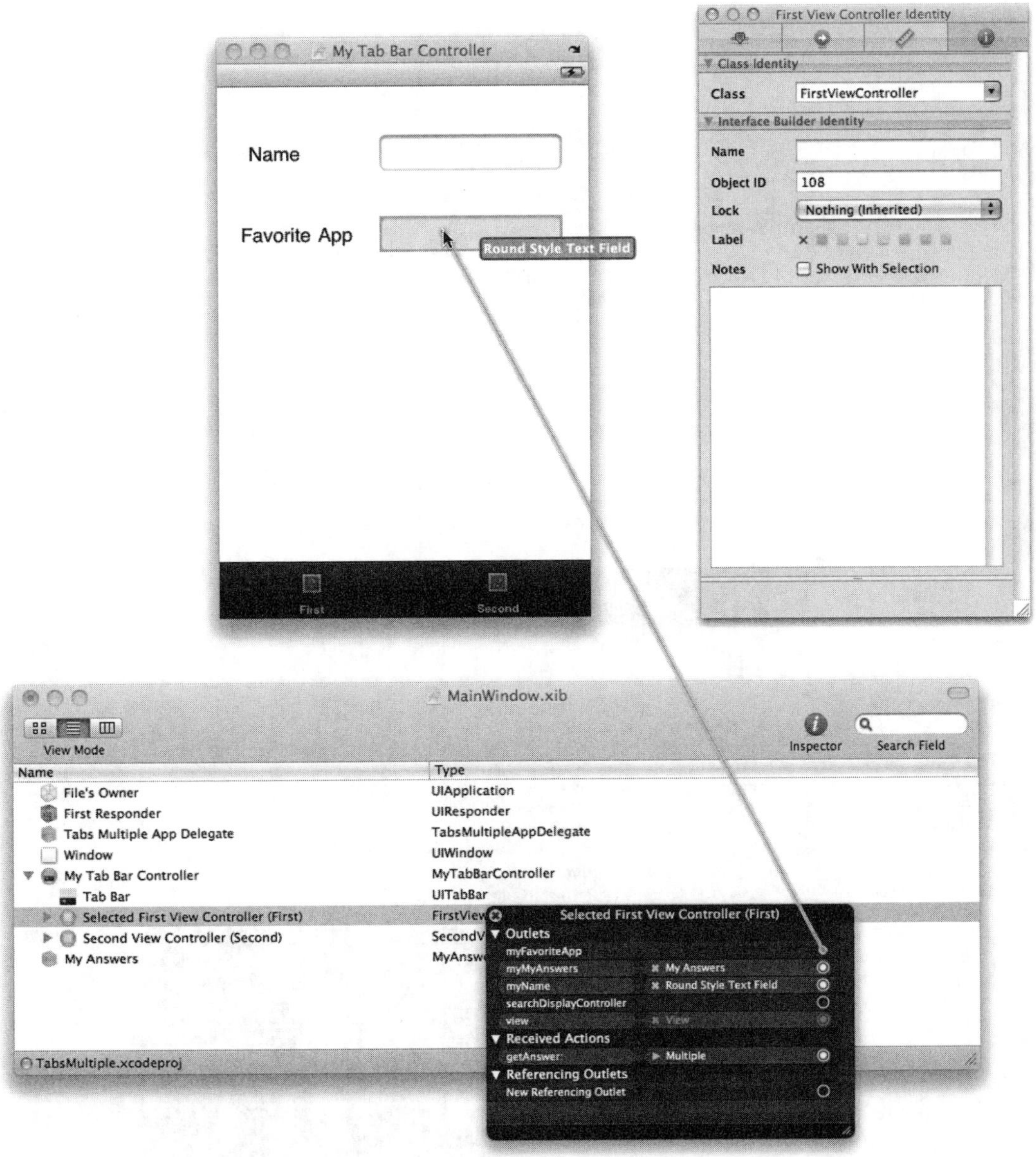

Figure 12-10 Connecting the `IBOutlets`

(continued)

13. Connect the `getAnswer` `IBAction` to both `UITextView`'s Did End on Exit events (Figure 12-11).

Figure 12-11 Connecting `getAnswer` `IBAction` to the text view's Did End on Exit event

14. Connect the `MyAnswers` object to the `myMyAnswers IBOutlet` in `FirstViewController` (Figure 12-12).

15. Select Second View Controller (Second) and change its class to `SecondViewController` (Figure 12-13).

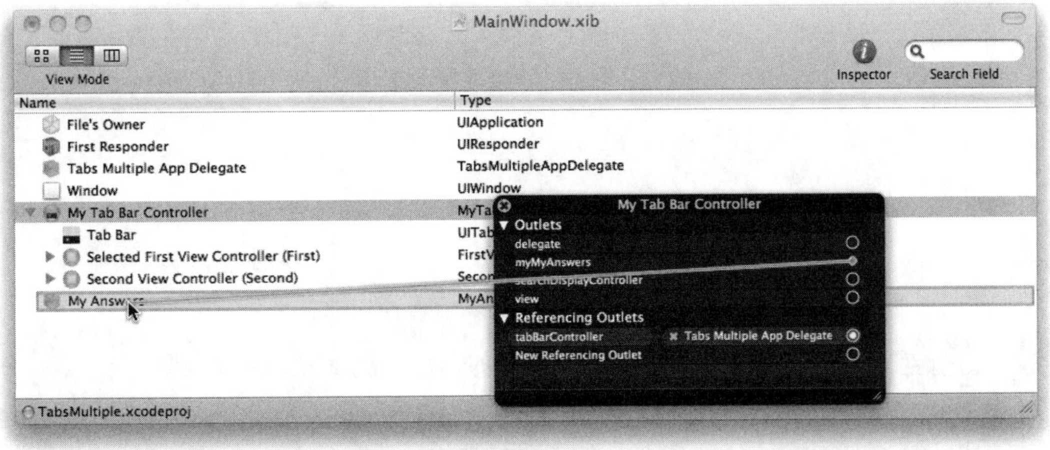

Figure 12-12 Connecting `MyAnswers` object to the `myMyAnswers` outlet

(continued)

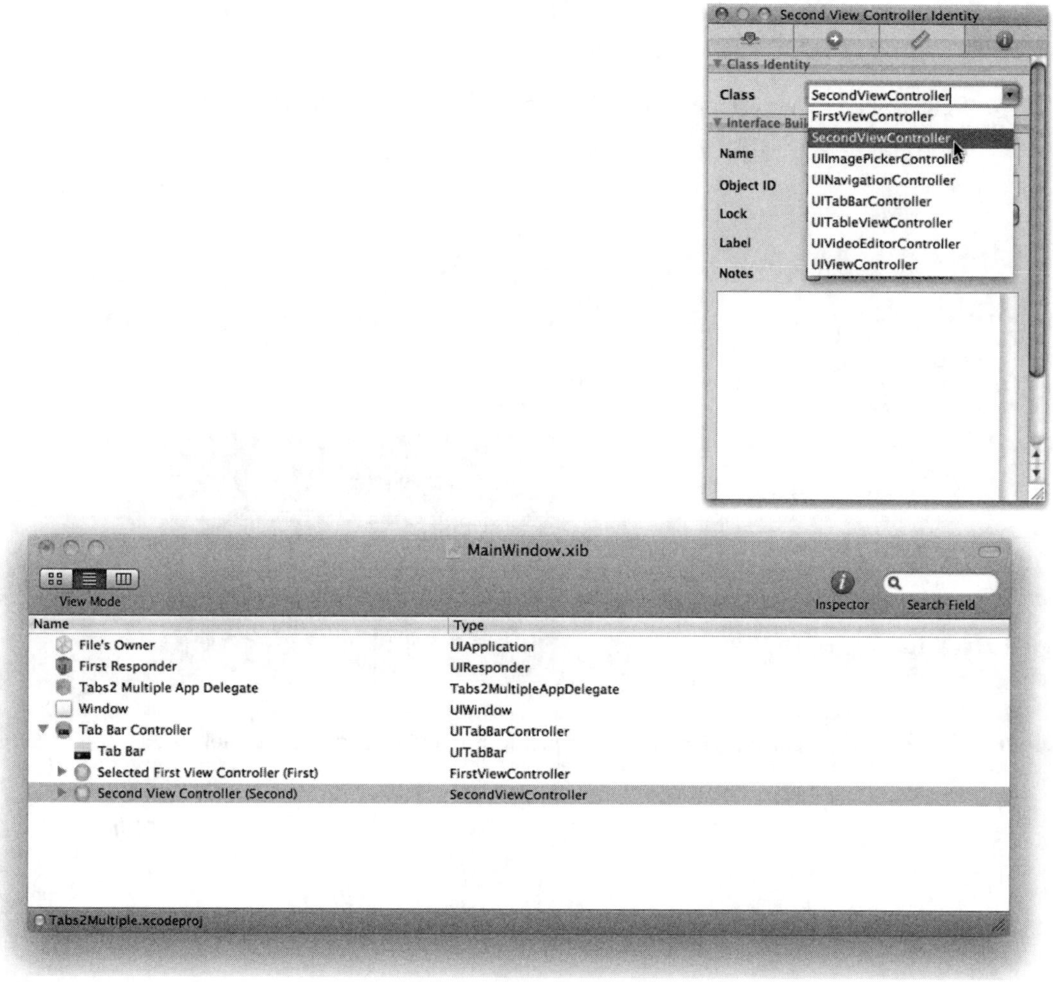

Figure 12-13 Changing Second View Controller

16. Connect the `MyAnswers` object to the `myMyAnswers IBOutlet` in `SecondViewController`.

17. Select MyTabBarController and change its class to `MyTabBarController` (Figure 12-14).

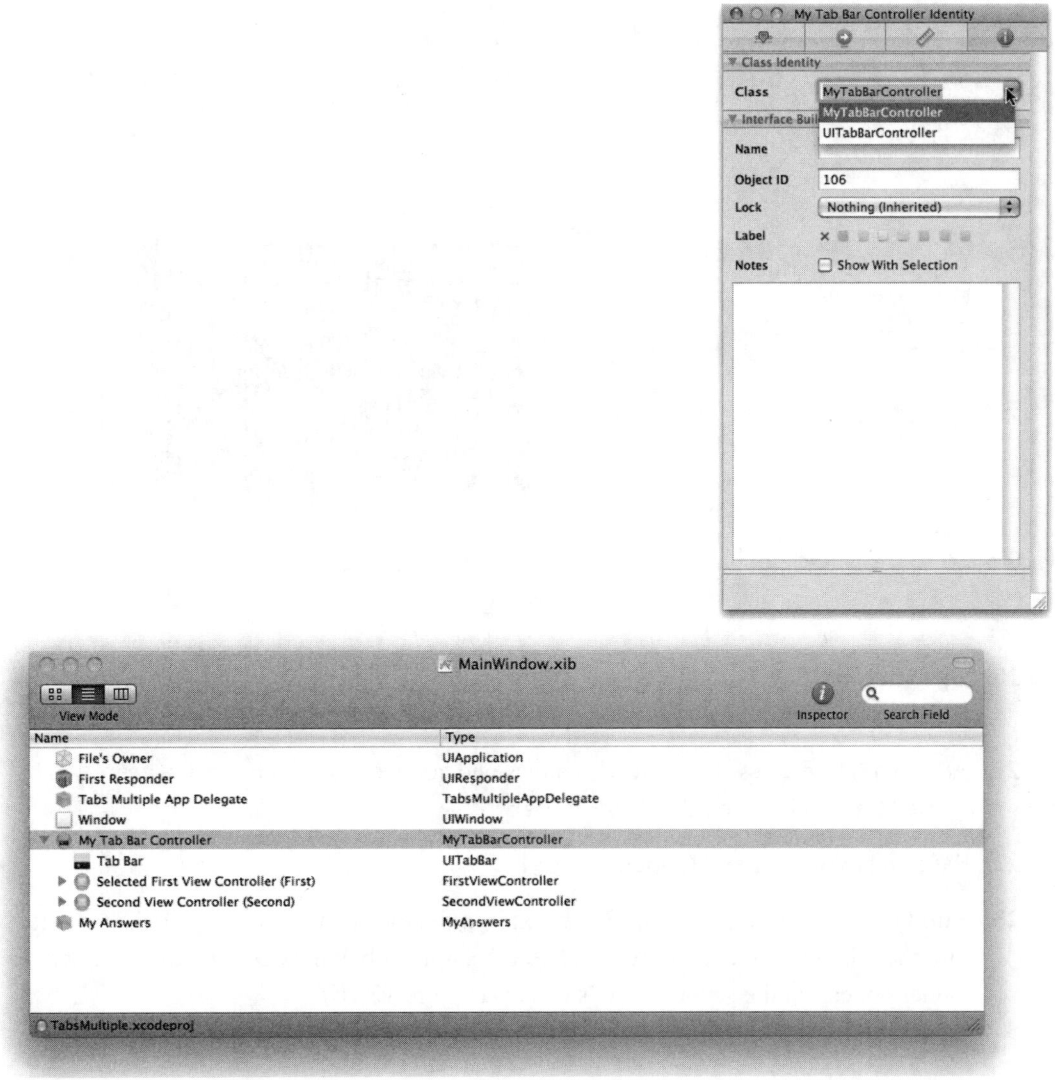

Figure 12-14 Changing the Tab Bar Controller's class

18. Connect the MyTabBarController's `myMyAnswers IBOutlet` to the MyAnswers object (Figure 12-15).

19. Save and exit Interface Builder.

(continued)

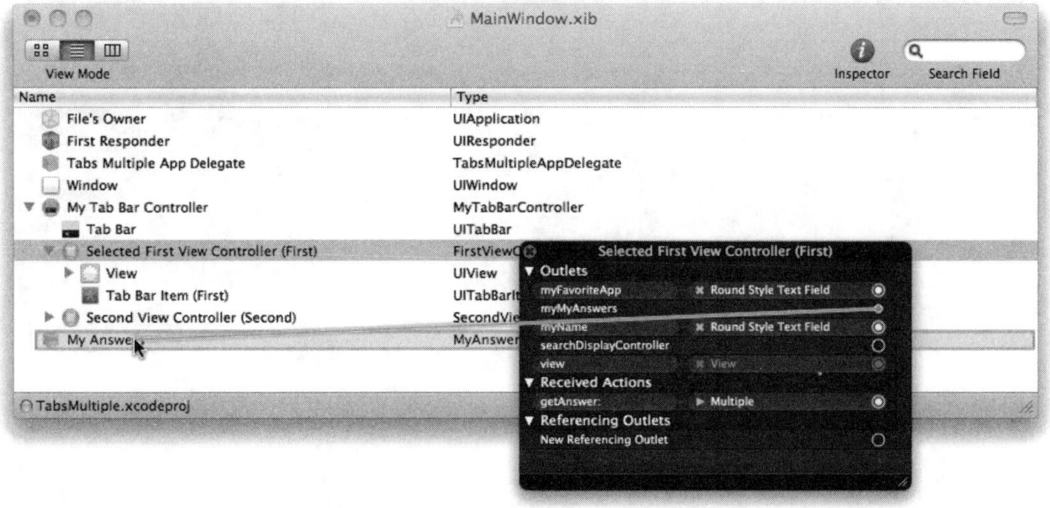

Figure 12-15 Connecting the `myMyAnswers` outlet to the object

20. Open SecondView.xib in Interface Builder. Change the File's Owner type from `UIViewController` to `SecondViewController`.
21. Add two `UILabels` to the view's canvas and connect them to File's Owner `labelOne` and `labelTwo` `IBOutlets`.
22. Save and exit Interface Builder.
23. Build and Run the application. Enter text into the top field and tap return. Enter text into the second field and tap return. After finishing, click the Second tab; the entered values appear on the second view's canvas (Figure 12-16).

Listing 12-9 MyAnswers.h

```
#import <Foundation/Foundation.h>
@interface MyAnswers : NSObject {
  NSString * myName;
  NSString * myFavoriteApp;
}
@property (nonatomic,retain) NSString * myName;
@property (nonatomic,retain) NSString * myFavoriteApp;
@end
```

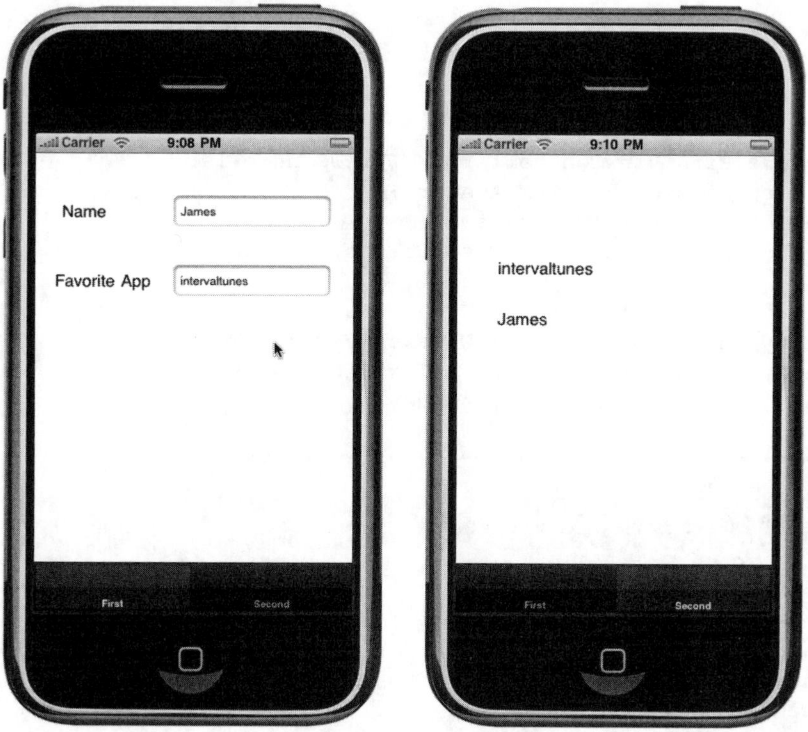

Figure 12-16 Entering the text and having it appear on the second view

Listing 12-10 MyAnswers.m

```
#import "MyAnswers.h"
@implementation MyAnswers
@synthesize myName;
@synthesize myFavoriteApp;
-(void) dealloc {
  self.myFavoriteApp = nil;
  self.myName = nil;
  [super dealloc];
@end
```

(continued)

Listing 12-11 FirstViewController.h

```
#import <UIKit/UIKit.h>
#import "MyAnswers.h"
@interface FirstViewController : UIViewController {
  IBOutlet MyAnswers * myMyAnswers;
  IBOutlet UITextField * myName;
  IBOutlet UITextField * myFavoriteApp;
}
@property (nonatomic,retain) MyAnswers * myMyAnswers;
@property (nonatomic,retain) UITextField * myName;
@property (nonatomic, retain) UITextField * myFavoriteApp;
- (IBAction) getAnswer: (id) sender;
@end
```

Listing 12-12 FirstViewController.m

```
#import "FirstViewController.h"
@implementation FirstViewController
@synthesize myMyAnswers;
@synthesize  myName;
@synthesize  myFavoriteApp;
- (IBAction) getAnswer: (id) sender {
  [sender resignFirstResponder];
  if([sender tag] == 1) {
    self.myMyAnswers.myName = self.myName.text;
  }
  else {
    self.myMyAnswers.myFavoriteApp = self.myFavoriteApp.text;
  }
}
- (void)dealloc {
  self.myMyAnswers = nil;
  self.myName = nil;
  self.myFavoriteApp = nil;
  [super dealloc];
}
@end
```

Listing 12-13 SecondViewController.h

```
#import <UIKit/UIKit.h>
#import "MyAnswers.h"
@interface SecondViewController : UIViewController {
```

```
  IBOutlet MyAnswers * myMyAnswers;
  IBOutlet UILabel * labelOne;
  IBOutlet UILabel * labelTwo;
}
@property (nonatomic, retain) MyAnswers * myMyAnswers;
@property (nonatomic,retain) UILabel * labelOne;
@property (nonatomic, retain) UILabel * labelTwo;
@end
```

Listing 12-14 SecondViewController.m

```
#import "SecondViewController.h"
@implementation SecondViewController
@synthesize myMyAnswers;
@synthesize labelOne;
@synthesize labelTwo;
-(void) viewDidLoad {
  NSLog(@"loading");
}
- (void) viewWillAppear:(BOOL)animated {
  [super viewWillAppear:animated];
  NSLog(@"name:%@", self.myMyAnswers.myName);
  self.labelOne.text = self.myMyAnswers.myName;
  self.labelTwo.text = self.myMyAnswers.myFavoriteApp;
}
- (void)dealloc {
   self.labelOne = nil;
  self.labelTwo = nil;
  self.myMyAnswers = nil;
  [super dealloc];
}
@end
```

Listing 12-15 MyTabBarController.h

```
#import <UIKit/UIKit.h>
#import "MyAnswers.h"
@interface MyTabBarController : UITabBarController {
  IBOutlet MyAnswers * myMyAnswers;
}
@property (nonatomic, retain) MyAnswers * myMyAnswers;
@end
```

(continued)

Listing 12-16 MyTabBarController.m

```
#import "MyTabBarController.h"
@implementation MyTabBarController
@synthesize myMyAnswers;
- (void)dealloc {
  self.myMyAnswers = nil;
  [super dealloc];
}
@end
```

In this example you created an application whose only coupling is in `ViewHandler`. `MultipleXibsViewController` knows nothing about `SecondViewController`. You share the data between the view controllers using the model, not the individual `UILabel`'s value. Although here this distinction is trivial, consider what happens if a view with many controls must share data with another view. The amount of sharing becomes unmanageable. By passing a single model object, sharing data becomes manageable.

In some respects, this example is a bit extreme. Usually coupling view controllers is acceptable. However, this example does illustrate that you can totally decouple views, view controllers, and views in xibs. Moreover, you can share data between them. The only coupling is that both view controllers must know about the `MyModel` data object. And of course the `ViewHandler` class is coupled with both view controllers.

In the preceding Try This you shared data between two xibs by using a shared data object that was added to the xib in Interface Builder. However, often you will wish to share an object between two xibs programmatically. Moreover, when using code to create views you do not have this option of sharing data. Instead, you must manually share data between xibs. Sharing data between xibs programmatically is arguably even more straightforward than using Interface Builder. The following Try This illustrates.

Try This Sharing Data Between Xibs Programatically

1. Create a new Window-based application named **MonkeySee**.
2. Create two `UIViewControllers` named `MonkeySeeViewController` and `MonkeyDoViewController`. Be certain to check "With XIB for user interface" when creating both so that you create xib files.
3. Create an Objective-C class named `Monkey`.
4. Open MainWindow.xib in Interface Builder and add a `UINavigationController` to the main window (Figure 12-17).
5. Expand the Navigation Controller. Select the "View Controller (Root View Controller)" and change its class to `MonkeySeeViewController` (Figure 12-18).

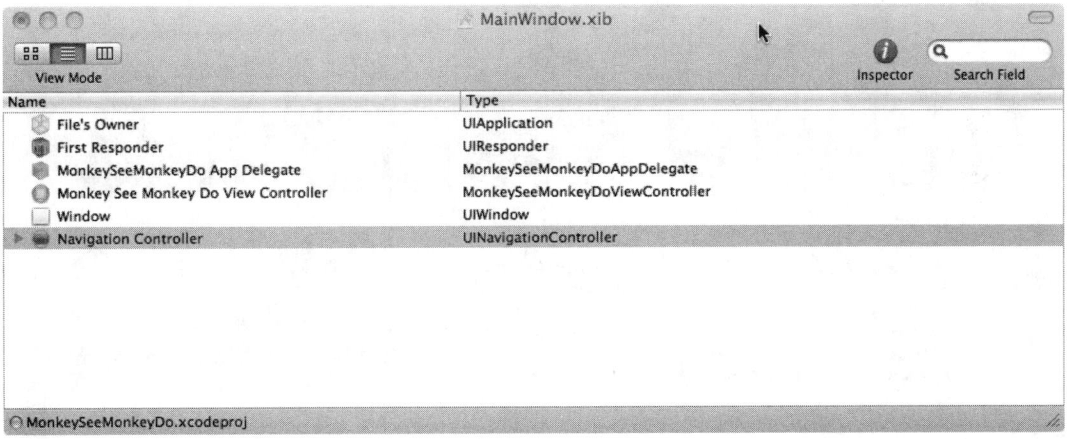

Figure 12-17 Adding `UINavigationController` to the main window

(continued)

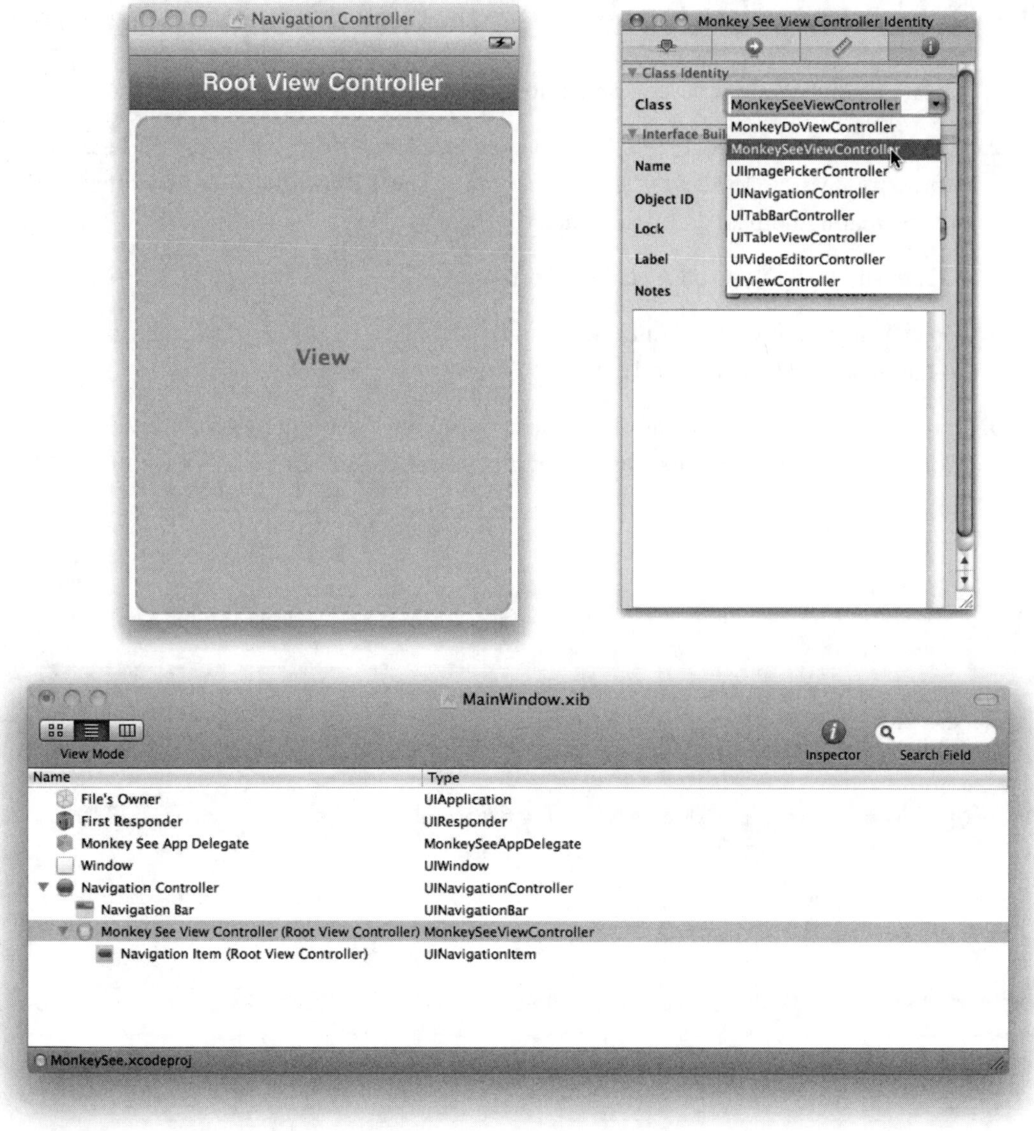

Figure 12-18 Changing the class to `MonkeySeeViewController`

6. Change its NIB Name to `MonkeySeeViewController` (Figure 12-19).
7. Save and exit Interface Builder.

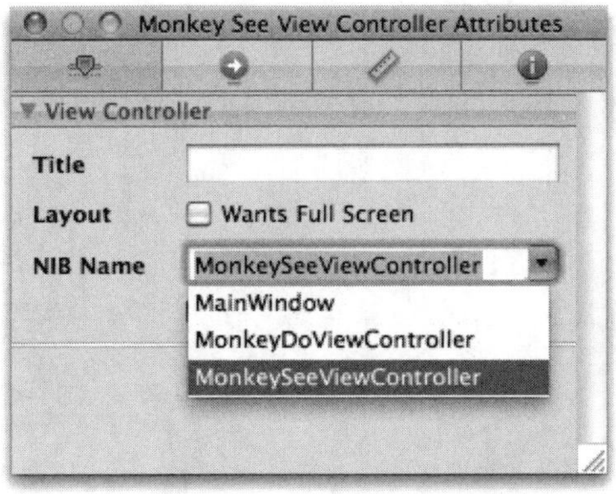

Figure 12-19 Changing the NIB Name

8. Open Monkey.h and add a property as an `NSString` (Listings 12-17 and 12-18).
9. Open MonkeyDoViewController.h, import Monkey.h, and add `Monkey` as a property (Listings 12-19 and 12-20). Also add an `IBOutlet` for a `UILabel`.
10. Also implement `MonkeyDoViewController`'s `viewDidLoad` method so that it sets the label's text to the monkey's name.
11. Open MonkeySeeViewController.h and add a `UILabel` as an `IBOutlet`. Add a `UIBarButtonItem` as an outlet. Also add a method declaration for an `IBAction` named `gotoNext:` (Listing 12-21). Import the MonkeyDoViewController.h header file.
12. Open MonkeySeeViewController.m and synthesize the label. Also implement the `gotoNext:` method and implement the `viewDidLoad` method (Listing 12-22).
13. Open MonkeySeeViewController.xib in Interface Builder and add a `UILabel` to the view's canvas. Change the label's text to be a name, like `Ralph`.
14. Connect the File's Owner `myMonkeyName` to the label added to the view (Figure 12-20).

(continued)

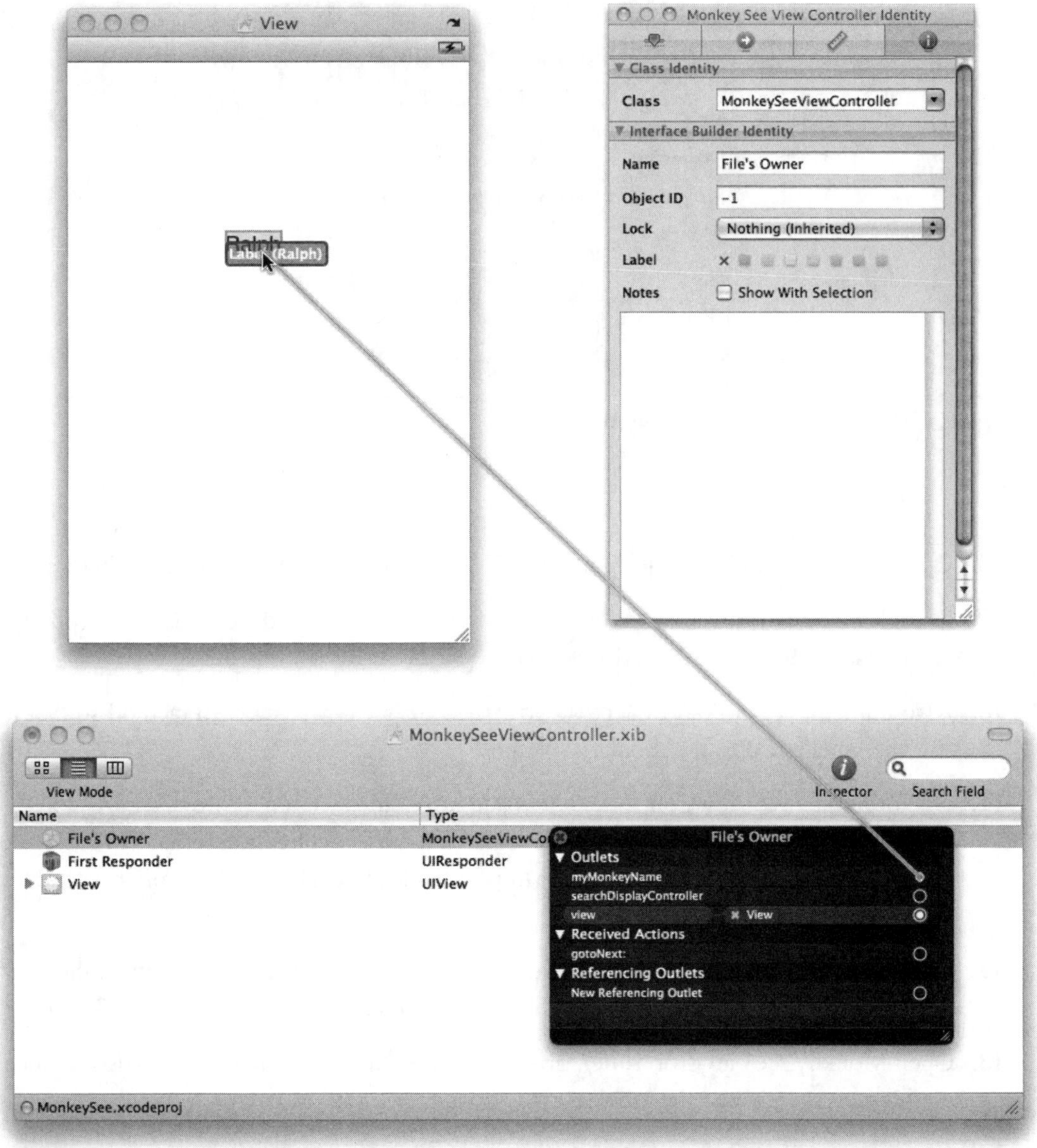

Figure 12-20 Connecting `myMonkeyName` outlet to the label

15. Drag a Bar Button Item from the library to the main window. Change the button's title to Next (Figure 12-21).

16. Connect the button to the File's Owner `nextButton` outlet (Figure 12-22).

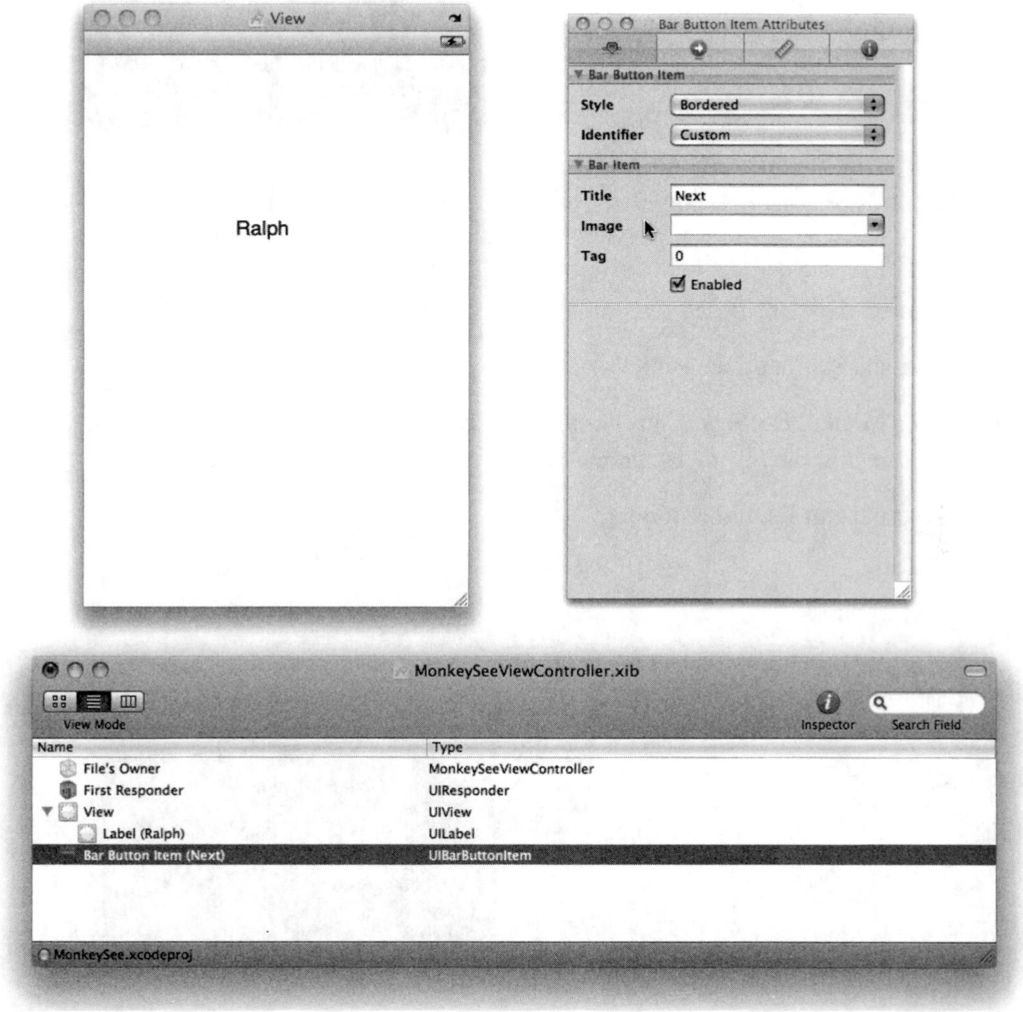

Figure 12-21 Dragging a button from library to the main window

(continued)

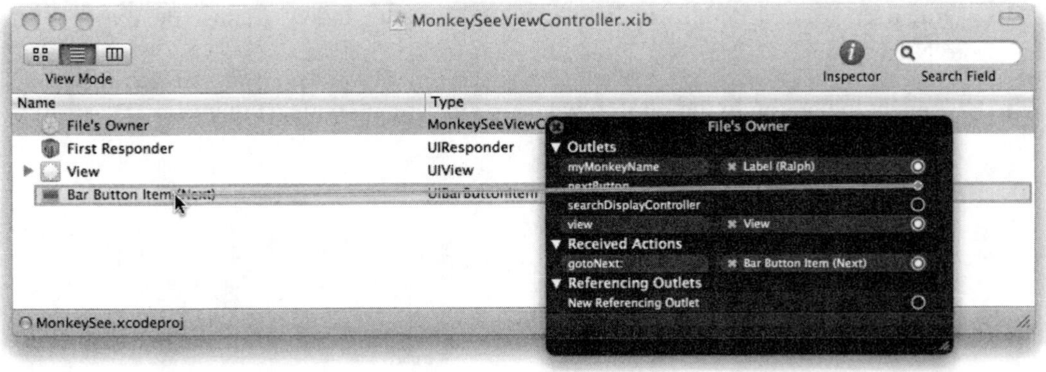

Figure 12-22 Connecting to the `nextButton` outlet

17. Connect the `gotoNext:` action to the newly added button (Figure 12-23).
18. Save and exit Interface Builder.
19. Open MonkeyDoViewController.xib in Interface. Add a `UILabel` to the canvas and connect it to the File's Owner `myMonkeyNameLabel` outlet.
20. Save and exit Interface Builder.

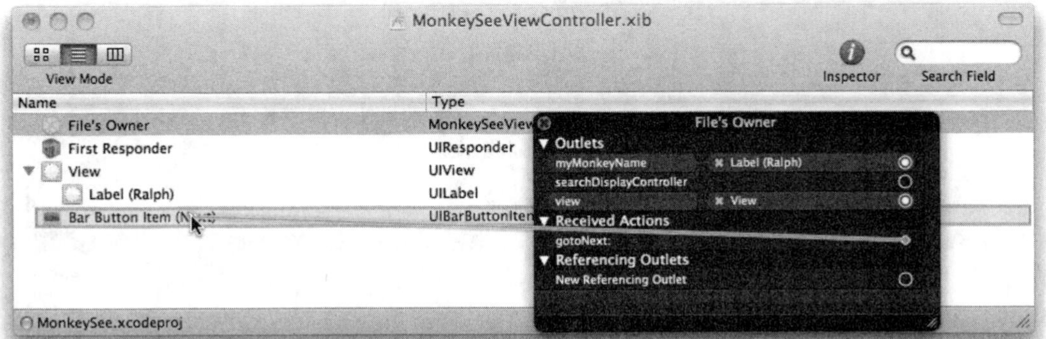

Figure 12-23 Connecting to the `gotoNext:` action

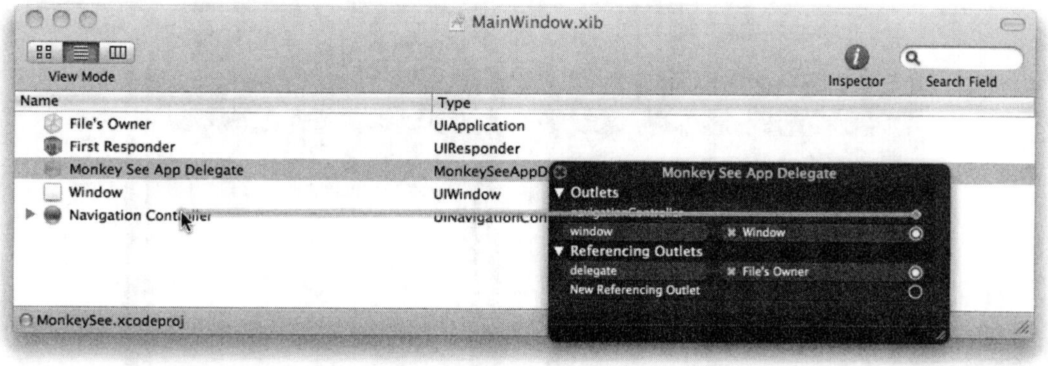

Figure 12-24 Connecting to the navigation controller

21. Open MonkeySeeAppDelegate.h and add the `navigationController` as an `IBOutlet` (Listing 12-23).
22. Open MonkeySeeAppDelegate.m, synthesize the navigation controller, and add it to the window in the `applicationDidFinishLaunching:` method (Listing 12-24).
23. Open MainWindow.xib in Interface Builder. Connect the `MonkeySeeApp Delegate`'s `navigationController` to the navigation controller in the main window (Figure 12-24).
24. Build and Run. The first screen shows the monkey's name (Figure 12-25). When you click Next, the next screen also shows the monkey's name.

Listing 12-17 Monkey.h

```
#import <Foundation/Foundation.h>
@interface Monkey : NSObject {
  NSString * myName;
}
@property (nonatomic,retain) NSString * myName;
@end
```

(continued)

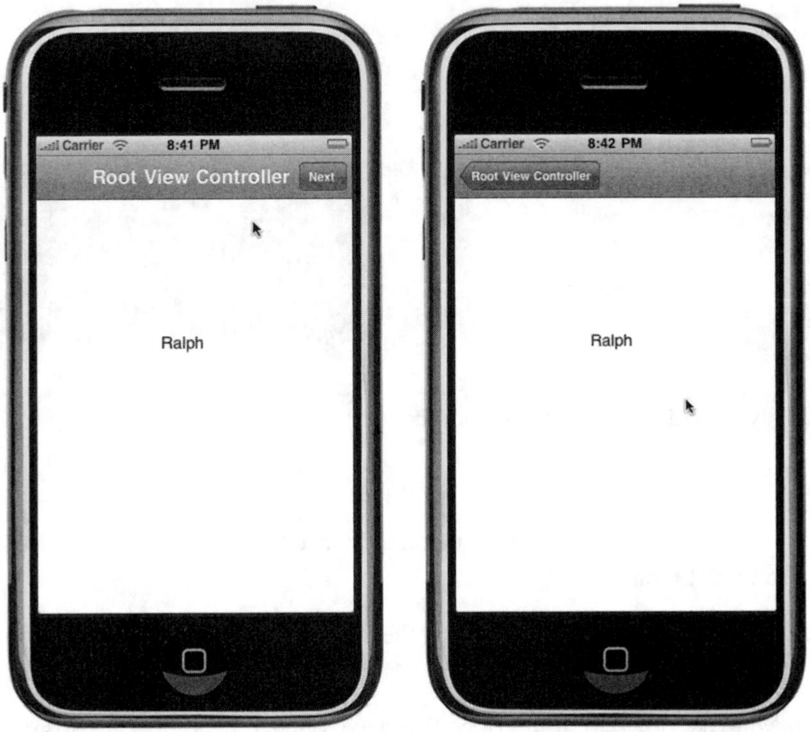

Figure 12-25 Running the application in iPhone simulator

Listing 12-18 Monkey.m

```
#import "Monkey.h"
@implementation Monkey
@synthesize myName;
-(void) dealloc {
  self.myName = nil;
  [super dealloc];
@end
```

Listing 12-19 MonkeyDoViewController.h

```
#import <UIKit/UIKit.h>
#import "Monkey.h"
@interface MonkeyDoViewController : UIViewController {
  Monkey * myMonkey;
```

```
  IBOutlet UILabel * myMonkeyNameLabel;
}
@property (nonatomic,retain) Monkey * myMonkey;
@property (nonatomic,retain) UILabel * myMonkeyNameLabel;
@end
```

Listing 12-20 MonkeyDoViewController.m

```
#import "MonkeyDoViewController.h"
@implementation MonkeyDoViewController
@synthesize myMonkey;
@synthesize myMonkeyNameLabel;
- (void) viewDidLoad {
  [super viewDidLoad];
  self.myMonkeyNameLabel.text = myMonkey.myName;
}
- (void)dealloc {
  [myMonkey release];
  [myMonkeyNameLabel release];
  [super dealloc];
}
@end
```

Listing 12-21 MonkeySeeViewController.h

```
#import <UIKit/UIKit.h>
#import "MonkeyDoViewController.h"
@interface MonkeySeeViewController : UIViewController {
  IBOutlet UILabel * myMonkeyName;
  IBOutlet UIBarButtonItem * nextButton;
}
@property (nonatomic, retain) IBOutlet UILabel * myMonkeyName;
@property (nonatomic,retain) IBOutlet UIBarButtonItem * nextButton;
- (IBAction) gotoNext: (id) sender;
@end
```

Listing 12-22 MonkeySeeViewController.m

```
#import "MonkeySeeViewController.h"
@implementation MonkeySeeViewController
@synthesize myMonkeyName;
@synthesize nextButton;
```

(continued)

```
-(void) viewDidLoad {
  self.navigationItem.rightBarButtonItem = self.nextButton;
}
- (IBAction) gotoNext: (id) sender {
  MonkeyDoViewController * monkeyDo = [[MonkeyDoViewController alloc]
initWithNibName:@"MonkeyDoViewController" bundle:nil];
  Monkey * aMonkey = [[Monkey alloc] init];
  monkeyDo.myMonkey = aMonkey;
  monkeyDo.myMonkey.myName = myMonkeyName.text;
  [self.navigationController pushViewController:monkeyDo animated:YES];
  [monkeyDo release];
  [aMonkey release];
}
- (void)dealloc {
  [myMonkeyName release];
  [nextButton release];
  [super dealloc];
}
@end
```

Listing 12-23 MonkeySeeAppDelegate.h

```
#import <UIKit/UIKit.h>
@interface MonkeySeeAppDelegate : NSObject <UIApplicationDelegate> {
  UIWindow *window;
  UINavigationController *navigationController;
}
@property (nonatomic, retain) IBOutlet UIWindow *window;
@property (nonatomic, retain) IBOutlet UINavigationController
*navigationController;
@end
```

Listing 12-24 MonkeySeeAppDelegate.m

```
#import "MonkeySeeAppDelegate.h"
@implementation MonkeySeeAppDelegate
@synthesize window;
@synthesize navigationController;
- (void)applicationDidFinishLaunching:(UIApplication *)application {
  [window addSubview:[navigationController view]];
  [window makeKeyAndVisible];
}
```

```
- (void)dealloc {
  [navigationController release];
  [window release];
  [super dealloc];
}
@end
```

In this application the two views shared data with each other programmatically using the `gotoNext:` method.

```
- (IBAction) gotoNext: (id) sender {
  MonkeyDoViewController * monkeyDo = [[MonkeyDoViewController alloc]
initWithNibName:@"MonkeyDoViewController" bundle:nil];
  Monkey * aMonkey = [[Monkey alloc] init];
  monkeyDo.myMonkey = aMonkey;
  monkeyDo.myMonkey.myName = myMonkeyName.text;
  [self.navigationController pushViewController:monkeyDo animated:YES];
  [monkeyDo release];
  [aMonkey release];
}
```

Both view controllers are subviews of the navigation controller. The first view's bar button invokes the `gotoNext:` action when tapped. This method loads the `MonkeyDoViewController`, creates a `Monkey` instance, and then assigns it to the newly created `MonkeyDoViewController`'s `myMonkey` property. After doing this, it pushes the `MonkeyDoViewController` to the navigation controller and the `MonkeyDoViewController` is displayed with the data passed to it before being displayed.

If you do not fully understand the navigation controller, or how the view was displayed, don't worry; for this example it is not important. What is important is that you understand how you passed the data between the xibs. The controller in the first xib instantiated the controller in the second xib. It then set the second controller's relevant properties. After setting the properties, it passed control to the second view controller, which loaded its view.

Summary

In this chapter you learned about the Model-View-Controller (MVC) design pattern, as implemented on the iPhone. As you encounter tutorials on the Web, you will see many examples that mix the controller with the model. Realize this mixture is out of convenience and not intended as production code. Always separate your model from your controller. It allows easier debugging and modification, and makes your code easier to understand.

Model data is often persisted between application invocations. On the iPhone, you can persist data using the sqlite C-based database, using property lists, by archiving, and through Core Data. You could, of course, implement your own persistence scheme; however, these four techniques are much easier. As this is a book on Objective-C and not the iPhone SDK, this chapter did not cover sqlite nor Core Data in any depth. You are encouraged to review both these topics in more depth.

Another problem that perplexes beginning developers is passing data between views. It is not as problematic as it might seem. The easiest way to accomplish this data passing is by passing a data object to a view controller after it has been initialized from the xib, but before the view has been loaded. Then, when the view calls its view controller's `viewDidLoad`, `viewWillAppear:`, and `viewDidAppear:` methods, the data object has already been set and the view can initialize itself accordingly.

Index

Symbols

A

B

C

D

E

F

G

H

I

M

O

P

R

W

X